# THE EXPERIENTIAL GUIDE TO LAW PRACTICE MANAGEMENT: OPENING AND OPERATING YOUR OWN FIRM

# THE EXPERIENTIAL GUIDE TO LAW PRACTICE MANAGEMENT: OPENING AND OPERATING YOUR OWN FIRM

Lynne Adair Kramer

Ann L. Nowak

CAROLINA ACADEMIC PRESS
Durham, North Carolina

ISBN: 978-1-6328-1906-2

eBook ISBN: 978-1-6328-1909-3

**Library of Congress Cataloging-in-Publication Data**

Names: Kramer, Lynne Adair, author. | Nowak, Ann L., author.
Title: The experiential guide to law practice management : opening and operating your own firm / Lynne Adair Kramer and Ann L. Nowak.
Description: Durham, N.C. : Carolina Academic Press, 2016. | Includes bibliographical references and index.
Identifiers: LCCN 2016004784 (print) | LCCN 2016005569 (ebook) | ISBN 9781632819062 (alk. paper) | ISBN 9781632819093 ()
Subjects: LCSH: Law offices--United States. | Practice of law--United States.
Classification: LCC KF318 .K73 2016 (print) | LCC KF318 (ebook) | DDC 340.068--dc23
LC record available at http://lccn.loc.gov/2016004784

Carolina Academic Press, LLC
700 Kent Street
Durham, NC 27701
Telephone (919) 489-7486
Fax (919) 493-5668
www.caplaw.com

Printed in the United States of America
2018 Printing

(2016–Pub.3401)

# *Dedications*

---

This book is dedicated to Ruth and Paul Kramer, who taught me at a very early age to
understand that it is the bottom line that counts
and
to Frederick Eisenbud, who has taught me so many other things.
LAK

This book is dedicated to my parents, Welville B. Nowak and the late Ruth G. Nowak,
for teaching me to believe in myself,
and
to my husband, Joseph R. Lombardo, for his encouragement and patience.
ALN

# Acknowledgements

There are a number of people to whom we will be forever grateful for their contributions to this book. They have made our days far easier and have made what has sometimes seemed an insurmountable task both manageable and, yes, fun. We would like to thank and recognize the talented librarians who work at the Touro Law Center library — in particular, Irene Crisci, Isaac Samuels, Laura Ross, and Stacy Posillico. We also would like to thank our hard-working research assistants — Luann Dallojacono, Gregory De Tolla, and Daniel Gili. Thank you, also, to faculty assistant Cathy Cembrale, who has always been willing to assist with good cheer. And thank you to all the students in our Law Practice Management classes for providing helpful feedback on the simulations in the teacher's manual that accompanies this book. Last, and certainly not least, we would like to thank our dean, Patricia Salkin, who has supported us, encouraged us, and cheered us on with this project.

Lynne Adair Kramer
Ann L. Nowak

# Table of Contents

# Table of Contents

# Table of Contents

# Table of Contents

# Table of Contents

# Table of Contents

# Table of Contents

# Table of Contents

# Table of Contents

# Table of Contents

# PART I

# OPENING THE OFFICE

## INTRODUCTION

This book was written with a very specific intent: We want to help you to learn how to open and maintain a successful law practice.

We are not going to provide you with lengthy articles to read about the history of the practice of law, nor are we going to ask you to read about the evolution of law firm practice management.

Rather, this book gives you the opportunity to take a "dry run" at opening your own law practice. A sampling of the tasks you will be asked to perform includes:

1) Finding your office space,

2) Choosing whether or not to have partners,

3) Naming your firm,

4) Forming your entity,

5) Choosing your field or fields,

6) Determining your division of responsibility,

7) Determining your division of profits,

8) Setting up the actual office,

9) Selecting and installing your management systems,

10) Marketing your business,

11) Hiring staff,

12) Choosing whom you want to represent,

13) Handling initial client meetings,

14) Preparing engagement letters and retainer agreements,

15) Preparing non-engagement letters,

16) Concluding your case,

17) Dealing with adversity, including but not limited to: grievances, malpractice, employee complaints, and actions.

If you are an admitted attorney opening your first office, this book should help you to avoid making some of the mistakes we made ourselves or have seen others make.

If you are a law student, the classroom simulations and assignments in the accompanying teachers' manual will give you a chance to learn how to handle office-related matters, decisions, and problems that you may face in the future. If you don't like the way you did something in this class, you will know to make a different choice when you open your office. On the other hand, if you like certain decisions you made here, you can model your office after the things that worked successfully for you. The nice thing about this class is that you can make mistakes now rather than in your law firm. Please feel free to thank us for that!

Lynne Adair Kramer
Ann L. Nowak

# Chapter 1

## SHOULD I OPEN MY OWN LAW OFFICE?

If you are reading this book, you are probably thinking about the possibility of opening your own law practice. And right at the outset, you probably should ask yourself, "Why am I having such a crazy thought?" Is the end result going to be a dream come true or an ugly nightmare? The answer, in part, has to do with your expectations and your motivations for going into your own business. Yes, the practice of law is a business, and it is critical that you understand this idea before you decide that you want to start your own firm. Although it is a wonderful thing to fight for the causes you believe in, and it is also important to provide services for those who may not be able to afford a lawyer, you will not be able to do those things if you do not run a successful business. You, therefore, must wear two hats when you open your own practice: one as the businessperson and one as the lawyer. Sometimes these roles may seem to conflict, but always remember this: if you run a sound business, then you will have the luxury of doing those things you deem right or good. With that in mind, you need to look at the reasons why you are thinking about opening your own office. Are you thinking about taking this step because you can't find a job, or are you motivated by one or more of the following thoughts?

1) I want to make a lot of money.
2) I don't like working for other people and/or I want to be my own boss.
3) I want to handle only the kinds of cases that interest me.
4) I want to have flexible hours so I can come and go as I please.
5) I like the idea of building something from scratch and making it into what I want it to be.

Chances are good that you identify with one or more of these statements. Chances also are good that as successful as you may become someday, it will take a good deal of time and patience before you are certain that what you chose to do was a good idea. That doesn't mean that you shouldn't try to build your own practice; it simply means that you have to temper your expectations with a dose of reality.

There will be an inordinate number of decisions that you will have to make, and it helps to consider the various options and opportunities available to you before you actually move forward. First and foremost, ask yourself whether you truly are suited to opening and maintaining your own office.

If you decide that this is the right path for you, then you must ask yourself where you want your office to be located, with whom you want to work, and what type of law you want to practice. As you read on, you will see that we are trying to provide you with enough information and tools to make reasoned decisions with regard to each of these issues.

## § 1.01   PROS AND CONS OF OPENING YOUR OWN OFFICE

When trying to decide whether you really want to go ahead and open your own practice, it is a good idea to confront some of the negative aspects of this choice right up front.

## § 1.02   CONS OF OPENING A PRIVATE PRACTICE

### [A]   Unpredictable Income

Probably one of the biggest problems associated with going into your own practice is the uncertainty surrounding your income. If you have no financial cushion, and you have significant bills to pay, you may be better off trying to find a job with a salary and staying in that type of situation until you have the necessary financial cushion to withstand at least 6-12 months without a paycheck. If you have a family member, or family members, who will provide the necessary financial support to allow you the luxury of going without a paycheck, then don't be ashamed to take advantage of that situation. You and your support network need to be prepared for at least 6-12 months of very unpredictable income. You need to acknowledge that likelihood and know whether those who are supporting you are willing to commit to assisting you financially for at least that period of time.

An alternative is to take a job as an attorney working for someone else until you have sufficient funds saved up to work full time in your own practice. Or, you can work part-time or full-time in an unrelated field while building your practice. This methodology has proved to be very effective for teachers, police officers, and accountants who have gone to law school with the plan of opening a law office. If you can manage to find something that provides you with enough income to meet your basic needs while opening an office "on the side," the financial pressure attached to opening your practice will in large measure be eliminated. You may be limited in the types of cases you can take because court appearances will conflict with a daytime position, but matters such as wills and estate plans, business formations, tax work, appellate brief writing, motion writing, and real estate closings generally will present little difficulty.

Even when you start to settle down and have a consistent stream of business, you will not necessarily have a consistent income. Sometimes clients do not pay their bills, and sometimes you may have cases with contingency fees where things do not work out as you had hoped. Plain and simple, your income can vary tremendously both month-to-month and year-to-year. If you keep your personal expenses down, the stress level from inconsistent income will be significantly reduced.

When I opened my practice, my husband and I had a cushion in the bank that could cover my share of the expenses for about a year, and my husband was working full time. We invested a small amount of our savings and agreed NOT TO BUY ANY take out, fast food, coffee or even lunch for 6 months. We did not go to eat out, rent a movie or buy anything other than necessities during that period. I made a time-for-space deal, but foolishly started out looking at WHAT I WASN'T EARNING each week. Quickly my accountants got me to view things more long term, forcing me to look quarterly and then eventually monthly. The practice started slowly, as will probably be true of yours, but it turned out to be the best investment we ever made . . . by far. At the time I closed the office to switch to teaching full time, I had 15 people in my employ and a thriving firm. LAK

When I started my practice, I had enough money in the bank to live on for 1.5 years. I had saved it from my job as a newspaper reporter. I knew from reporting on small-business startups and finance that it was a good idea to have savings that could pay for at least 1 year of expenses when you start any small business — and that included a law firm. I also learned from my reporting that it often takes small businesses from 3-5 years to begin really thriving. This was the case with my firm. It took me about 3 years until I was able to build my practice to a financial level where I could relax and not feel like dancing around the office with joy every time a client paid a bill. ALN

## [B] The Responsibility Is All Yours

When discussing the pros and cons of private practice with colleagues, they consistently reported that other than worrying about money, the most difficult part of opening and maintaining an office was the fact that there was no one to whom they could pass the buck; every aspect of responsibility and decision-making was theirs. If you open your own law business, you will be responsible for everything at the office, including obtaining business, organizing and prioritizing cases, making strategic decisions on cases, doing the work, making clients happy, sending timely and detailed bills, following up to make sure you get paid by your clients, selecting office management systems, keeping your calendar and meeting all deadlines, hiring and firing, and paying all the bills. The number of things for which you are responsible can be overwhelming for even the most experienced attorneys. Are you prepared to handle all of this? Does the upside make it worthwhile for you to try?

> When I started my practice, it didn't occur to me that I would have to juggle all of this. I have no idea why I didn't think of it, but I didn't. Many other lawyers who started their own firms have since told me the same thing. We were attracted by the excitement of starting a business, by the freedom of working for ourselves, and by the greed of being able to keep all the money we made. We didn't see it as greed, of course. ALN

## [C]  Irregular Schedule

Unless you have left a firm and taken clients with you, or you already have an agreement in place to represent someone or some entity when you open your own office, you are unlikely to have much legal work during your first few weeks or months of business. Are you disciplined enough to make a schedule of things that will be useful for you to do, whether or not you are receiving compensation for doing them? Are you creative enough, or a good enough businessperson, to understand the types of things you should be doing while you are trying to develop your business? Or will a lack of legal work and lack of predictability drive you crazy? These are things you need to consider if you are going to open an office.

If you make a modest effort, you can establish a somewhat regular routine while waiting for your business to grow. If you live where there is a legal newspaper, consider reading it first thing every day. For example, the New York Law Journal is the daily legal newspaper in the New York area that all practitioners should read to keep abreast of any changes in the law. Lawyers can subscribe to this paper both digitally and in print.

Similarly, if you want to be a litigator, but you are just starting you own firm and aren't busy yet, you may want to begin your mornings by visiting a courtroom and watching the proceedings. Whatever you choose to do, remember that you should find ways to utilize your time productively.

## [D]  Introvert?

Not anymore! If you are a person who waits for someone to come to talk to you at a party, rather than being the one who reaches out, it is time to change your ways if you want to open your own law business. This is particularly true for solo practitioners. Business is not likely to come knocking on your door. You are going to have to be a "rainmaker" unless you have a partner who is very good at bringing in the business. Even if you have such a partner, potential clients still will want to know about you. In essence, it may feel like you are always on display. In fact, you may find that people who have never met you are talking about you and sometimes saying untrue or contradictory things. For example, one person may say you are too tough while someone else may say just the opposite. Can you handle being the topic of talk in your town? As we all know, there are lots of lawyers out there. It will be your job to let people know why YOU should be their lawyer, and you have to be comfortable putting on a public face. We will talk a good deal about marketing later on in this book. For now, when you are deciding whether or not you want to open an office, you will need to consider whether you are comfortable being somewhat of a public figure as well as being comfortable trying to drum up business. If you feel that you don't like putting yourself "out there" and you are unwilling to sell yourself, then you should consider going into business with someone who is capable of carrying out these public functions. Bear in mind that you will have to participate in these functions at least to some extent. Public relations and business generation are subjects that cannot be given short shrift. You do not want to be a talented, starving attorney.

## § 1.03   PROS OF OPENING A PRIVATE PRACTICE

### [A]   You Can Chart Your Fate

The best thing about opening your own practice is that you do not have a boss, and it is up to you to decide what you want, or don't want, to do. You get to decide what to wear, what time you arrive at work (unless you have to be in court), what kinds of cases you want to handle and, most importantly, whom you want to represent and whom you don't want to represent. You are never faced with having your boss tell you that you have to represent someone you dislike or that you have to handle a case in which you have zero interest. Yes, in your own practice, there will be days when you have to decide which is worse: having no clients and no money or having clients and cases that you don't like but from which you will receive significant fees. But in your own practice, the choice is yours, and that is a great reward.

> When I opened my own practice, I had every intention of being a tort lawyer and trying big negligence cases. I took a course in medicine for lawyers at the local university, I went to all of the bar association's continuing legal education programs on negligence and trial law, and I even worked out a deal to open my office within the building of one of the premier negligence trial lawyers in the county in which I lived. Despite all of my strategy and planning, did I get the type of work I had hoped to do? Nope, not even close. I found that I was getting a particular kind of case in which I had little knowledge or interest. What did I do? I realized that I wasn't as committed to practicing tort law as I was to making a living. I was flexible. The more divorce cases I got, the better I got. Then the better I got, the more I got. I decided if this is what I was going to attract, then I was going to try to be the best at it. I started as a solo and ended up as one of the largest divorce and family law offices in my county. Am I telling you this story so that you don't stick with trying to do the kind of work you want to do? Absolutely not. I am telling you this to help you figure out who you are and what you want to do.
> LAK

If what you really want to do is civil rights law or criminal law or employment law, or any particular field of law, and that is truly what you want to do, then you must stay the course. If you have the financial wherewithal to be able to stick by your guns, DO NOT start taking cases in which you have little or no interest. The reason for this is that when you start making a living in another field, it will be very hard for you to go back as a beginner in the field of your dreams (yes, good name for a movie). Perhaps you have heard the term "golden handcuffs." It means you are making too much money in a job or business to give it up and do something else. Don't wear those bracelets. After you become fairly successful in one area of law, you are not going to want to start at the bottom in another field. Talk to lawyers in the field in which you want to practice, and see if any of them will let you shadow them. Offer to help them on cases for little or no money. Find ways to get active in the local bar associations, professional associations, or chambers of commerce where you can make the right contacts. Maybe there are assigned counsel plans or volunteer offices where you can work in the area of your interest. If you really want to become successful in a particular field, you should stick with your plan of action. You must, however, devise a plan — something we will discuss later on.

Opening a practice, and any business for that matter, can be a daunting and stressful task. Yet people open businesses all the time. Although it is true that a significant number of businesses fail, you can make business choices that will help you to prevent failure. For example, you have a considerable amount of control over the expenses you choose to take on when you open a professional practice and, by minimizing your expenses, you can increase your chances for success.

If you choose to open an office with partners, you will be making all of the decisions together, including decisions about the tenor of the office, the types of cases your firm will handle, and the division of labor. It is your decision at the outset whether you want to practice alone or work with others. If you decide to practice with others, you give up having total autonomy. Therefore, you must ask yourself — and honestly answer — how important is it for you to have that kind of control?

Another of the beauties of having your own firm is that you get to decide what kind of business you really want to run. You can decide that you want to build an "empire"; or you can decide that you want a somewhat leisurely life and, therefore, a somewhat leisurely practice; or you can decide that you want something in between. There is no question that the number of people your practice is supporting has a lot to do with determining the tempo and dynamic of the office. When you employ many people or you have several partners, you have to take in enough business to support everyone, which sometimes can lead you to be far less discriminating than you might be otherwise. On the other hand, when you work with many people in your own firm, you can pick and choose which work you personally want to do. For example, if you like making the court appearances and handling trial work, you may never have to write a motion or a brief if you have sufficient staff or the right partners. You may have specific people in your office who handle all of the document production and who respond to demands for bills of particulars and who answer interrogatories. You will likely select your partners based upon your different working strengths and interests.

By way of example, when I opened my office, I had to meet and sign up clients, draft my own pleadings, write my own motions and correspondence, deal with day-to-day problems, conduct my own discovery, and then conference and try my cases, as well handle the appeals. As my practice grew, I was able to hire folks to do the things I preferred not to do. I limited my work to meeting and signing up clients, writing the substantive correspondence including settlement proposals, negotiating settlements, writing settlement agreements, and trying cases. For the last 15 years I was in practice, I never drafted a pleading, answered an interrogatory or wrote a motion or an appellate brief. Of course I read the materials produced by my staff, but I determined it was not a profitable use of my time or talent to handle those particular tasks, and, quite frankly, I didn't want to do that work. LAK

I, on the other hand, enjoyed writing motions and appeals, so I did those things in my practice. I did not enjoy filling out forms in the firm's numerous bankruptcy cases, so I hired a terrific legal assistant to do that work. Of course, I always reviewed the forms carefully and made any necessary changes before we submitted them to the court. But offloading the task of preparing large stacks of paperwork greatly reduced my stress level and gave me time to increase my marketing efforts. Additionally, my legal assistant actually enjoyed preparing the forms because it allowed her to keep in close contact with our clients, who adored her. ALN

It is crucial to the success of any partnership that the partners (a) have similar goals in terms of the type of office they want to have and (b) that they understand, agree upon, and define their respective roles. Make certain to have those discussions BEFORE you open your office because they are integral to charting your course.

## [B]   Unlimited Possibilities

Owning your own business means that the sky is the limit in terms of the money you can make and the reputation you can develop. If you are a talented lawyer and businessperson, there is nothing stopping you from making a lot of money. No one else will determine your salary or income, and no one else will make decisions about whether you should take a case because it will or will not be profitable. With good judgment and good business sense, you usually will be able to tell which cases will be particularly profitable as well as which cases will be helpful to building your reputation. (Some minimally profitable or unprofitable cases may help build your reputation, especially if you can get press coverage.) Both types of cases will enhance your practice and stature within the legal community. This will lead to additional referrals from colleagues. There is no denying that "success breeds success."

Remember: the choice to open an office is not irrevocable; you can always try it and see if it fits.

# Chapter 2

## ARE MORE MERRIER?

Whether to open a solo practice or open an office with others is a very big decision. Some say it is just as serious as the choice of whom to marry. Some questions to ask yourself are:

1) Must I always be in charge?

2) Am I willing to share decision-making?

3) Am I a confident person?

4) Do I believe in my competence and/or my ability to learn as a lawyer?

5) Do I work well with others?

6) Do I take criticism well?

7) Can I keep my opinions and feelings to myself when I should?

8) Am I capable of bringing in business?

9) How are my organizational skills?

10) How are my managerial skills?

11) Am I a better businessperson than lawyer?

12) Am I a better worker than rainmaker?

13) Am I a better rainmaker than worker?

14) Am I a better speaker than writer?

15) Do I prefer preparing documents to conferencing with people or appearing in court?

16) Am I comfortable both on paper and in person?

17) Do I need to share the financial burden of an office?

18) Do I need to share the emotional burden of an office?

19) What kind of contacts do I have?

---

Although this list is by no means exhaustive, it should give you an idea of the types of things you need to think about before you decide whether to open an office by yourself or with other(s). If you reach the conclusion that you are probably not meant to be on your own, then the selection of the person you want to work with becomes just as important as deciding that you do not want to work alone. A business divorce, like a marital divorce, can be both personally and financially devastating. You must pick your partner(s) with care!

## § 2.01  POTENTIAL BUSINESS PARTNERS: FAMILY VERSUS FRIENDS VERSUS PROFESSIONAL ACQUAINTANCES

There are some very strong pluses and minuses to practicing with a family member, but there are definite differences to be considered depending on which family member you are considering.

### [A]  Family

SPOUSE: The biggest strength in having a spouse as a partner is the unity of interest. You both are seeking to maximize the benefits to your family. One of those benefits is money. When your partner is your spouse, the money you both earn goes to one household. You have little reason to argue about who gets what share of the profits. You have a pretty good idea of your partner's capabilities. You can almost assure that one of your children's parents will be available when necessary. That is, you can schedule appointments for each of you at differing times of the day, and you can do your best to make one parent's schedule significantly reduced if the other is on trial. And it is easy to plan for one parent to supervise a school trip.

On the other hand, there are very serious concerns that cannot be ignored if you are thinking about going into business with your spouse. If your spouse is your partner, and your marriage goes bad, so does your business. Divorce lawyers tell us that despite people's beliefs that they can work together after a divorce, that is almost never the case. Assuming that you are realistic in this regard and do not explore the option of trying to work together after a divorce, you are going to have to deal with who keeps the office, who gets which clients, who owes how much money to the other, and so on. The worst part about getting a divorce when your spouse is also your law partner is that you have no normalcy in any part of your life. You get stuck starting over not only personally but professionally. You have no safe haven to go to while navigating the divorce process, and you have to deal with chaos in every area of your life, which can be incredibly stressful.

The second most difficult issue to deal with when your spouse is your partner is never being able to get away from your work or your spouse. The number of years of your marriage should be considered to be doubled just on the basis of time also spent together at work. You may like being with your spouse 24 hours a day, 7 days a week, or you may not. The point is, it is something you need to think about and not dismiss as unimportant. One way of lessening this issue is to handle different areas of your practice. If you do this, you each will have different clients and, therefore, will be less prone to discussing work at home. You also will have less interaction at work and, therefore, fewer areas of discord.

My parents happened to be in business together so I saw from a very early age the strengths and weaknesses of this arrangement. While my parents' marriage and practice were both successful, I could easily see that almost any fights they had at home were related to the business. The funny thing is that in large measure, the arguments had little to do with the actual work performed, but really had to do with personal and working styles. I had a mother who was very organized and a father who was quite a bit less so. He was the one who might forget a file at home or, worse yet, forget altogether where he put it. He might forget to return a client call after promising he would do that. Needless to say, you could see how this could lead to some tension in the house from time to time. The great news was that my dad was very good at his work and quite detail oriented, and since it would have been quite difficult to find a partner as talented as my father, the partnership did in fact thrive. LAK

Another issue when practicing with your spouse is that if you are the only two attorneys in the firm, there won't be any attorney to generate billable time, speak with potential clients, or cover court appearances while you're both on a family vacation. This, of course, is also a problem for solo practitioners.

Many of the other issues that arise when having a spouse as a partner also arise with any partner(s). But the issues may seem more magnified with a spouse, so before we leave this topic, let's consider a few of them. Does one of you care a lot more than the other about appearances and, therefore, is more likely to spend a lot of money on furnishings and decorations for the office? Is one of you more likely to want to take more money from the business than the other? Is one of you more likely to want to have the newest equipment or software that comes out? Is one of you more conservative in your approach to the cases and clients you represent? These are just a few examples of the kinds of things that can come between partners and, more particularly, partner-spouses.

PARENTS AND SIBLINGS: Once again, you are more likely to have more unity of interest with family members than with non-relatives, but not nearly so much as when your law partner is your spouse. Partners who are family members tend to be more loyal to each other than to non-family partners. In some ways, it is easier to deal with a parent-partner than with a sibling-partner because parents tend to want to see good things happen for their children and grandchildren. The difficulty often arises with who is in control. Your parents have been telling you what to do since birth and often feel that this is how business should be handled as well. If you are a child joining a parent's already existing successful practice, you must be willing to accept the fact that at the outset, your parent — the senior partner — is, and should be, in charge. As the client base shifts and the ability to generate business changes, the roles should change. But sometimes this can be difficult in a parent/child partnership.

Another area that can be particularly problematic is when there are changes in technology that the child may see as a tremendous advantage while the parent may not. Changing how things have always been done is not easy, particularly when business has been good. Asking parents to spend money to make changes that will require them to learn something new may not elicit a positive response. These are things you are going to have to expect and learn to handle if you join your parent's law firm as a partner.

Sibling partners can be prone to experiencing the same jealousies they experienced as children. Older siblings may want to have more control just because of seniority. If you are joining a sibling with an existing practice, the level of success of that practice will impact on who will make the decisions in the beginning. If you are starting out as equals in a new endeavor and making equal investments, you have to set the ground rules from inception, making it clear that age has nothing to do with the decision-making process. Sometimes sibling law partners find that, based on their history, this is more easily said than done.

IN-LAWS: The problem here might be obvious to some of you. If you come in as a partner, it is unlikely that you will be an equal partner. If your marriage is good, your in-laws want you to succeed. If you succeed, their child will have the money to live well, which is what parents want for their children. In fact, in-law partners may decide to pay you far more than you would earn anywhere else. This is both the good news and bad news. If your marriage is strong, you all will live well. If your marriage falls apart, you may not want to continue working with your in-laws, or they may not want to continue working with you. The problem is that you might not be able to earn as much money elsewhere.

## [B]   Friends/Classmates

A real plus about going into business with a friend from law school is that you should have a pretty good idea about how bright that person is and what kind of work habits he or she possesses. Aside from honesty and integrity, which we hope you will find crucial to any relationship into which you enter, intelligence is critical. That is, even if your friend is honest and hard-working, you need to know if your partner is bright enough for you to rely on his or her work. Not all partners with whom you go into business — even friends — will work as hard as you do or be as bright as you are. You may take on a partner knowing that he or she is not a hard worker. But if that person has a lot of contacts and can bring in business that you can't, it might be a good match. The key here is that you must know the strengths and weaknesses of the people with whom you go into business. That way, you can have a good idea of your respective obligations and roles.

A major benefit of going into business with a classmate and or friend right after you both graduate is that you will be in the same place in your careers. Maybe one of you has had more clinical experience, but the difference in your skill levels should be close enough so that everyone feels on equal footing. If that is the case, the discussions about who will make which decisions and how profits will be shared will be very different from the conversations you would have with a prospective partner who has a well-established practice and years of experience. Nonetheless, you can never tell what it will be like to work with people until you actually work together. Are they really good at operating a business? Do they do things in a timely fashion? Can they deliver the clients they promised? Are they good at organizing themselves and your office? Do they have the same goals and values that you have for the office? Are they really going to put in the time and energy they told you they would? And are they putting in and taking out the money that was discussed? Unfortunately, when money is involved, partners can be very different from what you expected. Therefore, it will be very important that you and your partners discuss the issues we raise in this book, that you agree on a course of action, and that you memorialize you agreement in writing.

The major weakness of going into business with a classmate right after passing the bar exam is that neither of you will have any experience running a law firm. Yes, it would be great to know something about practicing law before you open an office, but you don't need to have practiced with another firm before opening your own office. This is because of the increase in clinical courses and training in law schools as well as the advent of concentrations and/or classes that prepare you for solo and small-firm practice.

## [C]  Professional Acquaintances

The biggest benefit to going into practice with an acquaintance/colleague who has been practicing law for a while is that he or she will have a proven track record. Not everyone opens a law practice right after law school. If you are someone who has been practicing law elsewhere for a few years and now want to open your own office, you may find that your best candidate for a partner is someone who was an adversary in one of your cases. If you have had adversaries who were sharp and honorable, you might want to consider approaching one of them regarding a partnership or some other type of working relationship. If you liked that person, other members of the bar and the judiciary may feel that way, too. Check with them to see if your instincts are right. People who practice in particular areas quickly develop a reputation — good and bad — among the bench and bar.

It is very important to be sure of what others think of your potential partner before you go into business with that person. Find out in casual conversation with your colleagues what they think of the person you are considering. If a lawyer is not liked by his or her peers, that fact can have a major impact on your practice.

If you don't know what your colleagues think of someone, and haven't been able to find out in conversation, consider looking in martindale.com. Martindale-Hubbell provides anonymous peer ratings, and every lawyer admitted over ten years throughout the country is eligible to be rated. Lawyers are rated A, B or C. These letters are reflective of a lawyer's competency. If someone has a C rating, it means the lawyer is not highly regarded by his or her peers or is not particularly well-liked. Lawyers don't give C ratings to peers they like, because a C rating can be harmful to business. Whether the person's C rating reflects their competence or personality, this rating usually indicates that this is a person you would not want as a partner. Most lawyers have B ratings, and the best in their fields receive A ratings. If a lawyer is rated either A or B, you can move on to other considerations for partner selection.

If you are thinking about partnering with a colleague who seems competent and likeable, you should consider that person's track record in business generation. Let's face it, chances are good that you are not going to want to partner with someone whose practice is failing economically. The exception is when you have so much work, and the lawyer whom you are considering is such a good lawyer that it doesn't matter whether that person is skilled at generating new business. Although there are many very good lawyers who are not very good business people, our goal in writing this book is, among other things, to make you a successful lawyer AND a successful business person.

There is absolutely no shame in making enough money to live well. As we have told many students and friends, the more money you make, the more money you have to help others.

If you see that your potential partner is doing well financially, you should try to understand the source of the profits. You may not want to join with someone whose lucrative practice is based only on one client. If that client leaves your law firm, your practice is doomed. We have seen that happen many times.

It is also worth reminding you that you do not want to be part of an operation where profit is made at the expense of quality. You also don't want to be part of an operation where the profits arise as a result of taking advantage of clients. A law practice can be profitable by running a streamlined and efficient operation and by providing the quality of work for which clients are willing to pay you well. If you are considering joining with an active practitioner, you should not be shy in making arrangements to examine the financial operations of the practice, which include not only examining tax returns but also all office management systems, billing systems, and costs associated with all equipment, leases, and other operations of the firm. If a potential partner is unwilling to share this information with you, walk away; clearly there is a reason that person does not want to share. Confidentiality issues can be easily dealt with and eliminated, so rest assured, that shouldn't be the basis for someone's reluctance.

## § 2.02   A BALANCED TEAM

Whether you choose to work with family, friends, or acquaintances, it is important to work with people who have complementary talents and strengths and who share similar values and goals. It also helps if at least one of you is technologically savvy. While this was not a big consideration in the past, so much of today's law practice relies on technology that it is important to have someone who understands computer operating systems and equipment.

Having at least one person with a good head for business is absolutely critical. Having more than one person who understands money is even better. As mentioned earlier, there are some very good lawyers who are not good business people. The bottom line is that a law firm needs to make money to stay viable. Many brilliant lawyers do not have good heads for business. These qualities are not mutually exclusive, but just make sure that you balance brilliance with business sense. If making money is not important to you and your partners, then you may feel otherwise.

However, if a firm is supporting several families, that firm needs to make money.

This brings us to the concept of the "rainmaker." Every firm needs at least one big rainmaker. If the partners split profits based on who generates how much business, your rainmaker is going to want you to take in every person he or she brings to the door. The office manager or managing partner will need to have a good idea about which files will and will not be profitable. That may be the person who decides whether or not the firm takes the case. Or, this decision may be made by a group. Either way, you are going to have to have sufficient financial information to evaluate the types of cases you are handling and whether or not they are worth your while.

Every firm must be able to generate business. Do not dismiss someone if that person's strength is attracting business rather than servicing it. You may be the most talented lawyer in town, but if you can't bring in any business, no one will ever know that. A well-balanced team, just like in sports, tends to be a stable and successful team.

# Chapter 3

# NAMING YOUR PRACTICE

If you are opening a solo practice, the easiest thing to do is to name the office after yourself. Calling your firm "The Law Office of Jane Doe" does not take a lot of imagination, and yet it may be exactly what you want to do. For example, if your family is well-known and well-respected in a particular geographical area, it makes sense to take advantage of that fact and use your family name as the name of your law firm. But even if no one knows your family or you, you may just decide that using your name conveys exactly what you want to convey: that this is your firm. And that is perfectly fine. Many lawyers do this.

Your firm's name can make a big difference in how the public perceives you. "The Law Office of Jane Doe" gives the impression of something more substantial than "Jane Doe, Esq." or "Jane Doe, Attorney at Law." As long as you are not doing something to mislead the public, you will be allowed to use your name in any reasonable way that you propose. But be sure to check the rules in your state when selecting the name of your firm. For example, some states prohibit you from opening an office called "The Law *Offices* of Jane Doe" if you are a solo practitioner with just one office. The reason for such a prohibition is that it implies more than one location and more than one attorney. Likewise, lawyers are specifically prohibited by the ABA Model Rules from using "Jane Doe & Associates" as a firm name if, in fact, there are no associates. Be sure to check the ethical rules where you live.

In addition, when selecting a name for your business, you will need to make sure that no one else in your state already has an existing business using the same name or a name so similar that there would be confusion if you were to use the name you selected. If someone else already is using your name, you may want to add something to your name, such as a middle initial or middle name, or you may want to refer to an area of law you will be handling to distinguish your office from the other business. States maintain a database of law firm names, and it is incumbent upon you to check out your selected name. You may access this information online and then reserve the name for a period of time until you complete your business setup.

You also will want to reserve and pay for one or more domain names. You can do this online. Just enter "purchase domain name" into your search engine to find companies that will do this for you. Usually, purchasing a .com domain name online costs only a few dollars. The domain name is important so that you can set up a website and people can find your contact information online.

In recent years, it has become more common to use a hook or an angle other than just your name when naming a solo practice. There are firms that add the field in which they practice to their firm name to try to attract the types of clients they want to service. For example, a lawyer might name her practice "The Family Law Office of Jane Doe" or "Jane Doe, Family Law Attorney." Some people choose a name that is totally unrelated to a specific area of practice because they think it might be catchier and thus more easily remembered. If this appeals to you, you might consider something like "Jane Doe: Lexicon Law" or "Lexicon Law: The Law Office of Jane Doe." ABA Model Rule 7.5 permits trade names as long as they are not false, misleading, or deceptive. That is not the case in New York, Texas, and a few other states that say trade names are misleading and prohibit them.

Another approach is to include a word that conveys something central to the core of who you are as a lawyer. An example of this notion is "Jane Doe, The Integrity Law Group." (If your state considers the word "group" misleading, consider using the word "firm" because almost all will permit that word.) What you name the firm may be important with regard to your ability to draw clients. Maybe you want to convey that your firm is not overly expensive. Maybe something like "Jane Doe, A Lawyer for the People," does the trick for you, but steer clear of names that imply that your firm is publicly supported.

Before you name your firm, make sure you have thoroughly checked the rules of your jurisdiction to see if there are any restrictions on naming a law office. Some states require that the name of the owners or partners be reflected in the firm name. Other states may not require the names of the attorneys but may still have a set of rules regarding misleading the public or promising the public things the firm can't deliver. Lawyers cannot claim in their name or as part of their identity that "every case is a winner." This is because no lawyer can guaranty the outcome of a case, although not every member of the public knows that. Thus, including that type of language in a name or on the letterhead is most likely going to be impermissible. Finally, your state may require you to use the initials PC, PLLC, or LLC in your name if you have formed such an entity. You do not want to invest in advertising only to find that you have to pull back everything you have done because you were too lazy to do the necessary legwork to make sure you were in compliance with your state's rules.

## § 3.01   NAMING A FIRM WITH SEVERAL LAWYERS

If there is more than one of you opening a practice together, naming your firm can sometimes be difficult. If you are newly admitted attorneys and believe that everyone is more or less equal in terms of investment, business generation, and experience, then listing your last names in alphabetical order is the obvious and simple way to go. On the other hand, such a simple solution may not be the right solution for you and your firm. For example, often people use the first initial of the last names to identify your firm. But if your names are **A**bromowitz, **S**mith, and **S**unshine, you might want to consider another ordering of the names.

Also, keep in mind that in a firm with many names, the ending names tend to be dropped when referring to a firm with many names. Therefore, you may want to have more identifiable names at the beginning of your firm name. Johnson and Jones, for example, may be too common to be distinguishable and memorable, so even if they are the first two names alphabetically, you may not want to use them at the beginning of your firm name. On the other hand, if some of the names are very difficult to pronounce, you may not want to put those names first unless the names may draw a particular demographic that you desire.

If the attorneys are not equal in terms of investment, talent, experience, and/ or business contacts, the choice of whose name goes first (or whose names are included in the firm's name) can create some heated discussions. For example, maybe you critically need the startup funds that one partner brings to the table. Or maybe you decide that one partner's ability to generate business is critical. Then you might decide to put that person's name first. You will have to take these things into account when formulating your firm's name.

Some attorneys have told us that it is a fantasy to believe that partners can ever be equal, because someone is always the leader or the more respected attorney. If you agree with that philosophy, then you might want to name the firm after that person — as in "The Jane Doe Law Group" (if that is permissible where you practice), or you might want to list that person's name first to make it the most dominant name in the firm.

Whatever you do, you have to be careful not to mislead. For example, you probably should not use something like "Suffolk County Law Services" because it might lead a potential client to believe that somehow you are affiliated with that county government.

If you do pick an unrelated name, you have to consider whether that name is something you should be trademarking. You also have to investigate if there is someone else who has used the name you want to use. Naming your firm is not an insignificant matter. The right name may make a difference in terms of potential clients searching for a lawyer. Attorneys and other business people now pay to find out which words are most commonly searched on the Internet by the people seeking the service they have to offer. There is nothing wrong with taking advantage of this type of knowledge. You are in business to make a living. Try to maximize that possibility, provided that what you do meets all rules and regulations of the jurisdiction in which you reside.

# Chapter 4

# WHAT TYPE OF BUSINESS ENTITY SHOULD YOU CREATE?

One of the more confusing things you will have to deal with when you open your practice is deciding what type of operating entity you want to form. Many lawyers form an operating entity without giving the matter much thought and often just do what their friends and colleagues have done. Although you might be comfortable with that, we believe you should get professional advice about the pros and cons of various types of operating entities and which type might be more beneficial for you.

We are not going to give you advice about which entity you should form. But we are going to give you some basic information, some guidance about whom to consult, things to consider, and questions to ask. Additionally, we're providing some basic informational forms and outlines in the Appendix to this book.

## § 4.01  WHOM SHOULD YOU CONSULT?

There are lawyers who spend their time assisting others in establishing business entities. Some identify themselves as corporate attorneys, some call themselves business attorneys, and others call themselves commercial practitioners. If you are renting space in an office where other lawyers have practices, ask them if they were happy with the lawyer who formed their business entity. If they give that lawyer a positive review, you may want to call that lawyer first. On the other hand, if you don't have an easy lead like that, your local bar association probably has a committee of lawyers who work in commercial practice. Check to see who is acting as the current chair of that committee. Then ask other practitioners whether they know of that person's qualifications.

You should also consult with your accountant concerning the tax ramifications of forming a particular type of business entity. If you do not have an accountant in mind to handle your business work, you should try to find a capable accountant with whom you feel comfortable. Your accountant will not only be able to help you with this issue but should be able to help you with any other matters. Accountants can assist you in making determinations regarding whether or not to take on certain financial obligations and, of course, they will assist you with preparing tax returns, paying estimated taxes, and setting up payment of withholding taxes. They also can be important sounding boards to assist you in making major business decisions. If your accountant is unclear when trying to explain important business matters to you, move on to someone else. You need to be able to understand what your accountant is doing for you. If your accountant's explanation makes you feel stupid, find another accountant. Remember: You were smart enough to get through law school and pass the bar;

therefore, you certainly are smart enough to understand accounting if explained clearly.

It is important not only to understand what your accountant is explaining but also to have a good level of communication with your accountant. Make sure that he or she answers all of your questions when you ask about the tax ramifications of forming a particular type of entity. While no decision is irrevocable, it sure is a lot easier to set things up correctly at the outset rather than having to dissolve or disband an entity and then incur the costs of setting up a different one.

Be careful about seeking free (or for that matter paid) advice from professionals who do not practice primarily within the venue in which you intend to operate. The laws vary from state to state, and not every state provides the same options for professional entities.

## § 4.02  CAN YOU INSULATE YOURSELF FROM CLAIMS OF YOUR OWN MALPRACTICE IF YOU FORM A PARTICULAR TYPE OF PROFESSIONAL ENTITY?

As much as we would like to tell you that you can shield your personal assets from claims of malpractice, the fact is that if YOU commit malpractice, your operating entity won't shield you. That is why, in this book, we will frequently remind you to obtain adequate malpractice insurance with a reputable company. We cannot say this too many times. You'd be surprised at the number of attorneys who are willing to take the risk of not buying malpractice insurance just so they can save the cost of the premiums.

The purpose of having a malpractice policy is to pay for any judgment against you for professional malpractice.

## § 4.03  SHOULD YOU BOTHER FORMING A PROFESSIONAL ENTITY?

Let's consider some options available to you as a solo practitioner.

### [A]  Solo Practitioner With No Entity

You certainly are able to open an office without forming a corporation or limited liability company. Some people prefer to do this because of the simplicity factor. Even if you choose this option, you may still have to follow some basic formalities. Some states require you to file a Certificate of Doing Business, often within the county or counties in which you operate. In New York and Texas, for example, you must file an Assumed Name Certificate (commonly referred to as a DBA) with the clerk of the county in which the business is conducted if you are operating under a name other than the proprietor's; no other filing is required. Information on establishing sole proprietorships is available on a state's department of state website or a county government's website.

Forms for a Certificate of Doing Business may be available to you in your county clerk's office, or you can download one for free or buy one online. There are companies that make these and other legal forms readily available for purchase both on the Internet and/or at a business stationer. The DBA certificate is simply a form that identifies you as doing business under a particular name. So, for example, it may be as simple as filing a certificate that says you are doing business under the name of Jane Doe, Attorney at Law. Make sure to check what you are required to file in your state and county and also where you must file the certificate or form.

Whether or not you choose to form an entity, make sure that you have insurance coverage for situations in addition to malpractice. For example, you will need liability insurance to cover you for claims as a result of accidents that happen on your premises. A miserable winter day can become a lot more miserable if you do not have liability insurance, and someone slips on the ice on the way into your office. You will also need Workers Compensation Insurance if you have employees. Do not make your decision about the type of structure you want for your business based upon the up-front cost of forming the entity. Those dollars will pale in comparison to the dollars you could place at risk by failing to form the entity.

While it is always important to have the appropriate insurance coverage, it is even more important to purchase enough insurance if you do not form a business entity that can provide you with an extra layer of protection. Meet with a knowledgeable broker and also discuss these issues with your accountant and/or attorney.

## [B]  Solo Practitioner With Entity

The most common types of entities used by solo practitioners are the Professional Corporation (PC) and the Limited Liability Company (LLC). As stated above, the most important reason for forming one of these entities is to limit your personal liability. Yes, there are costs attached to the formation of these entities, but there are also other advantages. Just the sight of PC or LLC after your name makes some people believe you are more established and that you have a more viable business, even though you know that you are just starting out and have only a couple of clients. If people perceive you as busy and high-powered, that may become your reality. This is because if people think you have a viable business, they will be more likely to hire you. And this isn't just our belief; we've heard it from other attorneys as well.

## § 4.04  MORE THAN ONE LAWYER FORMING THE BUSINESS

If you are going to be starting a business with more than one attorney, you should seriously consider forming a business entity of some sort. The reason for this is self-preservation. Lawyers have been advising clients to form an LLC or PC for years because you can insulate yourself from the malpractice committed by a partner or shareholder, provided you are not supervising that person's work.

The most common types of entities for more than one attorney are a PC, an LLC, or, in some states, a PLLC (Professional Limited Liability Company), depending upon the law in the jurisdiction where you will be practicing. It is critical that you not operate until you have your entity in place. If you are operational without forming an entity, the law will treat your firm as a general partnership, which means you are personally liable for the full amount of the obligations of the business — not just part of them — as well as any mistakes that your partners commit. Haste makes waste.

Whether or not to form a PC or an LLC/PLLC is a decision to be made with professional assistance. You may own a Professional Limited Liability Company only with other attorneys (i.e., not with anyone who isn't an attorney), which really should not be surprising given that the Model Rules, as well as state Codes of Conduct, do not permit the sharing of profits between a lawyer and non-lawyer. Ask your accountant if there are any specific tax advantages for you if you form one type of entity over another. In some states, there are costs associated with opening one type of entity that are not associated with opening another. Since you will be forming a new business and trying to save your dollars where you can, this may play a role for you in your decision.

Alternatively, one reason that many lawyers choose an LLC/PLLC is because of its flexibility. Flexibility is not an abstract concept. When operating a new business, you will make some initial decisions that you will want to revisit. Some attorneys believe that the process is easier with an LLC/PLLC than with a PC.

Some attorneys prefer the PC because they like the corporate structure. Your choice of operating entity will come down to a recommendation from your advisor or advisors. Be sure to discuss the potential tax advantages and or disadvantages of each structure in your particular case with your accountant. Please see the Appendix for sample forms.

The operating agreement is arguably the most important document in any LLC. The equivalent to this, if you choose to form a corporation, is the shareholders' agreement and corporate bylaws; in a partnership, it is the partnership agreement. The purpose of these agreements is to spell out all the rights, obligations, expectations, and rules of conduct so there will be no misunderstandings or surprises among participants.

Generally, these types of agreements will address the functionality of internal operations including: members' ownership (whether by percentage or shares owned); voting rights and responsibilities; powers and duties of members and managers or shareholders; distribution of profits and losses; holding meetings; and buyout procedures for transferring someone's interest (shares of stock or otherwise) when members/shareholders choose to do so or if a member or shareholder dies.

The parameters of what is required in the agreement are laid out in the governing statutes of the state in which the business is formed. You need to check to see which written documents are required by your state. Enforceability is key, so if your state requires documents to be written and signed in a particular fashion for the terms of your business relationship to be enforceable, then you have to be very careful to be sure that you are in compliance with your state's rules.

Although most states do not require operating agreements for LLCs, some do — New York and Missouri, for example. Also, the LLC statutes of some states, like New

York and Wisconsin, require the operating agreement to be in writing to be enforceable.

Regardless of whether your state requires a written agreement, we recommend that you have one in place. This helps you avoid being subjected to statutory default rules and protects the terms that you and your business associates worked so hard to agree upon.

## § 4.05   COMMON STEPS IN CREATING A BUSINESS ENTITY

1) Name your business.

2) File the articles of organization or a copy of your articles of incorporation (sometimes called a certificate of incorporation or certificate of formation) with the secretary of state or the appropriate body if applicable in your state. Note that there may be a legal notice publication requirement, depending on the type of entity formed and the rules in your state.

3) Create and execute a governing agreement, be it an operating agreement, shareholders agreement, or such other governing document that is applicable to the entity in your state.

Think about the following when drafting your agreement:

- Who will manage the LLC's affairs?
- What will be your respective interests in the entity?
- How do you remove yourself from the relationship?
- How will profits and losses be distributed?
- What are the voting rights? To move forward on a decision, what votes are required?
- How do you add new lawyers to the business? Do they need to buy in?
- What events will trigger the dissolution of the entity?

# Chapter 5

## LAWYER COMPENSATION

It should come as no surprise to you that one of the toughest aspects of forming a practice with other attorneys is figuring out the method of compensation.

Clearly, you want everyone to be an integral part of making the business successful, and you want to encourage teamwork while you are establishing your firm. Therefore, it is not uncommon, when you start, to share equally in the good and the bad. Under this scenario, if you have costs that exceed the firm's income, each partner would be equally responsible for either paying for those costs or for repaying the loan or line of credit that covered those costs. Under the equal-share scenario, if your firm's income exceeded the expenses, each partner would share equally in the monies that you chose to distribute.

When you first start your firm, you may have no idea of which partner will bring in the most clients or who will be the most productive worker. If this is the case, an equal division of profits and losses may make the most sense at the outset. As time passes, you may find that one or more partners are dissatisfied with an equal distribution of profits and losses for a variety of reasons. Therefore, you may want to revisit your arrangement. That, too, is not an unusual situation. As mentioned earlier, one of the reasons lawyers make agreements before they open an office is to establish rules for how their business will be operated and to set time frames for reevaluation. Businesses are ever-changing entities, and it is important for you and your partners to remember to reevaluate your compensation structure and make any necessary adjustments as your business evolves.

Dealing with who gets what percentage of the profits is a sensitive topic that can cause disagreement among partners. Another sensitive topic is deciding how much of the profits to distribute in total versus how much to retain in the firm. You might choose to have the firm retain some of the profits so that you can cover costs in the lean times, or to maintain a fund that is readily available if you need to spend money to increase your marketing; purchase new equipment, software, or furnishings; or hire additional staff.

As we will discuss below, there are also compensation arrangements that involve a holdback of a certain percentage of the firm's profits for later distribution.

Deciding how much to retain can be almost as difficult as determining the plan of compensation. Let's face it, sometimes one of you may need more money than another and, as a result, that person will not be eager to have the firm retain large sums of money that could be distributed to the partners. Also keep in mind that after the monies are distributed to the partners, it may be difficult or impossible to get those monies back from a financially needy partner if the firm needs those monies for expenses. Therefore, it makes sense to discuss the concept of retaining a financial cushion when you start your firm — before you actually have the money on hand — and to agree on what percentage of funds you will retain. You can revise this cushion when you have a better idea of how your business is doing.

In addition to thinking about retaining profits to pay for extra office expenses, you are also going to have to remember to retain profits to pay for taxes that you will owe on the money that the firm has taken in as well as on the money you have made personally. Remember that when you work for yourself, there is no employer to deduct taxes from your salary. This means that if you take a draw instead of a salary, there are no deductions out of the monies you receive for taxes and Social Security. You are going to have to make those payments at some point. Anticipating this expense is critical to having a realistic budget for your law business.

---

It just so happens that my parents were accountants, and, so, when I opened my office, I had the perfect accountants. My parents wanted me to succeed, and they were the right price. One of the first things my mother made me do was to open a tax account. She instructed me to put ⅓ of every fee I received into that account and told me I could not touch that money because it was needed for my taxes. Now remember, she had me take ⅓ of every gross fee. The bottom line was that I never needed the whole sum in the account to pay the taxes because there were expenses that came off of the fees. This way, I always had more than enough money to cover the taxes, and, at the end of the year, I had a nice little chunk of change to tide me over, or, if it wasn't needed, to invest or spend as I wanted. It was a great way to handle things! LAK

---

When I started my law practice, I decided that I would handle all the bookkeeping, payroll, and taxes myself to save money. I was good at these things, and I didn't mind doing them. I knew accountants who were willing to advise me, if necessary, and I liked the occasional diversion of dealing with numbers rather than clients. (Numbers don't get emotional.) But after a few years, I began to resent the time that I had to spend on these tasks and finally realized that it was a false economy to do them myself because I charged more per hour for my law services than I would pay a the bookkeeper and accountant. That is, instead of spending an hour of uncompensated time working on my payroll taxes and quarterly income tax filings, I could offload that work to someone else and make more money than I needed to pay them. The added benefit of sending work to a bookkeeper and accountant is that they got to know me and sent some of their clients to me. And I sent some of my clients to them. So offload your bookkeeping and accounting as fast as you can. ALN

# § 5.01  OVERVIEW

When preparing to write about the topic of partner compensation for this book, we interviewed numerous lawyers and confirmed what we knew from speaking informally over the last two decades with our colleagues in small-firm practice: small law firms, consisting of two to four partners, frequently do not have written compensation agreements. But when the number of partners becomes larger than that, firms tend to adopt written compensation systems. Some firms have compensation committees; in other firms, a senior partner is largely responsible for making the determinations. And in still other firms, all partners participate in an annual distribution meeting.

We believe that is it crucial that you discuss this topic with your potential partners BEFORE you decide to go into business with them. You need to know BEFORE you go into business whether you share a similar philosophy regarding how your firm should be run; what your goals are for the office; and how, when, why, and by whom monies will be distributed.

There are many issues that you will need to think about before determining your compensation plan. Included among them are the following:

1)  Do you want to compensate all partners equally, or do you want to enact a compensation plan that offers the partners incentives to work harder?

2)  If your firm establishes an incentive-based compensation system, which of the following categories will the firm reward more generously: the Finders (those who originate business), the Minders (those who maintain the clients), or the Grinders (those who do the work)?

3)  Who will decide partner compensation?

4)  Are you going to have a draw based on past performance?

5)  Are you going to distribute some monies prospectively and some monies based on what actually happened over the past year?

6)  Will you compensate one or more of the partners for managing the firm?

7)  Are there any jobs or tasks for which you will pay additional compensation?

While these questions may seem somewhat straightforward, they can actually be far more complicated than you can imagine. For example, if you credit someone with origination of business, what does that mean? If Lawyer A introduces the original client to the firm, and Lawyer B works on the client's matter, and then that client refers someone else to the office, which lawyer should get credit for the origination of business? Lawyers argue about this issue regularly. Lawyer A will suggest that Lawyer B was merely handling the work competently. Should the fact that a client is satisfied with a law firm's work, and, as a result, sends someone else to the office be considered origination? After all, do we punish a lawyer by withholding compensation if a client isn't overly enthusiastic?

If origination is going to be one of the factors in determining compensation, you are going to have to define what "origination" means for the purpose of your firm. Different firms will define it differently.

Here's why "origination" is hard to define:

Suppose, as we said above, Lawyer A brings a client to your firm. Then Lawyer B handles the case and makes the client feel comfortable enough to want to refer other people to your firm. Should you allow Lawyer B to get credit for "originating" the referral because Lawyer B made the existing client so comfortable that the existing client referred someone? If you allow Lawyer B (the worker) to get credit for the referral of a new case by an existing client brought to the firm by Lawyer A, then Lawyer A may want to do all the work on his or her own cases for fear of losing the future referrals. What if Lawyer A is better at rainmaking than at servicing cases, but Lawyer B is better at servicing cases than at rainmaking? Do you see how complicated things can get?

If you reward bringing in business and working on the files (including "minding" or cultivating the clients) equally, does that system promote more teamwork? On the one hand, if you have no business, there can be no reward for the worker. But if you have no one to do the work, then origination means nothing. On the other hand, the originator can argue that workers are interchangeable but rainmakers are not. There is a saying among lawyers that "you can always buy brains." But not all workers are good at client relations. Some are particularly skilled at making existing clients feel comfortable. This has to do with returning phone calls and emails promptly, explaining concepts clearly to people who know little or nothing about the law and the legal process, and choosing a tone and language that makes each client feel comfortable and valued. Many people who possess this skill are not good at rainmaking, but they are good at retaining clients. Is this as valuable as rainmaking, or more or less valuable?

There are no right or wrong answers when determining lawyer compensation. Lawyers who are going to go into business together are going to have to confront these issues, determine their values, and decide the most effective way to compensate attorneys in order to effectuate the firm's goals. Once again, we recommend that you deal with the issues raised in this chapter sooner rather than later.

## § 5.02   SAMPLE METHODS OF COMPENSATION

### [A]   Equal Distribution of Profits

This is the easiest and most obvious method of compensation and is frequently used by lawyers with a new practice. If everyone shares equally when the firm does well, then the lawyers can focus on the financial success of the firm rather than their personal financial successes. This method of compensation helps to insulate lawyers from the pain of years in which their personal cases aren't generating a lot of income. An example of this is where one partner handles negligence work and achieves a huge recovery one year but nothing major the next. Even if you choose this method of income allocation when you begin your firm, you should reevaluate your firm's method of allocating income annually.

Just as there are strengths to an equal compensation system, there are some major weaknesses as well. First and foremost, there is no reward for the partner who puts in far more hours than the others. If one lawyer works from dawn until dusk while another one attends his or her children's ball games most afternoons, the one who is there all day can become resentful. Likewise, when only one of the partners is networking and generating business, that partner may want to move to a firm where origination is rewarded.

## [B]　Equal Draws With Subjective Distribution of Profits

Another way to divide the firm's income is to have partners receive equal amounts of money but reserve an amount of the profits (sometimes called a bonus pool) to be divided subjectively among the partners. The division of this bonus pool can be made by a managing partner, a senior partner, a committee, or by all members of the firm working together to determine the value of each lawyer's contribution to the firm.

The arrangement where a senior partner is left to make the subjective decisions can often be found in small suburban practices where a senior partner had a successful practice before the addition of other partners. In this instance, the new partners agree to defer to that senior person because of that person's years of experience and obvious desire to see the firm succeed. More than likely, the senior partner's name is the lead name or the only name on the letterhead.

Where there is no senior partner, some firms elect a managing partner who will determine the distribution of the bonus pool. The partners elect this individual to be the managing partner because of that person's excellent business sense and management skills and because the partners are comfortable in relying on that person's judgment. The managing partner's goal must be the long-term success of the firm, and distributions must be consistent with that goal.

Some firms have a committee that is specifically charged with the duty of distributing the bonus pool. It is common for firms to keep the committee intact for a period of years so that a lawyer who is disgruntled one year won't be able to try to manipulate the compensation allocation the next year either by lobbying for a spot on the committee or by trying to put political blocs together to revamp the committee. Firms with a constant change in the management committee can face serious disruption — something that is not beneficial if experienced annually.

And finally, some firms require all partners to participate in the division and distribution of monies. In a small firm of two to five lawyers, this is not a problem. Colleagues have told us that this can create a great deal of fighting in larger firms and is not good for the morale or collegiality of the firm.

## [C]　Incentive-Based Compensation Where Percentages are Allocated to Different Functions

In this arrangement, partners may receive a base salary or a draw, and then the profits above the draws are divided based on percentages allocated to specific functions. The partners can agree to divide the profits based on their determination of the import of certain functions. For example, the firm can agree to an allocation of profits as follows:

- 25% for the origination of business
- 25% for the maintenance of the client(s)

- 40% for the billable hours/work actually done

- 10% left in a pool to be awarded for particularly positive contributions (for example, community leadership, bar leadership, or administrative work) or for marketing efforts such as speaking at civic association meetings or writing articles designed to bring in new business.

The categories and percentages can be revisited and changed at the partners' discretion. In their partnership agreements, the partners can choose to provide specific timeframes for the review of allocations, or they can write that the allocations may be readjusted. In addition to the flexibility built into this type of arrangement, another advantage of this type of compensation plan is that it allows each lawyer to be in control of his or her own financial fate. If one partner wants to work more hours and make more money, that person can do so. Alternatively, if a partner wants to work fewer hours and spend more time with the family, the partner's compensation will reflect that choice. Yes, the loss in income will affect the total income of the firm and, thus, will affect all the partners; but when one partner receives a smaller percentage of the total income, the other partners will receive larger percentages. This, in theory, should make the hard workers happy. Of course, if one partner is truly a slacker, the other partners are likely to be unhappy no matter how the percentages are computed.

There are also other negatives to this plan. (But, remember, there are negatives to all types of compensation plans.) First, because partners know what they will be rewarded for, they may focus their energy on one or two functions. So, for example, if the firm chooses to allocate the largest reward to the person who does the actual work on a file, then lawyers may well choose to perform the work on their cases rather than focus on other firm obligations that are less generously rewarded — such as maintaining relationships with clients. In addition, a lawyer may choose to work on a file although that person may not be the best suited to do that work, either because of lack of experience or lack of talent. This can present a host of issues: Who decides who does which work on a case? Does the originator decide, or does an office manager or management committee make that decision? Remember, the partners must share the goal of maintaining an excellent law-firm reputation, and this can be sorely tested when the desire for compensation comes ahead of competence.

## [D]  Limited Incentive-Based Compensation

There are firms that expect all the partners to work at every aspect of making the firm successful. These firms do not give financial rewards (additional compensation) to partners for being active in the community or for being well-known bar leaders. They do not compensate anyone for managing the firm, nor do they choose to ascribe value to anything other than billable time and business origination. This system is simple and creates little antagonism among partners because the factors being considered for the determination of compensation are clear and more or less objective, with the caveat of some possible disputes over origination. However, if you define origination clearly at the outset, then hourly billings and business origination are not subjective factors.

Some firms using this system make no payments of any sort, either draws or distributions, until all expenses are paid. The lawyers at such firms might have pre-established draws. The monies remaining after expenses and draws are immediately paid to the partners based on the agreed-upon credits for origination and billing time. There is no end-of-year distribution because distributions are made regularly throughout the year.

Some firms pay the lawyers both their draw and their share of profits weekly. If the firm's expenses are not covered, there is no draw and no payment of bonuses. Income can vary tremendously on a weekly basis, but with this system, all partners benefit during the good weeks, and there is little friction as a result. Remember, the positive side of this system is that if anyone comes up with a big client or a big victory, all of the firm's lawyers benefit.

## [E]    Eat-What-You-Kill Systems

Firms that operate with these types of systems may seem less like law firms and more like a collection of attorneys who are sharing overhead and not really sharing goals or clients. In these types of arrangements, lawyers are more or less operating their own practices within a practice. Overhead is shared among the lawyers such that each pays an equal portion of the rent, utilities, cleaning costs, shared equipment costs, and supplies; all of the income a lawyer generates remains his or her own. If a firm of this nature has associates, the firm can agree upon the costs to each partner to use the associates, and then it is up to the partner to charge the client for the use of the associates. If a partner brings in a type of case that he or she is not capable of handling, that partner can refer the case to someone else at the firm and negotiate to retain a percentage of the fee. This arrangement is not for lawyers who are anxious to build a firm where the lawyers share clients and are working toward the success of the firm. This arrangement also does not provide for anyone to manage the firm. Many lawyers consider this type of arrangement a firm in name only.

Nonetheless, this type of arrangement can be successfully executed by a group of attorneys who want the benefit of shared costs as well as the benefit of being able to pass clients to others with whom they are associated but who prefer to manage and control their own businesses. There is nothing wrong with this type of arrangement as long as everyone understands the philosophy at the outset.

## § 5.03    SOME ADDITIONAL THOUGHTS ABOUT COMPENSATION AGREEMENTS

## [A]    Can Partners Ever Really be Equal?

Some lawyers have very strong feelings about the notion of equal partnerships. They say they do not believe that people are ever really equal when it comes to business and that someone is always the leader. They say that in any firm of more than three lawyers, someone has to take the leadership role or the result will be chaos. That means that one person should take the dominant role in running all aspects of the business, from daily operations to lawyer compensation. The leader of a firm must be a good lawyer, good with people, and have good business sense. If you think you are not well suited to running a business — either by ability or by temperament — you have to decide if you would be willing to allow someone else to make the majority of business decisions on your behalf.

## [B]   Timing of the Distributions of Money

New lawyers who are opening a firm may recognize the need to explore and talk about the compensation issues we have discussed. They may talk about firm values, what should be recognized in their compensation plan, and who will make the determinations as to distributions. Nonetheless, a topic that these lawyers often fail to explore adequately is the timing of the distribution of money. This may be because most lawyers who are opening their own firms probably assume they will get a weekly draw and distributions either quarterly or at the end of the year. This may or may not be the best plan for you.

A plan that allows for draws and distributions only if the partners meet certain goals and/or expectations forces new lawyers to work harder and network more to produce more income. At the time the firm is created, the lawyers have to establish an expectation of profits — basically, an educated guess of what the firm should net. Then, you receive a distribution only if the firm makes at least that amount of profit.

So, let's assume that there are three partners, and at the beginning of your relationship, you agree that the anticipated first-year profit is $90,000. According to this expectation, you should have a law firm profit of $1,730 per week ($90,000 divided by 52 weeks). Under this compensation plan, the partners would not get any money during a week in which the law firm has less than $1,730 in profit. Thus, if the firm made only $1,500 in profit in one week ($500 for each partner), the partners each would receive no money that week because the firm did not meet the $1,730 expectation. The partners would have to wait until the next week and hope that the firm would meet its $1,730 goal that week. Some attorneys believe this method of payment forces young attorneys to make sure the firm meets its goal. Receiving no income in a week can be a tremendous motivator.

Remember that a draw is different from a distribution of profits. A draw is the amount that the partners have agreed to take weekly if there are sufficient funds to make the payment. The distribution of profits is a sharing of profits taken from the business when the partners choose to take all or some of the money. Salaries and draws tend to be regular payments in constant amounts; distributions are variable depending upon the amount of profit to be distributed. In the previous example, the draw was not paid because the firm didn't meet its goal.

Let's now look at what happens if the firm far exceeds its goal. If the firm had $3,000.00 in profit in one week, each of the three partners would receive the full amount of the draw: 1/3 of $1,730. Whether the other $1,270 is divided and paid to the partners is a totally different issue. Some firms make the division of these excess profits weekly. This can work only with either a simple plan for the calculation of the distribution of profits or one that makes the distribution based on the previous year's income. Doing the math weekly with subjective factors is almost impossible. However, distributions can be made quarterly if properly prepared for and certainly can be made shortly after the end of the year.

Make sure to have the conversation regarding the timing of draws and distributions before there is money to squabble over.

## [C]    The Firm Must Have the Ability to Evolve

Some attorneys believe that it is beneficial to limit how much is written in the firm's initial agreement. The agreement needs to contain compensation plans and management matters. But provisions for extensive pension contributions and/or costly buy-out arrangements for older attorneys can be a tremendous disincentive for young attorneys whom you may want to attract to your firm. If the firm's initial agreement commits too much of the profit to the past instead of to the future, you may limit the ability of your firm to grow.

# Chapter 6

# FINANCES

Let's say that you have determined that you have the desire to start your own law firm, and you believe that you have the personality to succeed at it. But do you have the money it takes?

If you're thinking of starting your own law firm, you have to think about finances for getting it off the ground. After all, starting a law firm is not just a big, exciting adventure. As we said before, it's a foray into the world of business. And in that world, the main goal is to make money. Yes, you are also hoping to help people. But you are opening a business in which you will be selling a commodity (legal services) with the intent to earn profits.

As the saying goes, "It takes money to make money." And law firm entrepreneurship is no different. You will need at least some money to start your law firm, even if you plan on operating from your home and using the trusty, old laptop that got you through law school.

Even if you don't buy any new equipment initially, and you use your cell phone as your only business phone (which we don't recommend, but we'll get to that in a later chapter), you will still need money to purchase malpractice insurance, stationery (although you can print your own, you still need the paper), business cards, a scanner, etc. This isn't a huge expense, but even the little things add up.

And while you're trying to get your new law business off the ground, you will need to have money to pay for your personal living expenses like health insurance, car insurance, gas, car repairs, medical copays, pet food and veterinary care, haircuts, food, etc. If you are not living with someone who is paying to keep a roof over your head at home (i.e., a parent, spouse, partner, sibling, or friend), you will also need to pay for the rent/mortgage on your living space, heat, electricity, access to the Internet, etc.

The question is: How are you going to do this when you're spending long hours every day trying to market your legal services so you can get clients who will pay you? And while you're doing that, you will have to spend long hours learning how to do the legal work for those clients.

That is, how are you going to earn money to pay all your personal bills when your law business still doesn't have many customers?

## § 6.01  HOW TO STAY AFLOAT WHILE YOUR PRACTICE IS NEW

Some new law entrepreneurs work at customer-service jobs in the food service industry to make money until their new firms begin to turn a large enough profit to pay all the bills. Still other new law entrepreneurs continue to work either full-time or part-time at their former profession — like nursing or accounting or teaching or construction — until their new law practices take off and fly.

Any of these plans is fine. But you need to have a plan, not just a vague idea of how you are going to make money while trying to launch and grow your law business. We'll get to how to construct a business plan later in this chapter. First, however, let's talk about sources of funding to start your law business and keep you solvent while you're trying to grow it big enough to sustain itself and you.

## § 6.02  SAVING MONEY WITH A HOME OFFICE

Although you certainly can start your law business from your home with just an old laptop and your personal cell phone, do you really want clients to come to your home? If you have the kind of practice where you don't need to see your clients in person, then this won't be an issue. If you do need to meet with your clients, and you have a home office, you could rent someone else's conference room to meet with your clients. That will cost money, and the conference room needs to be free when you want to use it. Also, what will you do when your clients want to drop in to pay you in person (for example, when they are paying with cash)? Do you want to have to clean up your house each time clients say they are coming over? How will you feel when you open the door to welcome a client and see that your cat has just coughed up a hairball where the client is about to step? And how will you feel about clients who decide to drop in first thing in the morning on their way to work when you're in the middle of brushing your teeth? Do you want clients stopping by your house without calling you first?

And do you want to be disturbed by your family members when you are trying to work? Do you think that your clients will want to talk on the phone with a lawyer when the lawyer's voice is almost drowned out by the background noises of children yelling and dogs barking? Will your clients think that this is professional?

Also, if you are sitting in your home, the humans who also live in that space will think that it's fine to ask you questions while you're trying to work. You'll also be able to hear their telephone conversations and television programs. You may think that you'll be able to tune this out, but soon it will begin to annoy you. And the humans in the house will begin to get annoyed when you tell them that you're busy and keep asking them to turn down the volume on the television.

Unless you have a totally segregated office space within your home or attached to your home, we recommend trying to find inexpensive office space outside your home, even if that will require spending more money.

## § 6.03  RENTING AFFORDABLE SPACE

You might want to rent a small room in another lawyer's office or in the office of another type of professional — like an accountant or a financial planner — where there is a potential for cross-referrals. In many parts of the country, commercial landlords are renting out one-person offices with shared bathrooms and shared conference rooms at a low monthly cost. Even in Manhattan, where rental space is extremely expensive, it is possible to rent this kind of small, private office space in a central, desirable location for a reasonable sum that will be affordable to many beginning solo lawyers. Often the space includes a desk, desk chair, locked file cabinet, electricity, heat, access to the Internet, and use of a conference room and printer. Information about this kind of arrangement at locations across the country can be found via an Internet search under "coworking office."

The question is: Where you are going to find the extra money to pay for this if you don't have any clients yet? If you bill by the hour, you need to bill only a few hours per month to pay for this, depending upon your hourly billing rate. (Note that we said "per month," not "per day" or "per week.") Even if you still are working at another job to make ends meet until your law business produces enough revenue to pay for itself and for your personal expenses, you can quickly earn enough money from your law practice to pay this monthly rent. You might need to charge the first month or two of your personal expenses on your credit card to get started, but it's an investment that is well worth it because the psychological factor of having a law office outside your home will spur you to feel more like a professional and, therefore, work harder to produce more revenue. It's a lot easier to slack off when you're working out of your home and don't have the recurring monthly expense of an office.

You might be tempted to think that you could use that same rental money to pay for some of your personal expenses — like your educational loan or your health insurance — instead of your office rent. But if you establish yourself in a home office, you are likely to find yourself less motivated to spread your wings and fly when trying to get your law business off the ground. Also, if you charge fees that are lower than those charged by other lawyers because you are operating from your home and you don't have much overhead, how will you justify raising your fees way up to the "going" rate in your community when you finally move into an office and have to pay for office expenses? Your existing clients are not going to be happy when you bump your fees way up because you suddenly need to pay for office overhead.

Similarly, many clients are going to expect you to charge much less than the competition if you are practicing out of your home with little or no office overhead. This is particularly true if you are a new attorney and haven't established a reputation in the community. New attorneys with professional offices outside their homes — even small rooms in an office building made up of various kinds of professionals who each rent a small room — can command higher fees because they have the patina of professionalism that comes with a commercial office space. It's just basic human psychology, and we have talked with enough clients during our many years of practice to understand client psychology.

## § 6.04   SO HOW MUCH MONEY DO YOU NEED TO START?

All of this having been said, how much money do you need to start a law practice? That depends. If you start in your home, and you already have a laptop and printer and a scanner and an Internet connection, you'll need enough money to pay for malpractice insurance. Policies for fledgling attorneys who are just starting out, and who don't have much business yet, can be fairly inexpensive.

So, if you are just starting out, and working out of your home, you might not need much, if any, startup money at all. Maybe you'll just need to buy a printer and scanner and malpractice insurance for the year.

## § 6.05   SHOULD YOU BORROW MONEY?

We caution you against borrowing startup money from relatives or friends because this could damage your relationship if you can't pay it back right away. Also, this is likely to lead those relatives or friends to think that you "owe" them free legal advice in return for the favor of loaning you money — even if you are paying them interest. Be warned that this kind of legal advice often involves a lot more than just a simple answer, and you will find yourself getting sucked deeper and deeper into the legal situation — for free. The time that you spend on this will be time that you could have spent marketing your services to potential clients who would pay you. Think of your product — legal advice — as a commodity. If you were in the business of selling t-shirts, would you want to give out a large part of your inventory to the people who lent you $1,000 to start your business? Of course not. Therefore, be careful about borrowing money from relatives or friends. And if you do borrow it from them, make sure to put the agreement in writing including whether or not there will be any interest and when the payment will be due (monthly increments or in a lump sum by a certain date). Do not be tempted to write that there is no specified due date for repayment. That may sound terrific to you when you are borrowing the money, but it won't sound like such a great idea down the line when the lender is asking you to repay the loan, and you don't have the money yet. Set specific dates and treat the loan with the same respect as a commercial loan. Remember: this is a business loan to start a professional business. Treat the loan in a businesslike and professional manner.

## § 6.06   FINANCIAL MATTERS TO CONSIDER WHEN STARTING

### [A]   Renting Space

If you decide to open an office in a rental space, you may not need much startup funding if you are going to use a small, furnished room. But if you decide to rent a larger office space — one that you can grow into with its own area for a receptionist and a legal assistant that you hire yourself (i.e., not personnel that you share with professionals who are not part of your business), you may need to borrow startup funds. This is also true if you are going to start a law practice with at least one other person. If you start a law business with more than one other person, you won't be able to operate from your home or from a tiny office space designed for a solo practitioner.

If you're going to rent a space that can accommodate more than one person, you'll most likely need to sign a lease and will need enough money for the first month's rent, the last month's rent, and a security deposit (typically equal to one month's rent). Even if your landlord allows you to rent a space without a lease, on a month-to-month basis, it is best to avoid this kind of arrangement because the landlord can suddenly raise the rent a lot or suddenly ask you to leave. If you have established yourself at that location, and have listed that location on your business cards and in advertisements, you will not be happy to learn that you have to scramble to find another office and move.

## [B]  Liability Insurance

As we mentioned earlier, you will also need to purchase liability insurance to protect you and the landlord in case someone sustains an accidental injury in your office. Many landlords require tenants to purchase this kind of insurance — often with aggregate coverage of $1-2 million. This sounds like a lot, but court awards for just one slip-and-fall case can be in excess of $1 million. Premiums can be as low as a few hundred dollars a year and are often payable in full before the policy takes effect.

## [C]  Furnishings and Equipment

If your office space does not come with furnishings, you will need to furnish it — including a reception desk and seating for clients, a conference table and chairs, art for the walls, bookcases, file cabinets, a paper cutter, a shredder, a central phone system that will transfer calls from one phone to another, etc. Although you can buy furniture used, you are likely to need at least several thousand dollars to outfit your new office.

Also, you will either need a photocopier or a high-speed scanner and a high-speed laser printer. We recommend both a copier and a high-speed scanner, because there are likely to be many times in your law practice when you will not want to have to reproduce a large document page by page through a small, slow scanner. If your scanner is a flatbed model, you will be able to scan bound documents, but you will have to scan them page-by-page, which is extremely time-consuming. A self-feeding scanner is better for loose pages, but the inexpensive ones are nowhere as fast as most photocopiers.

Our advice is to purchase or lease both a self-feeding scanner and a photocopier with a self-feeder. They serve different functions. If you need to copy a bound document, you can copy it on the photocopier, then feed the pages into the self-feeding scanner if you need to convert them to files in your computer. You will regret thinking that you can get by with just an inexpensive flatbed scanner and no photocopier the first time you have to copy a large document under time pressure. The process will seem agonizingly slow.

Some lawyers prefer to rent office equipment — especially photocopiers. In the case of photocopiers, renting will allow an attorney to get a super-fast, state-of-the-art copier that can also scan documents and send them to your computer. The prices begin at surprisingly affordable monthly rates. The good news about this kind of arrangement is that you don't have to lay out a lot of money to purchase one, and the rental companies usually provide quick on-site service if the machine breaks. Many of these machines also collate and even staple documents for you. This is a big help if you need to make many copies of a document and are pressed for time (for example, when you are up against a filing deadline and need to provide multiple copies). Litigators particularly appreciate this feature.

Alternatively — especially if you are just starting out and do not have much, if any, litigation — you might just want to purchase a mid-sized photocopier rather than a large one, charge it to your credit card, and pay it off over time if you don't have the money to pay in full now. See our chapter on equipping an office for more information about purchasing a photocopier.

Additionally, you will need enough money to pay for recurring monthly office expenses like utilities (electricity, heat, air conditioning, etc.) if they are not included in the price of your rent.

For a solo or small-firm practice, you may need to pay for web design and for the monthly cost of a domain name. Don't be tempted to design your own web site unless you are talented at this kind of thing. If you decide to do it yourself, look at the websites of a lot of other lawyers — not just in your location, but across the country. Get someone who is good at proofreading to proofread the writing on your web site.

There are many other small expenses associated with starting and running a small law office. For example, you will also need to pay for photocopy and printing paper, toner for the printer and the photocopier (unless you are sharing one that belongs to another business), manila envelopes, file folders, and assorted other necessities like a heavy-duty stapler that works on more than just a few pages, exhibit tabs, and litigation backs. Trust us: This list looks like a bunch of tiny expenses that seem so small as to be unworthy of mentioning, but these expenses add up quickly. You can easily find yourself needing to spend many hundreds of dollars on basic office supplies when you first start your law business.

## § 6.07  OTHER SOURCES OF STARTUP FUNDS

For all of these expenses and more, you will need a source of income while you are trying to build your law practice. For lawyers who do not want to work at an outside job during this startup period (i.e., during the first year or more), it is necessary to rely on savings, credit cards, or loans.

If you rely on credit cards, look for one with a low rate of interest. This seems obvious, but many new lawyers just use whatever card they already have. It is best to get a credit card that you use only for expenses related to your new law business. This makes accounting much easier.

Although it is theoretically possible to obtain a bank loan to start your new law business, this is extremely difficult to do. Banks are in the business of making money, so they want to loan money to people who have a proven ability to repay those loans.

The mere fact that you're a lawyer does not make you a good risk in a bank's eyes. This is particularly true if you are young and living with your parents and have a large educational loan to repay. The bank is likely to see you as someone who has not yet established a track record of repaying debt in a timely manner. The bank needs to be able to see that you are capable of managing your money responsibly and paying your bills.

Thus, unless you have a long history of paying debts on time, a bank loan (including a "small-business" loan) is not a viable option. By debts, we mean credit cards, car loans, mortgages, etc.

In deciding whether to give you a loan to start your law business, banks also will consider your track record in this kind of business — for example, have you practiced law before, and do you have a base of steadily paying clients that you are bringing with you to the new firm?

Banks also look to see what kind of collateral you have to secure the loan — a house, for example.

Additionally, to obtain a business loan, you will need to give a bank a very detailed business plan. As you will see when we discuss business plans later in this chapter, a detailed business plan requires a great deal of thought and work.

Another source of funding is a home equity loan or home equity line of credit. To qualify for one, you first need to own a home and have more than enough equity in that home to secure the loan. Equity is the difference between what you owe on the home and the home's resale value. (Note: the resale value can be less than the value that is listed on the statement that you receive from your municipality's tax assessor). If you think that this might be an option for you, you can read more about this through an Internet search (search under "home equity loans" or "home equity lines of credit"), through your mortgage holder, or through local banks/lenders. We caution you to think carefully before choosing this option. You could be putting your home in jeopardy if you are unable to make the payments.

## § 6.08   WHY YOU NEED A SPENDING DIARY

To determine how much money you will need to start and run your law firm, you will need to know not only your startup costs and monthly business expenses, but also your monthly personal expenses. Most people don't actually know how much money they spend each month. They know what their fixed expenses are — mortgage or rent, utilities, car loan, car insurance, health insurance, etc. But most people have no idea how much they spend on everything else. The only way to figure this out accurately is to spend one month writing down everything you spend and how much each thing costs for one month. That is, keep a spending diary.

Keeping a spending diary is easier said than done. It requires discipline. If you buy a cup of coffee and a doughnut on the way to work, you need to write it down. If you fill up the gas tank in your car, you need to write it down even if you pay by credit card and will have a record of that. You need to write down what you spent for a newspaper. Or what you spent for toothpaste. Or a pack of gum. Everything. This includes pet food, veterinarian visits, haircuts, and medical copays. Most of us will be surprised to discover how these little things add up and how much we actually spend on all of them. The key to making this plan work is to write things down right away. If you wait until the end of the day, you are very likely to forget things.

Note: You will need to cover all of these expenses every month. By listing your expenses, you are likely to find areas in which you can cut back. (Yes, we recognize that many of these expenses will vary by the month. For example, you might buy more packages of gum one month than another. But writing everything down for one month is likely to show you that you spend a lot more than you think.)

Next, list all of your expenses by category. This will include expenses that you pay annually, quarterly, or semimonthly, or that you need to pay sporadically. As a result, some of these expenses might not have come up in the month that you tracked your expenses. For example, you might not have had any medical copays or veterinarian visits that month. To figure out a monthly expense for something that you pay less frequently than every month, divide the expense by the number of months it covers to obtain the monthly expense for that item.

Categories of expenses include: rent or mortgage, homeowner's or renter's insurance, property insurance, electricity, heat, air-conditioning, cleaning service, lawn care, routine household maintenance, emergency household repairs, car loans, car insurance, car repairs (including new tires), car registration, public transportation, attorney registration fees, bar association fees, parking tickets, speeding tickets, cigarettes (and/or the cost of a program to help you quit), haircuts, hair coloring, toiletries (soap, shampoo, conditioner, razors, toothpaste, etc.), household paper goods (paper towels, toilet paper, tissues), trash bags, food, restaurant and takeout meals, entertainment (movie theatres, subscription services for movies and television shows), books, magazines, newspapers, legal publications (including online subscriptions), travel, recreation (including gym memberships), loan payments (including student loans), etc.

The Internet contains many websites that can help you determine your personal expenses. You can find them via an Internet search of "personal expenses categories."

The key is to figure out your average monthly expenses and then add enough extra money per month so that you will be able to amass savings to pay for the expenses that come up occasionally, semimonthly, quarterly, or annually. It is essential to accumulate savings so you can meet these expenses.

## § 6.09   A FINANCIAL WARNING, REPEATED FOR EMPHASIS

Although we have said this before, it bears repeating: If you are going to start a law practice (either solo or with one or more other attorneys), and you don't want to have to work at another job to pay your personal expenses while you're just starting up, you should have enough savings or a source of money — credit cards or some kind of loan — to cover your personal expenses for at least a year. We realize that this is conservative advice. Some people, especially people who are not very risk-adverse, start law firms with little or no financial cushion. But this is extremely risky and unwise unless you are coming from another law firm and are bringing clients with you.

One more time: You should not expect to make sufficient revenue from your law firm business to be able to cover all of your personal expenses for about a year. If you are able to make enough money sooner than that, terrific. You'll be ahead of the game. But don't count on it. You don't need that kind of pressure when you're trying to establish yourself, build your client base, and service your new clients. Don't be overly disappointed if, at the end of the first year, you still can't pay all of your personal expenses out of your business revenue. This is not uncommon. Just keep trying to build your law business and also see if you can cut some personal expenses.

## § 6.10  BUSINESS PLANS

Now it's time to talk about business plans. Although much has been written about business plans — both in books and on the Internet, most lawyers fail to write one when starting a new law practice, mostly because they think it's unnecessary. That is a fallacy. Even if you aren't trying to obtain commercial financing, a business plan is an essential tool to know where you're going and what your needs will be. Think of it as a roadmap. If you're traveling somewhere and you have a vague notion of where you want to go, you can just start to travel and hope that you'll wind up where you want to be — or at least in a good place. But as any of you know if you've ever driven somewhere new without a map or a GPS to guide you, getting lost can be time-consuming and annoying. It's a lot easier to have a map or a GPS to guide you. A business plan is like a map or a GPS for your law firm's trip toward success.

What are the essentials of a good business plan? Most book chapters and articles about writing business plans for your law firm tell you to think about your "vision" for your practice. But asking most lawyers who are starting their own firms to do this is like asking eight-year-olds what they want to be when they grow up. Most eight-year-olds either don't have a clue, or their visions for their careers are framed by the narrow vision of what they know of the world, so they don't have a good idea of what the possibilities are or will be.

We believe that a better place to start is to ask yourself what areas of law you want to practice in and what segments of the population you want to target as potential clients. Some lawyers find it easier to identify a target market before identifying practice areas, because those lawyers know that they have a potential source of clients in the communities or groups to which they belong. If you have access to this kind of ready market, then spend time trying to figure out what their legal needs might be.

Next, ask yourself how you intend to distinguish your firm from the existing law firms. Why would anyone hire you versus the other lawyers? Will the services that you offer be different from what other local lawyers offer? Or will you provide similar services but in a different manner? Perhaps you will provide the convenience of weekend or evening hours. Or the convenience of transacting business by video conferencing with your clients rather than making those clients come to your office in the middle of their workday.

To create a strong business plan, you first need to ask yourself why you are starting this business. Write down your reason. You'll need to think deeply about this. Don't just answer: "because I want to make money" or "because I want to be my own boss" or "because I think it will be an excellent adventure." All of those are fine, but you also need to think about serving your clients. Ask yourself questions like: Will I be providing a need that is unmet or insufficiently met locally? Will I be helping an underserved population?

A strong business plan includes details about your business concept, your prospective clients (who they are and why they will need your services), and the operations and finance of the firm (how you intend to run the firm including its projected income and expenses).

If you have no idea of what your "business concept" is, take heart: There are many examples of business plans on the Internet, including many discussions of how to write the "business concept" section for a new law firm. You can find them through an Internet search of "business plans for starting a law firm." One of the most interesting guides to writing a law firm business plan, with samples, is available at: http://masslomap.org/wp-content/uploads/2013/01/Building-a-Great-Business-Plan-for-Your-New-Law-Practice-Shoffner.pdf. We also have included a sample business plan in the Appendix to this book. You should use this solely as a guide; you and your partners must create a personalized vision for your firm.

# Chapter 7

# WHAT TYPE OF PRACTICE DO I WANT TO HAVE?

An important decision that you will have to make involves the type of cases you want to handle. That is, do you want to limit your practice to one or two areas of law or do you want to have a general practice? If you are very clear in your desire to work in one particular area of the law, I suggest you make the decision at the outset and try to stick with it. If you aren't sure, you have time to decide.

## § 7.01 ADVANTAGES TO LIMITING YOUR PRACTICE AREAS

There are several advantages to limiting your practice to one or two areas of law.

### [A] Expertise

It is virtually impossible to keep current in all areas of the law. Every day our courts make decisions, and if you want to be at the top of your game, you need to stay current with decisions that affect your area of practice. We strongly suggest that you read the law journal where you reside. Unfortunately, a lot of lawyers get busy and do not take the time to read it regularly. Because the material generally is available on line, you really have no good excuse for not knowing what is going on in your field. Legal newspapers, like the *New York Law Journal*, cover both federal cases and state cases. All decisions affecting practitioners in that state can be found there. Other states have similar resources. You will quickly gain a reputation for being a scholar of the law if you are a lawyer who can speak intelligently about the big changes as they occur.

Why is it important to stay current? The law is constantly changing, not solely by the introduction of new statutes, but by new and different interpretations of existing laws. A change in the law, or how the court views an existing law, can dramatically affect how you prepare and present your case. Even busy practitioners will find it possible to read cases and articles in one or two fields on a daily basis. But if you are busy in your practice, you will find it nearly impossible to read every case in every field on a daily basis.

In the earlier stages of your practice, you can make it your personal responsibility to read the new cases involving your field every day. As you become more successful and hire associates, you can require an associate — or even a law school intern — to read and prepare a memo regarding every new case in your field on a daily basis. You should circulate these memos to all of the attorneys in your office. This way, they can update their arguments, taking the newest cases into account.

A very important reason to be as current as possible in your area of practice is that you gain credibility with members of the bench and bar. Just like lawyers talk about judges, judges also talk about lawyers. It should not be surprising to learn that your reputation among the judges can dramatically affect the outcome of your cases and what you achieve for your clients.

> Several years ago I was handling a fairly large matrimonial case that I had spent close to two years preparing for trial. I had conducted depositions, hired expert witnesses, and spent hours prepping my client for trial. I was scheduled to start the trial and went to answer the calendar call the morning of the trial. As was my habit, I got to court early and was reading the New York Law Journal when I discovered that a decision published that morning had radically changed the law governing the most import financial aspect of my case. I answered the calendar call and explained to the judge what had happened. I got a 90-day adjournment so that I could have entirely new computations and reports prepared by my expert. My adversary was not aware of the change in the law but could not fight the adjournment when I put on the record the name of the case and the relevance of the decision. I subsequently tried the case to a successful conclusion, something that would never have happened had I not read the law journal that morning. Had I tried the case without knowing of the change in the law, I would have been lacking in necessary testimony and would have had to either request a new trial, the right to reopen testimony, renew or reargue, or I might have had to file a costly and time-consuming appeal. Staying on top of things can make a huge difference. LAK

## [B]  Your Attorney Rating

Another reason to consider limiting the scope of your practice is that it is hard to become an elite lawyer and receive an A rating from Martindale-Hubbell if you are handling cases in a wide variety of fields. Not only can you not be good at everything, but it is much harder to gain respect among your peers in any particular field if you do not practice regularly in that field. See our previous discussion of Martindale-Hubbell in § 2.02[C].

It is almost impossible to be named as a "Super Lawyer" if you do not restrict your practice to one or two areas. Super Lawyers is a lawyer-rating service that publishes an annual supplement listing top lawyers by field. Being recognized as a Super Lawyer is prestigious and can bring in business. The Super Lawyers list appears periodically in a printed insert in major newspapers and magazines like *The New York Times Magazine*, *The New Yorker*, *The Washington Post Magazine*, *The Miami Herald*, *Boston Magazine*, *San Francisco Magazine*, *Philadelphia Magazine*, *Los Angeles Magazine*, and *Texas Monthly*. Lawyers are recognized as being either a Super Lawyer or a Rising Star in various fields of law. Members of the public and bar use this resource to find top attorneys. Super Lawyers names no more than 5 percent of lawyers practicing in any given field in each state.

## [C]  Familiarity With Your Adversaries

Lawyers who practice exclusively in the same field get to know one another very well. As soon as you see whom your adversary is, you have a pretty good idea about how a case is going to be conducted. You know if someone is courteous. You know if someone likes to delay a case in order to bill more hours to the client. You know if someone is going to work with you and make reasonable offers. You also know if someone is or is not good as a litigator. All of these pieces of information help you to predict the length and sometimes even the outcome of a case — whether there is any chance of negotiating a settlement or whether you'll have to go to trial. You are, thus, able to give your client more information concerning what to expect.

Another benefit of knowing your adversaries is the ability to get coverage of matters if you are going to be out of town or you become ill. An adversary on one case could be a colleague willing to cover for you on another case. Knowing the reputations and abilities of your fellow attorneys makes it easier to select someone to assist you if you are a solo practitioner in need of coverage.

## [D]  Referral Work

One way to build and sustain your practice is to have attorneys in other fields refer work to you. It is easier to obtain referrals if you are not a general practitioner. There are two reasons for this. One is that if you limit your practice to one or two areas, attorneys in other fields will make an assumption that you are well-versed in those areas. The other reason is that they won't have to worry about whether you will steal their clients, either intentionally or unintentionally. Even if you don't intend to steal someone else's client, a client may like you better than the referring attorney. If the referring attorney operates a general law practice, and you practice in some of the same areas as the referring attorney, that client might decide to use you instead of the referring attorney. But if you limit your practice to one or two areas, and the referring attorney doesn't practice in those areas, there is no risk that the client will decide to switch firms.

## § 7.02  ADVANTAGES TO HAVING A GENERAL PRACTICE

### [A]  Being Able to Serve the Community as a Whole

One of the biggest benefits to being a general practitioner is the ability to represent virtually everyone where you live. If you are a general practitioner, you should be trained to handle routine events like house closings and will drafting. A large percentage of people within your community need to have someone render these non-adversarial services, and if you can handle all of the basic legal needs of many people in town, you will have lots of potential clients. If you also add the ability to handle drinking-while-driving cases, basic personal injury cases, and simple divorces, you should be able to stay pretty busy if you practice in a small town and there aren't many general practitioners there. If there are many, you will have to distinguish yourself in some way — perhaps by your warm and outgoing personality or by your promptness and attention to details. Almost every family for whom you do closings or wills will need you to handle one of these additional services at one time or another, and so you can count on keeping these clients for life unless someone cheaper or better establishes a practice in your town. The beauty of being a small-town general practitioner is that once you are known as the person who helped someone in town, you do not have to work overly hard to get additional referrals. You need to be pleasant and maintain a nice office atmosphere. Remember this: many people have said that clients choose lawyers based on whether the lawyer is likeable.

## [B]   You are Always Learning

Another bonus to being a general practitioner is that you are unlikely to get bored. If you are willing to take all kinds of cases, and you are willing to do the necessary research and hard work, you can practice in many different and interesting areas of law. A license to practice law gives you the flexibility to handle whatever you choose to do. So while you may never become a true expert in any one area, you may be the local "go to" problem-solver who has the respect of friends and neighbors.

## [C]   You Can Always Make Money

If you are a general practitioner, you don't have to worry if there is a downturn in a particular area of the law. If the real estate market is bad and no sales are taking place, you don't have to panic because that part of your practice has dried up. You can profit from the bad economy by handling bankruptcy cases and advertising that you do that type of work. You don't have to worry that a change in any one area of law might wipe out your business. You are used to doing new things, and you are not afraid of doing them. You have a totally different mindset than the lawyer who is only good at one or two things. You believe that you rarely will need to turn away clients because you lack expertise. You believe that you are capable of handling almost anything if you have sufficient time to learn.

## § 7.03   AREAS OF LAW THAT FIT WELL TOGETHER

Different lawyers have different perspectives on which areas of practice fit well together. Some lawyers group practice areas based on the skill sets each area needs. Some lawyers group practice areas by the types of clients that might have similar matters. And some lawyers group practice areas by the types of law that seem to fit well together. For example, a lawyer with good trial skills might look to handle both criminal law and negligence law. In each area, there is a lot of law to learn and to keep current with, but this combination has worked successfully for many lawyers.

When thinking about servicing clients who might have interrelated problems or issues, there are many combinations to consider. For example, criminal lawyers sometimes find themselves with clients who are not United States citizens and who will face serious immigration issues if they are found guilty of a crime or enter a plea deal. Without at least a working knowledge of deportation issues, a lawyer can do a serious disservice to a client. Thus, a lawyer might want to consider handling criminal law and immigration law within the same firm.

Disability law and employment law are two other examples of complementary practice areas, because many people experience health issues that cause disabilities that affect their employment.

A viable alternative to taking on more than one practice area in your firm is to handle just one of these fields and share space with someone who handles the related field — a topic that we will cover in more depth later.

Finally, you may decide that there are areas in which you believe you should become proficient because they are closely related to, or overlap with, your main area of practice. Thus, it would make sense to become knowledgeable in both. Some examples of this are: estate planning and tax law; elder care and health care law; commercial and real estate law; environmental law, zoning, and land use planning; commercial law and tax law; adoption law and family law; matrimonial law and family law; bankruptcy and debtor-creditor law. Choose whatever combination of fields makes you comfortable. Remember, though, that if you are trying to achieve recognition as a top practitioner in a particular field, it is not wise to spread yourself thin by practicing in too many different areas.

## § 7.04   DOES OFFICE LOCATION INFLUENCE THE KINDS OF CASES I WILL ATTRACT?

If you are certain about the area of practice in which you want to focus your career, then you should consider picking a location with a particular demographic because it will help you to attract clients in that field. For example, if you want to handle immigration law, opening an office where there is a large immigrant population will help you to attract immigration cases. If estate planning appeals to you, opening an office in a low-income area is not likely to be a good choice. Although your rent may be inexpensive in a low-income area, how many area residents are likely to have the large amount of assets necessary to require an estate plan? If you want to find out information about any town, village, hamlet, or city, just type the name into an Internet search engine. The results will provide you with information about the population's median age, income, ethnic breakdown, and educational level, as well as information about the industries generating the most work or income. Although it will take a little more work to find out information about each neighborhood, you can find this through an Internet search, too. To determine the general socio-economic level, visit the neighborhood and take a look to see if it appears prosperous, middle-income, working class, struggling, or poverty-stricken.

## § 7.05   WHAT IF I NEED TO LOCATE IN A PARTICULAR PLACE BECAUSE OF PERSONAL OBLIGATIONS?

Sometimes family obligations or physical limitations restrict where you may be able to open an office. If the location in which you open your office is more important to you than the type of cases you handle, then our recommendations about learning the demographics of that area applies to these situations as well. The only difference is that rather than picking the location to attract a type of work, this time you may be picking the type of work based on the location. By checking out the demographic information, you may be able to tailor your legal knowledge and expertise to suit the population in the location in which your office must be located.

## § 7.06 HOW TO COVER MORE AREAS OF PRACTICE

There is an easy solution to wanting to cover more than one or two areas of law without actually having to learn and stay current in all of them. You can practice in one area and go into a partnership with someone who practices in a complementary area or areas. This way, when you attract clients with cases that are not in your personal area of practice, you can have your partner handle them and still profit from the legal fees. If the fields are somewhat related, it is likely that you will attract cases that fall within your partner's area of practice; similarly, your partner is likely to attract cases that fall within your area of practice. You also can accomplish the same goal of expanding your business by sharing office space with one or more lawyers in a related field or fields. The lawyers who share office space can refer cases to each other.

It is important to remember, however, that even if you share space with someone and like that person, that person must handle cases competently and professionally and treat clients well, or the referral will do more harm than good to your practice. This is because you may be held responsible, and/or your reputation will suffer, if the other lawyer commits malpractice. This will cause your business to suffer. Please keep in mind that your jurisdiction may not allow you to share legal fees with other lawyers unless the client is specifically made aware of the fact that you will be sharing the fee and/or you may have to perform some work on the case to warrant the fee sharing. Make sure to learn the rules involving fee sharing within your jurisdiction. If your jurisdiction requires you to be involved in the case, then make a point of meeting with the potential client, take notes, and then participate in regular conferences with the lawyer to whom you are referring work, making sure to document your time. Offer to conduct research and or participate in strategy sessions to justify your sharing in any compensation.

## § 7.07 SOME FINAL THOUGHTS ON OFFICE LOCATION

Attracting business and making referrals from one professional to another are often the keys to starting and maintaining a financially successful law practice. Remember that all of your referrals from professionals need not be from other attorneys. There are professions that lend themselves to attorney referrals and vice versa. Financial planning and accounting are complementary professions for divorce lawyers or attorneys who focus on estate planning and or commercial work. They are also good sources of work for bankruptcy attorneys. Insurance brokers, likewise, also tend to be great sources of business for lawyers. Successful agents generally deal in volume and have a sizeable number of clients. All of the professionals mentioned here should have a very good idea about the net worth of their clients and should be able to tell if a case is one to which you are well suited.

Therapists can also be excellent sources of business for attorneys. Some believe it is not a good idea to share space with a therapist from whom one hopes to get business because these are clients who have to see their therapist and lawyer regularly, and if they sour with one, they likely will leave both.

While it makes good sense to maintain complementary relationships with other professionals, it is very important that you choose wisely if it involves sharing space. You do not want to have to move your office or be stuck in a long-term lease if your relationship with the other person sours.

Certain geographical areas are particularly well-suited for the practice of some areas of the law. Port cities attract maritime lawyers, and entertainment capitals such as Los Angeles and New York City attract entertainment lawyers. If you are interested in an area of practice that you think might be geographically specific, do your homework. Sometimes it doesn't matter where your practice is located. But sometimes it does. For example, if you want to practice immigration law, it helps to have an office that is not a five-hour drive from the immigration hearings.

# Chapter 8

# WHAT TYPE OF OFFICE SPACE IS BEST FOR ME?

When you decide to open a solo or small-firm practice, one of the first things you will have to consider is the cost involved in selecting the physical plant. There are a variety of options to consider, and your budget is going to play a large part in your decision-making process. The most common possibilities are:

1) Renting space

2) Buying a building or condominium

3) Making a time-for-space arrangement

4) Joining an incubator attached to a law school or legal services provider

5) Working out of your home

6) Setting up a virtual office

In order to explore these options properly, you need to understand your financial condition and know how much money you can commit to this aspect of your operation. Basic questions to ask yourself are:

- How much money do I have right now to invest?

- How much money can I borrow?

- How much money should I borrow?

- How much income will I realistically have during the next year? Do I have clients on whom I can count to pay a monthly retainer? Am I taking cases from a firm I am leaving? If so, based on past experience, how much income will I realistically earn from them? (Note that you may be prohibited from taking cases from your former firm.)

When opening an office, not only must you consider the initial cost, but you must also consider the continuing monthly expenses. Never underestimate either of these costs. Rather than underestimate, be conservative and slightly overestimate your costs. This way, you will have some breathing room in case something unexpected crops up. If you want to stay out of financial difficulty, underestimate your income and overestimate your costs. If you leave yourself no room for error, then you have just made your first serious error.

Let's look at each of the possible arrangements listed above and consider some of the pros and cons attached to each.

## § 8.01  RENTING SPACE

You may think that renting space is a simple concept, but it is more complicated than it seems. You need to consider a wide variety of issues for the lease, such as parking, financial stability of the landlord, zoning, shared expenses, etc.

Let's take a few minutes to look at some of the topics you need to be aware of with a lease:

1) What is the cost of space per square foot? Is that in keeping with the going rate for office space in that geographic area? You can consult a variety of websites for this information or enlist the services of a broker who is familiar with office space where you want to locate your office.

2) What is the amount of the security deposit, and what does it cover? Will it be held in an escrow account, will that account be interest-bearing, and will you or will the landlord receive the interest? Note that it is common for landlords to ask not only for a security deposit but also for the first and last month's rent when you sign the lease.

3) Who pays the utility costs? If you have to pay them in addition to your base rent, how is your share computed? Is each unit metered separately? Or is the bill for the entire building sent to the landlord, and the landlord computes your share? If the latter is the case, will your share be computed on the basis of the number of units or by the square footage of each unit? If you are sharing space in a suite, do you pay a share of the utility cost and, if so, how much? You can ask existing tenants about these costs. You do not want to sign a lease without any idea of your utility costs.

4) Are there other add-on costs? Do you have to pay for cleaning costs, outside maintenance (gardening and snowplowing), trash collection, or a percentage of the cost of any real estate tax increases and/or insurance increases? If you have to pay any of these, how does the landlord compute your share? And how often do you need to pay them — monthly, quarterly, or annually?

5) If you are in a suite of professionals, is there a shared copy machine or canteen (coffee, tea, milk, etc.)? Who maintains these things? Are you required to pay a cost for using them?

6) Is the space compliant with the Americans with Disabilities Act? Remember that you may have disabled clients, and this can be a very important issue.

7) Is there room for growth? Sometimes you can negotiate for the right of first refusal on any additional adjacent space that becomes available or larger suites that become available.

8) Are you allowed to sublet? This can be very important if you can't handle the rental cost; you want to be able to sublet part or all of your space so that you are not stuck with a rent obligation for the remainder of the term of the lease.

9) What is the layout of the space? Are you allowed to make changes?

10) Can you negotiate for exclusivity? That is, can you provide in the lease that the landlord cannot rent to an attorney with any of the same practice areas? In a large office building, this may not matter, but in a small building or suite,

this is very important. You do not want to find yourself stuck on a lease when someone else in your practice area can locate across the hall or in the same suite and divert your potential clients.

11) What is the term of the lease, and what are the renewal options? On one hand, new lawyers may find it advantageous to avoid getting tied into any sort of long-term lease. First, you don't know whether you are going to like running your own office; second, you have no idea of what your income will be and whether you can continue to afford the space; third, you have no idea of whether you will do well economically and will want to expand to a bigger space; and fourth, you may receive some wonderful offer to do something other than running a solo or small-firm practice. On the other hand, you may find that you love your location, have established a good client base in the area and do not want to risk having to move your office. Negotiating the right to renew for a longer term will take care of these concerns. Success is sometimes geographically dependent, and you do not want to lose out on what you have built because you weren't a good enough lawyer to protect yourself in your lease.

12) What is the escalation clause for the term of the lease? That is, how frequently does the rent increase and how much? Sometimes it makes sense to agree to a higher rate of increase toward the end of the lease term so that you will have more money available to you when you are starting out and spending money to set up your office and develop your business. Another important thing to consider when renting is who the other tenants are. In a small building or suite, the character of the other tenants can make or break your everyday life, so it is important to find out about them. How and where do you get this information? You can enter their names into an Internet search engine, and you can check with the Better Business Bureau. You also might want to consider checking the parking lot at various times over a week to see if there will be adequate space for your clients to park. Also, if you are thinking about joining a suite or taking space in a small office building, make sure you have an idea of the types of clients the others tenants attract. Is the constant coming and going of their clients noisy? Are the clients in the shared waiting area loud? In a shared suite, are the other person's clients so loud that you can hear them in your office? Is there room in the shared waiting area for your clients? Will the other person's type of clients make your type of clients uncomfortable? (For example, if the other tenant is a criminal lawyer who represents young gang members, and you are an estate planning lawyer who represents wealthy elderly women.) Will their type of clients make you uncomfortable?

> My suitemates in my first office were fabulous people who were very generous with me, but they had sedate practices. They handled real estate work and tort cases, neither of which have a constant flow of clients in and out of the door. Also, when clients were there they were not particularly loud. I was in the process of building a divorce practice and, as I became more successful, I had an endless stream of people coming in and out of the suite. Add to that the fact that divorce clients are rarely, if ever, happy, and often engage in shouting matches during conferences with their spouses and attorneys. While my suitemates were honestly happy for me in terms of the success I was achieving, they simply did not want to live with my clients. I was nicely asked to move elsewhere. As hard as it was for me, I understood why they were asking me to leave. We remained on good terms after my departure, and for more than twenty years, these gentlemen continued to refer me all of the divorce and family law matters that came their way. LAK

With any building, a few very important things for you to check are how promptly the parking lot gets plowed if it is in a snow area, how well-lit the parking lot is, and how clean the common areas are, including the bathrooms. Quite often, tenants have no control over these things, yet some of your clients will hold you responsible if they are dissatisfied with any one of them. Likewise, the quality of each of these services is critical to you personally. If you are living in a climate where the winter involves snow, you may lose business if the parking lot does not get plowed in a timely fashion. A badly lit parking lot can result in accidents because of ice or potholes that are not visible after dark. It can also be an invitation to crime.

Finally, we challenge you to find a female client who does not care about the cleanliness of a bathroom. Do you really want to hear a litany of bathroom complaints from your clients? Even if you have no control over the state of the bathroom that is shared by numerous suites, do you want to have to explain that to clients and seem like a powerless victim?

There are also a few terms with which you should be familiar before you go searching for office space. Since these terms are likely to be thrown at you, it is a good idea to have a basic understanding of them.

## [A]   Triple-Net Lease

This is a lease in which the tenant pays rent plus a portion of the taxes, insurance, and maintenance for the building. Some landlords vary this by asking the tenant to pay for a portion of the annual increase in taxes, insurance, and maintenance over the previous year.

This type of lease has its pro and cons. The base rent is lower than you might otherwise pay for that amount of space, and you might be able to have control over the additional cost. You will not have any control over real estate tax increases. Sometimes you can negotiate a cap on your responsibility for tax increases as well as a cap on maintenance and insurance costs. This helps you to avoid the surprise of a large, unexpected assessment for your share of the annual taxes, insurance, and maintenance at the end of the year.

Sometimes the landlord will require the tenants to pay money into a security fund. This gives the landlord protection in case the tenants do not meet their financial responsibilities above the rent. It also helps the landlord determine whether the tenant will be able to pay those additional costs. If a tenant can't or won't pay into a reserve fund, the landlord sees this as a pretty good indication that the potential tenant will not have the monies available to pay added costs when required.

If you enter into a triple-net lease, and your landlord requires you to pay a portion of the taxes, insurance, and maintenance at the end of each year, you should ask the landlord to estimate the first year's expense before you sign the lease. Then divide that sum by 12, and each month place 1/12th of the sum into a bank account that you have set up solely to keep the money segregated so that you will have it at the end of the year. If you don't put the money aside in a separate account, you might not have it at the end of the year when you are required to pay.

## [B]   Gross Lease

This is a lease in which the tenant pays rent, and the landlord takes care of everything else related to the building.

## [C]   Double-Net Lease

This is a lease in which the tenant pays rent and some of the costs associated with the building. Usually with this type of lease, the landlord will take care of the parking lot, the heating, and air-conditioning. The tenants may have to pay for electricity.

Most office leases specify that the landlord will pay for maintenance and repairs to the building itself, but the extent to which this applies varies with the lease. Be sure to read your lease carefully before you sign it. You may be able to negotiate the things for which the landlord is responsible. For example, who is responsible for repairing plumbing issues if there is a toilet within your office suite rather than in a bathroom that is shared by more than one suite?

My law office was in a one-story building with only four offices. Each office had an entrance directly from the outside of the building. One day, a gust of wind caught the door as a client was opening it and pulled the door open so wide that one of the hinges bent. The door would not close. This meant that the law office was wide open to the outside world. I called the landlord, and he said that the door was my responsibility because the hinges were on the inside and I had negotiated a lease in which I was responsible for all repairs on the inside of the office. It was true: I had negotiated this in return for a lower rent than if the landlord had been responsible for those repairs. But when I looked at my lease, I saw that it said that the landlord was responsible for repairs to all windows and exterior doors. As a result, the landlord fixed the door. I wish that I could say that I had been clever enough to have placed the exterior door provision into the lease, but it was part of the boilerplate language in the lease that my landlord used. I was lucky. Since then, I have seen leases that did not contain this provision. Do not leave your fate to luck. Be sure to read your lease carefully before signing it. ALN

Two final and important thoughts with regard to your lease:

(1) Always try to negotiate the rental cost including the add-ons to the rent — i.e., what they will be and whether there will be an annual cap. Virtually every landlord is expecting to have to negotiate the base rent as well as the other terms contained in the lease. This is an important time to put your lawyering skills to the test. If you are not experienced enough to handle these negotiations, or you don't feel comfortable handling them yourself, hire a lawyer who is experienced in the field. You will incur legal fees, but you are likely to save that amount and more by having a knowledgeable person negotiate favorable terms for you.

(2) Sometimes a fancy office is not a good choice. Although you might want a nice space to impress your clients, too nice a space might actually hurt your business rather than help it. If the office is too nice, your clients will think they are paying for it in higher fees. As you become more successful, you can choose to upgrade the appearance of your office. At that point, when clients are choosing you because of your reputation, they will not be surprised or deterred by a fancy office.

## § 8.02  BUYING A BUILDING OR CONDOMINIUM

If you have the money, owning your office can be a wonderful thing. The big difference between renting and owning is that every monthly payment you make when you are an owner goes toward your own equity. When you are a tenant, you have no equity, and your payments benefit your landlord, not you. When you own, you will have an asset that you can rent or sell to generate income after you retire from the practice of law. There are benefits and drawbacks to owning rather than renting.

Some of the benefits of owning are:

- Your monthly mortgage payments help you to build financial equity.
- You never have to worry about someone dramatically increasing your rent.
- You never have to worry about whether or not your lease will be renewed.
- You can configure and decorate the interior in any manner that suits you.
- You control the quality of both indoor and outdoor maintenance.
- When you eventually pay off your mortgage, your monthly expense for the office will be reduced significantly.

Some of the drawbacks of owning are:

- You can't just leave at the end of your lease term if you no longer want to practice in that location.
- You are responsible for maintaining the outside of the building including the parking areas, the building infrastructure, and the indoor maintenance of all the offices in the building unless you require tenants to be responsible for the maintenance of the interiors of their offices.
- You bear the economic risk of unexpected repairs and/or lawsuits if someone is injured on your premises.
- There is no landlord to complain to.
- You have to deal with tax increases, although you can pass these on to your tenants.
- You have to comply with all local building, zoning, and health and safety codes.

If the building has more space than you need for your own office, and you rent office space to other tenants, you will have all of the tasks and obligations required of a landlord plus you will have to deal with tenant issues (non-payment of rent, complaints, etc.) and will have to find tenants and negotiate leases with them. Additionally, if you are relying on rents to help you pay for the expenses of owning and operating the building, you will have to make sure that you have tenants for the available rental spaces and that they pay their rent. And if they pay it late, you will have to follow up to collect it. If they don't pay, you might have to go to court to evict them for nonpayment of rent.

There are many things you need to know if you are going to purchase a building or condominium. Because this is a general book on law practice management and not real estate management, we are not going to discuss all of the issues that can arise when purchasing and owning real estate. You may run into environmental concerns, zoning concerns, and title issues. Additionally, with a condo, there can problems with common charges and changes in rules and regulations. Suffice it to say that real estate is a sophisticated area of the law, and you should not represent yourself unless you are fully familiar with this area of practice.

## § 8.03 TIME FOR SPACE

This is an excellent option in which you give an attorney a certain number of hours of your time each month in exchange for free space within the office. Not only is there a tremendous financial benefit for you with this arrangement, but if you are fortunate enough to find space in the office of a highly competent attorney, you can learn a tremendous amount. It is not hard to find an attorney with excess space in the office and too much work to handle but not enough to keep a full-time associate busy. A time-for-space arrangement, therefore, may be mutually beneficial. As mentioned, this arrangement gives you the most benefit if the attorney from whom you are getting the space is someone with excellent credentials. Whether or not the attorney is a good teacher is another thing, but, at the very least, you will not be learning any bad habits.

---

I was fortunate enough to be in the office of two very fine attorneys when I opened my first office. I learned so much from them, not only by asking questions but by watching how they conducted themselves. Whenever I did work on their behalf, they expected the work to be of the highest quality. They had high expectations of themselves and of me. They helped to make sure what I did, I did well, and they answered not only legal questions I had but ethical questions that I confronted early on in my career. If I had had to work a few extra hours to be in their office, it would have been well worth it. Remember, too, that these gentlemen referred their matrimonial and family law cases to me for the remainder of their careers. I could not have had a better place in which to start. LAK

---

## [A] How Do You Decide How Much Time to Give for Your Space?

There is no definitive rule about how much time to give for the space you are getting. You could look for the comparable cost of rent per square foot and do the math, but that is only one factor to consider. Remember what we just said about the benefits of having quality mentors available. It may well be worthwhile to commit to more hours to have the right people to teach you.

---

I had no idea what a fair time for space deal was when I opened my first office and knew that the two gentlemen in whose suite I would be taking space had experience with that type of arrangement. Since they came to me with the suggestion of a time for space deal, and they had very fine reputations as both people and lawyers, (well deserved, I might add), I relied upon them to suggest the fair thing. I accepted their offer without negotiating. The burden was on them to give me enough work to equal the rent. If they didn't have the work to give, they nonetheless did not charge me rent. Make sure that is your arrangement. LAK

---

## § 8.04  STARTING IN AN INCUBATOR

Law schools are starting to see the wisdom of helping their graduates to open their own law practices. In the not too distant past, law schools did not encourage students to open an office right out of law school because the new graduates knew how to think like lawyers but not how to perform the skills necessary to do the work. New lawyers learned these skills at their first job, not in law school. In recent years, however, changes in the employment market as well as the need for lawyers to help underserved communities forced law schools to reconsider that position. As a result, many law schools have established incubators to help recent graduates start their own practices. The law school where we teach, for example, established an incubator that provides office space to approximately a dozen of our graduates. The rent is substantially below market value, and the graduates have a variety of basic necessities made available to them. Although incubator programs vary, it is certainly not unusual for copying equipment and Wi-Fi to be made available to occupants. In addition, our school has made a point of trying to provide both substantive and practical training to our graduates. A series of speakers visits with the occupants of the incubator, and the law school has designed and is designing courses that the incubator participants can attend at no charge. In addition, a professor who has practice experience serves as a liaison between the school and the incubator.

Some incubator programs have obtained funding to serve underrepresented communities and are able to pay incubator occupants who are willing and able to provide services to the members of those communities. This is a win-win because it gives legal work to new attorneys and gives legal representation to people who might otherwise have gone without representation.

Incubator programs differ from place to place, so it is important that you know the benefits and obligations associated with any particular incubator before you decide to open your practice there. For example, some incubators are "low-bono" service providers, where recent law school graduates promise to do a certain amount of legal work in return for a very low legal fee. Those attorneys generally work under the supervision of attorneys affiliated with either a law school, bar association, or charitable entity. This kind of incubator is similar to a clinic. The duration of each attorney's stay is limited; the attorney receives cases, supplies, and malpractice insurance. This type of incubator is designed as a training ground. The attorney is not building a practice but is getting training to be able to leave the incubator and start a practice in the future.

At the other end of the spectrum are incubators that provide low monthly rent but no supervision, supplies, or malpractice insurance. These incubators have no super-vising attorney or clerical staff. They may suggest that you handle low-bono matters, but you are not required to do so. The attorneys need to create their own business plans and develop their own practices, although the schools supporting this type of incubator frequently provide an experienced attorney or professor who is available to assist the occupants of the incubator. Additionally, some law schools provide their incubator tenants with lectures and even the ability to attend courses at no cost.

Probably the biggest drawbacks to opening a law practice in an incubator have to do with location. First, most incubators allow occupants to remain in the location for only a limited duration because of the need to make space available to newer graduates. This means that as incubator lawyers begin to establish their practices, they will have to relocate and may not be able to remain in the community convenient to their client base. Second, the incubators might not be in a location where the new lawyers would have established a practice otherwise, and they might not be in communities in which the lawyers want to stay. This is especially true in suburban and rural areas, because public transportation may be limited, and the established client base may not be able to follow the attorney to a different location.

As a new lawyer, you will have to weigh the benefits and disadvantages of whatever incubator might be available to you before making a decision about whether to join it. If you haven't figured out where you want to practice, what field you want to work in, or whether you even want to open your own law office, an incubator will allow you to try solo practice with only a minimal risk and minimal investment.

## § 8.05   WORKING FROM A HOME OFFICE

Working from home certainly has some advantages, but it also has some serious disadvantages as well.

### [A]   Disadvantages of a Home Office

#### [1]   Certain Types of Practices Do Not Lend Themselves to Home Offices

Criminal law is one example because you might not want people accused of serious crimes knowing where you live and coming inside your house. Two other examples are matrimonial law and family law, because clients in hotly contested cases often exhibit strong emotions and can behave in unpredictable ways. The same can be said for estate litigation, where emotions also tend to run high.

Exposing yourself and or family members to unnecessary risk should be a key factor in determining whether or not to have a home office.

---

As a divorce lawyer who has been threatened with car bombs, guns and rifles, as well as having had my office building doused with kerosene and dead fish left on my doorstep, I can say without hesitation that I would never have wanted to expose my children to any number of unstable parties with whom I was dealing. LAK

---

## [2]   Certain Types of Clients Expect Certain Types of Offices

It should come as no surprise that if you are trying to attract large corporations as clients, working from a home office might present the wrong image to your clients. With other types of clients, if you rarely have to meet with them in person, then you might be able to run your law practice from home using telephone and Internet communication, including video-chat meetings on the computer. If, on the other hand, the work requires frequent meetings, then a home office will not be suitable.

You may, however, be able to do something in between, in which you pay for the use of someone else's conference room, copy machine, and Internet access. Some lawyers will be happy to work out a deal with you to do this. There are also commercial companies that offer this kind of service — even including a shared receptionist, mail-drop, and phone answering — in an office suite used by professionals who also need this kind of service.

## [3]   A Home Office Will Test Your Ability to be Disciplined

Are you easily distracted? If so, a home office may not be for you. Sometimes it is very difficult for children to understand that mommy or daddy has to work, particularly when the child can see that mommy or daddy is there and could be available. This may put you in the position of constantly having to make a choice between your child and your work. When you set up hours that you will be working except in an emergency, be realistic about whether you can keep those hours if you are working from your home. Also, you have to think about what kind of practice you are trying to develop. If it really is not your intent to establish a full-time, client-intense practice, then a home office might work well for you. For example, attorneys who write motions or appellate briefs for other attorneys have no need to expend large sums on office space. Work can be done from any location and need not be done during normal business hours. People who handle small-volume real estate closings or estate planning can also find ways to make a home office very manageable.

## [4]   Isolation in the Home

Another problem many people encounter when working from home is isolation. The normal exchange of ideas is something lawyers often find useful when trying to hone arguments and decide strategies. In some offices, attorneys have regular strategy meetings when handling big cases. It is easier to bounce ideas off of other attorneys when you all work together in the same office. You don't need to make plans or set aside time to discuss an argument when colleagues are readily available. You can certainly reach out to colleagues from home, as well; you just have to make a bigger effort to make it happen.

## [5]   A Home Office Requires a High Dependence on Technology

If you do not want clients to come to your home every time they want to meet with you, and you do not want to spend your time traveling to a conference room elsewhere, then you will have to hold those sessions via video conferencing. The more meetings you must conduct via video conferencing, the more comfortable you become with the technology. But the more meetings you conduct via video conferencing, the more opportunity you have for technology to malfunction. Make sure that you have a backup alternative available — either an additional computer, smartphone, or tablet — as well as more than one method of video chatting. Also, if you are going to use a type of video conference that you have not used before, make sure that you test it before using it for your meeting.

### [6]   Additional Costs of a Home Office

There may be additional costs you have not considered when opting to open a law practice in your home. One very important thing to look into is whether you need additional liability insurance for your home. Your regular homeowners' or renters' policy may not cover you for injuries to clients on your premises. Make sure to look at the terms of your policy. If clients are not covered, you need to purchase liability insurance that will protect you if someone falls — including in your driveway or on your stairs.

## [B]   Advantages of a Home Office

### [1]   Lack of a Monthly Rental

The obvious benefit of a home office is the lack of a monthly rental expense. In addition, you may be able to qualify for a tax benefit from a home office, but you need to discuss this carefully with your accountant to see if you qualify and to discuss the pros and cons. The basic requirements for eligibility for a home-office deduction are:

> Regular and Exclusive Use: You must regularly use the office area of your home exclusively for business purposes. Occasionally meeting a client in your family room does not entitle you to a home-office deduction for that room.

> Principal Place of Your Business: You will have to demonstrate that you use your home as your principal place of business. If you use your home as your regular place of business, but you sometimes conduct business at a location outside your home, you may still qualify for a home-office deduction. Be sure to speak with your accountant about this before deciding whether or not to take the deduction.

### [2]   No Commuting Costs or Time

The next big benefit of a home office is the elimination of both commuting time and commuting costs. You don't have to worry about making it to appointments in your office on time because you'll already be there, and you minimize any wear and tear on your vehicle as well as reducing your expenditure on fuel.

## [3]  You Can Work at Any Time

Another positive aspect to having a home office is the ability to do your work regardless of life's inconveniences. For example, you will be able to work even if the roads are icy or flooded. You won't have to commute in torrential rain. And if you are working from a home office, you can work during the hours most convenient to you. You can also continue to run your full office while you are waiting for a repair person or a delivery, or when the childcare provider suddenly becomes unavailable.

## § 8.06  THE VIRTUAL OFFICE

The concept of a virtual office is one of the hottest topics in discussions about the future of the practice of law. Some lawyers believe that brick-and-mortar law offices eventually will become virtual law offices. Other lawyers believe that virtual law offices never will replace brick-and-mortar offices. And still other lawyers believe that the practice of law will evolve to a combination of both.

Let's take a look at some of the characteristics of a virtual law office, commonly referred to as a "VLO":

- The main difference between a VLO and a traditional practice is that a VLO does not have a home office base where the staff and files are housed. A VLO can be run from any location at any time.

- Cloud-based law practice management systems make all materials and information related to client matters available to attorneys working on the case, no matter where they are located. The attorneys easily can collaborate on the case because each is able to access the information at the same time and discuss it through a conference call or video conferencing.

- VLOs often automate common routine tasks such as time-tracking, billing, document storage and sharing, accounting, calendaring, and practice management.

- VLOs often outsource tasks such as answering the phone, setting up appointments, designing and maintaining the website, and marketing.

- VLOs are in large measure paperless. This means that storage costs are significantly decreased, and attorneys rarely waste time looking for hard copies of files and/or documents.

If you are thinking of starting a VLO, the supplies you will need will be very different from those you would need for a brick-and-mortar office. With a VLO, the most important startup items that you will need will be a laptop or desktop computer, a tablet, and a smartphone. You will need access to a secure, high-speed Internet connection. You also will need to set up and maintain a website; you can do this yourself or hire someone to do it. Additionally, you will need to establish a significant Internet presence, which you will be able to achieve in large part through social media. This means that you will have to become comfortable with blogging, tweeting, and posting things on Facebook. Virtual practitioners do not have a presence in a physical community, so they must distinguish themselves in the virtual world.

Additionally, you will need to learn to understand and properly use cloud software, backup systems, and encryption technology. You also should consider setting up client portals so clients easily can access documents, status reports, calendar items, and billing related to their cases.

## [A]   Some Issues You Must Consider If You Are Thinking About Opening a Virtual Law Office

1) Some states require you to have a physical presence if you are going to do most of your legal work with clients who live there. You MUST check the rules governing your jurisdiction. It may be that you can satisfy this requirement just by sharing a conference room there, but you will need to check with your jurisdiction to see if this is allowed. You probably will need a place for service of process because, at the time of publication of this book, that was a requirement of almost every state that had considered the virtual office issue. Again, check with your jurisdiction.

2) Where will your clients drop off documents if your state does not require a physical presence? Or will you require clients to scan in everything and email it to you? Will your clients feel comfortable doing this? Alternatively, will they feel comfortable mailing original documents to you so you can scan them?

3) When your entire law office is run through technology, privilege and security become increased concerns. It is critical that your attorney work-product, files, and communications be secure. You are bound by certain ethical rules to ensure the attorney-client privilege. You must be able to meet your state's requirements in terms of security. Cyber liability insurance is available, but it may not protect you sufficiently.

4) There is a big risk of becoming a slave to your virtual office because you are accessible at all times. Adoption of a virtual approach to your practice may imply to the public that you want to make yourself available at all times. If this is not the case, you will have to find a way to properly convey that fact. But if you let people know that you are limiting your schedule, you may be defeating one of your reasons for going virtual. This is something you really need to consider carefully.

5) Many professionals believe that client retention is based on relationships and that relationships cannot be developed and maintained easily if the attorney and client never spend physical time together. This may be true for some clients, particularly elderly ones who do not feel comfortable relying on an attorney they haven't met in person. As a result, you should consider what types of clients you want to attract. Will they feel comfortable never meeting you in person? Will they feel comfortable meeting you in a coffee shop or in the conference room of someone else's office? Even if your jurisdiction will allow you to operate a virtual office without establishing a physical presence in which to meet clients, will this arrangement work for the type of clients whom you want to attract?

## [B]  Final and General Thoughts on Virtual Practices

Even if you decide to set up a physical office rather than a virtual one, you will find telephone conferencing and video conferencing to be incredibly helpful as an alternative to always conducting in-office meetings. You will save travel time, and clients are often pleased to be able to meet with you from the comfort of their homes or the convenience of their offices.

# Chapter 9

## WHAT DO I NEED TO OPEN AN OFFICE?

So you've figured out whether to practice alone or with at least one other person, whether or not to incorporate, where to put the office, and what to call it. Now what?

You need obtain to obtain things — many things. And not just business cards, envelopes, pens, staplers, and something to sit on. If your clients are going to be coming to your office, as opposed to a virtual office, what kind of message will your choices send to your clients? For example, if you choose to print your own business cards, will the micro-perforations on the edges of the cards look cheesy compared with professionally printed cards that most other lawyers hand out? And should you invest in pens with your law firm's name printed on them? We will discuss these questions in this chapter.

You also need insurance — many kinds of insurance. Your insurance needs will depend upon your type of practice. For example, you won't need insurance to protect against claims for clients' slip-and-fall accidents that occur in your office if you maintain a virtual practice, but you will need cyber liability insurance.

To make this discussion easier, let's start with a checklist of things to consider:

__ Sign for the office door
__ Burglar alarm system and panic button
__ Fire/smoke alarms and carbon monoxide detectors
__ Business cards
__ Brochures
__ Stationery and matching envelopes
__ Computers
__ Photocopiers
__ Printers
__ Software
__ Telephones
__ Answering machine or service
__ Fax machine or service
__ Ink cartridges for printer, photocopier, and fax machine
__ Modem
__ Internet connection
__ Scanner
__ Shredder
__ Surge suppressors
__ Flashlight

__ Ruler
__ Message books
__ Legal pads
__ Pens (blue or black depending upon jurisdiction) and pencils
__ Black markers
__ Folders
__ Clips
__ Staplers and staples
__ Tape and tape dispensers
__ Hole punchers
__ Scissors
__ Rubber bands
__ Sticky notes
__ Legal pads
__ "Sign here" tabs
__ Exhibit tabs
__ Litigation backs
__ Postage machines or stamps
__ Postage scale
__ Desks
__ Desk chairs
__ File cabinets
__ Book shelves and bookends
__ Storage cabinets
__ Storage boxes
__ Desk trays
__ Conference table and chairs
__ Seats for the waiting room
__ Bathroom supplies
__ Cleaning supplies (including a can of hairspray — not for hair)
__ Legal publications
__ Research tools
__ Insurance
__ Permits
__ Decorations
__ Picture-hanging hooks
__ Hammer, screwdrivers
__ Vase
__ Coffee maker and supplies
__ Mugs and silverware
__ Small refrigerator (microwave: optional)
__ Window coverings
__ Wastebaskets
__ Wastebasket liners and trash bags

__ Tissues
__ Paper for photocopier and printers
__ First-aid kit
__ Fire extinguisher
__ Manila envelopes

This above list is not exhaustive, but it includes most of the things that you will need when you open your own law firm. If you start a law practice from home, you won't need many of these things — like furniture or a new refrigerator. If you start a law practice in a space that you share with other professionals (attorneys or professionals in other lines of work), you won't need many of these things because you will most likely be sharing a conference room and using office furniture that is already there. And if you're starting a virtual office, you also won't need many of the things on this list. You'll need to be concerned with how your website looks, which is a topic that we address later in this book.

## § 9.01  SIGNS

Let's begin at the top of the list. If you are renting space in an office building, you will need a sign either on the door or next to the door. If the building has a directory either inside the building, outside the building, or both, you will need a sign there, too. Often landlords have specific requirements about the appearance of the signs, including size, color, font and font size. They want all the tenants' signs to be similar-looking. Consult with your landlord about this before spending money to create signs. Some municipalities also have strict requirements about exterior signs, so be sure to check that, too. If neither the landlord nor the municipality has specific requirements, just remember that your sign is the first exposure a client will have to your office. You want it to convey professionalism, not ego. This means that it should not be so large, or contain print so large, that it looks like it's yelling at the clients. Similarly, you don't want it to look so lavish that it looks like it belongs outside a Baroque castle rather than a law office. In other words, avoid typefaces with fancy flourishes. Your professional sign is not the place to display your artistic alter-ego.

## § 9.02  ALARM SYSTEMS

You should seriously consider a hard-wired burglar and fire alarm system that will notify the alarm company and police if someone breaks in or a fire starts. Better safe than sorry, right? Even if you back up all of your information on the cloud or on a hard drive that you remove from the office, do you really want to arrive at your office one morning and discover that all the office equipment is gone? Or, worse, that everything has burned up including the notes on the legal pad on your desk? And the huge pile of financial documents that your client just dropped off yesterday and that you were going to scan in today?

Also consider buying a plug-in carbon monoxide alarm if your office is in a house — be it your home or a residential building devoted exclusively to office space. You don't want to come back to your office and discover that your secretary thought she was getting sleepy from eating a big lunch when, in fact, she was passing out from inhaling carbon monoxide. The same is true for you when you're working alone in the evening. That wooziness you feel may not be from eating a big dinner. Carbon dioxide alarms are inexpensive and are available at hardware stores and online.

## § 9.03   BUSINESS CARDS

Don't even think about printing your own business cards. Although it's tempting to shove sheets of micro-perforated business cards into your laser printer, those micro-perforated edges send a subtle message to the world that you're not as polished and slick as other attorneys. You don't need to hire an expensive printing company to produce your cards. There are numerous online companies that do an excellent job at an inexpensive price. Just be sure to proofread the words that you want on the cards — or better yet, ask someone else to do it — so that you don't have to throw them out and start again when you discover that you accidentally misspelled the name of the street. Or included a wrong digit in the area code. This kind of thing happens all the time. Be careful!

## § 9.04   BROCHURES

Brochures are a useful way to let the public know more about your firm and what it does. As with the business cards, do NOT print your own in your office unless you want to look like you lack a professional edge compared with other law firms. Yes, you can use Microsoft Publisher to design and print your own brochures on heavyweight paper, but if you want to avoid having them look like a home-grown arts and crafts project, get them professionally printed. This doesn't apply if you are highly skilled in this area or have a close friend or relative who is. There also are companies that produce brochures about numerous areas of the law — such as why you need a will or what you need to do if you want to sell your home. They will put your firm's name on the brochure so that it looks like it was produced especially for your firm. You can then display them in a holder in the reception area.

## § 9.05   STATIONERY

Stationery and matching envelopes: Buy a good quality. Your clients will judge you. You don't need to get stationery professionally printed. It's fine to print your own in the office. Just proofread it carefully so that you're not one of those attorneys who misspells his or her own name! (Yes, we have seen this.)

## § 9.06   EQUIPMENT

Computers: Either a desktop or a laptop is fine. Be sure that you utilize a good antivirus program.

Photocopiers: Some people choose to lease photocopiers rather than buy them. This usually allows them to get a bigger, faster machine. Leased machines usually collate for you. And you can get someone to come to your office to fix the machine when it malfunctions. But most beginning offices can get along fine with the kind of copier that you can buy in office supply stores. It's best to avoid the really inexpensive models that are designed for home use because they aren't designed for the kind of heavy use that will occur in a law office. They are also infuriatingly slow when you're under deadline pressure and need to get documents postmarked by 5 PM.

Printers: Try to avoid inkjet printers because they are much more expensive to operate than laser printers, not to mention slower. True, inkjet printers will print in color, and inexpensive laser ones won't. But you rarely need color in law office documents.

Software: At the minimum, you will need a good word-processing program. You should also consider timekeeping, billing, and law office management systems.

Telephones: It is best not to rely on a cellular phone as your main law firm telephone, no matter how much money you can save by doing it. There is often sound interference, and calls frequently are dropped. Also, you can't transfer calls from your receptionist to you. It's fine to use a cell phone when you're not in the office. But if you are in the office, you'll sound more professional if you are on a landline.

Answering machine, phone company answering service, or human answering service: Many law offices have moved away from using answering machines because phone company services are convenient and don't break. These services have the benefit of working when your power goes out. You can call into them from your cell phone or your home phone and find out who has called you. The benefit of using a machine in the office is that you can monitor the incoming calls after hours, hear who is calling you, and decide whether you want to take the call. Human answering services may seem more personal, but the prospective clients who call may assume that the person is affiliated with your firm and may become annoyed when that person can't answer questions. Also, the person who answers the phone needs to sound friendly, professional, and caring. Usually you can't control who at the answering service will be answering your phone. This is not an ideal situation, and it can run into significant money.

Fax machines or services: Although fax machines can now be purchased inexpensively, many lawyers have discovered that it is easier to use fax services, which cost less than ten dollars a month if you don't have heavy fax use. These services will use your dedicated fax number — and it is best to use a dedicated fax number so you can talk on your phone line while faxing at the same time. When people fax you something, the fax service routes it to your email address so you can pull up the documents from anywhere in the world. You no longer have to be in the office to receive faxes. It's easy to find these services in an Internet search of "efax services." You can even find reviews and comparisons (including costs) of the various services.

Scanners: Get the fastest one you can afford. When you're pressed for time and you're waiting for your pokey scanner to assist you, you'll wish you'd bought a faster one.

Shredders: The cross-cut ones are better than the strip-cut ones, but just make sure you get a shredder. There is no need to pay a lot of money for this. You'll just need it for shredding your own bills and personal documents. For client files, it's easiest and best to use a commercial shredding company. You can find them online in your location. Some will come to your office and shred your boxes of files right there. It will be cheaper if you opt to let the company take the files to be shredded at a remote location. It is usually even cheaper if you bring the boxes of files to the company. The companies will give you a written document stating that the files have been shredded. Check your local ethics rules to determine how long you must keep client files before you are allowed to shred them. Remember: even if you are allowed to shred most client files after a certain number of years, do NOT shred original wills and other documents that will be impossible or difficult to replace.

## § 9.07   MISCELLANEOUS

Hairspray: This is a useful cleaning tool. One spray removes ink on wooden tables. You'd be surprised how often the ink from notary stamps or leaky pens gets onto wooden conference tables. If you have a wooden conference table, keep a can of hairspray in the bathroom.

Message books: Even if you are working in a solo office, consider buying some message books. They are inexpensive and can be purchased at office supply stores — either online or in the actual store. The books usually contain three message slips to a page and make copies of the slip when you write on it. You can then rip off each slip and place it in the client's file at the end of the day after you have returned the call. If you are the only one in the office, writing the client's name and call back information on the slip will assist you in remembering to call clients back. It's all too tempting to scribble a client's name and phone number onto the side of a legal pad while you have another client on hold. Too often, that paper gets filed in the file of another client because the paper also contains notes for that client's case. You can also download computerized versions of a telephone message book. Just make sure that you put a copy of each message in the appropriate client's file.

Legal pads, pens, and folders: Even if you run an office that is mostly online, you will need legal pads. They are inexpensive and come in yellow or white and in either 8.5 by 11 inches or 8.5 by 14 inches. There is no advantage to any color or size. It is a matter of personal preference. But be sure to note that individual pages on some of the cheaper brands do not rip off cleanly when you get past the first few pages. That's frustrating and looks unprofessional if clients see your ratty-edged pages. So consider spending a little extra and getting the ones that rip cleanly.

As for pens, there is no need to get fancy ones. But be sure to note whether your jurisdiction requires filed documents (deeds, for example) to be signed in blue or black ink. This varies by the jurisdiction. Do not leave the wrong colored pens in your conference room. If you do, clients will use them on the documents, and you won't be able to file them. Clients also have a habit of absent-mindedly taking pens. Buy lots of spares; they're cheap. Unless you have extra money, you do not need to purchase pens with your law firm's name on them. Some lawyers think this is a good marketing tool. But we ask you: Have you ever consulted with a lawyer, doctor, dentist, accountant, or other professional just because you happened to notice that person's name on a pen? Probably not. But if you think that it's a nice touch to give them out, go for it. If you're a fairly new lawyer, this might make your clients think that you're more prosperous than you are. Personalized pens are, however, a nice giveaway if you're trying to market your services by holding free seminars at the local library or philanthropic organization.

File folders are essential even if you think that most of your practice will be conducted online and you're going to scan in and store all documents digitally. Nonetheless, unless your practice is a virtual one, clients will give you documents that you will have to store somewhere. When you first start your practice and have only one or two clients, you can store their documents in piles on your desk. But that quickly becomes impractical and, besides, it looks unprofessional. File folders come in many colors and sizes. Take a look at an office supply catalog online to see what's available. We recommend that you buy legal size rather than letter size. You also will need accordion file folders that will accommodate the smaller file folders. The outside file will bear the client's name. The inside files will keep the various parts of the file organized. For example, you might have one file for correspondence, another for billing statements, another for pleadings, etc.

Legal publications: You should seriously consider subscribing to legal publications in your field of practice as well as general-interest legal publications for your county and/or state (for example, the New York Law Journal). Reading these will help keep you up-to-date with new cases and changes in the law. Many of these publications, such as the American Bar Association's journal, are available online.

Research options: Online research options such as Westlaw and LexisNexis can be pricey, but these companies offer a variety of packages that are affordable to attorneys who need them for litigation practices. Check for special pricing for solo and small-firm offices. Some public libraries and courts offer free access to legal research. Also, many law schools offer their research capabilities to the public for a modest annual fee. Further, there are many free online legal research sources. Most notably, state statutes are often available online for free. Many years ago, lawyers needed to spend thousands of dollars buying and updating books for research, but this is no longer the case. Today, most resources for legal research are available online.

Insurance: At the very least, lawyers need to buy malpractice and health insurance. If you have a landlord, then you will most likely need to purchase liability insurance, too. But as you progress in your practice, you need to seriously consider purchasing other types of insurance — office interruption, office overhead, disability, and key person if you have partners. Office interruption insurance is especially important if you have a fire, flood, or other disaster that causes you not to be able to occupy your office during cleanup and renovations. Office overhead insurance is helpful if you become disabled and can't pay your office expenses for a while. Key person insurance is useful if you have a partner who brings in a significant portion of the revenue and isn't able to work for a period of time because of illness or injury. Disability insurance will pay a portion of your salary to you if you become disabled — either for a short or a long period of time.

Permits: You may need a municipal permit for a sign outside your office building — particularly if your office is in a building that doesn't have outdoor signs already (a house, for example). You may also need a permit if you make alterations to the walls of your office. Check with your municipality.

The other items on the list are self-explanatory. You may or may not need some of them depending upon whether you are renting your own office or sharing one with other people. In regard to the tissues, they are not just for you; they are for clients who cry. You will need more or less of these depending upon your areas of practice. Be kind: keep tissues where your clients can reach them.

# Chapter 10

# ORANIZATION OF THE LAW OFFICE

## § 10.01  PHYSICAL APPEARANCE

The manner in which you organize your law office matters, whether your office is a virtual one, a small rented room in a large suite of unrelated lawyers, or your own multi-room office with its own reception area and conference room. Why? Because if you can't find documents easily, you'll waste time. Also, it's easier to commit malpractice if you're disorganized. And, when clients see an office that looks disorganized, they often wonder if the lawyer who inhabits that office is also disorganized in thinking and handling cases.

Organizing a law office includes everything from the setup of furniture to what kind of storage systems you need for open and closed files. Let's start with the furniture and physical appearance.

Clients will judge you on outward appearances. This means that if your physical office is cluttered with piles of papers, clients will not conclude that you must be a good lawyer because you're busy. Some clients might not care, but many will conclude that you're disorganized or that you don't pay attention to details. Similarly, if a large part of your practice is virtual, make sure that your web presence is well-organized and intuitive with links that work. If your web page is cluttered, potential clients might give up in frustration or decide that you won't be approachable. Visual clutter is off-putting. So are those annoying little chat boxes that keep popping up on a website, asking if someone can help you. It's a lot like walking into a clothing store and having salespeople constantly ask you if they can be of assistance. Once is fine, but more than once feels like an annoying gnat buzzing at your head.

When designing your office — be it a virtual or a physical one — keep in mind the image that you are trying to convey. Do you want to appear intelligent, competent, professional, and caring? What about aggressive? If you want clients to think that you are aggressive — and some clients like this — will you be well-served by an office design that assaults the senses of your clients? Your clients might want you to aggressively defend their interests, but do they want to be the object of your aggressive nature? Probably not. Most people want their dealings with their lawyer to be calm and devoid of stress. This means that your office appearance — whether physical or virtual — needs to convey that this is a safe zone for clients.

Let's start with the physical office. Keep piles to a minimum. This includes not only papers but also newspapers, magazines, files, reference books, etc. Many lawyers have so much clutter in their offices that they have to move a pile from the visitor's chair so a client can sit in the lawyer's inner office. If you are prone to piles, and your office has a conference room, consider meeting all clients in the conference room rather than in your inner office. Keep the door to your inner office closed when clients are around. Keep the conference room free of piles. This way, clients will conclude that you're well-organized.

As for organizing your virtual presence, take a look at the websites of numerous other lawyers. Which ones inspire confidence? Why? Which ones annoy you? Why? Put yourself in the place of a client. What would those websites make you think about each of those lawyers? Now think about designing your own website. Learn from your colleagues' websites — both the good and the bad things.

## [A]  Layout

Now let's talk about the layout of your physical office — specifically the area in which clients wait to meet with you. If you do not have your own reception area, you won't be able to control the clients' waiting area. But for those of you who are planning to open an office that includes a reception area, please pay attention to this information: You must preserve the confidentiality of client information in the waiting area. Many lawyers overlook this detail. You should not.

Most solo and small-firm law offices contain waiting areas that are shared by a receptionist/legal assistant and clients. This means that confidential phone calls and paperwork sometimes aren't confidential. To avoid this problem, make sure that your front-desk person understands that files and correspondence should not be left uncovered on the desk where anyone other than office personnel can see it. The same is true for anything on the computer screen in the front office. Files with clients' names should not be visible to the public. This means that they should not be piled on the floor or propped against the side of a desk. If your office has an outgoing mail bin, make sure that the addresses are facing downwards. Phone conversations with clients or potential clients should not include any details that would reveal confidential information if people other than office personnel can hear. This includes using a client's name when saying hello on the phone. Ask your front-desk employee to discuss confidential client matters on a phone in a different part of the office or to call back the person when there is no one in the waiting area.

Another solution is to build a glass barrier with a sliding partition between the waiting area and the reception desk. Many doctors' offices use this method of preserving patient confidentiality. Yes, this may seem a bit cold and unfriendly to some people, but it is professional and preserves confidentiality.

Please also remember this if you meet with clients while you are sitting at your desk — as opposed to meeting in a conference room: Many clients can read upside down. Therefore, make sure that nothing confidential from another client is uncovered on the top of your desk. You'd be surprised how many lawyers neglect to cover or remove confidential documents. The same applies to documents — including time and billing records — on your computer screen. And remember that the rules for your front desk employee all apply to your workspace as well: Do not use clients' names when answering the phone if any person other than one of your employees is in your inner office. This applies not only to clients but also to other lawyers, title insurance salespeople, lunch delivery people, or anyone else. Some clients do not want anyone to know that they have visited with a lawyer for any reason. Not only should you respect that because it's the right thing to do, but you should do it because the ethical rules require it: All client contact must be kept confidential.

---

I learned my lesson about what kind of furniture NOT to put in a law office waiting room from going to visit a prestigious entertainment law office in Manhattan. I was a relatively new lawyer and had a case where I needed to meet with a lawyer in that firm. The reception area was furnished like a high-end living room, complete with a comfortable-looking couch. I sat at the couch and immediately sunk into it. The cushions were filled with down. The cushions enveloped me. I felt cozy and comfortable. A secretary served me tea in a beautiful china teacup. And that's where my problem began. I had sunk so deeply into the couch that it was barely possible to reach over to the coffee table in front of me to pick up the teacup and then put it back down between sips. So I had to hold the teacup and saucer in my lap and try not to spill tea on my light-colored suit. (A tea stain in my lap would not have looked professional.) Additionally, when it was time to go into the conference room, I had a great deal of difficulty getting up from my position deep in the couch. Elderly, portly, or out-of-shape people would have had an even harder time. This is where I learned to be courteous to clients in a waiting room: Make sure that the seating has solid enough seats and backs so that clients can get out of it easily. ALN

---

## [B]  Other Issues About the Waiting Area

After you've made decisions about the physical appearance of your waiting room, you must decide who will meet and greet people as they come in. Will you have a receptionist? If so, make sure your employee has a pleasant demeanor. This person is the face of your office. A pleasant receptionist can put people at ease and set the right tone for your interview. Someone who is sullen or cranky is not the right person to be meeting potential clients.

Your receptionist should note what time the client arrives. You need to have a good idea of your schedule and how long you keep potential clients waiting. Make sure that your receptionist lets you know when someone is waiting for you. If you have a receptionist, that person should offer your guest coffee, tea, water, or whatever non-alcoholic beverage you keep on hand. It is not very expensive to purchase a single-serving coffee maker. You should purchase small bottles of water or consider buying/renting a water cooler. We suggest buying a dorm-sized refrigerator and stocking it with milk and or cream. Some people believe that having a powdered creamer is adequate. That depends upon the type of impression you want to make. Many nervous clients will be grateful to you for giving them a beverage. If you have a receptionist, we suggest that you not keep the coffee machine or bottles of water where they are accessible to the clients. This can unnecessarily increase your monthly expenses. We have heard stories about clients in waiting rooms who, when they thought no one was looking, helped themselves to K-cups and water bottles to take home.

As we mentioned earlier, your receptionist should be noting the time when clients arrive. Tell your receptionist how often you want to be reminded that someone is waiting. Some clients arrive very early and, thus, may have to wait until the time they were actually supposed to be seen or shortly thereafter. You do not want to rush someone out of your office because someone else came way too early.

If you cannot afford a receptionist/assistant, or you choose not to employ one, there are still things you can do to make potential clients comfortable. First, make sure there is a bell or a system of some sort that lets you know that someone has entered the office. This is absolutely essential. You want something in place for informational purposes as well as for security. You need to know if an outsider is in your office. Second, with regard to refreshments, you have two options. You may decide that when you come out to meet a potential client, you will offer to make coffee or serve water. As an alternative, you can provide self-serve coffee and water in your waiting room. You can control how much is taken from your office by limiting how many K-cups and water bottles are available in the waiting room. People are less likely to take extras if they see that not many are available. As we mentioned above, you may decide that it is more economical to use a water cooler than provide individual bottles. Be sure to provide disposable cups and a wastebasket for the used ones.

## § 10.02  TECHNOLOGY

Despite great advances in technology, many lawyers enter their appointments in calendar books and keep paper versions of all their documents. Although some of these lawyers use billing software, many do not use timekeeping software. This is because they began practicing before personal computers and cell phones, and they are used to operating their law offices without technology. The earliest law office technology that was widely available to solo and small-firm practitioners was billing software. In those early years, it was common for lawyers to use a pen to write the time that they spent on cases and then give the pieces of paper to their secretary to enter into a billing program.

Keeping track of appointments, checking for conflicts, and searching for old documents to use as templates for new ones is so much easier than it used to be before the advent of inexpensive technology for the solo and small-firm lawyer. We strongly encourage anyone starting a law office to use a computerized law office management system that will oversee the calendar, client lists, file organization, and retrieval. The systems can make some initial conflict checking easier; the systems also compute statutes of limitations and notify you of upcoming deadlines; and if you're trying to remember an old case in which you wrote an affidavit that might be useful in a current case, the system allows you to run phrase checks to find the document easily. Computerized law office management systems will also keep track of your telephone messages and emails and file them in the appropriate case file.

Deciding which office management system to use can be daunting. There are many. Some are available for purchase; and you install the software on your computer. Others are available on the cloud for a monthly fee. For solo and small-firm practitioners who are just starting out, the cloud-based option is much more affordable. A comprehensive list of systems — cloud and computer based — is available in the Appendix to this book and on the American Bar Association's web site: http://www.americanbar.org/content/dam/aba/migrated/tech/ltrc/charts/pmtbchart.authcheckdam.pdf. The ABA's list includes features and prices.

Which practice management system is right for you? Don't just go by price. We recommend narrowing down the choices by features, then consulting the website of the companies whose systems you're considering. Many of the companies offer free trials. Test the systems. Some will seem more intuitive than others. Although many will have similar features, the features will work better on some systems than on others. Each system will have strengths and weaknesses, pros and cons. If you have colleagues who are using office management systems, ask them what system they use and what they like and dislike about it. Do your homework! But then test the system yourself.

It is also possible to purchase systems that just keep track of time and billing, but the management systems can do this and so much more — and at a price that is affordable. We recommend that you investigate what these systems have to offer you.

## § 10.03   FILING SYSTEMS

Traditionally, lawyers kept all case files and documents in large metal filing cabinets. Not only did this take up a lot of space, but lawyers also needed space to store closed files. Although many jurisdictions allow lawyers to destroy a wide variety of files after a certain number of years — commonly six or seven — lawyers often let the files accumulate until the lawyers run out of space, move, or retire. (The length of time for saving files varies by state. Check your state's rules. In New York, where we set up our practices, lawyers are required to keep documents for at least seven years before destroying them. Lawyers are not allowed to destroy irreplaceable documents — like wills and trusts.)

Lawyers with small offices and virtual offices have discovered that scanning documents and keeping only the electronic version solves the problem of lack of physical storage space. It also makes document retrieval a lot easier — particularly years after you've closed the file and are just looking for a template, as we discussed earlier. The paper copies of some official documents need to be saved — wills, for example.

If you're thinking about making your office "paperless," which almost always means "semi-paperless" because you have to keep some official documents in their paper form, just remember that you will need to invest in a very fast scanner. The inexpensive ones are slow and will cause you to spend too much time scanning your documents.

While we're on the subject of scanning documents, let's talk about naming those documents. A lot has been written about what to name documents when you file them electronically. Some people say that it's best to preface the name with the date. Other people disagree. You can read all about it in articles on the Internet. Whichever system you decide to use, just be sure that you're consistent in your naming. Opinions also vary about how to name the case files into which you place the documents. Many people say you should name case files the way you would name them if they were paper files: by the client's name. Other people say that it's better to name them by the type of case — for example, personal injury. But if every file in your office is a personal injury file, starting a file name with "Personal Injury" won't help you. It helps only if your office handles more than one kind of case.

Traditionally, lawyers have given subfiles names like "Pleadings" and "Correspondence." This can work for electronic files as well. Or you might want to use other divisions that seem more convenient to you. This might depend upon the type of case. For example, in a case involving the sale of a house, you might want subfiles that say, "Contract," "Appraisal," "Correspondence," "Closing Documents," "Billing," etc.

## § 10.04  BACKUP SYSTEMS

No matter what you name your files, you will have to implement procedures to back them up somewhere other than on your computer. Some people recommend external hard drives; others recommend the cloud. Still others recommend a combination of both. We fall into that last category. It is best to have more than one kind of backup — and preferably one that is not in your office in case the office is destroyed by fire, flood, or other natural disaster. External hard drives have become inexpensive, so you might want to consider purchasing two of them — one that you keep in the office and one that you bring home or store somewhere else outside your office. Or keep one external hard drive in your office and also back up files to the cloud. Please keep in mind that some practitioners have expressed security concerns about the cloud, even if you use encryption. Other practitioners think that the likelihood of a security breach, with decryption of files, is remote. But whatever backup option you use, be sure to test it regularly to make sure that your files are backing up properly.

## § 10.05  CREATING CHECKLISTS FOR PROCEDURES

Why do you need checklists for procedures? It seems like a waste of time to stop what you're doing for clients and make a list of all the steps necessary to do it — particularly if what you're doing is something you do frequently. But what if you eventually decide to hire a paralegal or an associate? And what if you want that person to take over that job? You have to stop to train that person. Wouldn't life be easier if you could provide a checklist? Or what if the task that you do frequently involves a large number of steps? For example, if you're representing a seller in a real estate closing. When you leave your office to go to a closing, you need to remember to bring the deed and other required transfer documents. You need your notary stamp or seal. What else? Without a checklist, you might get to the closing and discover that it needs to be postponed because one of your clients forgot to bring a photo ID. That's because you didn't have a checklist that reminded you to remind the clients all bring their photo IDs. If all sellers don't have a photo ID, the closing cannot occur. Or if the sellers of a house don't bring the keys, the purchasers can't enter their new home. Your checklist should include "Remind sellers to bring keys."

There are other excellent reasons to compile checklists. One is that if you handle certain kinds of cases only occasionally — every few years or even every few months — you are likely to forget important parts of the procedure. In the most egregious situations, this can lead to malpractice. But even if your omission doesn't cause a malpractice situation, do you really want to forget to do something and then rush around at the last minute to remedy the omission? An example of this comes from a checklist for representing clients who file for Chapter 7 bankruptcy protection. Your checklist should include "Send client directions for driving to court." If you don't do that, frantic clients will call your law office an hour before their court appearance to ask how to get there. If you are a solo practitioner, you won't be there to answer because you'll be on your way to the court. Or maybe in the court. If you are in the court, your calls will go to voice mail. Your client will be frantic and will most likely arrive late for the hearing. A simple checklist would solve this problem. You're going to be a busy attorney; why try to remember every little detail? Write them all down. It's a mental download that frees your brain and will ease your stress in the future.

Checklists are also very important for your personnel — everyone from secretaries to legal assistants to associates. The reason is simple: if they go on vacation, get sick, quit, or get fired, someone else can easily take over their tasks with the help of the checklists. Make sure you have access to those checklists. Make sure you have a copy of those checklists somewhere other than on that person's computer. Sabotage doesn't happen often, but if your employee is disgruntled, checklists could disappear from that person's computer. This is one very good reason why you should back up your computers to a hard drive as well as to the cloud and take that hard drive out of the office whenever you leave. Or lock it in the drawer of your desk. This is not paranoia. Stuff happens. We've heard the stories.

## § 10.06   BANKING

### [A]   Operating Account

Setting up a bank account for your office seems simple, right? Just go to the nearest bank and tell them that you want a checking account for your law office. That's a start. But then what? The bank is likely to ask you if you want a debit card. We caution you against using one for your office. Keeping track of your law firm's money is hard enough without having a debit card. Do you write down every withdrawal that you make with the debit card for your personal account? Have you ever tried to balance your account at the end of the month and discovered that you don't remember how you spent that $60 withdrawal? Your law firm is a business, which means that you will need to account for all the money that you remove from the business account. Do not be tempted to accept a debit card.

What should you ask the bank to write on the checks for your general operating account? Check your state's rules to see if you need to write something specific. If not, write the name of your firm and the words "Operating Account" or "General

Operating Account" or a similar designation below it. Include the firm's address. If you are bad at remembering to use a check register, get a checkbook that will make a copy of each check that you write.

If you are a solo practitioner, do not use this account as if it were a personal checking account. Yes, the funds in it are technically yours. (If the funds belong to someone other than you — a client, for example — they should be placed in an IOLA/IOLTA or escrow account. See below for the discussion of those accounts.) Using your operating account to pay for personal expenses that have nothing to do with your law office creates a bookkeeping nightmare. We have heard stories about solo practitioners who manage their own books and who say that they label anything that isn't an office expense as income. Although this bookkeeping system may work well for them, we advise against it. If you don't pay yourself a regular salary and, instead, want to take draws as you need them, then label those checks as "personal draw." Don't go to the mall and use an office check to pay for your new running shoes.

## [B]   IOLA/IOLTA Account

You will also need two kinds of escrow accounts (also known as trust accounts). The first is called either an IOLA or an IOLTA account, depending on the state in which you practice. The acronym stands for "Interest on Lawyer Account" or "Interest on Lawyer Trust Account." They are functionally the same. This type of escrow account should be used for either small sums of money from a client or larger sums that will not be held in escrow for long enough to generate much money. Typically, the amount generated would not exceed the legal fee to set up an escrow account that generates interest to be paid to a client. An IOLA/IOLTA account pays interest to a state fund that finances legally related public service projects such as providing civil legal assistance to the poor or other underserved populations such as the elderly or the disabled or that finances programs that help to improve the justice system. In many states, but not all, lawyers are required to open one of these escrow accounts. Lawyers withdraw money from the account via a checkbook. The checks should bear the firm name and the words "IOLA Account" or "IOLTA Account," depending upon the designation in your state.

These accounts should contain only funds belonging to someone other than yourself. They should not contain funds belonging to you or your law firm.

When you write a check on one of these accounts, be sure to either have your client endorse the check or have the client sign a consent for you to write the check. On the consent form, include the check number, the name of the payee, and the date.

## [C]   Escrow/Trust Account

In addition to an IOLA/IOLTA account, you should have a conventional escrow account. In some states, these are called "trust" accounts, but for purposes of this discussion, we'll call them "escrow" accounts. These are the accounts where you place all unearned monies as well as money that doesn't belong to you — for example, settlement proceeds, real estate sale proceeds, etc. Check rules in your state for requirements regarding the segregation of trust funds. (Note: some states do not require that you place retainers for legal fees in your escrow account or IOLA/IOLTA account. Again, check the rules for your state.)

All money that does not belong to you should be placed in either an IOLA/IOLTA or an escrow account. Place it in an escrow account — versus an IOLA/IOLTA account — if it is likely to generate more income than the legal fee that you charge to open the account for your client. Typically, a regular escrow account works like this: You establish an account in the name of your law firm that has a separate interest-bearing subaccount for each client. The bank gives you a checkbook with checks that bear your firm name and the words "Escrow Account." You then open a subaccount for each client when you are ready to deposit that client's funds. Each subaccount earns interest separately. When you are ready to withdraw the money and the interest, you transfer it into the main account and write a check to the client.

Escrow accounts also are used frequently for funds from a third party that will become your client's. An example of this is when you are the attorney for the seller in a real estate transaction. The purchaser signs the contract of sale and transmits it to you with a down payment check. You place that check into a newly-created subaccount. At the real estate closing, you write a check to the seller for that amount and the interest that it earned.

As with the IOLA/IOLTA accounts, please remember that when you write a check on an escrow or trust account, you should either have your client endorse the check or have the client sign a consent form for you to write the check. Include the check number, the name of the payee, and the date.

## [D]  Disbursement Account

In some states, lawyers are not required to place advance payments for filing fees, experts, appraisals, etc. in an IOLA/IOLTA account. In these states, some lawyers place the payments into their general operating account because this is not prohibited; but other lawyers use a "disbursement account." This is a checking account that contains only monies that are to be used to pay for expenses on behalf of a client. The account typically contains advance payments made by the client for the upcoming expenses, but the account can also contain funds transferred from the lawyer's general operating account when the lawyer is advancing the fee for the upcoming disbursement.

## [E]  Petty Cash Account

Some lawyers keep a small amount of cash in a box in the office for use when small purchases need to be made — for example, when they need to mail a package with postage that costs only a few dollars or perhaps to buy a birthday cake for one of the employees. Typically, the lawyers place a small sum of money in the box — perhaps $20 — and replenish it when it is nearing depletion. The lawyer keeps receipts in the box and enters purchases into a small logbook in the box. Some lawyers find this easier than writing checks for very small purchases. The money for the petty cash fund comes from the office's operating account (that is, the office's general checking account). The lawyers write a check to "cash" and also write "petty cash" on the lower left part of the check.

# Chapter 11

# LET'S MAKE SOME MONEY!

While many lawyers feel uncomfortable discussing the topic of money, we do not. You are reading this book so you can learn how to own and operate a successful business, and that cannot happen unless you understand how to get properly paid for all of your hard work. Traditionally, certain areas of law have structured their fees in very specific ways. For example, lawyers almost always work on a contingency basis when representing plaintiffs in negligence cases and in collection matters. Lawyers frequently bill on an hourly basis on commercial matters and on matrimonial matters, stating that they do not want to subsidize emotional clients who wish to fight about everything. But in many areas of practice, lawyers are rethinking the way they structure their fees.

Alternative Fee Arrangements (AFA) require some negotiating and creativity, yet you may find that both you and your client will be comfortable with something where there are up-sides and down-sides for both of you. In this chapter, we will be exploring traditional fee arrangements as well as introducing you to the possibilities of Alternative Fee Arrangements. Choosing the best fee arrangement for your office may differ on a case-by-case basis. We have provided you with some examples of retainer agreements in the Appendix.

## § 11.01   TYPES OF FEE ARRANGEMENTS

### [A]   Hourly Billing

Many large and small firms still use hourly billing. What this means is that you set an hourly rate for each lawyer and paralegal, keep track of the hours spent, and bill your client on a monthly basis for the hours spent at the respective hourly rates. While this may seem pretty straightforward, it is very important that your engagement agreement be detailed enough to leave no room for ambiguity. Some things that should be covered in your hourly billing agreement are:

- Whose time will be billed?

- What are the hourly rates for each person who can bill on the file?

- Do hourly rates change based upon the type of work being done by the attorney? For example, some firms bill a higher rate for the time an attorney spends in court.

- What increments do you bill in? Most firms bill in increments of 1/10 of an hour, although some have a minimum-billing amount of 1/4 of an hour.

- If you take on a large piece of civil litigation that is likely to take years, can you provide for increases in your hourly rate during the course of the litigation?

- If you have an increase provision in your retainer agreement, is there a limit on the amount you can increase the hourly rate and the frequency of such increases?

- Are there rules in your jurisdiction with regard to how often you must send a bill and with regard to how detailed your bills must be?

- Are there rules in your jurisdiction that require you to tell clients how they can dispute your bill?

- What is it that you actually bill for? We have found lawyers who bill for "cerebral time," and who put that language in their billing agreement. While we are certainly not advocating that you bill for the time that you spend thinking about the case while you are jogging or working out at the gym, it makes sense to let the client see what types of things you will be including in the bills.

## [B]    Variations on the Standard Hourly Billing Model

Some offices have modified the hourly billing model into something called a blended rate. A blended rate is an agreed-upon hourly rate for anyone who works on the file, from partners to associates to paralegals. For example, if your firm bills $100 per hour for paralegals, $250 per hour for associates, and $450 per hour for partners, the lawyer and client can agree to a blended hourly rate of $275 or $300 per hour. All of the same rules for hourly billing remain in effect except for the differences in rates. Some lawyers argue against the merits of this arrangement because they believe it encourages law firms to use their least experienced staff. Other lawyers argue in favor of this arrangement because, they say, the firms are likely to handle cases as they ordinarily would have, and clients believe that the arrangement is saving them money on hourly fees.

## [C]    Contingency Fees

Contingency fees are commonplace in certain areas of the law but impermissible in other areas.

A contingency fee is a fee that the client pays only if certain things (contingencies) happen. In a typical negligence case, the client is required to pay for the costs of the litigation but does not pay attorneys' fees unless there is a recovery. Make sure to provide in your retainer agreement what the fee will be and when the costs of litigation are to be paid. Most negligence lawyers charge 1/3 of the recovery after payment of expenses. In response to consumer complaints, some states now provide that attorneys' fees MUST be calculated on the net sum AFTER the payment of expenses. Make sure to check to see if there are any rules in your jurisdiction in this regard.

Contingency fees are also common in collection matters, but the fees are usually lower than with negligence cases, ranging anywhere between 20% and 33 1/3%.

## [D]  Reverse Contingency Fees

This is a somewhat novel, though logical, method of billing when you represent a defendant who has been sued for a large amount of money. You and the client must agree upon a sum that is the highest amount your client is willing to pay to settle the case. Once you and your client agree upon that figure, then you both need to agree upon a percentage that you will receive of the difference between that amount (the "baseline") and any settlement below that — i.e., any settlement that saves your client money. For example, let's say that your client's baseline is $100,000, and you have both agreed that your client will pay you will 25% of the amount between that baseline and a lower settlement. Then if you settle the case for $80,000, your client will pay you 25% of the $20,000 that you saved your client. This means that your client will pay you $5,000. Your client will pay you this in addition to your regular fee.

Defense lawyers, unlike plaintiff's lawyers, normally will not agree to a straight contingency fee because (a) the defense bar needs some predictable income, (b) the defendant usually has some percentage of liability, and (c) defense lawyers don't get to choose their cases when the are working as outside council for insurance carriers that represent defendants. Although plaintiffs' lawyers can choose cases where there is a likelihood of a recovery, defendants' lawyers are often just trying to limit their client's exposure. Thus, this type of reverse contingency actually may be better for defendants who are no longer billed strictly by the hour, regardless of outcome. Most clients are happy to agree to a fee arrangement that incentivizes the best possible outcome for them.

## [E]  Flat Fees

Flat fees are exactly what they sound like; you set a fixed fee that the client will pay regardless of the amount of time spent on a case and regardless of the outcome. This type of arrangement can be very risky in litigation, but some lawyers see it as a way to get business and are willing to take that risk. Costs and disbursements should be separate from the agreed-upon fee.

Some firms have clients that they will represent on a number of matters and agree upon a fixed fee for that representation, regardless of the number of matters handled. The fee may be paid on a monthly basis or at other agreed-upon intervals. Other firms have chosen to apply the fixed/flat fee notion in a somewhat unusual way. Where a client has an ongoing piece of litigation, the lawyer and client can agree upon a set monthly fee for as long as the case is active.

Flat fees help to make your income more predictable. In the past, many lawyers were hesitant to utilize a flat-fee arrangement because there was no consequence for clients who pestered the lawyer with calls or who prolonged a case with petty fighting. But the competitive nature of the law business has now made this type of arrangement much more commonplace. In fact, some of the largest firms in the country have worked out flat-fee arrangements with major clients as a strategy for winning or keeping their business.

During the Great Recession, companies and their in-house counsel were looking at ways to cut and predict legal fees. Many law firms were struggling and, as a result of the superior bargaining power of corporate clients, the law firms created new fee structures. Some companies negotiated flat monthly legal fees, regardless of the amount of work they needed, and others negotiated fixed fees for different parts of a case. The lawyer and the client in those cases agreed upon fixed sums for each phase of a case, such as investigation, pleadings, written discovery, depositions and so forth, with an additional large number for the trial (sometimes a fixed rate and sometimes hourly). Any of these arrangements might be workable for you as a small practitioner. You must, however, keep track of which arrangement was actually profitable to you so that you can determine whether to utilize it again and under what circumstances.

We will delve even deeper into the notion of segregating aspects of a case in our discussion of unbundling legal services in § 11.02.

## [F]   Hybrid Arrangements

Hybrid fee arrangements have been around for many years; however, there have been more variations on this theme recently. The basic hybrid fee normally involves an agreed-upon fee paid up-front and deducted from an eventual recovery. An example of this would be when a large potential client asks you to try collect on a significant judgment that he already has. You really have no idea if you will be able to collect the money, but you are willing to take the case if you are at least guaranteed some money for the work you do. You can charge a hybrid fee under these circumstances where you ask for a minimum up-front payment to be deducted from any money you recover. So, for example, you might ask for an up-front payment of $5,000 against 1/3 of any money recovered. The client would sign an agreement allowing you to keep the $5,000 whether or not you collected on the judgment. If you did collect on the judgment, you would get 1/3 of the money that you recovered for the client minus the $5,000 you already received.

Some states have statutory rules regarding legal fees. It is imperative that if you use a hybrid fee, you make sure that the fee does not exceed the statutory maximum legal fee in your state for the type of matter involved. You must also make sure that your fee is not "excessive." We bring this to your attention because many states have rules that say that lawyers cannot charge excessive fees.

A common hybrid fee seen in a variety of areas of the law is a flat fee up to the point of trial and then another fee for trial preparation and trial. This is very frequently seen in criminal cases where there is one fee for accomplishing a satisfactory plea bargain and another fee if the case goes to trial. Sometimes there is a flat fee for preparation and even trial. And sometimes the trial fee is billed hourly. This hybrid fee structure can also be employed in a variety of types of civil litigation, and is probably seen most commonly in cases involving contract disputes. Some lawyers have also used it as a marketing tool in matrimonial and family law matters.

Another type of hybrid fee is a <u>capped fee</u>. Here the lawyer and the client agree upon a maximum amount of a fee for a particular matter. The lawyer bills the client hourly pursuant to the retainer agreement. A variation on this is a written agreement in which the client pays a certain percentage of the difference between the total hourly fees and the fee cap. For example, suppose the parties agree to a fee cap of $10,000 with an even division of any amount between that and the lower sum of hourly fees. If the billing only is $7,000, the lawyer and client would evenly divide the remaining $3,000. Thus, the lawyer would receive $1,500 in addition to the $7,000 of hourly billing, for a total fee of $8,500.

The idea of a <u>fee collar</u> is an interesting concept that has recently gained popularity. A fee collar is when the lawyer projects a maximum hourly fee and earns bonus money if the billing comes in below that. If the billing exceeds the projected maximum fee, the lawyer receives only a portion of the hourly billing that exceeds the projected maximum fee by more than a certain percentage. It sounds complicated, but it really isn't.

Let's take a look at how this works. Assume that the lawyer and client have agreed to a fee of $10,000 with a collar of 10% and a 50% apportionment of any amount that is above or below 10% percent of the total. This means that if the lawyer's hourly billing is within 10% of $10,000 (i.e., between $9,000 and $11,000), the legal fee will be $10,000 as agreed. But if the lawyer bills only $7,000, the differential is more than the 10% collar, so the lawyer and client will equally share the $3,000 difference and, thus, the lawyer will earn $8,500 on $7,000.00 worth of billing. If the amount billed by the lawyer is $13,000 — which exceeds the projected fee by $3,000 — then the lawyer and client will equally share that sum. This means that the lawyer will receive $10,000 plus 50% of the excess, for a total of $11,500. Lawyers need to be good at estimating their fees to make these types of agreements. New practitioners are likely to have difficulty estimating the fee because they don't have a track record of handling cases and keeping track of time spent on them. Keeping good records of hours spent — even in fixed/flat fee cases — will help you to be able to project the total legal fee for a case.

## § 11.02  UNBUNDLING OF LEGAL SERVICES

When lawyers talk about unbundling legal services, they are talking about a type of legal representation in which the lawyer and client agree upon limiting the scope of the work that the lawyer does on a matter. Other terms used for unbundled legal services are "limited-scope services" or "discrete-task representation." These are situations in which a lawyer is hired to handle only a specific portion or portions of the tasks in a matter.

### [A]  Why Would Either a Client or an Attorney Consider This Type of Arrangement?

Clients tend to like this arrangement because it offers them a measure of control over costs and allows them to perform some of the work themselves. For example, clients may want the attorney to render general advice so the clients can represent themselves. This is common in cases where clients are participating in mediation or another alternative dispute resolution proceeding and are not sure if they are either giving up too much or are being too stubborn on a particular point. By hiring an attorney on a limited-scope basis, a client might have to pay an attorney only for an hour or two of time as opposed to hiring a lawyer to handle the entire matter. Or maybe a client needs a motion prepared on a case that the client is otherwise capable of handling. The client can hire a lawyer just for that purpose and not have to pay a lawyer for representation throughout the whole case. The possibilities are endless with regard to tasks a lawyer can do for a client without handling an entire matter.

Unbundling legal services helps clients with limited resources get legal assistance when they might not have been able to afford to hire a lawyer to handle the entire case.

Although commercial companies offer the public legal forms online (contracts and wills, for example), those companies do not provide advice or legal counseling. These services are not a substitute for an attorney who can provide explanation and advice.

Unbundling your legal services can free you to choose the tasks that you like to do and build a practice around that. If you have no interest in seeing a courtroom, you can still be involved in writing motions without having to worry about trying a case. Alternatively, you can choose to just make court appearances and let someone else to do the writing.

The economics of this type of practice can be very appealing to lawyers as well. Some lawyers discount their hourly rates — which can often be high — because clients are paying for only limited amounts of time, but other lawyers do not. Also because the services are limited, attorneys generally are paid when they render the services, so they have far fewer outstanding bills. Lawyers delivering limited scope legal services can insist upon payment at each appointment or before engaging in any task to be performed. Because the total fee for each service is comparatively low, clients are more willing and able to pay for the legal services.

Attorneys who provide services to clients with limited incomes speak very favorably about task-specific legal services for family court situations, because the lawyers can draft a petition or represent a client at a hearing without being obligated to do additional work. Although task-specific legal work can be billed hourly, it can also be billed at a flat fee. In some cases, attorneys and clients discuss the scope of the work and settle on a fixed fee that makes them both comfortable.

Courts throughout the country are showing support for the unbundling of legal services by allowing attorneys to make limited appearances. The courts in states promoting unbundling are finding that this helps significantly to reduce the number of pro se litigants who appear before them. In general, judges prefer to work with attorneys who are familiar with the workings of the court rather than work with pro se litigants. This is because cases with pro se litigants often take longer to wrap up because judges must take the time to explain things that lawyers would know already. In fact, state court systems, low-bono projects, and bar associations have designed, and are designing, notices of appearance for limited-scope representation to assure that this type of representation is available in their jurisdictions. These notices are unusual in that both the attorneys and the clients sign them, each agreeing to the limited scope of the appearance. Samples of these notices of appearance can be found in the Appendix of this book.

## [B]  Ethical Concerns About Unbundling Legal Services

When providing unbundled legal services, you should be mindful of the potential for your client to be confused over which one of you is responsible for particular aspects of the case — particularly if someone has to file the document that you prepared or follow up after it is submitted to a court. The way to avoid confusion is to spell out the client's follow-up duties, if any, in your written agreement.

Also, lawyers could potentially evade responsibility for the consequences of their work by limiting their work to document preparation and no follow-up. As a result, some states have restrictions governing the "ghostwriting" of pleadings and papers, requiring lawyers who draft pleadings to be identified. This helps to prevent lawyers from evading responsibility for inadequate work and also helps to keep them from preparing pleadings for frivolous matters without regard to the consequences. Make sure that you inquire about the rules in your jurisdiction if you are going to be using a limited-scope retainer.

## § 11.03  HOW DO YOU DETERMINE WHAT TYPE OF FEE STRUCTURE TO USE?

The first thing you need to do is to see if the state in which you practice restricts fee arrangements. Some states do. For example: New York has very clear rules regarding what lawyers can charge in medical malpractice cases and strictly prohibits contingency fees in both criminal and matrimonial matters. The New York Judiciary Law outlines a sliding scale cap limiting the percentage that an attorney can take as a fee in medical malpractice cases: 30% of the first $250,000; 25% of the next $250,000; 20% of the next $500,000; 15% of the next $250,000; and 10% of any amount over $1.25 million.

California also limits the percentage an attorney can charge in a medical malpractice case and prohibits contingency fees in divorce cases. A sliding scale limits the percentage an attorney can charge in a medical malpractice case in California to: 40% of the first $50,000 recovered; 33% of the next $50,000 ($50,001 - $100,000); 25% of the next $500,000 ($100,001 - $600,000); and 15% of any amount over $600,000.

Florida limits attorney fees in tort/negligence cases involving personal injury or property damage and medical malpractice cases if the client has waived a recovery right dictated by the state's constitution. In Florida, if a client and attorney settle the case before the filing of an answer or demand for arbitrators, the fee is 33 1/3% of any recovery up to $1 million. If the case is concluded after the filing of an answer or demand for arbitrators, the maximum fee is 40% of any recovery up to $1 million. If recovery or settlement is between $1 million and $2 million, the fee is 30%. If recovery or settlement is above $2 million, the fee is 20%. If all defendants admit liability and only want a trial on the question of damages, the fee is 33 1/3% of any recovery up to $1 million, 20% of any recovery between $1 and $2 million, and 15% of any recovery above $2 million.

The Florida constitution also limits the amount of the contingency fee that an attorney may charge in a medical malpractice case. As in New York, contingency fees in divorce cases are prohibited.

Texas does not limit attorney fees in medical malpractice cases, nor does it strictly prohibit contingency fees in divorce cases. But a comment to the Texas rules states that contingency fee arrangements in domestic relations matters "are rarely justified." In criminal cases, however, Texas does prohibit contingency fees.

Kentucky is an example of a state that also does not limit attorney fees in medical malpractice cases.

Some states with fee restrictions have form retainer agreements on their court websites, so you should look there. If you need someone to talk to, try your local bar association. For example, if you know you want to work in real estate law, reach out to the chair of the real estate committee of your local bar and ask for guidance about setting fees and preparing retainer agreements in the field. People who accept the chair role of a bar association committee usually are willing to work with other attorneys and may be an excellent resource for you. Be mindful of the fact that hourly rates and fee structures vary tremendously based on geography. The hourly rates from city to suburb are dramatically different, in large part because of the costs of rental space and services in the city. If you are asking other attorneys for fee information, try to be sure they have a real familiarity with your geographical location. There are cities where large firm partners bill anywhere from $400 per hour up to approximately $1,800 per hour. Also speak with local practitioners to see what the customary hourly rates are in your venue as well as to learn what type of fee arrangements are used for what types of cases. This is not to suggest that you must conform, but rather to suggest that if you are going to undercut the competition to attract business, or do something unorthodox, you should be well aware of what you are doing.

Another thing you must do is to keep careful records so that you can tell which type of fee structure results in the highest profit for your firm, while still being able to maintain good client relationships. If you make a lot of money on a case, but the client is unhappy, you are not likely to get repeat business or referrals from that client. Also, do not rely on what others tell you in terms of profitability. Listening to someone else who has different overhead costs, different staff, and different abilities may not give you the information you need to make a good decision on what YOU should be doing.

If you think you want to change the type of fee arrangement you have been making in a particular type of case, it is best not to make the change abruptly with all of your cases. Try it on a few cases and see how you make out. Does the new fee structure encourage you to do your best work? Are you really earning more while spending the same amount of time on the case? Are clients suddenly disputing more of your charges than ever before? And if they are not disputing the bills, are the clients displaying as positive an attitude with you and your firm as they displayed under the old method? Although some of the answers to profitability are obvious from the numbers, client relationships and satisfaction are far more subjective. Nonetheless, they need to be taken into account. Lawyers who want to have successful businesses have to learn to think about the long term. You want to maximize your client retention, satisfaction, and referrals so that you have to do less and less to attract new business as time passes.

## § 11.04   SHOULD YOU CHARGE A CONSULTATION FEE?

Whether or not to charge a consultation fee depends upon a variety of things, including what you think about the value of your time. There are, however, certain practice areas in which lawyers do not charge consultation fees because they do not want to risk the potential client going elsewhere. Negligence and personal bankruptcy are two examples of this.

Whether or not to charge a consultation fee on other types of matters presents a host of different questions. If the case is one for which you would normally bill hourly, charging a consultation fee may make sense because if the clients can't afford a consultation fee, how will they be able to afford your regular fee?

Through your local bar association and in discussions with colleagues, you can find out whether or not consultation fees are charged in given areas of law. However, even though some lawyers charge for a consultation, you may decide not to do so — particularly at the earlier stages of your practice. If you have a lot free time and little experience, meeting potential new clients and developing your interviewing skills may be more valuable to you than a small consultation fee.

When the time comes that people want YOU as opposed to just any lawyer, you may want to charge for consultations. Remember, a lawyer's time is money. If you spend all day seeing potential clients for free, you will have no time to do the work you already have.

What about the timing of taking the payment for your consultation fee, should you choose to charge one? Lawyers differ on when to take the payment. Some people think that you should take this fee before the interview, because if potential clients meet with you first and don't like you or what you tell them, they may be unwilling to pay the fee. Other attorneys think that asking for the fee before you see the potential client gives the wrong impression — that it makes you seem mercenary or unconcerned. We leave this choice to you.

You also will have to decide what form of payment you will take for the consultation fee. This, too, is an area where lawyers differ. Some attorneys will not allow credit cards for payment of a consultation fee because they do not like paying the associated service charges. We believe that the convenience to clients outweighs the fees to attorneys. Many people do not use checks or carry a lot of cash. We believe that you will be limiting your client pool if you do not accept credit card payments. It pays to conduct research to see what credit card processing company will give you the best deal with the lowest rate. Do your homework, and check again at least once a year because rates change, and the companies are competitive.

Some veteran attorneys have told us that they will no longer accept checks for consultation fees because of the frequency that they are returned for insufficient funds. Other attorneys believe that the more methods of payment you take, the more likely you are to attract potential clients. If you accept checks, just make sure you have all necessary identification information so that you have recourse if a check is dishonored. As your practice develops and you find that a certain method is not beneficial to you, you can always make changes. Remember that the more desirable you become as an attorney, the more selective you can be in your methods of payment and amounts required.

## [A]   Final and Important Note Regarding Consultation Fees

One way to make consultation fees more palatable to potential clients is to let them know that if they hire the firm, the amount paid for the consultation will be credited to their retainer fee or account. This makes you seem reasonable.

## § 11.05   RETAINER AGREEMENTS/LETTERS OF ENGAGEMENT

A "letter of engagement" is the document that you and your client sign to formalize your relationship. These agreements are contracts and, just like any other contract, must be written carefully. Remember, you are serving as your own attorney in this contract, and you will find out how good a lawyer you are when you have your first fee dispute.

Most letters of engagement are in the form of a letter from you to your client, and must be signed by both of you. But some letters of engagement look more like contracts than letters. And in some jurisdictions, lawyers call these engagement agreements "retainer agreements" or "retainer letters." In other jurisdictions, the term "retainer agreement" is used only when an engagement letter involves the payment of a retainer. The concept is the same, no matter what the name: The document is intended to clarify the terms of engagement as well as the rights and responsibilities of the lawyer and the client.

The requirements for the content of engagement agreements vary from state to state and field to field. Some states require written engagement agreements on all cases involving fees in excess of a certain amount. For example, New York requires a written agreement for all cases with a fee of $3,000 or more. It is a good idea to research the topic of engagement agreements in your state before opening your office. You do not want to have to delay a potential client from hiring you while you investigate your state's requirements for engagement agreements.

## § 11.06   REFERRAL FEES

Do not ignore the topic of lawyer referral fees. Many new attorneys believe that if they refer a case to another attorney, the attorney who takes the case will pay a referral fee even if the original attorney has done little or no work on the file. Why do many new attorneys believe this? They believe it because they have been interns in offices that do this. Yes, many small law offices have done this for years. And many lawyers have made a substantial amount of money referring cases to other attorneys. But this does not mean that the practice is permitted in the state where the office is located. Check the ethical rules in your state as well as the American Bar Association's Model Rules. States vary tremendously in what is allowed.

You should be aware that the Model Rules prohibit lawyers from sharing legal fees with non-lawyers.

Be aware that some states recognize referrals to be an integral part of the practice of law and, in particular, the economics of solo and small-firm practice. These states deliberately have omitted any provision in their rules suggesting that the division of fees needs to be in proportion to the amount of work done. Although every state requires the client to be aware of, and consent to, the referral fee, clients usually will not complain if they understand that the total fee cannot be any larger than it would have been absent the referral being paid to the other attorney.

MODEL RULE 1.5(e) STATES THAT ATTORNEYS WHO ARE NOT IN THE SAME FIRM MAY SHARE/SPLIT A FEE ONLY IF THE FOLLOWING THREE THINGS APPLY:

1) The division is proportionate to the work performed, or each attorney assumes joint responsibility,

2) The client agrees in writing, including the share to be received by each attorney,

3) And the total fee is reasonable.

Remember that if you assume joint responsibility for the case, you are, therefore, assuming joint liability for purposes of malpractice. Knowing that you will be liable for another attorney's malpractice should make you very cautious about the choices you make when it comes to referrals if you want to assume joint responsibility for the case so you can share the legal fee equally.

We recognize that you might be tempted to enlist the help of friends who are also just starting out, and vice versa, so that you can help each other build your practices in your respective fields. Be cautious in this regard. If you assume joint responsibility for a case — as opposed to handling one particular part and receiving a proportionate legal fee for handling just that part — you are responsible for the other attorney's errors. You will have to calculate whether the risk outweighs the reward.

Moreover, the Model Rules specifically warn attorneys that they must refer matters to attorneys whom they reasonably believe are competent to handle the matter. If you are not comfortable with the work product your friend will generate, then don't refer the case to that person.

## § 11.07   ACCEPTING CREDIT CARDS IN PAYMENT OF FEES

Think about how many times you have swiped your credit card in the last week. Nowadays, carrying cash — or even more archaic, carrying a checkbook — is quickly becoming a thing of the past. Even a baker at a farmer's market can accept payment for peanut butter cookies by pulling out a smartphone.

The same trend is evident in the law. And as a newly licensed attorney, not only will you need to accept credit cards, but you will also have to consider the ethical issues that come along with allowing clients to use them to pay you.

## [A]   Ethical and Professional Considerations of Accepting Credit Cards

To accept credit cards, you will have to choose a credit card processing company. But before you do that, it is important to understand the ethical and professional issues you might encounter when accepting credit card payments. You will need to know the right questions to ask to make sure the processor meets your needs and ethical obligations as an attorney.

### [1]   Client Confidentiality

One of the most important canons of the attorney-client relationship is confidentiality. This can be compromised when a third-party processor requires a client's name, address, and credit card number to pay you. However, as with most issues of confidentiality, this issue can be solved right from the beginning in your engagement letter by asking for your clients' consent to share their information with the credit card processor.

Additionally, to protect client confidentiality, do not include on the charge slip any information about the area of law, name of the case, or nature of the services provided. Instead, as recommended in a written opinion from the California State Bar Standing Committee on Professional Responsibility and Conduct, write only "for professional services rendered" (not even "legal services") on the charge slip.

### [2]   Automatic Credit Card Payments

The engagement letter is also where you should explain how your firm will charge the client's credit card for services rendered, especially if you want the client to authorize automatic payments. You can have the client authorize credit card payments in the engagement letter or in a separate document. Some lawyers ask clients to authorize automatic charges within a certain number of days after the bill is sent to the client unless the client disputes the bill.

### [3]   Risk of Commingling of Operating Account and Trust Funds With Use of Credit Cards

Lawyers have an ethical obligation to safeguard their clients' property, which in some states includes payments made for legal services that have not yet been rendered. States vary in their attitudes with regard to placing unearned legal fees into trust accounts. If you practice in a state that requires lawyers to place unearned legal fees into a trust account, you must remember not to deposit retainers into your general lawyer operating account. These retainers, and all other unearned funds — whether paid by a credit card or not — must be placed into a trust account. You are allowed to remove the funds only after you have earned them.

Not surprisingly, there are office management systems with billing systems that can coordinate these payments for you. If you practice in a state that requires the segregation of unearned funds as well as disbursement monies, look to see which systems can help you manage these funds. Do this before you set up your office. Any system that can make your life easier is a potentially good investment. In addition, credit card processors vary in their ability to place fees separately into the lawyer's trust account(s) and the lawyer's operating accounts. Check whether the credit card processor that you have in mind can do this.

### [4]   Disputed Fees and the Use of Credit Cards

Keep in mind that you may not be able to process your client's credit card payment if the client disputes the bill. In New York, for example, an opinion of the New York City Bar Association Committee on Professional Ethics stated that a lawyer cannot use a client's credit card to pay the bill if the client disputes the bill.

### [B]   Picking a Credit Card Processor

With your ethical concerns in mind, it is now time to pick a payment processor. One should consider several factors, namely:

1)   The software currently used by the firm,

2)   The aptitude and comfort level of the firm and its clients for cloud or online-based services,

3)   The firm's hardware needs, such as card-swipe machines or swipe devices for cellphones,

4)   The availability of the funds after processing, and

5)   The fees charged by the service provider.

For most businesses, the deciding factor is likely to be the fees charged for processing services. Each credit card processor uses a different pricing structure: some offer tiered programs with varying rates for different levels of service; others charge an array of fees. Some charge a start-up fee; others do not. Most charge a flat monthly fee and either a flat fee per transaction or a percentage of the transaction. Some charge different rates depending on the type of card used, or higher rates if the card is typed into a program as opposed to being swiped at a terminal.

In addition to the large, well-known credit card processors like PayPal and Square, legal-specific credit card processors have emerged to cater to lawyers' unique ethical considerations. Many of these specialized processors have the ability to direct payments into either trust or operating accounts.

### [1]   Credit Card Processing Companies

The field of credit card processing companies is ever-changing. Check the Internet for lists of providers.

## [2]  Or Head to the Bank

Many banks also offer credit card processing. Some attorneys like the convenience of having all their firm's financial dealings in one place — at their local bank — even though the bank's credit card rates may be higher than those of online providers.

# Chapter 12

# MARKETING

## § 12.01 WHAT COUNTS AS MARKETING?

When you open your own law business — either alone or with a partner — almost everything you do is marketing. If you go to a public hearing and speak, even if your comments have nothing to do with the law or any of your clients, that's marketing. People will hear you state your name. In some municipalities, public meetings are video recorded and televised several times that week via cable television and/or the Internet. Believe it or not, many members of the public actually watch these meetings. Weeks, months, or even years later, when they are looking for a lawyer, someone might recommend you to them. Or they might see your website or advertisement. The person who saw you speak at the meeting is likely to remember that you sounded either: (a) intelligent and persuasive or (b) like a disorganized, unprofessional mess. If you were a client who needed a lawyer, which would you prefer?

Remember: the manner in which you conduct yourself in your private life can have an impact on whether people will want to hire you. Remember this when you're thinking of getting drunk at a party or a wedding. And remember this when you are thinking of rushing out to the supermarket in old, ripped sweat pants and a food-stained t-shirt. Which clients would want to hire a drunk who acts stupid or out of control? Which clients would want to hire someone who looks like he or she is disheveled and pays no attention to details? You may be disagreeing with this paragraph, thinking that clients understand that your conduct in your personal life does not reflect your conduct and abilities in your professional life. But trust us, we have heard a lot of comments from a lot of clients, and many clients DO judge lawyers by their conduct and appearance in their private life. So be warned, especially if you are both living and practicing in the same geographic area, and that area is a town or village.

## § 12.02 MARKETING CHOICES

But let's talk about why you should care about marketing. You should care because unless you are already well-established as a lawyer and can bring clients with you or get a lot of referrals from your old firm, you are not likely to have many clients if you don't market your services.

Traditionally, lawyers looked to advertising in newspapers and telephone books as primary ways to market their services. Lawyers with bigger coffers advertised on the radio and on television. Some lawyers gave free seminars to small groups at local libraries or community centers as a method of marketing their services. Others spoke to community action groups or civic associations. In recent years, more and more lawyers also have begun to spend time and resources on building websites and posting content there, including short blogs. Additionally, lawyers have been turning to social media as a marketing tool.

How you market your services depends, in part, on your areas of practice. It is much easier to market legal services if you stick to one or two specific areas rather than trying to brand yourself as a generalist. You may actually be a generalist, but that's a hard concept to "sell" when you're appealing to potentially interested members of the public. If you're a generalist, it is a lot easier to pick an area or two to market, and then tell clients that you will also serve their needs in other legal areas. The exception to this advice is if you live in a small town where people feel good about getting to know their lawyer and knowing that the lawyer will be there for any of their routine legal needs — much like a family doctor is there for their general medical needs. In a small town, it is likely that clients will seek your advice because they either: (a) know you and trust you as a person or (b) someone they trust knows and trusts you as a person or has heard that you are friendly, approachable, competent, and trustworthy.

## § 12.03  MARKETING STRATEGIES

Marketing a lawyer's services involves a lot of the same strategies as marketing a bar of soap. The bottom line is that the purveyor of the product or service has to figure out what the public wants or needs, then present the product or service as something that will fill a want or need of the public — possibly even a want or a need that members of the public aren't even aware that they want or need.

For example, if you are an estate planning attorney, many of your potential clients might not even be aware that there is something you could do to help save them money in the future. It is your job, as a marketer of legal services, to inform the public that they need this service and why. Better yet, rather than informing them of what you can to for them, consider flipping the model and informing them of the consequences of not investigating what you can do for them. In other words, tell your potential clients what their children could lose if your potential clients don't plan for the future. Or tell your potential clients what they, themselves, could lose if they don't help their elderly parents plan for the future. Don't just wait for potential clients to figure out for themselves that they need to engage in estate planning. Think about it: How many times have you purchased a product that you didn't even know you needed — and that you didn't even know existed — until you saw a compelling advertisement for it? If you carefully construct your marketing efforts to educate people about what they don't even realize they might need, you will be helping yourself enlarge your client base.

## § 12.04   MARKETING VEHICLES

### [A]   Advertising

Many lawyers think that they are advertising effectively if they place a full-page advertisement in a telephone directory listing the firm's name in large letters across the top of the ad, then listing the firm's many practice areas in smaller type. But if you are a potential client and you are looking for an attorney to help you in a subject area, are you going to be attracted by the name of the law firm if you have no previous notion about what the firm's practice areas are? Wouldn't it make more sense from a marketing point of view to advertise one or two main subject areas in large, bold print, and then put the firm's name below that? But how many potential clients still look through the yellow pages of the telephone book for an attorney? Is this the best way to spend your marketing money? Might it not be better to think about where your potential clients will be looking in their quest to find an attorney?

Where would you look if you were a client in search of an attorney? You might ask your friends, but only if your legal needs were in a subject area that you were willing to discuss with friends — like real estate or personal injury. But what if you were looking for a divorce attorney or a bankruptcy attorney and didn't want your friends or relatives to know this? Where would you look for an attorney? The Internet.

### [B]   The Internet

One of the keys to establishing a vibrant Internet presence is creating a web page. This is easy to do. Many people do it themselves with the help of templates and step-by-step instructions provided by Internet companies that specialize in this at a very low cost. You can find them easily online. Alternatively, for more money, you can hire a person or company to speak with you directly and create a website for you. Some of these companies are also able to offer advice about analytics including how to obtain a higher position in lawyer listings when potential clients search the Internet.

Getting your name onto the Internet is not enough, though. You need to create an Internet presence. This means that you need to start writing blogs (short opinion or informational pieces) to display on your website and on other people's websites. The more exposure you can get, the better. Thus, if your little informational pieces appear in places other than your website, more and more people will learn your name. If you target websites for business that are in the community in which you practice, then you will be making yourself known to potential clients. That is, if you practice law in Massachusetts and are not admitted in Arkansas, putting your blog on a website of a local Arkansas business will not help you market your legal services in Massachusetts.

### [C]   Blogs

What kinds of things can you blog about? For your own website, you can create a lot of quick and easy blog posts by looking for interesting cases in your field. By "interesting" cases, we mean cases that humans who are not lawyers would find interesting. The cases do not have to have been decided by a court yet. But if a newspaper has written about the case — even to mention that it was filed, it's in the public domain and fair game for your blog. Just write a few sentences about it and follow that with a short paragraph about the general law on which the case is based. Do not take a position on the case. In the third paragraph, write that you handle cases in this area of law and that you offer consultations on matters in this area of law. If you offer free consultations, write that. And that's the end of the blog.

Try to write a blog like this every few weeks. If you don't have time to research and write them, consider hiring a law student to write them. Note: It may be more economical to pay the student by the blog entry than by the hour. You must, however, review anything a student does very carefully. An inaccurate statement in a blog can be very damaging.

Be sure to include a statement at the bottom of the web page with the blogs that says that they are attorney advertising and that they are not intended to provide legal advice or form an attorney-client relationship.

One easy and free way to alert people to the existence of your blogs is to add an automatic link to them below the signature block in all your emails.

## [D]   Articles

If you like to write, consider writing occasional, short articles about the law for newsletters published by non-legal organizations such as dental or medical societies, charitable or fraternal organizations, or business groups. The newsletters can be either printed on paper or distributed online, but most organizations now have websites with information about the newsletter. If there is no guide for submission of articles, just send an email to the editor with a proposal for an article. Include a sentence or two about your credentials in the field about which you are going to offer advice.

As an example of the kind of article you might offer, if you are writing to the editor of the journal published by your county's dental society, you might state that you are a lawyer who practices in the field of real estate law and who has created office leases for numerous dentists. You might then state that your article is about the top five things that frequently are missing from leases for professional office space. Then, in your article, you can say that these are only some of the things that are either missing or that need to be taken out of standard boilerplate leases provided by commercial landlords. Be sure to write in your article that you have had experience in this field and that you are writing from experience. Include your email address at the end of the article and invite readers to contact you for more information. When they contact you, do not just give them tips for free on the phone. Offer to represent them in reviewing or creating a lease.

## [E]   Social Media

Social media can be a good marketing tool for lawyers — including Facebook, LinkedIn, and Twitter — but there are dangers. Remember not to post any information about ongoing cases. And do not post any information about any clients without their written permission. It's best to use social media to remind people that you exist and that you practice law in certain areas rather than to tell them about your actual cases. Also, if you are thinking of using Facebook as a marketing device for your legal business, be sure to establish a separate Facebook page for your firm that is not associated with your personal Facebook account. Do NOT link them. Keep your personal Facebook page private. That is, be sure to limit it to friends. Even then, be careful what you post there because even if you limit viewing to friends, those friends can repost things, and the re-postings may carry your name. If you have a law firm Facebook page, consider limiting it to photos of you at conferences and meetings, and links to interesting articles written by you or others.

Important: If you are using Twitter, do NOT send tweets while you are sitting with a client, waiting for the client to read legal papers. It does not matter what the subject of your tweet is, do not send it while a client is paying you for your time. Not only is that unprofessional, but it is likely to anger the client.

## § 12.05   OFF-DUTY MARKETING

Don't pass up chances to market your services when you are "off-duty" and in your personal time. These include time spent almost anywhere — in a grocery line, at a doctor's office, participating in a community theater group, or anywhere else. Most people do not know any lawyers well and think of lawyers as strange, unapproachable creatures. So when they are talking with you informally and feel comfortable with you, and they think that you seem intelligent, responsible, caring, and professional, they will probably want to hire you if you practice law in a field in which they need assistance.

I have been lucky enough to get a substantial amount of legal work from medical professionals who treat me. I'll admit that it was a little strange at first to have someone peering into one of my body cavities ask me what kind of law I practice and then try to hire me. When I say "body cavities," I mean all of them. The first time it happened, my instinct told me to mention only the real estate and contracts part of my practice. Although I was a general practitioner, I focused on contracts, real estate, and bankruptcy. I was pretty sure that the doctor wasn't interested in declaring bankruptcy, so I didn't mention that part. The doctor perked up when I mentioned real estate and asked to hire me for the sale of a house. After several of my doctors asked to hire me for house sales, office leases, and other similar matters, I learned to respond to inquiries from my additional doctors by saying, "I do a lot of real estate and contract work, especially for doctors," because by then it had become true. Saying that I did this work for other doctors turned out to be a good marketing technique. The truth is that I have never quite gotten over being hired by a potential client while that person is looking up my nose or into my mouth or into elsewhere. ALN

## § 12.06 NOT-SO-OBVIOUS MARKETING STRATEGIES

### [A] Volunteering

What else can you do to market your legal services? You can volunteer to work with community groups — not as a lawyer but just as a member. When people learn that you're a lawyer, at least some of them will be likely to hire you for the same reasons that we discussed in the paragraph above. And they will recommend you to friends and relatives for those reasons. Some people like to reward an attorney with business after seeing the attorney's willingness to serve the community for free.

### [B] Testimonials

You can also ask your friends and clients to write testimonials about your services on Avvo and Yelp and your website. Potential clients will look there when deciding whom to choose as an attorney.

### [C] Business Cards for Support Staff

Want an easy marketing idea? Give each member of your support staff business cards with that person's name on it. As we mentioned in an earlier chapter, you can order cards online inexpensively — sometimes for as little as $10 for 500. Encourage your staff members to give out their business cards when they're not in the office.

### [D] Sponsoring Community Organizations and Events

Some attorneys find that sponsoring or co-sponsoring community organizations and events is a good potential source of business. Consider sponsoring a Little League team and putting your law firm name on the back of each child's t-shirt. Or consider co-sponsoring a charity walk-a-thon.

---

For many years, I sponsored several softball and Little League teams, my favorite of which was "Kramer's Alleged Base Stealers." LAK

---

### [E] Cultivating Relationships for Referrals

Another great way of marketing your services is to cultivate a relationship with lawyers in fields other than yours. Even if there doesn't seem to be a large opportunity for cross-referrals, you never know who that attorney knows — possibly people who will need your services. The same is true for cultivating relationships with non-law professionals. Accountants and financial planners are often an excellent source of referrals for lawyers, as are psychologists. Make friends with these professionals. Refer clients to them. Sooner or later, you are likely to receive referrals in return.

## [F]  Speaking Engagements

Many lawyers find that speaking on panels brings them sufficient attention in their field of practice to cause other lawyers to refer cases to them. Additionally, you may meet lawyers who are willing to pay you for referring cases to them after you perform the client intake and do some initial work. Ethics rules cover this kind of arrangement, so check your local ethics rules before arranging with another attorney to accept a referral fee or pay one to an attorney who refers a case to you.

## [G]  Brochures

Another way to market your services is via a law firm brochure. If you're skilled at layout design, you can format and print one yourself. But be sure to proofread it carefully. Otherwise, check the Internet for companies that will do this for you. Send the brochure — by regular mail, not via email - to every potential client who calls you to inquire about services, pricing, etc. Send the brochure to every client who hires you if you didn't already send it to that person before. And send the brochure to every client at the conclusion of that client's case if you practice in subject areas in addition to the one involving the client's case — or if you offer services in addition to the services that you provided for that client. You may be thinking, "That's a waste of money because my client knows what services I provide. And, besides, I already sent that person a brochure when the case started." Trust us on this: many clients forget that you provide services other than what you have provided for the client.

---

Early in my practice, I handled divorces. Eventually, I stopped doing this because I preferred practice areas in which clients were not as angry at their situation in life. But before I gave up that practice area, I helped one divorce client obtain a settlement in a long and contentious battle. I got to know him pretty well, and he seemed to like me and the job that I did for him. A couple of years later, he called me to ask if I had a copy of his divorce agreement because he needed it for the attorney who was handling the sale of the marital house. I was surprised that he had not asked me to handle that sale because the law firm brochure that I sent to all clients at the conclusion of every kind of case listed all of the firm's practice areas. Real estate was one of those areas. I immediately thought that perhaps he hadn't been as happy with my representation as I'd thought he was. So, after a lot of soul-searching about whether I should ask him why he hadn't hired me for his house sale, I finally asked him. And here's what he said: "You do real estate? I had no idea! I would definitely have hired you if I'd known." And then he apologized profusely. And I apologized for putting him on the spot by asking. Then we both laughed. All was well between us. The incident taught me to make sure to have a conversation with clients about my other practice areas. I learned not to assume that clients read my brochures. ALN

---

Brochures are good marketing tools, but just don't expect that everyone will read them. Some lawyers like to give away pens and refrigerator magnets as marketing tools. We don't see a lot of value in doing this, but if you can get the stuff inexpensively enough, go for it. Getting free "party favors" from a lawyer is never a bad thing.

## [H]  Cultivating Relationships With Newspaper Reporters

And, finally, consider cultivating a relationship with one or more local or regional newspaper reporters. Reporters for local weekly newspapers are often young and relatively inexperienced. Because of this, many of them are eager to establish a connection with a lawyer who is friendly and who can give them context about lawsuits — background information about the law and procedure. In return, they will quote you. Just be careful about what you tell them because sometimes reporters will print information that you intended to be confidential. Thus, when speaking with reporters, it is best to assume that everything you tell them might end up in print. This means that you should not express an opinion on the merits or possible outcome of someone else's case. It's fine to explain the background law and/or procedure. Make sure that the reporter isn't using you solely to gain a personal education rather than as a source for a good quote. Your goal in this is not to just make a new friend; your goal is to get quoted saying something about law and/or legal procedure that sounds interesting and intelligent.

## [I]  Responding to Newspaper Reporters

And while we're on the subject of sounding intelligent, here's a tip for responding to a reporter who calls you and asks for a quote: Don't respond right away. Tell the reporter that you are close to finishing up a meeting or a brief and ask if you can call back in about ten minutes. Then spend those ten minutes figuring out something cogent to say. Write down your quote. Remember to write it in plain English that an eighth grader could understand. If you try to write in language that makes you sound like a pompous professional, the reporter probably won't use the quote. Or the editor will cut it out. Or the readers won't understand it. Your goal is to make the quote understandable. So make the sentences short. Write only a couple of them because editors are likely to cut anything more than one or two sentences in a quote. And if you leave it up to editors to make that cut, you may discover that your quote is no longer accurate or it's out of context. Try to connect your sentences so that no one can cut one of them or parts of them. Use words like "and," "but," and "because."

Please remember that if you decide to take the risk of trusting a reporter with "background" information that is not to be printed, make this clear to the reporter by saying, "I am going to tell you something but you need to agree not to write this, and that means not even writing that it's from a source that you can't name. Do you agree to that?" Do not assume that when you say that something is "on background," the reporter will understand that the information is not to be printed — even without attribution. And remember, also, that some reporters will agree not to print information, and then put it into the story anyway. To protect yourself, assume that everything you say to reporters might appear in print, and don't comment on the merits of anyone's case.

When I was in my 20s and worked for a small-town newspaper before I went to law school, I learned a valuable lesson about why lawyers should be careful to use plain English when explaining things to reporters. I had called the town's attorney for a quote about a lawsuit that the town had lost. The lawyer said, "We're going to file an Article 78!" I had no idea what an Article 78 was. Worse, I was too embarrassed to ask because the town's attorney had said it as though everyone should know what it was. This was his loss because he didn't make me feel comfortable calling him to explain other legal concepts. I called other lawyers instead. And, as a result, I quoted them when I needed a lawyer to explain a legal concept. This was good for their business. He never got this kind of publicity from me because he didn't make an effort to explain a concept simply. ALN

## [J]  Greeting Cards

And here is one final idea about how to remind your clients that you care about them: send them birthday cards. It may sound hokey, but if you sign the card personally, this reminds the client that you have a personal touch. Many attorneys don't. This will make you stand out from the crowd. Do not send pre-printed cards. Insurance companies sometimes do this. When we get one of those cards, we don't think, "Gosh, my insurance company really cares about me." We think, "My insurance company had my birthday in its database and used this card as a marketing ploy." You don't want your client to think that the card is marketing. You want your client to think that you care about him or her personally. By the way, this does not apply to holiday cards. Feel free to send them to clients, but clients will not necessary feel as loved when they receive a holiday card as when they receive a birthday card from you. Lots of businesses send holiday cards. But most businesses do not send birthday cards, particularly personally signed ones. You can order them in bulk online. You can send the same card to all your clients each year. Get a different card for everyone the next year. Do not pre-print your name or your firm's name on the card. This makes the card look pre-meditated — i.e., like marketing. If the card looks like you went out to the store to buy it yourself, the client will be much more impressed with your gesture. It also helps to write a short message inside — just one of two sentences. Try to make it something personal, but if you can't think of anything appropriate, just write something like, "I was just thinking of you. Hope all is well!" You can write the same thing to every client, but write something different to everyone the next year. (The second year, you can write everyone a message like, "Another birthday! Hope it's happy!" Yes, some of your clients may compare notes, but it is unlikely that they will conclude that you send cards to all your clients. And even if they conclude this, they will still view you as more caring than the average attorney. The low cost and low effort of this marketing strategy makes it worth trying.)

PART II

MANAGING THE OFFICE

# Chapter 13

# HIRING PERSONNEL

## § 13.01 HOW WILL YOU KNOW WHEN IT'S TIME TO HIRE SOMEONE?

Attorneys who are thinking of starting their own firms frequently ask how they will know when it's time to hire personnel and outside contractors. Our answer is pretty simple: It's time when you find that you are busy enough that you could be billing a client for working during the time that it takes you to do a task that you could delegate to a staff member or a consultant.

This is where you finally will be using those mathematics skills that seemed pretty useless to you in grade school.

Here's an example of how to figure out whether it's time to hire someone:

You are billing clients at $200 per hour. You also are good at bookkeeping and accounting, so you do all of your business's bookkeeping and accounting yourself. You think: Why pay someone to do this when you can do it yourself? But as you get busier and busier with clients, you begin to resent the time that you need to spend doing the bookkeeping and accounting. You find yourself having to stay late to either finish that work or finish your clients' work. If you could work for your clients during the hour that you spend doing the bookkeeping or accounting, you could make $200. Will you need to pay a bookkeeper or accountant $200 per hour or more to do this work? No? Then the answer is simple: offload the bookkeeping or accounting to the bookkeeper or accountant and do your legal work in the time that you just created for yourself.

This sounds like it's obvious, but it is not obvious to most attorneys with firms that are less than a couple of years old. Attorneys who start their own solo or small-practice law businesses generally have an entrepreneurial spirit, which means that they aren't afraid to tackle the tasks necessary to start and run a new business. This includes bookkeeping and accounting. These entrepreneurs often look for any way to save money while they are trying to grow their businesses. But not offloading bookkeeping and accounting is false economy when you begin to become busy with legal work.

## § 13.02   WHOM CAN YOU CAN HIRE?

### [A]   Office Cleaners

Assuming that there are no provisions for office cleaning services in your lease, consider hiring someone to do this for you. Even if you and your partner(s) take turns vacuuming the rug and scrubbing the toilet, is this something that you want to be doing when you have a pile of clients' work waiting for you on your desk? Sure, it's fine to clean the office yourself when you first open the place. Every penny that you can save is important. But when you get busy, don't keep cleaning your own office just because you've always done it and it doesn't require much thought. If you actually enjoy scrubbing the toilet, and you find the task relaxing, then, sure, continue doing it. But for most people, this is a task that should be offloaded to make more time for a busy attorney to earn money working on a client's file. Remember your basic math: If it takes you a half hour to vacuum and dust the office and clean the bathroom, that is a half hour of money that you could earn working on legal matters. If you bill clients at $200 an hour, you could earn $100. How much would you pay a cleaning service to do this? Less than $100. Also, you do not want clients to arrive unannounced and see you vacuuming the office carpet yourself. This makes you look less professional and less prosperous. Yes, some clients might conclude that you are down-to-earth and thrifty, but many others will think that you must not have enough work to keep you busy and wonder why you are not successful. This can erode their confidence in you. What is the takeaway from this discussion? If you are going to clean the office yourself, do it after hours or on the weekend, and lock the office door.

### [B]   Support Staff

How do you know when to hire a receptionist, secretary, legal assistant, paralegal, or additional attorney? And should you bring in an intern/extern, even if you do not have to pay that law student? Keep reading for these answers.

### [C]   Interns/Externs

Let's start with the easiest part: the interns/externs. As you begin to become busy in your solo or small-firm practice, you may think that you can get free help by agreeing to take on a law student through a local law school's internship or externship program. Just keep in mind that no matter how capable a law student is, that student probably is not experienced enough to be able to work on any cases without supervision. Additionally, the purpose of an internship or externship is to teach the student practical skills, not to get free labor. You might, however, have tasks for a student to do that are mutually beneficial. For example, you might ask the student to read the legal newspapers and bar journals to summarize the important cases and articles for you. The student also can assist you in investigating accident cases by going to the scene and taking photos, obtaining weather conditions on the day in question, locating witnesses, etc.

## [D] Additional Staff and Attorneys

Now let's move on to the subject of receptionists, secretaries, legal assistants, paralegals, and attorneys. Should you hire one? If so, when should you hire one?

Let's start with how you will know if it's time to hire someone to help you. This decision is somewhat subjective, but basically it boils down to the same financial analysis that we performed in our discussion about accountants, bookkeepers, and office cleaners: Can you make more money in the time that it was taking you to do the task? If so, offload the task to someone who charges less per hour. But there is also another factor to consider when making a decision about whether to hire a receptionist: Will you seem more professional and established if someone else is answering the phone and greeting clients?

The answer is that a receptionist who looks and sounds polished and professional will put a professional patina on your law business. That is, clients will think immediately that you seem professional. We understand that there is a trend for solo lawyers to answer their phones themselves, but we caution you to be careful when making a decision about whether to do this. Although this may be a cost-effective measure when your law business is young and you are working from your home, this will make your law business appear like it isn't well-organized or prosperous when it is located outside your home. As an analogy, what would your clients think of you if you showed up in court carrying your files in a paper bag? A paper bag is an economical and sensible container, but is it a good alternative to a briefcase or a tote bag when clients expect lawyers to carry files in a briefcase or tote bag? Similarly, clients expect prosperous law firms to have a person to greet them. Please note that if you already know your clients or have the kind of practice where clients will not ever come to your office, you do not need a receptionist to impress them.

## [E] Shared Receptionists

Many office suites will rent you an inner office that includes the use of a shared receptionist. This is fine. But will this person also answer your phone? Do you want this person to answer your phone? Might your clients prefer a receptionist who will get to know their names and the sound of their voices and, as a result, greet them as though he or she is pleased to hear from them? We know that we feel good when we call a doctor's office and the receptionist's voice brightens up with recognition when he or she hears who we are. We feel valued as customers of that office. The same is true for your customers (clients). And a client who feels valued is a client who is not likely to switch lawyers and who is likely to recommend you to other potential clients.

## [F] Virtual Receptionists/Answering Services

If you cannot afford a full-time receptionist, or even one that you share with other businesses, consider purchasing the services of a virtual receptionist service. The upside of this is that the service is an outside contractor, not part of your office, so you won't have related payroll tax or insurance issues. The downside is that you won't have control over who answers your phone unless you hire a service that assigns you a dedicated person. But keep in mind that even then, that person might be answering phones and taking messages for other businesses, so your clients' calls might go straight to a recording that asks them to hold. And then they might be on hold for so long that they hang up. Although this also could happen if you hire a full-time receptionist, it is much more likely to happen if you contract with an outside service that serves numerous other businesses.

Another downside of hiring a service to answer your phone is that the phone answerer will not know any details about a client or the client's business. When clients use a small law office — as opposed to a large one — they expect a personal level of service rather than an impersonal one. This means that if your virtual receptionist sounds very warm and caring, relatively new clients will be tempted to start talking about their case as if the receptionist should know whom they are. And when the receptionist doesn't know, the clients are likely to feel just a little frustrated or unsatisfied. This undermines all of your efforts to make your clients feel comfortable with your law business.

So, if you don't have the funds to hire a full-time person to answer your phones (and maybe do other work as well), is it better to use a virtual receptionist or answer your phones yourself? A third option is to let calls go to voice mail, but many lawyers find that they lose new business that way, particularly in a practice area like bankruptcy when potential clients go down a list of bankruptcy attorneys, calling them all to figure out who seems caring and affordable. If they do not reach a live person when they call your office, they are likely to hang up and not even leave a message. We know this because our clients have told us this — that they hired us because we not only had a live person to answer the phone but because the live person was pleasant and reassuring.

If you contract with a virtual receptionist service (i.e., a telephone answering service), periodically ask your friends to call in and leave messages that are slightly complicated including the name of a person that sounds simple but that could be spelled more than one way. Also ask a friend to leave a specific message, not just a message to call back.

Ask your friends to report to you about their experience with the service: How long did it take someone to answer? Were they automatically placed on hold? If so, how long were they on hold? Was there music on hold? If so, what kind? Was it extremely loud (i.e., annoyingly loud)? Did the person who answered seem warm? Did the person who answered ask how to spell the name that could be spelled more than one way? Did the answerer get the complicated message right? Did the answerer just give you the name and number of the caller but not include any or all details of the message? You need to know these things because this will have an impact on your clients' comfort level with your business.

If your answering service is not providing the level of attention to detail that you seek, try talking with the owner/operator of the service. If you are not able to obtain an improvement in service, either try another service or consider answering the phone yourself until you have money to hire a full-time or part-time employee to answer the phone. (Having a part-time employee answer your phone is better than having to answer it yourself or letting calls go to voicemail all the time.)

## § 13.03   WHEN IS IT TIME?

Question: When is it time to think about hiring a secretary or legal assistant to perform non-legal duties like assembling court packets, collating copies of documents, sending routine letters (e.g., status letters, engagement letters, and file-closing letters)? Answer: It is time when you find yourself getting bogged down with these duties and you need the time to do work for clients so you can bill them. Again, this is where basic math kicks in. The amount that you can bill a client per hour is much greater than the amount that it will cost you to pay a non-lawyer helper per hour. (Note: The same thing applies if you bill clients by the job instead of by the hour. You can get a legal job done a lot faster, and presumably get paid a lot sooner, if you aren't delayed by having to do a lot of routine tasks that a secretary or legal assistant could do.) Again, you can hire someone part-time or share someone with another professional (not necessarily an attorney).

## § 13.04   CONFIDENTIALITY AGREEMENT

Remember to be very forthright and specific about your confidentiality requirements when hiring either full-time or part-time employees, including receptionists and phone-answerers. Commit your requirements to writing and include a statement at the end that says that your employee has read the rules, has had a chance to ask you questions about those rules, has a copy of those rules, and understands and agrees with those rules. Have the new employee sign and date this statement. Make sure you give a copy of the rules and the signed statement to the new employee.

One downside of hiring a virtual receptionist service is getting the phone answerers there to sign your confidentiality agreement. You might have to settle for a written statement or policy from the service stating that all calls and information in those calls will be confidential. If your practice includes any high-profile clients (i.e., well-known clients, celebrities, government officials, etc.), you may want to think twice before contracting with a virtual receptionist service because you will be hard-pressed to keep the phone answerers from telling everyone they know that they spoke with a well-known person. At least if the phone answerer is one of your employees, you will be able to speak with your employee about the importance of never mentioning to anyone that the well-known person called. That will not insure total confidentiality, but at least you have a greater likelihood of achieving it.

## § 13.05   BE CLEAR ABOUT DUTIES

Be warned that if you decide to hire more than one part-time non-lawyer to help you with routine tasks, you will need to be very clear about the duties of each person. Otherwise, the afternoon person might rip up and re-do the work done by the morning person because the afternoon person believes he or she can do it better. (This actually happens.) Not only should you commit the tasks to writing, but you should also write down your expectations that each person will not try to change or recreate work done by the other person. And you should give each employee a written policy statement that you expect your employee to speak with you if he or she has any problems with work done by another employee.

## § 13.06   INDEPENDENT CONTRACTORS VERSUS EMPLOYEES

Some of you might be tempted to try to save money by hiring a secretary, legal assistant, or paralegal as an independent contractor to avoid paying payroll tax and insurance. Do not do this. The IRS rules clearly delineate guidelines to determine whether someone is an independent contractor. If a person has set hours and works inside your office, that person is not an independent contractor. Don't take the risk of claiming otherwise. Also, your so-called "independent contractor" is not likely to be happy about having to pay self-employment tax, which the person would not have to pay if he or she were your employee rather than an independent contractor. And that unhappy worker might report you for violating the law.

Please note that if you hire a self-employed accountant or bookkeeper to come to your office to look over your records on a set day of the week at a set interval (say once a week or twice a month or once a quarter), this person does not necessarily fall into the IRS category of "employee." If the person operates his of her own business and serves numerous other professionals, that person is most likely an independent contractor for tax purposes.

Each January, you should furnish an IRS 1099 form to each independent contractor who performs services for you. This form states the amount that you paid the person for services. This is an IRS requirement. The IRS regulations also require you to file a copy with the IRS.

If you need a secretary or legal assistant on only an occasional basis, you can contract with an employment agency that specializes in providing temporary employees. These people are not actually your employees. They are employees of the agency; thus, you are not responsible for payroll tax withholding and any other ancillary tax form filings.

You are responsible for payroll tax withholding and both quarterly and annual tax form filings for your own employees. Rather than discuss them in detail here, we are advising you to consult an accountant for details. You may choose after that to do the work yourself, but at least find out what you need to do to comply with federal and state rules.

## § 13.07   OTHER CONSIDERATIONS

When you begin to get so busy with legal work that you are feeling overwhelmed, it's time to think about hiring a full-time or part-time paralegal or associate. Also consider, as an alternative, bringing in a self-employed attorney on an of-counsel basis, which means that the other attorney helps you only on occasional projects on a part-time basis. Or now may be the time that you are able to offer a time-for-space arrangement. This can work well for you if you have extra space. The lawyer can work for you in exchange for the office space you provide. The decision about whether to bring in a lawyer or paralegal to help you should be based on whether you can make money from that relationship.

Things to consider: (1) Will the hourly rate that you pay someone be less than the amount that you bill a client for that person's work? If so, you will make money on this arrangement. (2) Will the hourly rate that you pay that person be the same as the amount that you bill a client for that person's work? If so, will delegating that work to the other paralegal or attorney allow you to perform other legal work for which you can bill clients? In this case, the arrangement will be beneficial to you.

Just remember that when you delegate work, you will need to review it and possibly make changes to it before sending it out to a client. That will take up some of your time, but this will take you significantly less time than if you had done all the work yourself. Also, remember that if you are billing clients at a lower rate for that person's work, your clients will appreciate the cost savings. If the total bill is substantially less than what the clients would have spent for you to do all the work yourself, most clients will not mind being billed a small sum for your document review and revisions. They are likely to appreciate seeing that you cared enough to review the work yourself and will be happy that your decision to bring in assistance saved them money. One thing to remember is to tell them ahead of time that someone else will be performing some of the work to hold down their legal costs, but reassure them that you will be reviewing everything and working closely with the other person on all aspects of the client's case. You also will want to reflect this arrangement in the engagement agreement where the client can see the difference in the hourly rates.

## § 13.08  HOW TO FIND PERSONNEL

So how do you find suitable personnel without paying a lot of money for advertising? You can advertise in local newspapers. You can also advertise on Craig's List. If you are looking for a part-time secretary or someone you can train as a legal assistant (but who does not need the in-depth skills of a paralegal), you might want to send an email to other local attorneys and other non-lawyer professionals to ask if they have any part-time employees who are looking for additional work. Or you may speak to the support personnel whom you know at other firms; they often know who is available. Other sources of secretarial candidates — either part-time or full-time — are post-secondary schools in your area with secretarial programs, and the career services offices of local community colleges. If you are looking for a paralegal, contact the career services office of area schools with paralegal programs. If you want to hire a lawyer, contact area law schools and bar associations.

If you're placing a help-wanted ad, what do you say in the ad? Some people advise against stating the salary, but you might want to consider stating it because that will rule out a lot of people who want a job that pays more. Definitely state whether the job is full-time or part-time. If it's part-time, state the number of hours. If you want the person to possess excellent writing skills, write that. If your firm concentrates in certain fields of law, write that. (For example, "Secretary wanted for office of attorney with matrimonial practice.") If you're paying by the word for your ad, you will want to make it as short as possible. But don't be penny-wise and pound-foolish. That is, don't skip some important words in the interest of saving a small bit of money on the ad. If you want a secretary who is experienced in helping to prepare bankruptcy petitions, say that in your ad.

Just remember that if your ad is too specific, you may not garner many applicants. If your ad is too vague, you may receive a deluge of applications but many of them will be from people who aren't qualified for the job. Sometimes it's better not to be too specific in the expected experience or qualifications because you can always train someone who is smart and hard-working. On the other hand, if you have limited time, it may be worth it to spend a bit more money to hire someone experienced in your field.

## § 13.09  PRECAUTIONS BEFORE HIRING SOMEONE

If you are trying to hire someone whose duties include answering the phone, make sure that you speak with the person on the phone before bringing in that person for an interview. If the applicant's voice is grating or does not seem polished or professional-sounding enough to be the voice of your law firm, there is no need to waste time — yours and the applicant's — bringing in that person for an interview.

If there are significant typographical errors in an applicant's resume and/or cover letter, do not invite that person in for an interview because that person does not possess the requisite attention to detail to work in a law office.

---

A young woman applied for a job as a secretary in my law office. She sent me a resume that said she had lived in and worked in Westhampton, NY for many years. But she repeatedly misspelled Westhampton as "West Hampton." Although her work experience seemed solid, I didn't call her for an interview because that repeated error in her resume showed me either that she did not create her own resume and also did not proofread it or that she paid no attention to obvious things like the spelling of the name of the community in which she lived and worked. Her lack of attention to this basic detail caused me to wonder how much attention she would pay to details in a job in my firm. ALN

---

If you do call an applicant in for an interview, pay attention to these factors:

- Was the person on time?

- Was the person dressed appropriately for an interview to work in a law office?

- Was the person well groomed?

- Did the person's appearance indicate an attention to details? For example, if the applicant was a woman who wore nail polish, was it so chipped that it looked like a small rodent had snacked on it? Or if the applicant was a male, were his shoes so scuffed that they looked like they hadn't been polished for two years? Little details like this can indicate that your applicant is lazy or not concerned with details. How hard is it to either remove or repair severely chipped nail polish or shine shoes before a job interview? These may not be deal-killers for you, but they should raise red flags.

- Also, during the interview, pay attention to whether the candidate slouches into the chair as though he or she is getting comfortable for a casual night watching a movie. This kind of inappropriately casual body language also raises a red flag about the candidate's inclination to comply with the conventions of working in a law office.

---

A candidate for a secretarial job in my law office came in for the interview with long hair that was still very wet. She did not say that her hairdryer had broken or give any other explanation for why her hair looked as though she had just come out of a shower. (It was not raining outside.) She also produced a resumé from an envelope that looked like it had been made for a small greeting card. The resume was folded into quarters. The inappropriately wet hair and the inappropriately folded resumé signaled to me that this job candidate did not understand the professionalism necessary to work in a law office. ALN

---

Always ask for, and check, references. Call the references and ask specific questions that will force the former employer to say more than just general praise. For example, ask what the candidate's strengths were. Also ask what the candidate's weaknesses were. If the reference says that the candidate didn't have any weaknesses, be suspicious. Everyone has at least one weakness. Ask if the candidate had a chance to demonstrate whether he or she was proactive about figuring out what needed to be done before being asked to do work. If the answer is yes, ask for an example. Also ask if the candidate was better at large-scale tasks or at things that required a high level of detail. Ask if the candidate had an opportunity to display whether he or she could defuse situations where a customer was annoyed, upset, or difficult. If the answer was yes, ask for an example. These are just some of the specific questions that you can ask to get answers that will be more meaningful than just general praise of the candidate.

Matters that you might want to discuss with a candidate in an interview include, but are not limited to, the following:

1) The candidate's responsibilities and functions should he or she get the job

2) How you organize the office, the office calendar, and the work load

3) The salary for the position and your policy regarding increases in salary and or bonuses

4) Benefits, if any

5) Time off and hours of work

6) Policy with regard to cell phone use during work

7) Policy with regard to email and Internet use during work

8) Dress code, if any

9) Expectations re: behavior (i.e., no sexual harassment, no dirty jokes), pleasant but professional atmosphere

10) Drug policy

## § 13.10  HOW TO TREAT EMPLOYEES

The office environment in small law firms often is less formal than in large ones. It is up to you to set the tone in your office and decide what type of office atmosphere you want. You can opt for a casual and friendly atmosphere, a formal atmosphere, or something in between. Whatever you do, try to be consistent and let your employees know your expectations.

## § 13.11  CONFIDENTIALITY CONVERSATIONS

When you've found someone to hire, make sure to talk with that person about what kinds of information that person must keep confidential and why. Although it may seem obvious that all matters need to be kept confidential, most people think that it's okay to talk about clients with their spouse or their best friend from childhood who lives out of state. For example, if a famous person walks into your office to consult with you, and she is wearing a hat that makes her look like she has a beehive on her head, your receptionist will find it difficult not to tell anyone that the famous person walked in — let alone that she walked in wearing a hat that looked like a beehive. So it is your job to explain what information needs to be kept confidential. You should also explain why because humans usually appreciate knowing the reason for being asked to comply with rules. They also comply with them more often if they realize why the rules have been enacted.

This means that you should explain that attorneys are required to comply with ethics rules and that those rules hold attorneys accountable for the conduct of their employees. Explain that not only can you lose a client if anyone in your office even mentions to an outsider that the client was in your office (let alone any information about that client including that client's demeanor, legal problem, etc.) but that you might have to defend yourself against a grievance filed by the client because your office didn't keep the confidence. Explain that the grievance committee can suspend or disbar lawyers and, even though it may not seem like a big deal to tell someone that a celebrity was in your office (let alone a celebrity wearing an odd hat), you will have to spend time answering the complaint instead of doing moneymaking work for other clients.

One of the best ways to make sure that your employee understands this is to give the employee a short quiz after he or she reads your confidentiality rules. You might want to ask questions like, "Can I tell my spouse if I swear him or her to secrecy?" Or, "Can I tell my sister because she lives out of state and will never meet this client?" Although your new employee will most likely guess the answer that you are expecting, this kind of mini-quiz hammers home the point: Tell no one. And make sure that your confidentiality statement delineates a clear penalty for violating your rule: "immediate loss of job 'for cause,' which will disqualify the employee for purposes of unemployment compensation." Or words to that effect.

## § 13.12  OBLIGATIONS OF EMPLOYERS

Whether you opt for a casual or a formal business environment, there are certain things that you must do as an employer. Among them is the requirement that you post certain notices where they are visible to your employees. Both the federal government and your state government have rules in this regard, and it is essential that you be in compliance with both. The federal government has a United States Department of Labor website that will tell you what posters about federal law you need to display in your office. (See http://www.dol.gov/osbp/sbrefa/poster/main.htm.) On this website, you will be asked a series of questions. After you supply accurate answers, you will receive a list of the posters you are required to display. You can obtain free copies of those posters, and it is your responsibility to make sure they are posted in a place where all employees can see and read them. Also, check to see what posters your states requires.

States vary on their minimum wage laws, and you must post what is required by the state in which you operate your office. Make sure to check to see if your state requires postings about any other matters such as safety, smoking, criminal convictions, and/or discrimination.

### [A]  Payroll Taxes

If you are paying employees, you will have to take certain deductions from their paychecks and then make sure that those funds are properly deposited as per the requirements of your state.

Because your obligation to pay federal taxes on behalf of your employees is so critical, we are including some basics from the Internal Revenue Service website, just to remind you of your obligations as an employer.

The following directive about your responsibility as an employer is from the Internal Revenue Service website. (See: http://www.irs.gov/uac/Employer-and-Employee-Responsibilities---Employment-Tax-Enforcement and http://www.irs.gov/Businesses/Small-Businesses-&-Self-Employed/Understanding-Employment-Taxes.)

Employer's Responsibility
Employers must report income and employment taxes withheld from their employees on an Employer's Quarterly Federal Tax Return (Form 941) and deposit these taxes in full to an authorized bank or financial institution pursuant to Federal Tax Deposit Requirements. Employers are also responsible for filing a Federal Unemployment Tax Act (FUTA) return annually, and depositing those taxes.

Employers who do not comply with the employment tax laws may be subject to criminal and civil sanctions for willfully failing to pay employment taxes.

Understanding Employment Taxes
Employers must deposit and report employment taxes. See the Employment Tax Due Dates page for specific forms and due dates.
At the end of the year, you must prepare and file Form W-2, Wage and Tax Statement to report wages, tips and other compensation paid to an employee.

Use Form W-3, Transmittal of Wage and Tax Statements to transmit Forms W-2 to the Social Security Administration.

Federal Income Tax

Employers generally must withhold federal income tax from employees' wages. To figure out how much tax to withhold, use the employee's Form W-4 and withholding tables described in Publication 15, Employer's Tax Guide.

You must deposit your withholdings. The requirements for depositing, as explained in Publication 15, vary based on your business and the amount you withhold.

Social Security and Medicare Taxes

Employers generally must withhold part of social security and Medicare taxes from employees' wages and you pay a matching amount yourself. To figure out how much tax to withhold, use the employee's Form W-4 and the methods described in Publication 15, Employer's Tax Guide and Publication 15-A, Employer's Supplemental Tax Guide.

You must deposit the wages you withhold. See requirements for depositing. For 2013, the employee tax rate for social security increased to 6.2%. The social security wage base limit increased to $113,700.

Additional Medicare Tax

Beginning January 1, 2013, employers are responsible for withholding the 0.9% Additional Medicare Tax on an employee's wages and compensation that exceeds a threshold amount based on the employee's filing status. You are required to begin withholding Additional Medicare Tax in the pay period in which it pays wages and compensation in excess of the threshold amount to an employee. There is no employer match for the Additional Medicare Tax. For additional information see our questions and answers.

Federal Unemployment (FUTA) Tax

Employers report and pay FUTA tax separately from Federal Income tax, and social security and Medicare taxes. You pay FUTA tax only from your own funds. Employees do not pay this tax or have it withheld from their pay. Refer to Publication 15, Employer's Tax Guide and Publication 15-A, Employer's Supplemental Tax Guide for more information on FUTA tax.

Self-Employment Tax

Self-Employment Tax (SE tax) is a social security and Medicare tax primarily for individuals who work for themselves. It is similar to the social security and Medicare taxes withheld from the pay of most employees.

We suggest that you not only look at the IRS website yourself but that you discuss with your accountant all of your obligations regarding both federal and state tax payments. Your accountant can help you to set up all of the protocols necessary to insure that you properly comply with all filing requirements.

## [B]   Compliance With Other Federal Laws

As an employer, you may be subject to any or all of the following federal laws either when you start your office or if it grows larger in the future:

- The Equal Pay Act (a Section of the Fair Labor Standards Act): This applies to you if you have $500,000.00 in gross sales or business in a year AND you have two or more employees either engaged in interstate commerce, or the production of goods through interstate commerce, or the selling, handling or in some way working on goods or materials produced for interstate commerce. This act requires an employer to give equal pay for similar work requiring equal skill, effort, and responsibility.

- The Age Discrimination in Employment Act of 1967: This applies to you if you have 20 or more employees and prohibits you from discriminating against employees who are 40 or older regarding hiring, firing, compensation, terms, and conditions of employment.

- The Americans with Disabilities Act (ADA): This applies to you if you have 15 or more employees. This act prohibits discrimination in hiring, firing, compensation, promotion, training, or any other privilege of employment against anyone qualified under the ADA. The law is intended to protect those with mental or physical disabilities.

- Title VII of the Civil Rights Act of 1964: This applies to you if you have 15 or more employees. Title VII prohibits employers from discriminating against employees on the grounds of race, color, sex, national origin, or pregnancy status.

States vary in terms of how many employees are required before employers are subject to state rules concerning harassment, discrimination, disability, and the like. Make sure that you check to see what is applicable to you where you maintain your office and whether you are required to comply with rules in other states in which you do business.

If you have employees, you must comply with your state's minimum wage laws, unemployment, and workers compensation laws. Make sure that you know all of the applicable rules in your state and that you remain in full compliance. You must also make sure you are aware of the laws in your state governing overtime. Check the laws where you practice.

If you don't understand whether any of the rules apply to you, or what they mean, consult an attorney who works in the field of employment law.

## § 13.13   EMPLOYEE MANUALS AND EMPLOYEE POLICY GUIDES

There are numerous books and websites with templates for employee manuals. We recommend that you use something that is geared for an attorney's office or a professional practice. We have included a sample table of contents for an employee manual to remind you of the things you and your partners should agree upon before hiring employees. (See Appendix.) Some employment lawyers believe that employee manuals are not necessary for firms with four employees or fewer because of the close contact and informality that the lawyers and their small staffs often share. If you have a very small firm and do not opt for a formal employee manual, consider writing a less formal employee policy guide. The purpose of this guide is to let your employees know what you expect of them.

An employee manual should include all of the applicable federal and state labor laws that apply to your practice. You will need to say that your office policy requires full compliance with each of the laws applicable to your firm, and you need to provide a procedure for dealing with any alleged noncompliance. You should update your manual from time to time, especially if the size of your firm grows big enough to trigger compliance with labor laws that did not apply when your firm was smaller.

It is important to state that your office manual is a guide for your employees, not a contract.

Consider including the following matters in your employee manual:

- Equal Opportunity, harassment, and sexual harassment
- Employee classifications
- Attendance and tardiness
- Dress code
- Compensation and work hours
- Payroll procedure
- Medical and retirement benefits
- Job evaluations
- Bonuses
- Employee reimbursement
- Vacations and holidays
- Sick time, bereavement, and personal time
- Leaves of absence
- Religious observances
- Jury duty
- Drug and alcohol policy
- Telephone use
- Recordings
- Confidential communications

This list is by no means exhaustive, but it should give you a good idea of the types of things for which you need to develop policies before you hire employees. If you choose to write your own manual, you might want to have it reviewed by a labor and employment attorney in your state before you distribute it to your employees.

## § 13.14   HOLIDAY CALENDAR

Each year, you should give your employees a list of the days on which the office will be closed during the upcoming year. Also give this list to new employees when you hire them. It is important to list the dates of the holidays rather than just listing their names (i.e., "New Year's Day") because the days of the week on which a holiday falls may affect what you do during a particular year. If a holiday falls on a Thursday, and you are going to keep the office closed on Friday, let your employees know in advance so they can make plans. This is a small gesture, but it is the type of thing that demonstrates to your employees that you are considerate of them.

# Chapter 14

# DEALING WITH POTENTIAL CLIENTS

## § 14.01 HANDLING THE INITIAL PHONE CALL

Yes! A potential client is actually calling your office. Of course you are excited; you should be. But, in your excitement, don't forget the many things you have to deal with before offering that person the opportunity to retain your firm.

As a new attorney, if you have chosen to go it alone, you most likely will be answering your own phone(s) for a while, and, therefore, will be screening your own clients. Here are a few questions to consider:

- Will you have an office landline or just a cell phone?
- If you have a landline, will you have any calls forwarded to your cell phone after a certain number of rings?
- Are you going to use a Google number, which is free?
- Will you be able to distinguish office calls from other calls?
- How are you going to answer your calls?
- Do you want potential clients to know that you are answering your own phone?

This last question is one that you need to think about carefully. Lawyers often have strong opinions about this. Some say that clients regard a law office as more professional and more successful if someone other than the lawyer answers. Other lawyers say that clients don't care one way or the other. Still other lawyers say that some clients appreciate being able to speak to the lawyer directly. The question is, what type of impression do you want to give?

If you do answer your own phone, what will you say? Know in advance how you plan to handle this. You might just say your name or you might announce the name of the firm. Whatever it is that you intend to do, know it in advance so you do not stammer and mumble on the phone. You need to instill confidence. Also, the tone of your voice will convey a lot about who you are. If you sound abrupt and impatient, potential clients may not want to hire you. Do you want to sound neutral and professional? Is that enough? Or do you want to sound patient and caring? You should think about this carefully. Your decision will hinge, in part, on the subject areas of your practice. For example, if you are planning to practice bankruptcy law and hope to have a clientele of people who need to file personal bankruptcies, you might want to answer your phone with a voice that sounds caring. This involves softening your tone just a bit but still remaining firm and professional-sounding. If most of your practice involves corporate litigation, you won't need to adopt a slightly softer edge to your phone-answering voice. The same applies to the voice of any person who answers your phone for you. Remember this especially if you are thinking of using a live answering service. Will the person who answers your phone use the kind of tone that will inspire potential clients to wait for you to call back, or will the tone propel them to call the next attorney listed under a Google search for attorneys in your field?

If you have opened an office and you have staff or an intern, you must give instructions as to how you want your phone answered. You also need to tell anyone answering your phone what questions you want them to ask potential clients. Some offices actually provide a script and have a copy of that next to the phones and on computer screens so that no one is ever at a loss about what to say. Some offices don't have a script but have a list of information that the phone answerer must obtain. That is easier than a script because the individual speaking on your behalf needs to sound responsive and NOT scripted. But your employees or interns might feel more comfortable with a script. Talk to them about the two options before deciding which one is right for your office. You might make different decisions for different employees and interns depending upon each person's temperament.

## § 14.02   WHAT IMPORTANT PIECES OF INFORMATION SHOULD BE OBTAINED DURING THE INITIAL CALL?

This will vary with the attorney and type of practice. But usually the following information is helpful:

- The name of the potential client
- The type of case
- Who made the referral
- The current status of the matter
- Information necessary to screen for conflicts (for example, in divorce cases, ask for the name of the spouse)
- Phone number where person can be reached
- Whether there is a preferred method of contact — email, text, home phone, cell phone, or regular mail — or a method by which they do not want to be contacted
- Also, if you charge a consultation fee, state the amount

You can create a sheet similar to this, listing the information you need. You can use a physical sheet, or you can design a form on your computer that is accessible to everyone who answers phones in your office. You also can buy software that has intake forms. The point is to have a system of some type, whether you create it or you buy something already in existence. You are more likely to get the information you want and need if you have a consistent manner of handling the initial client telephone contact.

As mentioned earlier, when you first begin your solo or small-firm practice, you should take advantage of almost every opportunity to meet with potential new business. You want to do this for a variety of reasons, not the least of which is honing your interviewing skills. As you become more experienced as an interviewer, not only will you be able to learn more quickly whether or not a case has merit, but you will also become a better judge of your potential clients. There will be people for whom you will not want to work, for any number of reasons, including:

1) They are not pleasant.

2) They are not forthright.

3) They have unrealistic expectations.

4) They are too demanding.

5) They are too eccentric or not always rational.

6) They can't afford you.

7) They can afford you but will not pay you what they owe you.

8) They have a value structure that makes it impossible for you to work for them.

If you handle predominantly one area of practice, both you and your staff will become very good at reading potential clients. An experienced telephone interviewer will often be able to determine, with some accuracy, whether any of the problems listed above apply to the potential client on the other end of the phone. Whether or not you entrust someone else to do this for you involves an important judgment that only you can make. As you become busier and your staff becomes more capable, you may choose to see whether to allow someone else to perform some or all of the initial screening. Many small firms offload the initial telephone screening to the secretary, receptionist, or paralegal. If you do this, be sure to train that person well. That person needs to do two things: (1) obtain all the necessary information to help you decide whether to take the case, and (2) provide more subjective information about whether the client is demanding or impatient or evasive — all qualities that may make you consider whether you want to take the case.

Some small firms use a secretary or receptionist to ask a small list of initial questions, and then turn the more detailed screening over to one of the attorneys. For many law firms, this practice works well.

Firms with ten or more attorneys often choose one partner — often the managing partner — to be responsible for screening most of the potential new business. That attorney conducts the telephone interview and then makes an appointment either to meet with the potential client or have the potential client meet with someone at the firm who handles the type of work that the potential client needs.

Many experienced lawyers will never let anyone else screen for them, but many other experienced lawyers say that they are too busy to spend time screening clients. There is no right or wrong choice.

## § 14.03  INITIAL CONTACT THROUGH A WEBSITE

Almost everyone who opens any kind of business invests in a website. If you open a law business, you should have one, too.

One important aspect of your website that is relevant to our discussion here is how it gives a potential client an opportunity to initiate contact with you and your firm. Most websites will send you a copy of all inquiries. Your job is to respond promptly and in such a way that the potential client is anxious to get to meet with you. If you are not able to respond to inquiries quickly, assign this task to another attorney or staff member at your firm. The reason for this is that many people think that a lawyer who isn't responsive in the face of potential business is likely to be even less responsive after the pressure to secure the new client is over — i.e., after the retainer is paid. This is a case of a first impression being a lasting one. You do not want to convey either a lack of interest or a lack of time.

### [A]   Responsibility for Giving Legal Advice

If you are going to make your first contact with a potential client via email, you must be very careful with your response. The following applies to inquiries not only via email or website but also to inquiries made over the phone and in-person:

Do not EVER give advice to a potential client unless and until you have had an opportunity to ascertain sufficient facts to give a knowledgeable and well-thought-out opinion. There are important reasons for this. One is that you might be committing malpractice if you give advice that is not based on a complete set of facts and other pertinent information. Another reason is that giving advice imparts the impression that you are forming an attorney-client relationship with someone who has not signed an engagement letter with you. You most likely do not intend to form an attorney-client relationship with a stranger who tries to get free information in an initial email or website inquiry.

It is bad enough if *you* give legal advice when you shouldn't, but it is inexcusable if your staff does so. Make the rules with regard to giving advice very clear whenever you interview and hire someone. It may also be a good idea to circulate basic reminders about this when you give out your holiday schedule at the beginning of the year.

### [B]   What Can You Discuss?

If you can't give advice to people who seek you out through your website, what can you do?

You can discuss the types of cases that you handle, as well as your experience in certain areas of law. You can also arrange appointments through your website, but we caution you that it might be a better use of your time to ask people to call for an appointment. Although you can obtain a great deal of information about the potential case via a website questionnaire, talking on the phone will give you a better idea of the potential client's temperament. If the client is not one you want, you will not have to spend time in an office meeting.

## § 14.04   SCREENING POTENTIAL CLIENTS

It is essential that you screen your prospective clients carefully. If you choose to schedule appointments without conducting the screening that we suggested, you may discover a conflict during your meeting. And if that happens, you will not be able to represent that party. Worse, you may well have put yourself in the position of being unable to represent the person who is your existing client. Why? Because the potential client may have revealed confidential information to you during your meeting. After you have heard it, you cannot pretend that you didn't hear it. One of the most painful things you will experience as an attorney is having to return unearned monies that an existing client paid to you. This problem can be avoided with the exercise of appropriate care.

Unfortunately, you may learn that conflicts arise more frequently than you expected. In certain fields, the conflicts are pretty easy to identify. For example, in matrimonial cases, there are typically only two parties, and so you usually can determine any conflict easily. You need to ask only some basic information like the full name and birthday of the spouse. With a case involving commercial litigation, however, there can be numerous parties and a variety of witnesses. It is far more difficult to gather the necessary names and information to determine whether a conflict exists.

Moreover, there are other potential conflicts that only seasoned practitioners might recognize because they are likely to ask the kinds of questions that would reveal a potential conflict.

## § 14.05   CONFLICT CHECKS

We have mentioned the issue of conflicts many times. You can never think about the issue too much or too often. Your malpractice carrier will inquire about your conflict-checking systems. If, as mentioned above, you meet with someone and you discover that representing them might cause a conflict with an existing client, you cannot ethically represent that new person unless you investigate and believe that you can represent both parties without a conflict of loyalty and unless both parties sign an agreement waiving the conflict. What can you do to avoid the problem of conflicts of interest? The good news is that there are many software programs that will assist you in the process of screening for conflicts. A word to the wise though: Conflict-checking systems are only as good as the information that has been entered into the system.

Having a good conflict-checking system and protocol in place is step one in avoiding a mistake that can cause you difficulties. As we have said, virtually every law practice management system has a conflict-checking element. But these systems are not magical in terms of finding conflicts. They are only as good as the person who inputs the information. Most systems operate by checking for words (typically names) that already appear in your case files. For example, if you have a potential client who wants a divorce, you might miss a conflict if you merely check your list of current and previous clients, as well as the list of people who have consulted with you, for people with the same last name. The reason is that there are many married couples with different last names. If the person who screened the client did not ask for the spouse's full name, the conflict checking system wouldn't have found a problem. The same principle applies in any type of legal matter, be it litigation or transactional.

Before anyone in your office makes an appointment to meet with a potential client, you or your staff should ask for the names of all adversaries. That information needs to be entered into your data bank so the conflict check is truly meaningful. Some law offices even ask for the names of important witnesses to make sure that they are not clients of the firm and/or that the witnesses have not met with anyone from the firm. It is important to realize that having the adversary as a client is not the only way for a conflict to occur. Just having met with the adversary and having obtained confidential information can give rise to a conflict. Make sure the name of every person who meets with someone in your office is entered in your databank.

Your malpractice carrier will probably want to see that your office has more than one conflict-checking system in place before issuing a policy. Therefore, you may have to design an additional process yourself. Any office with more than one attorney should make it a practice to check directly with each of the firm's attorneys prior to accepting a new client to assure that there is no conflict. This is most commonly done by having the attorney who is seeking to take in the new business fill out and circulate a form, usually via email, that contains all of the following:

1) The name and address of the potential client

2) If the client is a business, the name of the business and the names and addresses of all principals

3) The names and addresses of the adversary or adversaries

4) A brief description of the matter

If the firm is circulating this information in a physical document rather than in an email, each attorney must initial the document to indicate that he or she has no known conflict.

Delay in taking this action can jeopardize your chances of being hired by the potential new client. It is best to perform this conflict check within 24 hours of obtaining the information from the potential client.

## § 14.06  SCHEDULING APPOINTMENTS

If you charge for consultations, and you are a lawyer who screens your own telephone calls, you will want to limit your time with potential clients on the telephone and meet with them in person if you think that you might want to take the case. This is because you make money at the consultation and because clients are more likely to want to hire you after they have bonded with you in person.

If, after speaking with a potential client on the phone or in person, you decide that you don't want to take the case, be nice anyway. Some lawyers are abrupt when they realize that they won't be able to make money with the potential client. Be careful not to convey the idea that you think your conversation was a waste of your time. You do not want the person to form a negative impression about you because that person might have a future legal issue with which you can help. Also, if you act interested and then turn down the case for some credible reason, that person might recommend you to friends and relatives.

If you do not charge a consultation fee, you still might want to get people in the door so that you can gain experience in interviewing. Making people think that you are generous with your time can be helpful in trying to establish your business.

## § 14.07    STICKING TO YOUR DESIRED SCHEDULE

Some lawyers believe that opening the office during weekends and evenings will give them an edge, which is probably true. When you have not yet established a reputation and are trying to build a business, this can be a way of distinguishing yourself.

When, where, and how you choose to meet with clients is a major quality-of-life decision. If you feel strongly about the need to balance your personal life and your professional life, you may choose to make strict rules. If you determine that there are hours you wish to reserve for your family, then be honest with yourself about that fact and set your rules accordingly. There are some lawyers who will NEVER go to their office on a Saturday because they have decided that that day is reserved for their family. The temptation to break the rule can be strong, particularly when someone is offering a significant retainer if you will meet on a Saturday morning. The trouble with this is that you are placing yourself on a slippery slope. When clients know that you were once willing to meet on a Saturday, they will have little hesitancy in reminding you of that fact when seeking to be accommodated in the future. They might even say, something like, "You sure were willing to come in on Saturday when you wanted my money."

Once you come in on one Saturday for the money, you'll find it easier and easier to do it again. It is not our job to tell you when and when not to work. What we are trying to do is give you meaningful information by which to make a choice that works for you. We have learned that if you mean to reserve time for things other than your work, whether it is family or an important avocation, you must make a meaningful schedule that you, your staff, and your partners understand and are willing to accommodate. If you are in a partnership, you might have to forfeit some percentage of partnership income if you want to limit your hours to accommodate your outside activities. But that will be your choice. There is no right or wrong choice. You need to decide what is right for you. After all, isn't that one of the main reasons why you chose to start a solo or small-firm practice?

If, on the other hand, you are single-minded in your desire to build a busy law practice, you may choose to work nights and weekends. By making yourself available on nights and weekends, you will be making yourself available to people who find it difficult to get time off to meet with an attorney during the workweek. Those people will be happy to have an attorney who will accommodate their needs. If you choose to offer evening and weekend appointment hours, you should log how many clients you obtained as a result to see if it is worth your while.

## § 14.08   SHOULD YOU TAKE WALK-IN APPOINTMENTS?

The choice whether or not to take walk-in clients is a personal one. If you decide to open a storefront office in a downtown area, your intent most likely is to make yourself or your staff available to the public for walk-in visits. Other lawyers, however, discourage walk-in visits because they say it is intrusive. They prefer to ask walk-in visitors to make an appointment to come back later that day or on another day. If you want to discourage walk-in visits, just tell walk-in visitors that you have other appointments but that you would be glad to meet with the visitors at a time when you can devote your undivided attention to them.

## § 14.09   HOW TO HANDLE PRICE SHOPPERS

You are likely to receive communications from potential clients who want to know, first and foremost, how much you charge. This is likely to be someone who is price-shopping — someone who is contacting numerous lawyers to try to find the least expensive one. If the work is very simple and straightforward, you might want to take the case and charge a price that will be competitive with other lawyers in your area. But before you set your price, be sure that you have obtained all important information. You should not propose a fee without knowing the pertinent facts. Otherwise, you may discover that the case is far more complicated than you anticipated, and you'll be sorry that you agreed to take it at such a low fee.

# Chapter 15

# POTENTIAL CLIENTS IN THE WAITING ROOM

You have a potential client! Someone is interested enough in you to want to speak with you in detail. The person might just be shopping for free advice — and, thus, wasting your time. If you offer free consultations, this is always a possibility. As a result, you might decide not to offer free consultations. Or you might decide to offer them but limit them to 20 or 30 minutes.

We discussed the subject of consultations previously. But you should know that many attorneys find it difficult to decide whether to offer free consultations. Often the decision depends on your practice area and what other attorneys in that practice area are doing. If most attorneys in that practice area are offering free consultations, then you probably will decide to offer them, too. Then again, as you get busy in your practice, you might not want to spend time offering free consultations except when you think the case sounds potentially lucrative. Otherwise, you can wind up spending a lot of time giving free advice. Keep in mind that you can offer free consultations in one of your practice areas but not in another — for example, you could offer them for potential bankruptcy cases but not for consultations about divorces or separations.

No matter what you decide about whether to charge a consultation fee, what do you do when the client is sitting in your reception area waiting for a consultation? Do you provide an intake form? If so, what information should it request? And should you ask the potential client to bring any information or documentation to this initial meeting? If so, what should the client bring?

Unlike doctors, many attorneys do not use intake forms. Lawyers who use them say that they save a lot of time that you would otherwise spend sitting with the client, asking the client questions and writing the answers. Also, clients fill out intake forms in their own writing, so if answers on an intake form contain incorrect information, the client can't blame you for the mistake. Lawyers who don't use the forms prefer to speak with the potential client and learn the facts from their conversation.

The content of intake forms varies by the practice area. A criminal attorney will want or need different information from a personal injury attorney. Whether the attorney asks the client to complete the form or whether the attorney completes the form is the attorney's personal choice. At a minimum, you will want the client's first name, middle or maiden name, last name, physical home address, address for post office mail, email address, home phone number, and cell phone number, as well as an indication of which number the client would prefer you to call.

Whether you ask a potential client to fill out an intake sheet in your waiting room is a topic that generates a lot of discussion among lawyers. Some believe that asking for a lot of information from someone who is not yet your client can seem rude and intrusive. That group of attorneys believes that if you ask anything, ask merely for basic contact information and referral source. Attorneys practicing in family law and criminal law are most vocal in their opposition to intake sheets in the waiting room. On the other hand, attorneys handling accident cases often believe an intake sheet is a good idea, as do lawyers who handle commercial and/or general civil matters.

Lawyers who utilize an intake sheet that seeks anything other than contact information commonly also include a brief written explanation of the purpose of a consultation. If you do this, you should explain that the purpose of an initial consultation is not to provide advice about what the client should or should not do. You should explain that the purpose of the consultation is for the attorney to give the client an overview of the area of law involved in the case along with an explanation about what the attorney might be able to do for the client. You can also write that the attorney will be able to answer questions about the fee structure during the initial consultation.

Lawyers handing accident cases might want to ask for information about how the accident happened along with a description of the injuries. Lawyers handling commercial or civil litigation might want the intake sheet to ask the reason for the consultation, along with the names of the parties involved in the matter or dispute. Some attorneys obtain this information at the outset so they do not make the mistake of meeting with someone with whom there is a potential conflict. If you do not obtain the names of parties at the time the appointment is made, be sure to get the names involved in the dispute before meeting with the client. Your staff might recognize some of the names, but they should also make sure that they enter all of the names in your office's conflict-checking system to see if there is a conflict that requires you to avoid any conversation with that potential client.

Most lawyers will ask who referred the client or how the client learned about you and decided to call you versus any other lawyer. It is important to do this for a variety of reasons:

- So you can call and thank the person for referring the client
- So you can learn the most effective method of business generation
- So you can know if the client requires special attention because of who made the referral

If you decide to give a potential client an intake form, you may want to add language that says that the purpose of the initial consultation is to investigate the nature of the client's legal needs and to determine what, if anything, the lawyer can do to help the client with those needs in the future. Include language that makes it clear to the client that (a) this initial consultation does not mean that you represent the client and (b) you do not represent clients until they sign an engagement agreement with your office and pay a retainer (if you require one for that type of work).

Lawyers differ widely on whether or not to accept checks for initial consultations. Many lawyers accept them, but some lawyers do not.

Some lawyers believe that if you charge for an initial consultation, you or the member of your office who schedules the consultation should make it clear at that time how payment can be made and when it is due.

Note: occasionally a potential client will appear in your office for the consultation and say that he or she forgot to bring a wallet. If that means that the person didn't bring money, credit cards, or a driver's license, you will have to decide whether to reschedule the consultation. Keep in mind that the client may have traveled a long distance, taken off time from work, or paid a babysitter to come to the consultation. You will have to decide whether the person will pay you after-the-fact and whether you are willing to take that risk. What if this is the kind of person who never intended to pay you, never intended to hire you, and just wanted some free advice? Also, if the person didn't bring an ID, how can you verify his or her identity?

If you ask a client to fill out an intake form, consider attaching it to a clipboard so the potential client will have something to lean on when filling out the form. Also offer the person a pen. Consider asking the client to fill out the form in blue ink so you can distinguish the original from a photocopy.

We have provided sample intake sheets in the Appendix.

But let's step back in time for a moment. When the potential client first calls your office to set up the consultation, the member of your office who schedules that consultation should remember this important detail: Ask the potential client to bring all documents that a lawyer would need to review to be able to make an educated statement in the consultation. But don't say those exact words to the potential client, or the person will be confused and will bring you a shopping bag crammed with papers. Instead, ask for specific documents depending upon the area of law that is involved. For example, if the potential client is coming to speak with you about a traffic ticket, your office should ask the client to bring the traffic ticket (or a copy of it). If the potential client is coming to speak with you about a lawsuit in which he or she is a defendant, ask the person to bring either the original or a copy of the summons, complaint, and any other legal documents that he or she has received in connection with the lawsuit. If the potential client wants to speak with you about writing a new will, ask the person to bring the last will he or she has — either the original or a copy — if he or she ever had one drafted.

And, finally, when you greet your potential client for the first time, smile and shake hands. You might be tempted to show the client how forceful you can be by shaking his or her hand in a vice grip. Do not do this. We have had our hands nearly crushed in handshakes. This did not impress us with the strength or force of the other person. Instead, it made us think that the other person had no clue about the sensitivities of others. This is not a good sign if negotiation might be necessary in a case. Conversely, don't offer your client a limp fish of a handshake. When someone does this to you, do you think that the person can be forceful? Probably not. Strive to offer a handshake that is firm yet not overpowering. If you are not sure about what level of strength might be appropriate, practice with friends or relatives. This might sound silly, but you can make a first impression only once. Strive to impress your potential client, even if that person turns out to be someone you don't want as a client.

This brings us to what you should do in the initial consultation.

## § 15.01   INTERVIEWING THE POTENTIAL CLIENT

You're face to face with your potential client.

Begin with a bit of small talk. Do not get right to the main event. (This advice applies to many kinds of human interactions. Humans like to feel as though you care about them.) Ask the person how the traffic was, or whether it was hard to find parking in the lot, or comment that the person's tie/necklace is attractive. This may be obvious to some of you, but it is not obvious to everyone, so we are mentioning it.

Remember our chapter about marketing? Your conduct in this initial interview is marketing. If the potential client likes your personal style, he or she is more likely not only to hire you but also to recommend you to other people. This will translate into future business. So be nice; find something to say that does not involve the main event in your interpersonal relationship that day. We realize that many of you might be thinking, "I can't believe that I paid good money for these authors to tell me to be nice." Trust us, there are many lawyers in the world who have never thought about the message that is conveyed by your handshake and the way in which someone begins interactions with others. Indeed, in some cultures, people expect a brief exchange of small talk before getting down to business. In the United States, this attention to detail will distinguish you from your colleagues. We'll say this important word one more time: marketing. Remember that everything you do and say is marketing — either obviously or subliminally. Marketing is supposed to send a positive message about you. But it can also send a negative message. You're the one in control of this, so pay attention to these details.

---

I once accompanied a family member to the office of a small firm that handled only probate work. The family member was going to retain the firm to handle the probate of an estate. Waiting for each of us in the firm's conference room was a bottle of water, a legal pad, and a pen. This attention to detail told me a lot about the firm. It immediately increased my comfort level about the attorneys who worked there. And I was right: The firm was meticulous in its work. That small gesture was a memorable visual cue that constantly reminded me to refer people to the firm. ALN

---

## § 15.02   ALLOWING POTENTIAL CLIENTS TO BRING FRIENDS OR RELATIVES INTO AN APPOINTMENT

Depending upon the type of case, it may or may not be appropriate to allow third parties to attend a consultation. In any type of case, you must consider privilege issues, because the attorney-client privilege is waived as soon as another person is in the room when you are speaking with a potential client. This is a very serious issue that must be explained to people who want to bring a friend or relative into the meeting. Often potential clients will tell you that the person knows everything they are going to say. You must carefully explain to the potential client that the issue is not whether the third party knows something; the issue is that the presence of a third party can cause the lawyer-client confidentiality to be waived. You need to explain to the potential client that this means that what would have been a secret between the potential client and the lawyer will no longer be a secret in the eyes of the court and that the court might require you to disclose that secret information.

One situation in which this often arises is divorce consultations. People consulting with a divorce lawyer are often upset and want to bring a friend or relative for emotional support. We suggest you allow that support to be available with one caveat: Explain the privilege issue to the potential client and say that the friend or relative is invited but that if, during the course of your meeting, the potential client is going to talk about unreported income (a common problem in divorce cases) or drugs or anything illegal, you are going to ask the friend or relative to step out of the meeting, and you will invite the person to return when that discussion is over. In that way, you have protected the privilege.

With a potential criminal client, you usually will want to meet with the client in private when discussing the substance of the case. You may choose to begin a meeting on a criminal case with a client's friend or relative present as you explain the procedure of a criminal case, what you will be doing, and the costs involved. We suggest that you explain the privilege rules to the people who are attending the initial part of the appointment and further explain that because of those rules, you meet privately with potential clients who are accused of a crime.

With real estate transactions and plaintiff's negligence cases, lawyers tend not to be as concerned about the type of information that needs to be protected. Nonetheless, we strongly suggest that whenever a potential client (or, for that matter an existing client) wants a third party to attend a meeting, you should always remind everyone of the privilege issues.

---

I used to explain the attorney-client privilege to everyone who came to see me, but I had not really seen the application of my warning come into play until I represented a wife in one of the highly publicized phony mortgage scandals. The government and I were fighting over who should get the very expensive marital home. The government wanted to liquidate the house and receive monies to give restitution to victims. I wanted to keep the house for the wife and children because almost everything else had been seized by the government. When the prosecutors tried to question me with regard to issues surrounding the home, I could very comfortably assert the privilege, and no matter how many times they asked, I was never required to disclose information that they very much wanted. If you are not happy with the fact that I was not willing to help the victims, bear in mind that my first obligation was to my client, who would have suffered a serious loss if I had revealed the information she confided in me. LAK

---

One type of case that may require some privacy is when a husband and wife come to your office to have wills drafted. Sometimes one spouse wants to leave everything to the other spouse, but the other spouse does not want to reciprocate. Or one spouse wants a trustee to be appointed for the money he or she might leave to the other spouse because the potential recipient has spending issues. Having both parties in your office at the same time to discuss their intentions can cause a serious problem. Consider meeting with each party separately.

## § 15.03  QUESTIONING CLIENTS

After the brief preliminary small talk, ask the potential client an open-ended question to learn why the client is there. After a few minutes, begin to ask your potential client more focused questions. And as time passes, you will get to the details you believe are necessary to understand the case.

Excessively stubborn clients with tunnel vision are difficult to deal with. It's now your decision whether to just give in and state the price/price range or stand your ground and show that you cannot be manipulated easily. The worst that can happen is that the person won't like your desire to maintain control over your involvement in the proceedings. Pay attention to this signal. If the person becomes your client, this behavioral trait is likely to resurface. If you resist the person's effort to micromanage your behavior when the person is your client, the client might file a grievance against you, and you will have to waste your time justifying your behavior to the grievance committee. We have seen this happen. So pay attention to your potential client's behavior in the initial consultation. For more details about signs that your potential client might be one with whom you do not want a relationship, see Chapter 16.

### [A]  Script or No Script?

What do you do after you have asked your initial question during the consultation? Many attorneys just ad lib — that is, they talk without a script. We're not suggesting that you write down every word of what you're going to say. In fact, we advise against that. Imagine how you would feel if you went to a lawyer and watched him or her read from a script in the consultation. We do, however, advise that beginning attorneys consider going to the consultation armed with a subject-specific form for you to fill out. This form will contain a list of things that you should ask and places for you to write the answers. For example, if the potential case involves a personal injury, your form should prompt you to ask for the nature of the injury and the date of the injury. Or, if the potential case involves a bankruptcy, your form should prompt you to ask the client approximately how many debts he or she has and the approximate total of those debts not including mortgages and home equity loans.

This form will serve as an agenda to keep you on-track during the consultation. It's a good idea to begin the meeting with the potential client by reiterating that the purpose of the meeting is for you to gain enough information to determine whether the client's matter is something that you will be able to help with in the future and to give the client a broad overview of options for resolving the matter.

## [B]   Should You Take Notes or Not?

Some attorneys take a lot of notes when meeting with a potential client; some attorneys take only a few notes; and some take no notes until immediately afterwards. What you do will depend upon your strengths for recalling and for multitasking.

Some attorneys believe that if you are looking down at paper or typing, you will have limited eye contact and, thus, a limited time to bond with the potential client. Many experienced attorneys who have developed a good listening style believe it makes sense to get the general facts of the case and understand the situation before taking any detailed notes.

But other attorneys like to take notes on as many details as possible before taking a case. This is particularly true if remembering details about a case is not one of their strengths. Some attorneys are able to skillfully blend taking notes and making eye contact because they take notes only about the most important details.

> One of my strengths as an attorney was my ability to interview a potential client and remember some unusual fact about the case. I never took notes during an appointment because I was skilled at remembering details and knew that if I listened carefully and paid attention, I would get a better feel for the case and the client. I also knew that I would be able to pick out a detail that would make it clear to the client that I had listened carefully. After meeting with a potential client, if I did not take the case on the spot, I wrote down at least 4 or 5 sentences about the case including that one unusual detail and what might be the challenging part of the case. I also always wrote down the fee I had quoted. If and when a client made an appointment to return, I was always able to repeat the unusual fact I'd noted, and the potential client was always impressed that I remembered a detail of the case. This is an easy way to assure clients that you are attentive and interested in representing them. LAK

## [C]   Should You Record the Interview?

We urge you not to record your interview. In our experience, people are not always candid when they know they are being recorded, and it is unlikely that you will get all the information you would have gotten had you not recorded your meeting. Attorneys also choose their words far more carefully when they are being recorded. Remember this client meeting is not an interrogation. This should be a pleasant experience where you and your potential client comfortably explore the case and the potential for a good working relationship.

## [D]  Purpose of the Initial Interview

You must think carefully about the purpose of an initial client interview. There are many things that you must do during that first meeting.

You must:

1) Find out why the person is in your office.

2) Find out if the person has an expectation of what he or she wants you to accomplish and what that is.

3) If the matter involves litigation, find out what response can be made to the other side.

4) Discuss what you can do for the potential client. It is your job to sound intelligent and to make the client believe that you know what you are talking about. Be careful not to misrepresent your knowledge. This is where lawyers can get into trouble.

5) See if there are any conflicts.

6) Decide if the person you are meeting with is someone you want to have as a client.

7) Determine your fee and let the potential client know what it is and how you expect payment to be made.

Additionally:

8) Depending on the type of case, you may provide an engagement letter or a retainer agreement at this meeting and ask the client to sign it and pay the retainer.

9) Give the client a roadmap of how you expect the case to progress with your respective assignments for the next meeting.

## [E]  How to Get Started

How do you get started on your task? There are a number of studies that say that starting with broad questions makes clients feel comfortable and more likely to hire you. Although some attorneys prefer not to ask broad questions in order to control the interview and save time, many attorneys will, after the initial small talk, ask something like "What brings you to my office?" or "What can I help you with?" Allow the person a few minutes to speak broadly. As the interview moves forward, you can ask more specific and focused questions. This is called funneling.

For example, let's assume the potential client was involved in an automobile accident. Most lawyers will ask that person to tell them how the accident happened. You will want to hear the client's rendition and know what the potential client thinks is important. After he or she has told you the story, then you can ask specific questions like, "Were you wearing a seatbelt?" Or, "Were you speaking with anyone on your cellphone?" You can ask all about when the person saw the other car and how fast the cars were going. As you move forward with your inquiry, your job is to elicit the important details. This will help you to determine the merits of the case as well as any defense that can be raised.

## [F]  The Road Map

Members of the general public often have no idea about the procedure that is involved in legal matters. Make sure to ask your client whether he or she has had experience with matters of the kind the client is asking you to handle. Explain what you intend to do, including meetings that you intend to hold and your client's role in both attending and participating in those meetings. You may want to explain what documents you will need to draft and review and the time it can take to finalize those documents. Giving a client a basic understanding of how the case will proceed can relieve the client's anxiety and provide reasonable expectations.

If the case involves litigation, it is important to give the client a basic understanding of the litigation process. Although more than 90% of lawsuits are settled, a client may have to go through a lot of the legal process before a settlement is achieved. It is a good idea to explain the steps that you will most likely take in the case. Emphasize that even if you move promptly, you cannot guaranty how long the case will take. Some courts move more quickly than others, and some adversaries like to engage in delaying tactics. Emphasize to your client that you cannot control how long a case will take.

## [G]  Show Potential Clients That You Care

It is very important that you convey your sympathy or empathy to the potential client and let the person know that you are listening. The easiest way to show that you are paying attention is to use the person's last answer in your next question. For example, if the client tells you that she jammed on her brakes in order to try to avoid crashing into the other car, your next question might be something like, "After you jammed on your brakes, did your car go into a skid?" You need not do this with every question, but you do want to use the technique enough to make it clear that you are listening.

At some point, the potential client may begin to ramble. Your job at all times is to focus the interview without being rude. Sometimes the person on the other side of your desk will say that he or she is embarrassed to tell you something. Remind that person that you can do a good job only if you know all of the facts. Assure the person that you are not judgmental. Let the person know that the best way for you to be an effective lawyer is to know more information than the other side knows. Tell the person that if you learn something that may be damaging too late in the case, this could be devastating to their position.

## [H]  A Tip for Getting the Whole Story

What do you do when you think your potential client is not telling you the true story? A good tactic is to ask the person if there is anything that person may have forgotten to tell you and then to say something like, "You know, if you don't tell me the whole story, I am not going to be able to do a good job for you." If that doesn't work, one of the most effective ways to get to the truth is to ask the potential client "What will the other side say happened?"

## § 15.04  WHAT TO DO IF YOU WANT THE CASE

If, at the conclusion of the consultation, the case appears to have merit and you would be willing to work for this person, say this. Then ask the person what he or she would like to do. If the person wants to hire you, prepare an engagement letter for the person to sign. You can do this while the person is waiting, or you can email or mail it to the person later that day. If the person wants more time to think about what to do, you might want to explain that the matter may be time-sensitive even if there is no applicable statute of limitations because you cannot predict what other people might retain you, possibly causing a conflict or such a heavy work load that you would not be able to accept this person's case in the future. In other words, make it clear to the person that you might not be available to start this case in future if the client delays for a significant period of time. Given that many potential clients come for consultations and then disappear for a while and fail to make a decision about taking any legal action, it's a good idea to let potential clients know that your agreement to handle the matter today may not apply to the future because of extenuating circumstances that you cannot predict today. Most clients don't realize that this is a possibility. In their minds, the decision whether to hire an attorney is theirs alone; they don't realize that an attorney might choose to decline representation. Beware of potential clients who argue with you when you decline representation. Their argument should confirm your decision not to represent them because they will be difficult to deal with if they become your clients.

---

A potential client explained the details of her case and asked me to represent her. When I explained some options for handling the case, she began to argue with me, telling me that she wanted it handled differently. I listened patiently, then explained the drawbacks to handling it the way she wanted. She again argued with me. This happened three times. After the third time, I politely declined the case. She asked why, and I said that I thought she would be happier with an attorney where she didn't have to argue. She argued with me about that. I said that I thought this did not bode well, that she was already unhappy with me. She again argued with me and said that she wanted me, not another attorney, to handle the case because someone had told her that I was a good attorney. I held my ground, and she eventually gave up. But it took me years to learn to trust my instincts on this kind of thing. Trust your instincts. You are not likely to regret it. ALN

---

## § 15.05  WHAT TO DO IF YOU DON'T WANT THE CASE

After you have turned down the potential client or case, be sure to confirm this in writing with a letter of non-engagement.

## [A]  What Is a Letter of Non-Engagement?

A letter of non-engagement is a letter that a lawyer sends to a person after a consultation when the lawyer is not going to represent that person. The letter states that the lawyer has not been retained, is not representing the person, and that any discussion about possible action was just discussion and not intended by the lawyer to be legal advice.

If you research the topic of non-engagement letters, you will find a variety of articles suggesting that you send such a letter when you meet with a potential client and decline to take his or her case. Most articles do not discriminate with regard to the types of cases in which you should send such a letter. Although it is necessary to send such a letter in many types of cases, particularly where there are statute of limitations issues (for example, in negligence, medical malpractice, and contracts), there are some types of cases in which sending such a letter might actually create problems. An example of this is when someone comes to your office to explore the possibility of a matrimonial action (a divorce or separation) and then decides not to pursue it. If you send a non-engagement letter to that person's home, that person's spouse might recognize your name on the envelope. Yes, you could email the letter. If you select this option, be sure to ask the person if the email address is private.

In situations where there are statute of limitations issues, it is important when you decide not to take a case that you send a letter saying you are declining it and giving a warning regarding time limit risks. We do not suggest that you give exact dates, nor do we suggest that you tell the person that they have no case. This is because you could be wrong on either or both counts, opening yourself up to potential liability. Rather, write that you are not making a determination on the merits of their case and that they should see another attorney right away if they are interested in pursuing the matter because time limits are involved.

There are other situations when we believe that it is very important to send a letter stating that you have declined to take the case. The first is when you represent someone on other matters and you choose not to handle a particular new matter for that client. If you don't send a letter making your intention clear, that client could claim that he or she expected you to take care of this matter because you were already handling other matters for that person.

Another time in which caution is required is when someone consults with you in that person's capacity as an officer of a corporation and also as an individual. There are many situations in which you can represent a person in only one of the two capacities. Therefore, you must send a letter to that effect. Make it clear in which capacity you represent the person and say that you cannot represent the person in the other capacity because there could be a conflict of interest. In the letter, suggest that the person hire another lawyer (not someone at your firm) to represent him or her in the other capacity.

We have provided some sample letters in the Appendix. You should modify them in accordance with the facts and circumstances of the matter involved.

# Chapter 16

## MANAGING CLIENTS AND CLIENT RELATIONS

In this chapter, we will discuss handling difficult clients and how to break bad news to your clients.

### § 16.01  DIFFICULT CLIENTS

When you set up your law office, you usually don't think much, if at all, about what you'll need to do if any of your clients are difficult. But you definitely should think about this before you start your own firm. You may have had experience dealing with difficult people — either in the practice of law or elsewhere. This, however, does not fully prepare you for dealing with them when you are trying to get a small practice off the ground and grow it. Extremely difficult clients can absorb all or most of the energy that you would have spent marketing your services to attract more clients. This will significantly affect your potential revenue stream. So please pay attention to what we have to say here. It will help you.

All lawyers in solo and small-firm practices eventually encounter difficult clients. No matter how hard you try to avoid working for this type of client, you'll wind up with some of them. Sometimes there is no indication in the initial consultation that the client will be difficult. Sometimes you just can't tell until you begin to work together.

By difficult, we mean clients who:

- are demanding, or
- think they know more than you do, or
- ignore you or are mentally erratic/irrational, or
- are dishonest, or
- want you to lie/distort/stray from the rules.

### § 16.02  DEMANDING CLIENTS

Let's start with the demanding clients. They are the ones who believe that because they are paying you to work for them, they have the right to instant responses from you and your staff and that you should drop everything in your law practice and your personal life to make their work your number one priority — even if there is no legal reason why you should do this (for example, a statute of limitations issue).

These clients are the ones who call you at 9:01 AM if they know that your office opens at 9. They will send you emails at all hours of the day and night — often several emails each day — because they saw that you had a smartphone sitting on your desk during the consultation. Some of them will even call your office at 3 AM and leave a long, rambling message, then call the office again at 5:30 AM to add additional information, then call again at 9:05 AM to talk to you about it. (This kind of client assumes that you arrive at the office well before 9 AM and that you, therefore, will have listened to all the phone messages and researched all relevant points by 9:05 AM because, of course, you have nothing else to do — or, at least, nothing else that is as important as this client's work.)

Typically, this client's work is not time-sensitive. The client just believes that "buying" an attorney's time means that the attorney is at the client's beck and call.

## [A]  Controlling Your Client

So how do you deal with a client like this? If you are charging by the hour, you often can take control of a client like this by politely reminding the client that you are charging for listening to all the phone messages and reading all the emails. If you are not charging by the hour — for example, if you are charging a flat fee or a contingency fee — you frequently can control the client by setting up your email to send an automatic response that you will answer all of your phone calls and emails before you leave work for the day. You can also either record this same message on your voice mail or ask your assistant or answering service to say the same thing.

You can also try to control these clients by setting up a FAQ page on your website and direct clients to that page. Additionally, you can set up a client portal and post all pertinent information in the client's portal. For example, you can post upcoming court dates, information about documents that the client needs to submit to you, etc. Between the FAQ and the portal, most routine client questions will be answered.

If this doesn't work to curb your client's instinct to touch base with you in a manner that feels demanding, talk with your client. Explain that you have many clients and that if they all expected this level of constant contact, and all expected you to drop everyone's work to do theirs, you would never get anything done for anyone. If this doesn't work to calm your client, you might want to suggest gently to the client that he or she might feel more comfortable working with an attorney at another firm. Believe it or not, many of these demanding clients respond that they don't want another attorney — that they want you. At that point, you have to ask them to back off a little. If they don't, then you need to seriously consider discharging them as clients. If you're in the middle of litigation, you might have to file a motion with the court to get permission to be discharged as counsel. Check your local court rules.

## [B]  How to Spot a Demanding Client

The clients who are demanding are often hard to spot initially. In your first meeting with them, they are frequently personable and even easy-going. They often are polite and respectful, hesitant to ask a lot of questions, and will tell you how happy they are that you have time to represent them. You think: "Wow. This is a dream client!" And then the trouble begins.

These are the clients who you wish you had never agreed to represent because they are so annoying. Unfortunately, these people are sometimes old friends or relatives, or close friends or relatives of your friends or relatives. Don't be surprised if someone you thought you knew well for years turns out to be one of these annoying clients. Sometimes people display different sides of their personality when they're under stress. And legal issues often cause stress for your clients. Even something as simple as a lease to rent a house can cause stress.

Suppose that your client is an old friend who has decided to go away for the summer and wants to rent out his house during that period. Let's say that you start with a "boilerplate" lease that you found on the Internet. You read it carefully, modify many of the provisions so that your client will be better protected, and then you add a Rider with additional provisions. Your amiable client takes one look at the lease and says, "This looks like the lease that I saw on the Internet." You say that it is because most leases have the same basic provisions, but you add that you changed numerous things to better protect your client. You further explain that you created a Rider to add important provisions. Your client then says, "There is too much here. It'll scare off the renters. Can you make it a lot simpler?"

You try not to sigh, and you explain patiently that if you take out a lot of provisions, your client won't be protected. Your client then says, "But I trust these renters. They have excellent credentials and seem like the kind of people who would take good care of my house." You immediately think of all the horror stories you've heard from friends, relatives, and colleagues who mistakenly thought the same thing.

You wind up spending hours exchanging emails with your client in an effort to produce a lease that will make him happy but still will protect him adequately. You had anticipated that this would be a quick and easy job, but now it's taken more than five hours of your time. You didn't discuss your fee with him because he's an old friend, has plenty of money, and made it clear that he wanted to "hire" you — i.e., pay you for your services. The problem is that you're pretty sure he thought this would be an easy job and that the only reason he hired you instead of using a lease that he found on the Internet was that he thought it would take up a lot less of his time to just have you do it. You then realize that he probably thought you would charge him just a small sum of money — like maybe $50 — because it was such an easy task and because you're old friends. Worse, you're wondering if he thinks that you'll charge him so little because you found the basic lease on the Internet and didn't have to create it yourself.

## § 16.03   TIME-CONSUMING CLIENTS

Even though most lawyers know that they should use engagement letters for every client, even those who are old friends or long-time clients, lawyers often don't do this when it comes to old friends and longtime clients. And here's what often happens when one of those turns out to be a time-consuming client because the client is picky, asks seemingly endless amounts of questions, and appears to have checked his common sense at the door:

You will wind up writing off most of your time. We have seen lawyers do this time and time again. They don't want to jeopardize their relationship with the person, so they chalk up the experience to a lesson learned, and they bill for a small amount of time — often just one hour. They write the actual time spent on their invoice, then write something like "professional courtesy" next to the excess time and don't charge for it.

Here's what often happens: The client gets the invoice and writes a politely worded email in return that thanks you for the invoice but says that he was very surprised that the job took so long and that if he'd realized this at the outset, he just would have used one of the form leases from the Internet. In other words, he is saying that it's your fault that you didn't anticipate that he was going to be difficult and ask you a million questions that wound up taking hours of your time. Worse, his comment shows that he didn't value or care about your efforts to protect him from possible adverse consequences of using a form lease without annotation and additions.

This is a no-win situation for you. The best response is often to write back politely and say that you were pleased to have been able to help protect him. And then sit back and hope that he'll pay you. And hope that he will never, ever, hire you for a legal matter again.

## § 16.04  CLIENTS WHO TRY TO SAVE MONEY BY ALTERING DOCUMENTS THEMSELVES

One big problem with this kind of client is that he may well try to annotate what you drafted — add new provisions and alter existing provisions — so he can use the document again in the future. And then, when his attempt at lawyering backfires, he'll come back to you and ask you to save him from the mess he created. Just remember how difficult this person was before. Unless you're starving, seriously consider saying no and referring him elsewhere because difficult clients usually don't get less difficult with age.

Clients who decide to reuse and alter forms that you've created also fall into the category of "clients who think they know more than you do." They think that because your document is written in plain English, they can change it just as easily as you can. This is like looking at a Hemingway novel and thinking that because it's written in plain prose, you can write something like it and your book will be excellent, too. Often these clients will wind up in a dispute over some provision of their altered document and come back to you for help, acting as though your document caused the problem. They don't tell you that they have altered it. You initially panic because you're thinking that maybe you forgot something or did something wrong. But then you read the document and notice provisions that you are pretty sure you would never have written. You pull out your version of the document and compare. Nope, you didn't write these things. When you ask the client, he confesses to having added just a few things. This is a client who thinks he knows more than you do.

## § 16.05   CLIENTS WHO SECOND-GUESS YOUR ADVICE

The even-more-annoying clients who think they know more than you do are the ones who say they've run your advice past their brother-in-law, sister-in-law, college roommate, etc. The other person is a lawyer, and your client just happened to bump into them at some sort of function, so your client took the opportunity to get a second opinion on the case. (Yes, an opinion after presenting 1.5 minutes of information to the other lawyer, often after both parties have consumed cocktails.) Your client reports back to you that this person thinks you should handle the matter differently. Most of us have one immediate thought when this happens: "If you doubt my ability to handle this case, let that lawyer handle it!" But we don't say that. Well, sometimes we do. But mostly, we remain polite and ask what kind of law the person handles. The majority of the time, it's an area that's unrelated to the area in question. But even if it's the same area of law, how do you handle this kind of situation — when the client reports to you that someone else thinks you should be handling the case differently?

You could say politely that obtaining a second opinion is always good and that you would be happy to turn the case over to the other person if that would make the client more comfortable. Your client will most likely assure you that he or she does not want to switch lawyers. And you will explain why you decided not to pursue the method that the other lawyer suggested. Or you will say that you'll look into that method and thank the client for bringing this to your attention.

## § 16.06   CLIENTS WHO THINK THEY ARE LEGAL RESEARCHERS

Worse, though, is the client who decides to research the legal issue or legal solution on the Internet and then keeps making suggestions to you about how you could handle the case based on that. The information is usually either faulty, just plain wrong, or doesn't apply in your jurisdiction. Non-lawyer clients usually do not understand that law in one jurisdiction may not apply to another jurisdiction. But this won't deter the client who knows more than you do. That client will keep trying to function as your paralegal — researching the case endlessly online and through conversations with other people.

One efficient way to keep this kind of client from annoying you with phone calls and emails about this "new" information is to ask the client if he or she could write you a memo about it. This often works if you explain that this is what you would ask a paralegal to do, and you say that it would be extremely helpful to you to have this in writing so you can refer to it. Tell the client that fancy legal language is not necessary and that plain English is fine. This way, you'll keep the client busy and away from you so you can do productive work. And you never know, it's always possible that the client who thinks he or she knows more than you do might actually know more than you do about something. Keep an open mind but learn to control your clients. Clients are like puppies: They need to be trained. Even the best ones need to learn what your expectations are. Just be gentle but firm.

## § 16.07   CLIENTS WHO IGNORE YOU

Some other types of problematic client behavior have no clear-cut solutions. For example, what do you do about clients who ignore you? These are the clients who don't answer calls from your office when you call about an upcoming court date. Or when you call for additional information that you need as you're approaching a deadline. Very few clients are unresponsive like this, but from time to time, you'll encounter one. What do you do? And what do you do when their lack of responsiveness causes them to default on a court date or a deadline, and then they blame you? If you're lucky, you've documented all the times that you called them, and you also put your requests into writing. You can make a motion to the court to be relieved as counsel. But that takes time, and you don't get paid to do that.

## § 16.08   CLIENTS WHO EXHIBIT STRANGE BEHAVIORS

Or what do you do when your client acts mentally erratic or irrational? For example, what do you do if one of your clients walks through the front door of your office and stands in the reception area and yells down the hall to you she is going to "killlllll" herself? And then she laughs. You think she might be kidding, but you're not sure. She's acting a little odd. And then another client comes to you with a notebook that's a half-inch thick and contains a hole from the front cover to the back cover that she's drilled by hand with her pen. What do you do? These are true stories. You don't know for sure if the client will be a danger to herself or others. Do you gently suggest that she see a mental health professional? We suggest that you call your local or state bar association for guidance. Perhaps there is a mental health committee. Ask for advice from some of the more experienced practitioners who serve on it. The committee is designed to deal with mental health issues of attorneys, but the committee chair or other members might have wisdom and experience that will help you.

## § 16.09   CLIENTS WHO WANT YOU TO LIE FOR THEM

What about the clients who want you to lie for them? You know that your ethics rules prohibit you from lying, but how do you handle saying no? Although the ethical rules are clear, how you choose to meet your obligation is up to you. Be firm. Do not compromise your ethics.

## § 16.10   HOW TO DUMP A PROBLEM CLIENT

With any of the above categories of problem clients, you may get to a point where you no longer want to represent them. Can you just write to the client and say that you want to sever your ties? Sometimes, but not always. If you are in the middle of litigation, your client might not be able to substitute a new lawyer without the court's permission. This means that you might have to draft and file a motion to be relieved as counsel. If you are in the middle of a transactional case, and changing attorneys won't jeopardize the case, you might just be able to get your client to sign a simple document agreeing to change attorneys. Then you can just ship the file to the new attorney. But if changing attorneys will jeopardize the case — for example, if you are up against a deadline to finish a prenuptial agreement and changing attorneys would delay the matter past the deadline — then you might have to tolerate the difficult client through the conclusion of the matter. There are no hard-and-fast rules here. Our best advice is that if a client is extremely difficult (versus just somewhat annoying), don't delay in your decision to break free. This is particularly true in the case of clients who lie, want you to lie, or want you to bend the ethics rules for them.

## § 16.11   HOW TO TELL BAD NEWS TO YOUR CLIENT

What do you do if your problem is not a difficult client but, rather, a difficult situation that you need to discuss with your client? For example, how do you tell a client that you lost a case at trial after recommending a trial instead of a settlement? Or, how do you tell your client that you just won a big case for him but that the adversary is going to appeal, and you know that the adversary has deep pockets to pay for the appeal, but your client does not?

Your method of breaking bad news to your client should depend not only on your personal style but also on the temperament of your client. For example, if your client is high-strung, you should consider informing your client in writing with a copy of the court's decision attached. In your letter (or email), you should carefully explain the decision and the options for an appeal. By opting for a written communication, you are giving your client time to process the bad news before calling you. If you inform the client on the phone or in person, a high-strung client might have an immediate emotional reaction before fully processing the information. This will be unpleasant for you. Wouldn't you rather give the client a little time to process the bad news before calling you to discuss it? The client might call to vent, but at least the client will have all the necessary information to discuss the situation instead of just reacting to it.

If your client is more easygoing, and you know the client fairly well, you could call the client and deliver the bad news. When you work closely with clients, as you often do in solo and small-firm practices, clients will expect you to call them with news — either good or bad. If the news is bad, and your client isn't high-strung, you can always preface your bad news by saying something like, "I have bad news and I have good news." The bad news, of course, is that you received an adverse decision. The good news is that there are points on which you can appeal. And you can explain these points to the client. That will give the client hope. You can say that many lawsuits are won on appeal.

This is not hopeful advice if the adversary has deep pockets and your client does not. In a case like this, you might want to suggest a payment plan. This would allow you to appeal the decision and would allow your client to make monthly payments toward the legal fee.

The bottom line is that we do not recommend a one-size-fits-all method of delivering bad news to clients. It's never pleasant to deliver bad news to a client, but your job will be easier if you pay attention to the client's temperament and package your delivery of the bad news in a way that will be more palatable to that temperament.

# PART III

SURVIVING TURMOIL

# Chapter 17

# FEE DISPUTES

Almost every lawyer will, at some point in his or her career, have a disagreement with a client over the amount of a billed legal fee. As we discussed earlier, it is important to be aware of your jurisdiction's rules about fees. There are several issues with regard to fees that you need to be aware of if you are going to be successful in a fee dispute with your client. The most important questions to which you must have answers are:

1)  Was the fee agreement in writing?

2)  Was the fee set by the jurisdiction in which either (a) the work was performed or (b) the attorney was retained or licensed?

3)  Did the jurisdiction impose any requirements on attorneys with regard to billing procedures, and did the attorney comply with those requirements?

4)  Does that jurisdiction have any procedures that an attorney must follow in a fee dispute with a client?

Check your state for the rules and/or regulations with regard to attorneys' fees. All of these rules and regulations are not necessarily found in the same place; therefore, it is incumbent upon you to perform a thorough search of the topic of attorneys' fees — both by researching and by getting advice from other practicing attorneys — before you enter into any fee agreement with clients. Ignorance is not bliss. If you fail to follow the rules by which you are bound, chances are good you will lose all or part of the fee for which you worked so hard. If you are doing work in a state other than where you maintain an office, be sure to check to see which rules apply to you. Attorneys are now easily able to conduct business in a state without actually setting foot there. If you are doing work in a state other than where you maintain an office, be sure to check to see whether there are any rules with regard to fees by which you may be bound. This includes work done by telephone, email, web chatting, video conferencing, etc. Being able to work in more than one jurisdiction can be a good thing, but make sure you know the risks when you accept the benefits.

Many states seek to have fee disputes resolved by way of arbitration or mediation and have set up programs for bar associations and other groups to administer fee-dispute hearings to avoid tying up the courts with these matters. You usually are entitled to a trial de novo if you are not satisfied with the results, or you and your client can stipulate in advance to be bound by the determination of the arbitration panel. But let's not get ahead of ourselves; let's talk about what you can do to minimize your chances of being involved in a fee dispute.

## § 17.01   TYPES OF CASES

There are certain types of cases where the likelihood of being involved in a fee dispute increases dramatically. Matrimonial and family law matters are notorious for such disputes. Clients involved in these types of cases generally are stressed out from the situation, and that stress is increased by having to incur attorneys' fees. Additionally, these types of cases can be someone's first involvement with an attorney, and a client's uncertainty about dealing with lawyers can cause stress. Although business clients tend to think of attorneys' fees as just part of the cost of doing business, this is not the case with a family law client. Our county bar association told us that in the year before we wrote this book, more than 75% of the fee disputes files involved matrimonial and family law matters. So, if you are worried about dealing with fee disputes, matrimonial and family law may not be the right fit for you.

Civil and commercial litigation with hourly fees also can be fertile areas for fee disputes. Because no one can predict how much time litigation can consume, clients can be shocked by the large amount of their bills. Even though you may have provided clients with an estimate of the hours involved in their case, your estimate might have been way off — perhaps because of unforeseen circumstances. <u>Do not underestimate the fees when you are meeting with a potential client because you are afraid of scaring the client away with a realistic estimate.</u> If you minimize the estimate, you maximize the chance of a fee dispute. Some of the alternative fee arrangements discussed earlier in Part II of this book, such as a fee collar, can help you to avoid a fee dispute. The problem for you with a fee collar is that if you are incorrect in your estimate, you are limited in how much of your bill will be paid. Yes, you will avoid the fee dispute, but you can do that without a fee collar simply by compromising on the amount you will accept if the client complains about your fee. But there is a benefit to using a fee collar if you bill fewer hours than the amount agreed upon, so, once again, you will be making a difficult choice. Bear in mind, though, that because you don't have to have the same fee arrangement on every case, you can try something on a case or two and see whether it makes sense to implement the arrangement more widely.

It is also a good practice to have discussions with your clients about the costs associated with different options for handling the case as it progresses. When clients are knowledgeable about the costs and participate in the decision-making, they often complain less in the end.

## § 17.02   COMPLYING WITH ALL RULES REGARDING YOUR FEE ARRANGEMENT

There is no excuse for writing an engagement agreement that runs afoul of the rules for attorneys in your jurisdiction. If you accept a case and are not familiar with the usual fee structure for that type of matter, there are a variety of things you can do to protect yourself. The first thing is to research the fee rules before you meet with the potential client so that you do not make an improper quotation when trying to sign up the person. If your potential client does not reside in the jurisdiction where your office is located and you will be doing work in the jurisdiction where he or she resides, make sure to check the rules regarding fees in that jurisdiction in addition to your own.

Do not hesitate to communicate with someone from your local bar association to discuss the rules regarding fees. A good place to start is with the chair of the committee that covers the type of case you are thinking about taking. Most committee chairs are appointed not only because they have knowledge of the topic about which they are serving as chair but because they have the respect of their colleagues. Chairs of bar association committees are well aware that their position comes with a certain amount of responsibility. They generally will not have a problem answering reasonable questions about commonly charged fees. Experienced attorneys are a very valuable resource for new attorneys. Make friends with older colleagues and treat them with respect; you will be rewarded with their wisdom and guidance.

## § 17.03  WRITING YOUR ENGAGEMENT AGREEMENTS IN PLAIN ENGLISH

In certain types of matters, boilerplate engagement agreements are required. In all other matters, you have the freedom to draft an engagement agreement. But be careful about this. Yes, it is easy to copy the format of another lawyer's agreement or one that you found online. That is fine if the document suits your purposes. Just be sure that it isn't missing provisions that will be important for you and your client. Also, if you do not understand everything in that agreement, do not use it. You must be able to understand and explain the terms of any agreement that you ask a prospective client to sign. To make your job of explaining easier, give your prospective clients agreements that are written in plain English.

## § 17.04  COMPLYING WITH ALL RULES AND BEST PRACTICES REGARDING YOUR BILLING PROCEDURE

Not only must you be knowledgeable about all rules concerning the fees you can charge, but you must also be equally knowledgeable about any billing requirements that may apply to your case. For example, some states require that you send an appropriately detailed bill for services rendered every 60 days. If a client disputes your fee and you do not comply with this requirement, you might lose a portion of your fee. Some jurisdictions provide that if a lawyer does not send a bill within 60 days of performing the work, the lawyer will forfeit the fee earned during the period of noncompliance if the client disputes the bill.

When you make your billing notes, it is extremely important to be as detailed as possible about the work you performed. The details will assist you in recalling the circumstances surrounding the work that was performed and will be useful to you in a fee dispute situation, grievance proceeding, or malpractice lawsuit. Having the details about the work you performed — including whether you discussed it with your client — can help you to prevent and defeat claims that you did work without your clients' knowledge and permission.

Be aware, though, that you must consider the potential risk/harm to your client and/or the case if you disclose too much in your bill. If you need to make an interim fee application in a litigated case, you most likely will be required to submit your bills, which should include a description of the work performed. A problem can arise if you speak to a witness whose name is indicated on your bill, and your adversary had no idea that the witness was cooperating with you. By including the name of the witness on billing records that you submit to the court, you will have tipped off the other side as to what will come at trial and may have put the witness in jeopardy. Therefore, if you anticipate having to use billing records to make an interim fee application in a litigated case, you might not want to name the witness on the billing record and, instead, write merely that you spoke with "a witness." In your case file, rather than in your billing records, you should make note of the name of the witness, the time of the meeting, and the place it was held. Then, if you do become involved in a fee dispute, you will have the information you need.

## § 17.05   KEEPING RECORDS OF YOUR TIME, EVEN IF YOU CHARGE A CONTINGENCY FEE OR FLAT FEE

Keeping track of your time may seem like an unnecessary waste of your time in a contingency fee or flat-fee case. After all, your fee is not based on the hours that you worked.

Keeping track of your time in contingency fee and flat-fee cases serves two purposes: (1) Keeping track of time helps you to calculate how much you made per hour and determine whether or not that case was profitable. This helps you to plan whether or not you should accept cases like this in the future. (2) Keeping track of time helps you to support your position in a fee dispute because revealing the large number of hours that you worked helps you to prove the reasonableness of your fee.

Some states permit an inquiry into the reasonableness of a contingency or fixed fee even if the client signed a clearly written fee agreement. When states require legal fees to be reasonable, lawyers must justify their fees if the fees are particularly large — for example, in negligence or medical malpractice cases. Keep detailed timesheets. This helps you to show that you are entitled to your large fee.

## § 17.06   COMPLYING WITH THE RULES FOR HANDLING FEE DISPUTES

As we mentioned earlier, not only must you know the rules about how you are permitted to set fees and bill clients, but you must be aware of whether the jurisdiction has rules about how fee disputes must be resolved. Consider these questions:

- Does your jurisdiction have a mandatory fee arbitration program?
- Is the program applicable to all types of cases?
- Is the program limited by the amount in dispute?
- Must you give your clients notice of the arbitration program and, if so, when?
- If the client does choose to arbitrate, what happens?
- Can a lawyer initiate a fee dispute proceeding?

- Under what circumstances can you sue to collect your fee?
- Can you put provisions in your retainer agreement/engagement letter as to whether a fee arbitration is binding or non-binding?
- Does the fee dispute program in your jurisdiction have a format for answering the complaint?
- How many arbitrators does your program require? Does the number vary by the amount in dispute?
- Are the arbitrators lawyers, non-lawyers, or both?

While these may seem like a lot of questions, they are basic to the fee dispute process in many states. It is important for you to check the rules when you open your practice. Although it may seem premature to worry about fee disputes before you even have clients, you should be aware that some states require lawyers to provide prospective clients with the fee dispute rules. Because the rules for fee resolution differ from jurisdiction to jurisdiction, we cannot provide you with a one-size-fits-all set of rules.

# Chapter 18

# GRIEVANCES

One of the most unpleasant experiences you can have as a lawyer is learning that someone has filed a grievance against you. If you have a busy practice, it is likely that you will be required to deal with one eventually, no matter how diligent and careful you have been. This is because some clients make unreasonable demands and, then, if you don't comply, get angry and retaliate by filing a grievance. With that thought in mind, let's explore the most common cause of grievances, how to avoid a grievance, and what to do if you receive one.

## § 18.01  WHAT IS A GRIEVANCE?

Different states have different disciplinary rules governing attorneys. One of the first things you should do when you begin practicing law is to look at your state's rules for attorneys' conduct.

If you violate those rules, someone can file a grievance against you. A grievance is a complaint filed with the body that governs attorneys' conduct in the state in which the attorney is licensed. The purpose of the grievance system is to protect the public against attorneys whose behavior calls into question their honesty, integrity, or professional competence. It should be obvious that you can't steal or borrow funds that don't belong to you (i.e., trust/escrow funds), and it should be obvious that you can neither put your own needs ahead of your client's nor engage in misrepresentations. But not all grievable behaviors are that obvious, and that is why you must familiarize yourself with your state's rules and regulations.

## § 18.02  COMMON CAUSES FOR GRIEVANCES

### [A]  Failure to Communicate

One of the most common causes for grievances is the failure to communicate properly with your client. This means that if a client calls you or contacts you via another medium, you should respond within a reasonable amount of time. Grievance committees usually impose a standard of reasonableness upon an attorney. What is "reasonable"? There is no exact definition. We recommend trying to return all calls the same day. In no event should you let more than 24 hours pass before responding to a client. Be sure to log in calls right after you receive them and right after you return them. Do not wait until later when you need to guess at the time and length of the calls.

As your practice grows, you will have less time available to return calls. Consider responding by email if your client uses email and you have informed the client that you may be responding by email. There are certain benefits to email, one of which is that you can respond quickly and from almost anywhere, including places from which you could not respond by telephone — for example, while waiting for a hearing to start. Email has serious pluses and minuses. Remember that anything you put in an email is there forever to come back and haunt you. Be careful about putting answers and legal advice in an email when you don't have all the facts and information to give proper advice. Your words can be directly quoted in a future proceeding against you if you have given incorrect advice. Further, be sure to inform your clients that their workplace email address might not be confidential if they work for someone else, even if the individual passwords are confidential. Ask clients to give you a private email address instead.

You can respond to a call by emailing that you will be available to speak at a particular time, or you can send an email in which you offer to schedule an appointment to meet to discuss the client's questions. You also can delegate someone in your firm to return calls when you are unavailable. Some attorneys specify this in their engagement agreement; that way, clients are on notice about the attorney's availability and the process to be followed when a client needs relatively straightforward information that a non-lawyer employee could provide.

Having language of this nature does not absolve an attorney of the obligation to communicate with a client personally, but it puts clients on notice and provides a method of dealing with responses, which helps you avoid a sustainable grievance for failing to communicate with your client in a timely manner.

If you are a solo practitioner, you might want to think about having a coverage arrangement with another lawyer that is similar to what doctors use when they are away or not scheduled to be working. If you do this, clients have to be made aware of the arrangement. Even more important, you should arrange to do this only with a lawyer whose level of competence makes you feel comfortable. This is important not only for your peace of mind but because you may be held liable if the other lawyer gives poor advice on your behalf.

Be aware that a very common communication complaint/grievance involves lawyers' failure to keep clients informed about what is happening with their cases.

There are two simple ways to ensure you can prove you have met your obligation to keep a client informed.

First, send the client copies of all pleadings, motion papers, and important correspondence. This way, if clients complain to a disciplinary committee that you did not keep them informed, you can defend yourself by demonstrating that you provided the clients with everything needed to keep them apprised of the progress of their case.

Second, as we mentioned earlier, keep detailed time records and create detailed bills that show what you worked on and whether you spoke with the client or anyone else on their matter. Include the specific subject of the conversation and some details. When we suggest being detailed, we are not suggesting that you include privileged or strategic information on your bill. Rather, we are suggesting that you include enough information to demonstrate communication without giving away too much — in case you have to submit your bills to a court when you are making make a fee application during litigation. As we said earlier, be careful not to jeopardize a case by including too much information on the bills.

## [B]  Neglect

Another very fertile ground for grievances is neglecting a case. We all know that there is certain work we just don't like to do. In law school, it might have been a paper for a class you didn't like or being forced to work on a project with someone who was difficult or lazy. As a lawyer, you will run into the same types of problems. There are tasks you might not like to do — be it drafting a contract or writing a complaint, motion, or brief. There are also clients you may discover you really don't like, so you might procrastinate about doing their work.

In all of these situations, it is common for lawyers to keep moving the assignment or file to the bottom of the pile of the things to do. Remember this: if you take the case, you have to do the work. Don't neglect it.

## [C]  Rule Number One: Don't Take a Case You Shouldn't Take

Lawyers opening their own practices generally think that they want as many cases as they can get. They want to be busy, to get experience, and to earn money. One of the most difficult things to do is to turn down potential new business, particularly if you don't have that much going on in your office. But sometimes a case that you shouldn't have taken will turn out to be an albatross around your neck.

Here is an example: You may have known that a potential case wasn't particularly good, but you thought you could make some money on it. You took it on a contingency fee basis, and now a good deal of time has gone by; you have spent hours and hours working the case, and the more you learn, the less you believe in your chances of winning. The insurance carrier is refusing to make a settlement offer, and now you know you will be stuck trying the case. If you lose, you will make no money for all of your work. Because the client is not paying you an hourly fee, the client does not care if you have to spend hours at trial.

Worse, you are close to the trial date, so it is too late to make a motion to be relieved as counsel without jeopardizing your client's position.

But if that isn't bad enough, your retainer letter did not include a provision requiring the client to advance money to pay for experts' fees, so now you have to pay them out of your own funds. Worse than that, the trial probably will take a few weeks, so you won't be able to generate billable time for other cases in your office. And because you have become relatively certain that you are not likely to win this case, you will not only make no money on it, but you will not be reimbursed for the experts' fees because there will be no recovery from which to reimburse you for paying them.

What is the moral of this story? The moral is that you shouldn't have taken the case.

But there are things you can do to avoid making this mistake.

First: Take your client-interviewing process very seriously. Find out enough facts to have a reasonable understanding of the case. What is the potential client's goal? Is it a valid one? Is it an achievable goal?

Second: If you need another opinion and you have a partner, invite your partner into the meeting and see what he or she thinks.

Third: Consider using a limited retainer agreement. You can be retained for the purpose of investigating to see if you think there is a good claim. You can't employ this technique if a statute of limitations is about to run out, but if there is sufficient time, this strategy gives you the opportunity to see whether you want the case without obligating yourself to do anything more than an investigation. The investigation should be thorough enough to tell you whether the combination of facts and law warrant accepting the case.

Sometimes you should not take a case because you have an instinct that the potential client is going to be a problem.

---

Every lawyer thinks that he or she can smell a problem client a mile away. Of course that isn't always so, but I did develop one rule of thumb that was invariably correct. It was that any woman who had lipstick up to her nose was wacky. We made it a rule not to take those clients. People like that are a disaster waiting to happen. LAK

---

Trust your instincts. A potential client is usually on his or her best behavior during the initial meeting. If you sense trouble then, things generally will not get better when that person becomes your client. Sometimes a potential client will say something during an appointment that makes it clear that he or she isn't someone for whom you are going to want to work. Maybe the person has shown himself or herself to be a bigot during your first meeting, or maybe the person has done something you cannot in good conscience defend. The good news is that as your own boss, you can choose whom you want to represent.

The term "access to counsel" does not mean that everybody has the right to have you as an attorney. You are in business. You are not required to represent every person who walks through your door. If a potential client has been arrested, and you find the person's act reprehensible, you do not have to represent that person. Rather than accept the case and then start avoiding the client and the work, just don't take the case. Otherwise, you are likely to end up with a grievance because of your delays in dealing with the client and the case.

Just to be clear, we strongly believe in the need to do pro bono work. It is a good thing to provide legal services at no charge to people who need legal assistance and who do not have the income and resources to pay for it.

> I also decided that there were people who engaged in certain activities that I could not in good conscience defend. If I believed that someone sexually or physically abused his or her own child or children OR engaged in such conduct with another child or children, they just were not going to have me as their attorney. I never felt I could represent someone accused of such actions with the type of zeal a lawyer should demonstrate on behalf of a client. The beauty of being my own boss is I could make that decision and stick to it. LAK

## § 18.03   INCLUDING LANGUAGE THAT IS IMPROPER IN AN ENGAGEMENT AGREEMENT

Although you must look at the rules within your own state, certain themes are consistent throughout the country:

1)  Limiting a client's ability to sue you: Language in your engagement agreement that says the client waives his or her right to sue you for malpractice is unenforceable in most places. Additionally, the inclusion of such language in and of itself in your retainer agreement may sustain a grievance in your jurisdiction. Model Rule 1.8(h)(1) states that a lawyer shall not make an agreement prospectively limiting the lawyer's liability to a client for malpractice unless the client is independently represented in making the agreement. In California, which has not adopted the Model Rules, Rule 3-400 is comparable and states that a member shall not contract with a client prospectively limiting the member's liability to the client for the member's professional malpractice.

2)  Limiting the client's ability to file a grievance against you: Language of this nature may be enough within your state to sustain a grievance. Model Rule 1.8(h)(2) states that a lawyer shall not "settle a claim or potential claim for such liability with an unrepresented client or former client unless that person is advised in writing of the desirability of seeking and is given a reasonable opportunity to seek the advice of independent legal counsel in connection therewith."

3)  Providing for a non-refundable retainer: Many practitioners are confused about the difference between a non-refundable retainer and a minimum fee. It is important that you understand the difference because even in very strict states, a minimum fee is usually acceptable while a non-refundable retainer is not. Generally speaking, fees paid to a lawyer in advance are refundable if they have not been earned, according to Model Rule 1.6. Some states get more specific. In New York, for example, lawyers are not allowed to enter into an arrangement for a "nonrefundable retainer fee" according to Rule 1.5(d)(4) of the New York Rules of Professional Conduct. However, this rule states that a New York lawyer may charge a "reasonable minimum fee" if the retainer

agreement "defines in plain language and sets forth the circumstances under which such fee may be incurred and how it will be calculated."

So what is a non-refundable retainer? It is exactly what it sounds like. It means that once the client gives you the money, it's yours, even if you don't finish the case or the client changes his or her mind about proceeding. This is unacceptable, because you shouldn't be able to keep money that you haven't earned. A minimum fee is something very different. A minimum fee is a fee you establish as the least you will take to handle a particular case regardless of the amount of work or time it takes you to complete the case.

Let's take a look at an example to make sure the concept is clear:

Suppose that Smith and Jones is a well-known divorce law firm that asks a prospective divorce client to sign a retainer agreement providing for a minimum fee of $10,000. The firm's hourly rate is $400. After spending only 10 hours on the case, attorneys Smith and Jones are able to achieve a very favorable settlement for the client. At $400 an hour for 10 hours, their billed time amounts to $4,000. Does the client get $6,000 back? No, because the minimum fee was $10,000. The lawyers would argue that it might well have taken someone less experienced 40 hours to achieve what they did for that particular client. Moreover, if they weren't honorable, they could have expended 25 hours of time working more slowly or doing unnecessary work in order to make it look like they earned all of the money they had been paid. It makes sense that Smith and Jones can set fees reflective of their skills and efficiency. The terms of their compensation were written in plain English in their retainer agreement, and the client believed it was worthwhile to have that firm advocating on his or her behalf. Just as ballplayers and artists can be rewarded for their talents, so, too, can lawyers. The client should be happy that the case was resolved quickly and favorably, that litigation was unnecessary, and that he or she did not suffer from the stress that lengthy cases cause.

If you are going to charge a minimum fee, be sure that you make the terms very clear in your retainer agreement. Minimum fees generally are used by experienced attorneys who can be selective about the cases they take and who, by virtue of their experience and reputation, can justify charging a minimum fee.

## § 18.04 MAKING A FEE ARRANGEMENT THAT IS PROHIBITED IN YOUR JURISDICTION

Some states have very clear rules about the types and amount of fees that can be charged in particular fields of law. For example, contingency fees in matrimonial cases are strictly prohibited in New York. Also in New York, there is a fee structure that lawyers cannot exceed in medical malpractice cases.

Ignorance of the rules in your jurisdiction is not a viable defense to a grievance. Do not merely rely on the word of another practitioner when setting your fees; some lawyers keep up with rule changes and some don't. You can ask for advice, but check the rules yourself. You do not want to find yourself with a sustainable grievance because you relied on what someone else said instead of checking for yourself.

Remember, too, that many states do not list all of their fee restrictions in one obvious place. Make sure that you and your partners find out as much information as you can in this regard and then catalogue the rules so that they can be located easily by each person in your firm who has the authority to set fees and sign retainer agreements.

## § 18.05   WHAT TO DO AFTER YOU RECEIVE A LETTER FROM YOUR GRIEVANCE/DISCIPLINARY COMMITTEE

Before writing this chapter, we met with lawyers who represent people who have had grievances and/or malpractice cases filed against them, as well as lawyers who have served on grievance committees in their jurisdiction. An important adage that we learned during these meetings is that if you receive a letter from your disciplinary committee, remember the three Cs: Cooperation, Candor, and Contrition.

Let's assume that you get a letter with the return address of your grievance or disciplinary committee. The first thing to do when you get that letter is to TAKE IT SERIOUSLY. That means that you need to stop panicking and open it. Do not bury it under a pile of mail until you can face whatever accusation it contains. (We are not joking about this. Many people don't open mail if they fear that it contains bad news. We know this from talking with our clients.)

Regardless of whether the complaint was filed by your client, by the opposing client, by the opposing attorney, or by someone else, you must respond. Even if you believe that the complaint is ridiculous and without merit, you must provide a thorough, detailed, and serious response. Lawyers who have served on grievance committees told us that just as many problems result from the failure to respond to a complaint properly as from the complaint itself. Failure to respond in most jurisdictions is the basis of a grievance. Don't put your career in jeopardy for this reason.

If this is the first time that you have received a letter of this nature, you may want to consider consulting an attorney who is experienced in handling grievance procedures. Many local bar associations have an ethics committee. If you receive one of these letters and you are a member of your local bar association, consider contacting someone on the ethics committee to discuss the allegation. Ask the following questions:

1) Did I do anything that was inappropriate or unprofessional?

2) If my conduct was problematic, do I need a lawyer?

3) If I do not need a lawyer, is there is some specific protocol, format, or language I should use when responding?

Don't be embarrassed to ask questions. Most people who serve on their bar association's ethics committee are more than willing to assist a colleague.

If you need time to put together a proper response, make sure to call the issuing committee and request time. Most committees will be willing to extend that courtesy because they are looking for a thorough response. Do not just file a late response without obtaining an extension of time. Make the call, record when you made the call, and get the name of the person with whom you spoke to obtain the extension of time.

If you have documents to refute the allegations contained in the complaint, supply them. For example, if the grievance involves an alleged failure to communicate, provide the committee with the proof that you did communicate — emails, correspondence, etc. Provide copies of your billing notes that reflect the issues that you discussed in a telephone conversation with your client. Specific notes on your bills, which include the subject of the conversation as opposed to the details of the conversation, preserve your client's privileges while still protecting you. If your notes do not supply the topics discussed, they should at least show when the call was made to the client. If the time billed was extensive, it will appear to the committee that your discussion probably was substantive.

As affronted as you may be by a complaint, it is not a good idea to be flip or aggressive with the committee. Although being contrite is not always possible, particularly if the complaint you receive is a total fabrication, you must show the appropriate respect for the process.

## § 18.06   POSSIBLE RAMIFICATIONS OF A GRIEVANCE

Not only is it important for you to be well-versed in the rules of professional responsibility in the jurisdiction(s) in which you practice, but it is also important for you to understand the scope of the jurisdiction of your grievance/disciplinary committee, as well as the procedures and the ramifications of an affirmative finding.

A very controversial and hot topic in the grievance world involves if and when the public should be made aware of the fact that a grievance has been filed against you. States vary in their approaches, and you should learn what the rule is where you practice.

Most states do not make records available until a disciplinary action has been taken. In New York, for example, the Judiciary Law requires that all disciplinary proceedings against lawyers remain confidential until an Appellate Division court decides to discipline or disbar the attorney. In Texas, information about a grievance is public if the lawyer is found to have committed professional misconduct and receives a public sanction. In California, bar association investigations and inquiries are confidential; the complaint becomes public only when disciplinary charges are filed against an attorney in State Bar Court.

Only a few states make all or most complaints a matter of public record. In Florida, for example, the matter becomes public information when the case is closed or the matter is decided by a grievance committee and further proceedings are undertaken.

Only Oregon treats all information as public. According to the Oregon State Bar's Rules of Procedure, disciplinary proceedings are open to the public except in circumstances when they are exempted or protected by law.

Because more and more complaints are being filed against attorneys, many states are discussing the issue of transparency — that is, whether to make the complaints public. Of course, the mere filing of a complaint is no indication of its validity, and so most lawyers oppose making complaints public until the grievance process on the complaint is complete. This prevents the public from judging a lawyer — and deciding not to hire that lawyer — on the basis of a complaint that later is found to be baseless.

States vary with regard to their grievance processes and the sanctions that can be imposed upon an attorney.

Suspension and revocation of a license to practice law are the ultimate sanctions that can result from violations of a state's disciplinary code for attorneys. Again, states vary in terms of the process.

Make sure to understand your state's process BEFORE you respond to any complaint you receive.

# Chapter 19

# MALPRACTICE

We think that it is important to discuss a subject few lawyers want to raise when encouraging you to open your own law practice. That subject is malpractice.

It is our belief that if we discuss this subject openly and honestly, we will be able to help you to avoid certain pitfalls and help you to be better equipped to deal with problems if they occur.

IMPORTANT: DO NOT EVEN CONSIDER WORKING FOR ANY CLIENTS UNTIL YOU HAVE A MALPRACTICE POLICY IN PLACE.

## § 19.01   WHAT IS MALPRACTICE INSURANCE?

Malpractice insurance is exactly what it sounds like; it is insurance to cover you for mistakes you make while acting in your professional capacity. Let's face it: We all are likely to make some mistakes during the course of our professional careers. Sometimes the mistake is a little one that you can fix easily. Sometimes the mistake is a large one — like missing a statute of limitations deadline. Your goal is to make sure that you have adequate insurance so that if you make a mistake and your client sues you, your personal assets will not be at risk.

Most malpractice policies are "CLAIMS MADE" policies. This means that you will be covered for claims that are made during the term of the policy unless your insurance company includes exceptions.

If you are an experienced attorney, the area that can make things a little sticky is the RETROACTIVE DATE (also known as a "retro date"). When your carrier gives you a "retro date," this means that your policy will not cover any acts or omissions that occurred prior to that date. So even though your policy is a "claims made" policy and the claim is made during the period of the policy, the company will not cover you if the act or omission occurred prior to the retro date. If you are an experienced attorney, you will want your retro date to be as far back as possible. That way, you will have more of the years covered during which you could have made an error. Carriers are not foolish, though; they try to make your retro date closer to the date of the policy so they have less exposure.

Two experienced attorneys joining together to start a firm may have different retro dates. If your partner has a history of claims (be wary of this) or had a different carrier than the one you are using for your new firm, your new carrier is likely to want to give that person a very short retro date.

You can ask the carrier to make yours different from your partner's. There is no guaranty that this will happen, but there is no harm in trying.

If you are the senior attorney joining in the creation of a new firm and had a different carrier, you may want to consider getting "tail" insurance, which covers occurrences in your past.

A word to the wise: although there is no current national database for lawyers to see if someone has committed malpractice, there are things you can do to check on a potential partner. You can search e-courts (or whatever similar system is available in your state), LexisNexis, West, Google, and Google Scholar to see if your intended partner's name appears as a defendant in the caption of a lawsuit or lawsuits. It is certainly better to go into a relationship with your eyes wide open.

If you are a new attorney, the retro date is normally the date of your policy. For you, this should not present a problem because you have not practiced before. For you, the retro date only becomes an issue if you are going into practice with someone who has already been a practicing attorney. If you go into practice with someone who has practiced before, your firm could have to defend itself against mistakes from your partner's past.

## § 19.02   WHERE DO YOU GET MALPRACTICE INSURANCE?

Almost every state and large local bar association has a deal with a malpractice carrier to provide its members with a group rate. This is a win-win for the carriers and the bar associations because the carriers don't have to spend time finding lawyer-customers, and the bar associations get lawyers to buy malpractice insurance. Most of the time, the money you save with the group rate will exceed the amount it costs you to join the bar association through which you are obtaining the insurance. Check to see if your state or local bar offers this.

## § 19.03   OTHER RELATED INSURANCE

Consider getting cyber coverage. This is relatively new, but it can be very important. Cyber insurance covers you in case someone hacks into your computer system.

If you plan to have employees, also consider getting employment practices insurance to cover you for claims alleging sexual harassment, age discrimination, etc. Again, it makes sense for you to discuss these things with your broker or agent. Remember, you do not have to have done something wrong to be sued. And if you are sued, the cost associated with defending such a claim is likely to be high. Much or all of this cost will be covered if you have appropriate insurance.

## § 19.04   HOW MUCH COVERAGE SHOULD YOU BUY, AND HOW BIG A DEDUCTIBLE DO YOU WANT?

When it comes to buying insurance, the more coverage you want, the more you will have to pay. Also, the higher the deductible is, the lower the premium will be. Balancing these realities and making good choices is not an easy task.

We know that certain fields of law involve higher risks and higher rewards than others. If you handle medical malpractice cases, large negligence matters, and large commercial and/or corporate matters, your individual cases involve more money and risk. For example, if you miss a statutory deadline in a medical malpractice case, you could be dealing with millions of dollars in damages. If you handle big-money cases, your firm should not economize in the area of malpractice insurance.

Malpractice insurance disclosure remains a hot topic nationally. States vary about requiring attorneys to disclose whether or not they have malpractice insurance. Some states make you disclose this to potential clients up front, and some states even require you to note on your letterhead if you do not have malpractice insurance. Some states require lawyers to fill in a form when they register to practice, indicating the amount of insurance coverage they have. It is critical to look into your state's malpractice insurance requirements and adhere to the requirements. You also will need to keep up with any changes to your state's requirements because this is an evolving area, and states are looking into making more changes.

How much malpractice insurance should you acquire? We believe, based on our conversations with malpractice insurance consultants, that you should purchase no less than $1 million in coverage per incident. The consultants told us that the price differential for a lower amount just isn't worth it. You might also want to explore getting additional umbrella coverage from another carrier.

There are many issues to consider in selecting a deductible. First, there is something called a "loss only" deductible. This means that you pay the deductible only if you lose the case or the claim is paid. If you do not have a loss-only deductible, you have to pay the deductible even if you win. The deductible that you pay in these circumstances goes toward legal fees and the costs of defense. You pay more for your policy if you buy a loss-only deductible. So, if the choice is made available to you, you need to consider the cost differential before making your choice.

Next, you have to decide how much of a deductible you want. Although it is true that your premium is lower if you select a higher deductible, you must recognize that if you are selecting a higher deductible, you actually have to have the amount of the deductible on hand. Remember, too, that that deductible amount must be available for each and every claim that you have during the term of the policy. As a new attorney, you probably will not want too large a deductible even if the premium is lower. Insurance carriers have made it clear that they will be expecting payment of the deductible, and if you don't have the funds available, the carrier might sue you for the money.

An unfortunate reality is that your premium will be higher if you have had a claim in the past. Ironically, this can be true even if you prevailed in the case. The reason for this is that insurers had to pay legal fees to defend you, and they want to make up for that cost by increasing your premium. The good news is that you still are likely to be insurable.

## § 19.05   BE TRUTHFUL ON YOUR POLICY APPLICATION

It is absolutely essential that the information contained in your malpractice policy application be accurate and complete. It will not help you to leave off information in the hope of getting a cheaper policy rate. A carrier may deny coverage if there is any material misrepresentation in the policy application. You defeat the purpose of obtaining coverage if you give your carrier an excuse not to defend and/or pay any claim against you.

What is the take away from all of this? Spend time with a malpractice insurance professional to help you choose your carrier, the limits of your policy, and the amount of your deductible.

## § 19.06   WHAT CAN YOU DO TO AVOID COMMITTING MALPRACTICE?

### [A]   Conflict Checks

In setting up your office, it is important from the outset to use a conflict-checking system. What is a conflict of interest? The Restatement of the Law Governing Lawyers states that a conflict exists "if there is a substantial risk that the lawyer's representation of the client would be materially and adversely affected by the lawyer's own interests or by the lawyer's duties to another client, a former client or a third person."

To determine whether you or your firm has a conflict, you must consider many things. You need to know what assets and involvements you and your partners have. These can cause a conflict of interest. Then you have to explore the question of whether you represent or have represented a person or entity — or even been consulted by a person or entity — with regard to a matter that might compromise a current client's interests.

Even if there is no actual conflict, it is a good idea to avoid the appearance of impropriety. You do not want to be the subject of a newspaper article that makes you look like you might have acted in an improper or inappropriate manner.

We highly recommend that upon opening your firm, you and your colleagues read articles on the topic of conflict of interests to give yourselves a clearer understanding of the issue. Our purpose in mentioning this is to raise the issue with you and give you information about how to act proactively to prevent problems.

Many law offices have more than one system in place to deal with conflicts. This is a good idea because in the application for insurance coverage, your carrier usually will ask for information about your conflict checking. Your carrier might even require that you have more than one such system.

Let's look at some different things you can do:

1) A simple and effective method is the old-fashioned conflict-check sheet that circulates throughout the firm before you accept a client. That sheet usually contains the name of the client(s), the name of the adversary or adversaries, the type of matter, the name of the person who referred the case to the firm, and the names of any known witnesses involved in the matter. All lawyers must indicate whether or not they have a conflict of interest. If there is a conflict, depending on the type of the case, you and your colleagues might decide to explore the question of whether the conflict can be waived. Be careful in making this decision, because sometimes the appearance of impropriety to the outside world is not worth the fee that you might receive.

2) In addition to this manual method, most firms now have software that includes an electronic conflict checking system. As we discussed in a previous chapter, there are many office management systems that will search the data you enter to see if anyone with the same or a similar name shows up in the database. You can check your database not only for the names of the clients and adversaries but also for the names of witnesses and anyone or anything else possibly related to the matter. Remember, though, that the system is only as effective as the data you enter. You, your colleagues, and your staff must not delay in entering all relevant data. Delay can present a major problem. You also have to remember not to purge information regarding old matters. You have to continue to maintain good records of the people you represented in the past because a conflict can live on. If you err and take a case where the new client causes a conflict with a client whom you were already representing, chances are very good that you will have to withdraw from representing both parties. It is unpleasant to have to withdraw from representing clients as a result of this type of error. It is even worse if you have gotten a large retainer and are required to return those funds to your now-former client.

## [B]   Maintain a Top-Notch Calendar System

Computer software for calendar control is now quite plentiful, and these systems vary greatly in terms of the different options available to you. You can use something as basic as Microsoft Office to enter statutes of limitations dates and other important dates, or you can invest in software that will actually compute the statutes of limitations for you and then include them in your calendar. Prices of systems differ, so you should investigate the systems carefully. (See our previous discussion about office management systems.) Many companies offer free trials. Don't just pick a system because your friends use it. Test some of the leading ones to see which one you like best. You might decide at the outset to spend as little as possible because you have few cases and not a lot of opportunity for error. There is no right or wrong answer as to how much to expend at the early stages of your business, as long as you spend enough to adequately protect yourself. As you gain a larger inventory of cases, you will have more dates to keep track of, and your need for a more complex calendaring system will increase. If you are joining with another lawyer who already has a significant caseload, you may decide to invest in a larger management system because that caseload will involve many dates that you must not miss.

Be aware that there are many critically important dates in each and every litigation case. These include but are not limited to:

- Statutes of limitations dates

- Notice of Claim dates (dates by which you must serve a municipality with a notice of your intention to sue)

- Dates by which you must serve an answer to a complaint or a reply

- Motion dates, including dates for answering papers and reply papers

- Court conference dates

- Discovery dates of a variety of kinds — including dates by which to answer interrogatories or bills of particulars, and dates by which depositions are due

- Dates by which pretrial information must be exchanged — for example, witness lists and experts' reports

- Trial dates

Please remember that you do not want to make your first entry about a due date on the date that your time runs out. You have to decide how much of a warning you need for each type of deadline so that your software can give you reminders at whatever intervals you believe are needed to ensure that you have time to gather the information and create the documents necessary to meet your deadlines.

It is critically important to be aware of statute of limitation dates because this can help to prevent malpractice claims not only with regard to cases that you take, but also with regard to those that you do not. If you choose not to accept a case that has a statute of limitations consideration, be sure to send a non-engagement letter to the person. This helps you to avoid claims by people who say that they thought you were representing them and then blame you for missing the deadline. (See sample non-engagement letter in the Appendix.)

## [C]   Limit the Scope of Your Representation

Although not all jurisdictions require written engagement agreements, we strongly recommend that you use them. Putting things into writing greatly decreases the possibility of a misunderstanding between you and your client about your respective duties and obligations. Of course, just having a written engagement agreement is not enough; you must draft an uncomplicated and understandable engagement agreement where the scope of your representation is set forth very clearly. You need to identify the matter being handled as well as the aspects of the matter to which your representation is limited.

So, for example, if you are being hired to negotiate a settlement between two brothers concerning their individual financial contributions to a parcel of real estate, your engagement agreement should identify the parcel, identify the parties, indicate what issues you are being hired to negotiate, and clearly state that your representation is limited to negotiations. The engagement agreement also should state that it does not cover litigation and that you are not required to commence or participate in any aspect of litigation. (In a situation like this, your engagement letter should state clearly that you are representing only one of the two parties. It would be a conflict of interest to represent both parties.)

Likewise, if you are retained to handle a matter that you expect to litigate, you should indicate in the retainer agreement that your representation DOES NOT cover any aspect of an appeal. If you do not want to file the notice of appeal, or whatever the equivalent is in your jurisdiction, you may want to add that language to your retainer agreement as well.

Why would you want to limit the scope of your representation? In the first case that we mentioned, clearly stating that you are not required to participate in any aspect of litigation informs the client that he or she may have to retain another attorney if the matter does not settle. Sometimes just knowing this will encourage a client to settle the matter.

In the second case, clear and unambiguous language states that your obligation to represent the client ends with the trial. If there is an appeal, and the client wants you to handle it, the client will have to enter into a new retainer agreement with you.

But there are other less obvious things that may need to be in an engagement agreement. For example, let's assume that you are handling a malpractice case. A variety of jurisdictions have held that these types of cases cannot be tried properly without an expert witness. Therefore, your engagement agreement must include who is going to advance the fees for the expert. If you don't include language stating that the client must advance the expert fees, and then you do not call an expert because you either couldn't or wouldn't advance the fees, you will be guilty of malpractice in any jurisdiction in which it is malpractice to fail to call an expert witness in a malpractice case.

Remember that when you are drafting your engagement agreement, you are drafting a contract in which you are representing yourself. Be a good lawyer on your own behalf. Know what you want to put in your retainer agreement before you draft it, and then make sure that you write clearly and unambiguously. Any ambiguity is going to be construed against you, so take the time to do your job well when drafting your engagement agreement.

## [D]   Be Sure to Document When a Client Is Acting Contrary to Your Advice

As surprising as this may sound, your clients are not always going to listen to you.

Worse yet, it is not uncommon for clients who ignore your advice to conveniently forget what you told them and blame you for the result of their failure to follow your recommendation. You can and should be proactive by giving your clients a written reminder of your recommendation and the fact that they have chosen to act in a manner that is contrary to your advice. Letters of this nature should be reserved for substantive matters, not whether you disagreed over an adjourned date or something of a similar nature. If there is a proposed settlement and you feel confident that you cannot do better at trial, let your client know in writing. This is the time when you want to make it clear to the client that he or she is acting against your advice. If you then are forced to try the case because the client refused the settlement, and the outcome is what you feared it would be, your client will be hard-pressed to blame you for his or her poor judgment.

If you are concerned because your client is refusing to allow you to conduct discovery that will enable you to give your client an educated opinion about how to proceed with the case, you should let the client know of your concern. Often clients will want to avoid the cost of extensive discovery and expert evaluations or appraisals, and then will ask you to tell them whether a proposed deal is fair. This is like a patient asking a doctor whether he or she has a fracture, but refusing to allow the doctor to take an X-ray. If you don't have the opportunity to educate yourself sufficiently, you must let the client know that you cannot give an educated opinion with insufficient information. Chances are good that you will encounter this situation fairly frequently during your career. If you handle these situations properly, you can protect yourself against future malpractice claims while allowing your clients to proceed in the way they prefer.

## [E]   A Few Final Thoughts

Some malpractice experts say that it is easiest to avoid claims when you limit the areas in which you practice. They say that when you practice in many areas, you have a lot less experience or knowledge than you would if you practice primarily in a particular field. It is not easy to stay current in numerous areas. This is not to say that you cannot be an effective general practitioner. Just make sure to protect yourself by purchasing sufficient malpractice insurance and by adopting the strategies that we have discussed with you in this book.

Do NOT ask a client to waive malpractice claims in your retainer agreement. Model Rule 1.8(h)(1) states that a lawyer must not make an agreement to limit the lawyer's malpractice liability unless the client is represented by independent counsel when making the agreement. The comparable rule in California, which has not adopted the Model Rules, is Rule 3-400. It states that a lawyer must not contract with a client to limit the lawyer's malpractice liability.

In some jurisdictions, not only are malpractice waivers unenforceable, but the mere act of having that language in your retainer agreement is a basis for a sustainable grievance. Make sure to read your state's code of professional responsibility. Ignorance of the rules is not a defense to a grievance proceeding.

## § 19.07   WHAT SHOULD YOU DO IF YOU THINK YOU MADE A SERIOUS MISTAKE?

## [A]   Notify Your Carrier

If you think that you may have made a mistake that could give rise to a claim, NOTIFY YOUR CARRIER IMMEDIATELY. You need to make sure that your carrier will not be able to decline to cover you because you gave untimely notice of your error. Look carefully at your policy to see if there is a required method for you to use in giving notice. Many carriers have something called pre-claims assistance. Check with your carrier to see if this process is available to you. Carriers with this type of assistance usually have hotlines for you to call to find out what to do. It is never a bad thing to get advice from your carrier.

In fact, if you make a mistake, do not try to fix it without first notifying your carrier. Unless there is some real exigency, let your carrier tell you what to do so the carrier has no basis for denying you coverage.

Also, many states require you to notify your client if you make a mistake. Let your carrier guide you through the process and advise you about how and what to tell your client.

What should you do if someone makes a claim against you for a sum of money that is less than your deductible? For example, if the claim is for $10,000, and your deductible is $10,000 or more, your instinct will be to try to settle the claim. However, you must find out from your carrier if you are allowed to do this and if there is any particular process that you must follow. Whatever you do, make sure all appropriate releases are signed. Your release must make sure to cover any and all claims that may have arisen or that may arise as a result of your action or inaction. Do not be embarrassed to get advice so that you don't compound your original error.

## [B]   Cooperate With Your Carrier

1) If a claim is made against you, do not hide anything from your carrier. You must disclose the whole truth. The carrier will want as much detail and information as you can provide. If you sent your client emails and or correspondence regarding the subject of the claim, make sure you give those emails and correspondence to the lawyer supplied by your malpractice carrier. There is almost nothing worse for a lawyer than getting blindsided when the adversary brings up something negative that your client said or did and "forgot" to tell you. You are the client here. Don't do this to your lawyer.

2) If, during the course of your representation, you think that your lawyer forgot something or missed the boat on an argument, let your lawyer know. You are likely to know more than your lawyer about the substantive law in the case that is the subject of the claim. Your lawyer's expertise is malpractice. Do not hesitate to give your input. In fact, provide that input in writing so that you have a clear record should you need it in the future.

3) If you want to settle the case, you must tell this to your lawyer. Let your lawyer know the parameters that you have in mind for any settlement. If you believe that you committed malpractice, and you think you are at risk for a verdict in excess of your coverage, you must put that in writing to your attorney. If your attorney fails to attempt to settle the case within the policy limits, and there is a verdict in excess of your coverage, you may have a remedy against your carrier for the excess if you documented your settlement instructions, and they were ignored.

## § 19.08   AVOIDING PERSONAL LIABILITY FROM MISTAKES MADE BY YOUR PARTNERS

If you are in a practice with more than one attorney, you should seriously consider forming a limited liability company or some type of corporate entity. As we discussed earlier, one of the main purposes for practicing under a legal entity is to avoid personal liability for mistakes made by others with whom you practice. Please note that there are situations in which a limited liability company or a corporate entity will not protect you from liability — for example, if you personally make a mistake or if you were responsible for supervising a person or person(s) who made one. Nonetheless, your best hope for insulating your personal assets from liability for mistakes made by your partners is to practice under one of these entities.

# Chapter 20

# EMPLOYEE ISSUES

Although we believe it is important to give you advice about how to deal with problems that may arise in your law firm, we hope that we can help you to avoid these problems in the first place. The more employees you have, the more likely you are to experience some type of employee-related problem. Sometimes problems arise from an employee's perceived slight or insult; other problems arise from an employee's lack of understanding of an office policy, procedure, or protocol.

## § 20.01   UNEMPLOYMENT CLAIMS

These cases are difficult to win unless there is gross misconduct. Someone who gets fired for not being good at a job is likely to receive unemployment benefits. You need to have a meritorious position if you are going to oppose the benefit. If you feel strongly about a claim, consider consulting an attorney who is knowledgeable about unemployment benefits. Our advice is to evaluate the conduct leading to a dismissal before contesting the unemployment insurance claim. Although unemployment claims can increase your insurance premiums (and no one likes incurring an increase in unemployment insurance costs), be realistic before engaging in this kind of battle.

## § 20.02   WHAT TO DO IF YOU RECEIVE AN IN-HOUSE COMPLAINT

If you are a very small office, and you have no institutionalized procedure to follow for in-house complaints, you likely will meet with the employee yourself to see if you can remedy the situation. We do not recommend admitting error. If an employee makes a complaint that you think might be legitimate, make sure to ask the employee how he or she would like to see the situation remedied.

If you have an employee manual, the manual should specify <u>a clear process for making complaints</u>, and should include:

1)   The name of the person to whom a complaint should be made. If the manual provides for a complaint to an immediate supervisor, you may want to offer an alternative in case the supervisor is the subject of the complaint.

2)   A statement that an investigation will be undertaken promptly. (You may or may not include the investigation process. Some people do not like to detail the process because if you do not follow it exactly, you could be found to have lacked compliance if you end up in court or arbitration.)

3) A statement that the complaint, investigation, and findings will be confidential to the extent feasible.

4) A statement that appropriate action will be taken based on the findings of the investigation.

5) A statement that there will be no retaliation for filing a complaint and that if the employee believes there was retaliation, he or she should file an additional complaint about the retaliation.

You should investigate promptly and thoroughly. Obtain details like:

- When did the incident take place?
- Where did it happen?
- Were there witnesses?
- Has it happened before?
- Did the complainant talk with anyone else about the event?

Also, if the complaint is about some type of unwelcomed behavior, you should find out if the complainant indicated that the behavior was unwelcomed.

It is very important that a neutral party be in charge of the investigation. That person should interview everyone with potential information about the claim. At the conclusion of each interview, the witness should be reminded that if he or she remembers any further information, it should be provided to the investigator.

You must be careful about taking interim measures. For example: Do not reassign the complainant or move that person's work area to another part of the office unless the complainant requests it. Otherwise, the complainant might see this as retaliation.

Upon completion of the investigation, you should write a report. Do not make legal conclusions. What you want to do is say that you believe a certain act did or did not take place. Make your report factual not conclusory. Before you finalize the report, you may want to have it reviewed by counsel. Remember, this report will be important if you are sued. You will need a record showing that you followed your process properly. This will be helpful if the complainant takes any further action.

The last step is to take corrective action where appropriate. We suggest that you ask the complainant what he or she believes that action should be. See if the suggestion makes sense. If so, consider taking that action. After your investigation, you may need only to send a memo to the staff reminding them of prohibited behavior. Or you may have to fire someone. The action that you take must be designed to end the problem. You also should conduct a follow-up investigation to see if your penalty or solution was effective.

The investigation report (including dates and times of interviews), notes, and action taken should be maintained in a file that you and the employee keep. We also suggest that you place an additional copy in the files of all affected employees.

## § 20.03  WHAT DO YOU DO IF YOU RECEIVE AN EQUAL EMPLOYMENT OPPORTUNITY COMPLAINT, HUMAN RIGHTS COMPLAINT, OR YOU ARE SUED BY AN EMPLOYEE

The Equal Employment Opportunity Commission (EEOC) is the agency charged with monitoring compliance with Title VII.

If an employee files a charge against you, the EEOC will send you a notice within 10 days of the charge, and an investigator will be assigned to your case. The EEOC may, at the outset, dismiss a charge that it believes has no merit or is not covered under Title VII. If the EEOC decides there is at least some basis for the complaint, then the EEOC will conduct an investigation to determine if there is reasonable cause to believe that discrimination occurred. At the very least, you should contact your attorney about the complaint. If you have Employee Practices Liability Insurance (which lawyers in solo and small-firm practices normally do not), you must advise your carrier of the claim.

Assuming that you do not have this insurance, you will need to make decisions quickly after learning of the complaint. If appropriate, the EEOC will offer you the opportunity to engage in a mediation process to resolve the matter. If your investigator does not mention this to you, ask if the process is available to you. Mediation is the fastest and easiest way to take care of this type of matter. If you can resolve the matter through mediation, the case will be closed.

During the EEOC investigation, the investigator is going to seek a statement of your position. This is your chance to tell your side of the story. Check to see if your lawyer wants to review anything that you prepare prior to submission. Chances are good that you also will be asked to respond to requests for information. This is akin to the discovery process in litigation. You might be asked for personnel records or documents, such as any steps you took when you received an initial complaint.

The investigator may want to visit your place of business or talk with other employees. You should speak with your lawyer about how to proceed, but the general rule is to respond promptly and appropriately. If you have a reason why you cannot get something done in a timely fashion, ask for an extension. Do not ignore requests. You are allowed to be present during interviews with management, although you do not have the right to be there when other employees are being interviewed. Even with an employer's cooperation, these cases generally take at least 6 months to be investigated and possibly longer.

At the conclusion of the investigation, the EEOC can make the following determinations:

1) That there is no reasonable cause to believe discrimination took place. If this happens, the EEOC will state this is a letter to the complainant and further state that the complainant can still file a lawsuit within 90 days of receipt of the letter.

2) That there was reasonable cause to believe discrimination took place. The EEOC will invite the parties to participate in conciliation to see if the matter

can be resolved. If conciliation is not effective, the EEOC can file a lawsuit, Usually, however, the EEOC opts to issue a "Right to Sue" letter advising the complainant that he or she has 90 days in which to file a federal lawsuit.

If you are sued in federal court for discrimination and or retaliation, hire a lawyer who knows how to handle these matters. This is a very specific area of practice, and it makes sense to hire someone with the knowledge that will give you the best chances for success. Be aware that attorneys' fees can be awarded if the complainant prevails against you. That is why it makes sense to try to settle a case if you think that some type of prohibited behavior took place. If the other side is making unreasonable demands, it behooves you to have a competent lawyer in the field to expedite the process, help to minimize any verdict, and reduce your exposure to attorneys' fees.

# Chapter 21

## YOUR PARTNER IS A DISASTER

Law partnerships are like marriages because partners in both law and marriage enter the union with high hopes, great expectations, and excitement about the benefits — tangible and intangible — of working as part of a team. Even when partners craft a written prenuptial or partnership agreement that speaks to the division of assets, liabilities, and responsibilities in the event of a dissolution of the team, the partners don't really expect that a dissolution will occur. These agreements are similar to insurance policies — protection for you just in case you ever need them. When you purchase home insurance, do you expect that your house will burn down? No, of course not. You do it to be safe, just in case. The same is true with a prenuptial or partnership agreement.

We spoke about partnerships earlier in this book. Your partnership agreement should contain provisions for dissolving the firm, for one or more partners buying out one or more others, for death, for short-term disability, and for long-term disability. There are many sample partnership agreements online.

But what happens if the unthinkable occurs? Lawyers who partner to form a law business rarely start their business with the following thoughts:

- That a partner would steal from them
- That a partner wouldn't perform his or her share of the work
- That a partner wouldn't bring in any business
- That a partner would divert cases
- That a partner would incur law firm debt without the knowledge of all other partners

Even if you've heard stories about these things happening, you think that this couldn't happen to you. After all, you've chosen your new partner well. Perhaps you were in the same study group all through law school. Or you ate lunch together for two years while you were associates at a big law firm. Or the person is your first cousin. Or you have known each other since you were both in diapers. There is absolutely no way that this person could ever be a slacker or a cheater or a thief. Right? People don't change their essential natures, right? Wrong. Honest people can become dishonest if they are forced into desperate situations. They can become addicted to alcohol or drugs. Things can happen.

Our purpose in writing this is to tell you not to delay action if your partner begins doing any of the things listed above: taking firm money, diverting cases, incurring debt, not bringing in business, or not doing his or her share of the work. Do not try to ignore it and hope that life will get better. Don't think, "I'm too busy; I can't cope with this now." This is what many lawyers do. But the situation only gets worse. Talk with your partner, as hard as that may be. If your partner is in denial or keeps offering excuses, take some time off — a week is best, but even a weekend is better than nothing — and get away from the situation. Try to envision your future with that partner. What if the situation doesn't improve in a year? What if it gets worse? Are you willing to work harder, bring in more business, do more than your share of the work, all to support a situation created by your partner? Are you willing to pay back the law firm debt that you did not know your partner was incurring? Are you willing to live with the knowledge that your partner is diverting cases? Are you worried that your partner might take some of the escrow money? At what point will you decide that you want to sever relations? Why are you waiting and not doing anything about the situation now?

At the very least, take a look at your partnership agreement. You don't have one? This is the time when you realize why you needed one. If you have one, what does it say about dissolving the firm? What if one partner doesn't want to dissolve it? How are the assets and liabilities distributed?

Now look at the liabilities. How many of them required you to sign personally? Many landlords require the principals of a corporation to sign personally. If yours did, then you and your partner each are personally liable for the full amount of the rent for the remainder of the lease period. If your partner doesn't pay any of it, the landlord has the right to sue you for the full amount.

If your partner is having alcohol, drug, or other personality-altering issues, will that person try to grab the money in the firm bank account when you announce that you want to dissolve the firm? What about client files? Will your partner try to take them? What can you do to prevent that? If this sounds like planning for a marital divorce, yes, the emotional upheaval and the necessary pre-planning and strategy are similar. Don't do anything rash. Think carefully.

Please understand that if your partner is exhibiting this kind of behavior, that person might not readily agree to follow the protocol for law firm dissolution that is in your partnership agreement. You might be forced to sue your partner. Think long and hard about whether you want to do this. If you do, you could be tied up in a time-consuming and emotionally tumultuous court battle for years while you're trying to run or even rebuild your law practice. For some people, it is easier to just cut their losses and move on. As some lawyers have explained, you can always make more money but you cannot regain the time and emotional energy that you will need to spend fighting the partner who has wronged you. (Also, you may not want everyone to know the details of your private business.) These lawyers say that during the time that you spend fighting for what's yours, you could be working hard to build your firm to an even bigger and more successful position than it was in before. But that is a matter of personal choice. All we are saying is that (a) you should try to solve partnership issues before they fester, and (b) you should think through your strategy very carefully before taking action.

This having been said, let's talk about the egregious situations that can happen in a solo or small-firm practice. For example, what do you do if you suspect that a non-lawyer employee is stealing money from the firm? This happens more often than any of us would want to believe. Just look up the stories on the Internet. Type in "law firm theft and embezzlement." You will most likely be shocked at what you discover. Even a lawyer with a solo practice can be the victim of embezzlement by an employee. For example, if you give your legal assistant the authority to deposit clients' checks into the office operating account and reconcile the account, would you know if your employee was embezzling? You might be thinking that you won't have enough money in the office checking account for your employee to embezzle, but you're wrong. Even firms with small balances can be subject to embezzlement. It can be $50 here, $100 there. And as your firm becomes more prosperous, an employee with a flawed moral compass is likely to become bolder — taking larger amounts because you'll be busy and you don't monitor the account closely.

You're probably thinking that you'll just be careful about whom you hire and that you'll avoid this problem by hiring someone who comes highly recommended or whom you know well. Read the stories on the Internet. Many lawyers who trusted their long-time employees have fallen prey to embezzlement by those very employees.

How can you avoid this? If you have more than one legal assistant, make sure that neither one has total control over the office accounts. Also:

(1) Institute an office policy where every check has to be scanned in and emailed to you so that you can forward it to your accountant.

(2) Audit the checkbook yourself, and let your bookkeeper or the person in charge of the books know that you're doing this.

A few other tips to cut down on the likelihood that an employee will have an opportunity to pilfer:

- Do not get an ATM card to facilitate deposits into your office accounts if your employees are going to make deposits for you.

- Consider writing in your employee manual or policy guide that you must at all times be able to access the office email account of each employee. This would mean that they would be prohibited from changing the password without notifying you. Also consider including a prohibition against employees using the office email account for any personal purpose.

- Consider eliminating signature stamps and not giving employees permission to sign your name to things.

Be mindful of the fact that the American Bar Association's Model Rules of Professional Conduct — Rule 5.1 and Rule 5.3 — require lawyers with "managerial authority" to make "reasonable" efforts to ensure that non-lawyers in the firm confirm to the Rules of Professional Conduct. The rules note that this includes lawyers with "direct supervisory authority" over non-lawyers as well as lawyers. Rule 5.3(c) specifies that such a lawyer "shall be responsible" if the conduct of a non-lawyer employee violates the Rules of Professional Conduct. This means if your employee steals money from your trust/escrow account, you WILL be held responsible.

But what if it's a lawyer-employee (an associate) who is stealing? Rule 5.3(c) states that you must make "reasonable efforts" to ensure that lawyers over whom you have supervisory authority conform to the Rules of Professional Conduct. The Rule states that you "shall be responsible" for another lawyer's violation of the Rules if you order the conduct or ratify it "with knowledge of the specific conduct." Further, the Rule states that you "shall be responsible" for the lawyer-employee's violation of the Rules if you have "direct supervisory authority" over that lawyer and know of the conduct "at a time when its consequences can be avoided or mitigated" but you do not "take reasonable remedial action."

What if the person is a partner in your firm? Did you know that Model Rule 8.3 requires you to "inform the appropriate professional authority" if your partner or any other lawyer "has committed a violation of the Rules of Professional Conduct that raises a substantial question as to that lawyer's honesty, trustworthiness or fitness as a lawyer in other respects"?

How do the Rules define "professional misconduct" by a lawyer? To quote Rule 8.4:

It is professional misconduct for a lawyer to:

(a) violate or attempt to violate the Rules of Professional Conduct, knowingly assist or induce another to do so, or do so through the acts of another;

(b) commit a criminal act that reflects adversely on the lawyer's honesty, trustworthiness or fitness as a lawyer in other respects;

(c) engage in conduct involving dishonesty, fraud, deceit or misrepresentation;

(d) engage in conduct that is prejudicial to the administration of justice;

(e) state or imply an ability to influence improperly a government agency or official or to achieve results by means that violate the Rules of Professional Conduct or other law; or

(f) knowingly assist a judge or judicial officer in conduct that is a violation of applicable rules of judicial conduct or other law.

The bottom line is that if your partner steals from the trust/escrow account, a sufficient remedy is not just to use your own money to replenish the account and sever your professional ties to your partner. The Model Rules also require you to report your partner's action.

Please note that individual states may have even more stringent requirements than the Model Rules. Contact your state's bar association for information about "the appropriate professional authority" to which you must report lawyer misconduct in your state. And above all, don't be so busy with generating business, serving your clients' needs, and making money that you don't pay attention to the financial aspects of running a business — including monitoring the books and bank accounts.

# Chapter 22

# OTHER DISASTERS

Have you thought about what you would do if a natural disaster or personal catastrophe prevented your law office from functioning normally? Few lawyers think about this in the heady anticipation of setting up their law business. But you MUST think about this. Hurricanes, tornadoes, and floods often give you little or no notice before arrival. The same is true for the disability and/or death of partners or office staff. Will your office be prepared to function well if any of these disasters occurs?

## § 22.01  NATURAL DISASTERS

What steps can you take to protect your law practice against natural disasters such as hurricanes, tornadoes, fires, and floods (including floods caused by burst pipes in the building)?

Consider taking these actions:

If you have enough warning, make sure that all of your files are backed up to an outside server — either in another physical location or in the cloud. The problem with the cloud is that if you don't have electricity or Internet service (i.e., the cable is out), you won't be able to access your files.

Make sure that your laptop and cell phone are fully charged. If you have backup chargers, make sure they are fully charged, too. If you have a car, make sure that it has a full tank of gas because you might not be able to get gas for a while if electricity is out in your region. (Gas pumps are generally powered by electricity.) You may need your car to get to the courthouse. You may also need to use your car to charge your cell phone and laptop.

If you store files in the basement of your office, make sure that file boxes are not directly on the floor where they can flood. If you store file boxes in the basement, it is best to store them on metal shelving to keep them off the floor. Also consider placing basement file cabinets on wooden pallets so the bottom file drawer will be elevated more than a few inches off the floor. Even if the basement of your office is dry and doesn't get wet in bad rainstorms, one broken pipe is enough to ruin years of stored files. We know of law offices where this happened. Metal shelving and wooden pallets can be purchased inexpensively. Seriously consider taking this precaution.

If you have even a few minutes of warning before a disaster that requires you to evacuate your office, forward your office calls to your cell phone until the disaster is over and you can return to the office. Be sure that you are out of harm's way first. That is even more important than forwarding your calls.

Now that most landlines are electronic, make sure that you have at least one non-electronic phone in your office and that you have a way to plug it in. Non-electronic means that they do not need electricity to work. An example of this is the old-fashioned Princess phone. If you can't find one in a store, check eBay. Do not rely exclusively on your cell phone because if the electricity is out, you may not be able to recharge it quickly or often, and you will miss office calls. Remember, though, that if your office's telephone service is provided by a cable company, the electrically powered modem won't work, which means that even an old-fashioned phone won't work. Also, that phone won't work if the storm caused a cable outage.

Make sure that you have contact numbers for your employees. This means that you should list them on a printed sheet and/or in your cell phone contacts. You also should have a printed copy of your client list with phone numbers, addresses, and email addresses. Consider, additionally, saving a copy of this information onto a flash drive that you can grab and take out of the office. But you still will need the printed copy if your power is out and you cannot recharge your laptop.

Other essential items for your office are a fire extinguisher and flashlights. Some municipalities require all offices not only to have fire extinguishers but to have them professionally inspected every year. If you are not required to do this, make sure that your fire extinguisher is large enough to be useful. The kind that is made for a stove-top fire in your kitchen is not big enough for your office. Check the date on your fire extinguisher and flashlight batteries every year. Also test your flashlights every year. The flashlights will prove useful if the power goes out at night. Also consider purchasing a smoke detector (preferably one with a carbon monoxide detector, too). Although it is expensive, consider purchasing a defibrillator. You never know when you might need it.

Consider photographing or videotaping your office so that you will have a record of all furniture and equipment in case you need to make an insurance claim.

If you have warning about an impending natural disaster, be sure that you take at least the following items out of the office with you:

- Laptop computer
- Notary stamp
- Safe deposit box keys
- Copy of computer backup if you have one that is not cloud-based
- Hard copy of employee manual and/or office policy manual (in addition to the electronic copy) for easy reference in case you have a limited ability to recharge your laptop
- Copy of all insurance information

If you will be unable to return to your office quickly after the disaster, contact all of your clients to tell them about the situation and how they can reach you. Be sure to reassure them that your will be able to continue to handle their legal matters even though you are temporarily unable to use your office in the normal manner.

# § 22.02  PERSONAL DISASTERS

What would you do if you were temporarily disabled and could not perform your job — for example, if you suffered a stroke? Who would take over for you if you were a sole practitioner? What if your partner or secretary suffered a stroke or died? Would you be able to get into their files? Do you know where on the computer they filed documents?

Make sure that you plan for this. Will someone else be able to take over easily? Don't assume that personal disasters will never happen. This is why there are understudies at Broadway shows. Things happen. Take time to be prepared.

# Chapter 23

# CONCLUSION

We hope that our work on this book will help to make your work in opening and maintaining your own law practice somewhat easier.

While nothing can totally prepare you for what it is like to actually own and operate a law office with all of its accompanying responsibilities, the information in this book should alleviate some of your apprehension and stress.

We want to remind you that what works for one lawyer may not work for another, and what is customary and proper in one state may not be acceptable in another. You will learn these things as you move forward. Be careful to take the time you need to do the research and think thoroughly enough to make good judgments.

The two of us spent much of our adult lives owning and operating our law offices. Although the areas in which we practiced were different, and the size of our staffs and offices were different, the conclusion that we each reached is the same: If either of us had the chance to do things over and reconsider whether or not we wanted to start our own law firms, we would not hesitate to do it again.

Being independent and having the ability to make a difference in so many peoples' lives makes for a wonderfully rewarding professional life. We wish you the same success and satisfaction that each of us has experienced in our legal careers.

# APPENDIX A

## SAMPLE FORMS

### APPENDIX A INTRODUCTION

We have spent a good bit of time reminiscing about what it was like when we started our own practices, including the kinds of forms and information we wished we'd had at our fingertips.

As a result, we decided to make your lives much easier than ours were, and we assembled sample documents that you should use for reference purposes only. They should not be copied in their entirety. Instead, use them as inspiration when you create your own agreements, forms, and letters. We have included items that you can use to help you form business entities, as well as a variety of forms that will help you with the process of meeting clients and signing up cases. In addition, we have included some checklists and forms that will help you manage various types of cases, as well as a detailed chart of office management systems prepared by the ABA.

We are grateful to lawyers and bar associations throughout the country for allowing us to reproduce the materials in this Appendix, and we appreciate the collegiality that they displayed in helping us to make them available to you. Please keep in mind that by including these forms, we are not endorsing either the forms or the providers. Please also keep in mind that what works in one state may not be appropriate or complete in another. Make sure that you check the rules of the state in which you practice to determine what is proper there.

Lynne Adair Kramer
Ann L. Nowak

## *Special Thanks*

The authors would like to thank the following lawyers, law firms, and companies for giving us their time and allowing us to use their documents as samples for our readers:

The American Bar Association

The Florida Bar Association

The Louisiana State Bar Association

The New York State Bar Association

The Suffolk County Bar Association

The Judicial Council of California

Harvey B. Besunder, Esq., of Bracken Margolin Besunder LLP

Allen B. Breslow, Esq.

Frederick K. Brewington, Esq.

Joseph N. Campolo, Esq., of Campolo, Middleton & McCormick, LLP

Anthony V. Curto, Esq., of Forchelli, Curto, Deegan, Schwartz, Mineo and Terrana, LLP

Richard A. Gurfein, Esq., of Gurfein Douglas LLP

Maureen S. Hoerger, Esq., of Perini & Hoerger.

Dean T. Kirby, Jr., Esq., of Kirby & McGuinn, PC

Vanessa Kirker Wright, Esq., of Kirker Moore, LLP

Bryan P. Kujawski, Esq., of Kujawski & Kujawski,

Anthony M. La Pinta, Esq. of Reynolds, Caronia, Gianelli & La Pinta, P.C.

Lawyers Mutual Liability Insurance Company of North Carolina

Meredith R. Miller, Esq., Associate Professor of Law at Touro Law Center

Scott Michael Mishkin, Esq

Forrest S. Mosten, Esq

Edward J. Nitkewicz, Esq., of The Sanders Law Firm

Crystal Osborne, Esq., of Britton Osborne Johnson PLLC

Todd S. Page, Esq., of Stoll Keenon Ogden PLLC

Jon Polenberg, Esq., of Polenberg Cooper, PLLC

Rubin & Rosenblum PLLC.

Brett A. Scher, Esq., of Kaufman Dolowich Voluck, LLP.

Lois Carter Schlissel, Esq., of Meyer, Suozzi, English & Klein, PC

Madhu Singh, Esq., MBA, Foundry Law Group

Howard M. Stein, Esq., and Michelle Schmitt, Esq., of Certilman Balin Adler & Hyman, LLP.

Richard L. Stern, Esq., of Macco & Stern, LLP.

Gary H. Tabat, Esq., of Tabat, Cohen, Blum & Yovino, PC

Marshal S. Willick, Esq., of Willick Law Group

# Business Plan

**[Firm Name], P.A.**

**123 Any Street**
**Anywhere, New York 11722**

**[Partner's Names]**
**Shareholders**

## *BUSINESS PLAN*

Prepared (date)

**[Firm Name], P.A. Start-up Business Plan**

**TABLE OF CONTENTS**

**[Firm Name], P.A. Start-up Business Plan**

**[Firm Name], P.A. Start-up Business Plan**

## Executive Summary

[FIRM NAME], P.A., is a new law firm established on August 28, 20XX. The firm's attorneys are (list names of partners). The firm's partners are not in this start-up alone, but wish to memorialize the help and efforts of friends and family in making [FIRM NAME], P.A., a reality.

The last quarter of 20XX will be spent planning and implementing the start-up phase of the law firm. The firm will be open for new clients on January 6, 20XX. The firm will hold an open house on January 10, 20XX.

This business plan is designed to document the planning and implementation information agreed to by the partners during start-up meetings. The business plan covers the firm's structure and governance, financial projections, equipment, software and supplies that will be in place by opening day. During the start-up phase, additional information will be added and this plan will be updated as a guide for operations of the firm.

## Structure and Governance

The firm has (insert number) partners working in firm. The firm is organized as professional association, and there is an elected managing partner who serves a term of two years. As compensation for management duties, the firm pays the Managing Partner $1,000 per month. The initial capital contribution of each partner is $5,000.00.

## Legal Services Offered

Each partner has three years of legal experience in state government, in addition to two years experience as associate attorneys in private practice. As a group, the partners have solid working experience in the areas of civil litigation; elder law; family law; real estate; and trusts

**[Firm Name], P.A. Start-up Business Plan**

and estates.  These services will be offered to new clients.  It is a goal of the partners to have 350 active client matters by the end of the second year of operation.

It is possible that the firm's partners may be asked to assist clients with matters in practice areas not listed above.  Acceptance of work for prospective clients in practice areas not listed above requires the approval of all the partners to ensure the firm has the expertise to handle the work in the client's best interests.  At this time, the firm has no defined referral network, but sees the need to develop one during the first year of operations.  In the alternative, prospective clients the firm cannot serve will be referred to The Florida Bar's Lawyer Referral Service.

**Administrative Management**

**Personnel.**  Firm management does not anticipate hiring associates until 20XX.  When the firm commences operations, there will be an on-call contract paralegal and part-time office manager/bookkeeper on staff.  The firm will utilize Receptionists ($240/mo) as its virtual receptionist and answering service.  If it is determined there is sufficient paralegal work of at least 30 billable hours per week, and this work is no longer manageable using on-call contract paralegals, the partners will hire a full-time paralegal in order to hold down the cost of work to the clients.

**Accounting.**  Mr. Accountant, C.P.A., a relative and friend of Partner (name of partner) has agreed to provide discounted accounting services during 20XX.  The firm has purchased the cloud-based version of QuickBooks Professional Version financial management software for general ledger accounting, trust accounting, and timekeeping, billing and collections.

**[Firm Name], P.A. Start-up Business Plan**

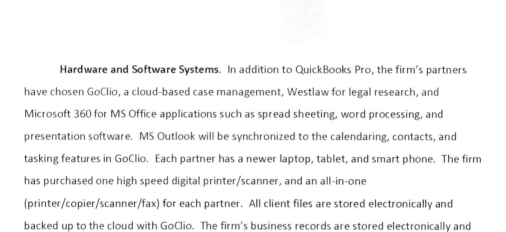

**Hardware and Software Systems**. In addition to QuickBooks Pro, the firm's partners have chosen GoClio, a cloud-based case management, Westlaw for legal research, and Microsoft 360 for MS Office applications such as spread sheeting, word processing, and presentation software. MS Outlook will be synchronized to the calendaring, contacts, and tasking features in GoClio. Each partner has a newer laptop, tablet, and smart phone. The firm has purchased one high speed digital printer/scanner, and an all-in-one (printer/copier/scanner/fax) for each partner. All client files are stored electronically and backed up to the cloud with GoClio. The firm's business records are stored electronically and stored in the cloud via QuickBooks Online. Practice specific software has been purchased and is available on the firm's server. Each partner has remote access connectivity to the firm's main server.

With the assistance of a local IT consultant, firm management will take the necessary steps (appropriate firewalls and e-mail encryption) to prevent access to client data. All employees and vendors for the firm must sign confidentiality statements. All paper documents will be shredded when no longer needed or their retention period has run.

**Location and Security**. Mrs. (insert name), aunt to Partner (insert name), has agreed to rent space next to her company's home and office furniture and supply store; space that is currently vacant. The space has a separate waiting area, a break room, a 14 x 16 room suitable for conferencing, a 10 x 12 room suitable for conferencing or a private working environment, and one open space (former showroom) that is suitable to be divided into work cubicles for the partners and staff. The firm will pay $1,500 per month (utilities included) for rent. The firm has purchased recently de-installed (used) cubicle furniture and

**[Firm Name], P.A. Start-up Business Plan**

dividers for $2,000.00. During 20XX, the partners (and their friends and family) have acquired used furniture and accessories to outfit the rest of the space. The Furniture Store has nighttime security, and for $200.00 per month, security personnel also will provide nighttime security for the firm. Visitors to the firm during business hours will be confined to the waiting area until escorted into the main space by firm personnel.

    **Insurance Portfolio.** The firm has acquired basic lawyers' professional liability insurance for $7,000.00 for the first year. The firm makes quarterly payments on the LPL policy. The firm has acquired general liability insurance on the premises, contents and valuable data for $2,400.00 for the first year. per year. Each partner is required to obtain his/her own disability insurance. For 20XX-20XX, the partners will be covered on their spouses' health insurance.

**Marketing Plan**

    **Market Opportunity.** There are over x,xxx Florida Bar members in the Second Judicial Circuit (the six counties comprising the greater Tallahassee service area). However, a large portion of these lawyers are employed by government. The population of the firm's service area tops 400,000. In Leon County, the rate of adults holding advanced college degrees is twice the national average. As the capitol of the third most populous state, the local populace includes a large middle class. We have determined through local research that the middle class is underserved by the available lawyers; there are not enough lawyers to serve the populace in the Second Circuit. It is well known that state capitols tend to be recession proof. Furthermore, legal plans (insurance) are popular among the middle class. The firm has joined ARAG Group legal plan as a provider of legal services.

**[Firm Name], P.A. Start-up Business Plan**

**Acquiring Clients and Initial Marketing Strategy**.  The firm's partners have an excellent network of trust relationships in the service area.  Each partner is required to belong to two community-based organizations.  The partners have met to ensure that memberships in these organizations do not have conflicting missions.

In order to create a positive firm image (branding), the partners will vote and agree to make time and/or monetary contributions to only two charities in the first two years of operation.  This limit does not include "tombstone" promotions and advertisements in charitable, civic and school event programs.

The firm plans to establish itself as an affordable alternative for legal services in the areas of civil litigation; elder law; family law; real estate; and trusts and estates.  The firm already has commitments from over 125 prospective clients wishing to retain the firm.

The firm's partners have committed to cross-selling efforts.  We will strive to promote all of the firm's services in marketing situations, and have made provisions in the firm's compensation system to reward cross-selling originations.

**Competition.**  Our market research indicates that [FIRM NAME], P.A., will be able to offer legal services for ten to twenty percent less than other firms by leveraging forms software, utilizing superior records and knowledge management processes.  The partners are also willing to accept less compensation during the first two years of operation to ensure there is sufficient operating capital.

**Website.**  The firm's website will be launched in December and will prominently announce the firm's opening date.  The firm's partners have chosen a local website designer and have reviewed several well-regarded law firm websites.  The website designer and the

**[Firm Name], P.A. Start-up Business Plan**

partners have met on numerous occasions to review the Florida Bar Ethics Department's Advertising Handbook. The website will include enhanced contact information. It will include numerous ways to contact the firm's partners. The partners have prepared articles describing the firm's services along with helpful links to important education for clients about the sale and purchase of real estate, title insurance, estate planning, elder law and family law. This information also will be available in paper format to visiting clients and prospective clients.

**Client Service.** The firm's case management system, GoClio, includes a client portal feature. This will enable clients to view their documents and messages anytime. Nonetheless, the firm's intake process includes asking clients how they wish to communicate with the firm's partners. In this way, the firm can accommodate their requests and avoid misunderstandings. The firm's partners will meet every two weeks to discuss case status and workflow, as well as other management issues. In the first two years of operation, regular bi-weekly meeting dates will be set on the office calendar to discuss the status of cases and marketing efforts. Depending on the needs of the clients and management needs, regular partner meetings may be moved to a monthly basis.

The partners have agreed to undergo additional training in time management, client relations and how to handle difficult people.

The firm will utilize a client survey to be given to the client after work is completed. The survey can be returned anonymously to the firm's accountant.

**Pro Forma Financial Documentation**

**Projected Case Loads and Total Investment Time.** The firm's partners have agreed upon certain work/life balance principles. At all times, the firm's partners will operate under a

**[Firm Name], P.A. Start-up Business Plan**

compensation system that rewards each partner's total investment time in the firm. This investment time includes origination, case management, case processing, and firm management.

The partners will record all time worked on behalf of firm operations. The attached pro forma financial documents will reflect that no partner will work more than 2,400 hours on behalf of the firm (46 weeks x 50 hours). If any partner finds the need to work longer hours, the firm's partners will take the matter up a partners' meeting and will discuss the need for an associate attorney(s). Individual time budgets are attached to this business. Individual time budgets provide for a fair distribution of work based on the partners' individual talents. That is, it is acknowledged that some are more suited to management whereas others are more suited to marketing activities.

**Projected Fees.** Insofar as firm management intends to concentrate on middle class clients. Fees for residential closings are expected to fall in the $1,000 to $2,500 range. Preparation of basic estate plans will range from $500 to $750. In the first year of operations, hourly rates for partners will range from $175 to $225. Paralegal work is outsourced and so is a pass-through cost to clients.

**Attachments:**

**Projected Cash Flow Statement**

## Operating Agreement


**[Firm Name], PLLC**
**Company Operating Agreement**
**Members**


**[Street Address of the PLLC]**

Operating Agreement – [FIRM NAME], PLLC

## LIMITED LIABILITY COMPANY OPERATING AGREEMENT
## OF
## [Firm Name], PLLC

## [MEMBER MANAGED]

THIS OPERATING AGREEMENT ("Agreement"), is made and entered into as of this 1st day of May, 20XX, by [Firm Name], PLLC., a _____ Limited Liability Company (the "Company"), and its Members _____.

The Members hereby adopt this Agreement as the "Operating Agreement" of the Company to set forth the rules, regulations, and provisions regarding the management and the business of the Company, the governance of the Company, the conduct of its business, and the rights and privileges of its Members.

NOW THEREFORE, the Members and the Company, intending to be legally bound, hereby agree as follows:

## ARTICLE I
## ORGANIZATION AND BUSINESS PURPOSE

1.1     **Formation**. On ____, 20XX, the Company was formed by filing a Certificate of Formation with the [State] Secretary of State under the [State] Limited Liability Company Act (Revised Code of [state and insert code number).

1.2     **Name.** The name of the Company shall be [Firm Name], PLLC. The Company may do business under this name and under any other name or names which the Members select. If the Company does business under a name other than that set forth in its Certificate of Formation, the Company shall file a DBA (Doing Business As) name as required by law.

1.3     **Term.** The LLC will commence its business as of the date of the filing of the Certificate of Formation and will continue until dissolution pursuant to Section 9 of this Agreement.

1.4     **Principal Office.** The location of the principal place of business of the Company within the State of _____, as may be updated from time to time.

1.5     **Registered Agent.** [Firm Name] shall be the registered agent in the State of _____. The location of the registered agent's office in [State] [insert address]

1.6     **Members**. The name, present mailing address, initial capital contributions, and percentage interest of each Member is set forth in Schedule A, as amended from time to time.

Operating Agreement – [FIRM NAME], PLLC


1.7    **Member Disqualification.** Each Member shall be qualified to practice law in the state in which the Member's principal office is located unless otherwise specifically agreed to under this Agreement.

1.8 **Admission of Additional Members.** No additional members may be admitted to the Company without the prior unanimous written consent of all of the Members. Each such additional member must be licensed to practice law in the state in which they maintain their principal office, unless otherwise waived in writing by the Members provided that such waiver does not violate any applicable rules of professional responsibility.

1.9    **Business Purpose.** The purpose of the Company is to engage in or provide professional legal services to the public and to engage in any other lawful acts or activities for which a Professional Limited Liability Company may be formed within the State of _____.

## ARTICLE II
## CAPITAL CONTRIBUTIONS

2.1    **Capital Contributions.** Capital contributions shall mean the money, property, promissory note, certain binding obligations, or services contributed to the Company in exchange for an ownership percentage interest in the Company.

2.2    **Initial Capital Contributions.** The initial capital contributions made by each Member to the Company is set forth in Schedule A.

2.3    **Additional Capital Contributions.** At the request of a majority of the Members, the Members shall make additional capital contributions to the Company in proportion to their respective percentage ownership interest in the Company. In the event the Company must reimburse costs attributable to capital contributions then such reimbursements shall be made in proportion to the Member's respective ownership interests. For purposes of this section, time spent by Members serving the Company or its clients shall not qualify as or be deemed additional capital contributions.

2.4    **Percentage Interest.** Each Member will own a percentage of interest in the Company. Each Member's ownership interest is set forth on Schedule A.

2.5    **No Interest on Capital Contributions.** Members shall not be paid interest on their capital contributions.

2.6    **Return of Capital Contributions.** Except as otherwise provided in this Agreement, no Member shall have the right to receive any return of any capital contribution or to demand distribution.

2.7    **Investment Risks.** All capital contributions in Membership interests of the Company have not been registered under the Securities Act of 1933, as amended, or other applicable state securities laws and are offered in reliance on exemptions provided by such acts. The Membership interests of the Company are to be acquired for investment only and not for

Operating Agreement – [FIRM NAME], PLLC

distribution, transfer, or resale to others. The Company is not required or in any way obligated to register the Membership interests or assist anyone in complying with any exemption from registration. The Members agree that there is no market for the Membership interests and none is expected to develop, and such interests are illiquid investments.

## ARTICLE III
### ALLOCATIONS OF PROFITS AND LOSSES, DISTRIBUTIONS, WITHHOLDINGS, AND METHOD OF ACCOUNTING

3.1    **Duties to the Company.** Except as otherwise permitted by the Company, each Member shall devote his or her best efforts and substantially all of his or her professional time to serving the Company and its clients. The Members agree to exert best efforts to comply with the Company's "Practice Management Principles" provided in Exhibit 1, as amended from time to time and mutually agreed upon by the Members.

3.2    **Allocation of Profits and Losses**. The Company's net profits or net losses shall be determined on an annual basis and shall be allocated to the Members in proportion to each Member's ownership interest in the Company as set forth in <u>Schedule A.</u> Such special allocations shall be in accordance with Treasury Regulation 1.704-1(b)(2)(ii)(d).

3.3    **Distributions.** The Members shall determine and direct the Company to distribute available funds in such amount and at such time as the Members mutually agree. Available funds shall mean the net cash of the Company available after the Members have allocated appropriate provisions for expenses and liabilities. Distributions for purposes of liquidation of the Company or in liquidation of a Member's interest shall be made in accordance with the positive capital account balances pursuant to Treasury Regulation 1.704.1(b)(2)(ii)(b)(2). In the event that a Member shall have a negative capital account balance, there shall be a qualified income offset, as set forth in Treasury Regulation 1.704.1(b)(2)(ii)(d).

3.4    **Distribution of Assets**. If any assets of the Company are distributed in kind to a Member, those assets shall be valued on the basis of their fair market value. Unless the Members decide otherwise, the fair market value of the assets shall be determined by an independent appraiser who shall be selected by the Members. The profit or loss for each unsold asset shall be determined as if the asset had been sold at fair market value and shall be allocated as provided in Section 3.2.

3.5    **Withholding.** The Members are authorized to withhold from distributions, profit allocations, or payments to other Members, in order to pay appropriate federal, state, or local government authority any amount required to be withheld pursuant to the provision of the applicable state or local law. All amounts withheld pursuant to this section shall be treated as amounts distributed to such Member pursuant to Section 3.3.

3.5    **Method of Accounting**. The Company will use the method of accounting previously determined by the Members for financial reporting and tax purposes.

Operating Agreement – [FIRM NAME], PLLC

3.6    **Amendments to this Section.** The Members are authorized, upon the advice of the Company's tax counsel, to amend this Section 3 to comply with the Internal Revenue Code (the "Code") and Regulations promulgated under Section 704(b) of the Code.

ARTICLE IV

MANAGEMENT

4.1    **Member Managed.** The management of the Company shall be vested in its Members. The Members shall be agents of the Company for the purpose of the business and its affairs. Except as otherwise limited by this Agreement, each Member shall possess all power on behalf of the Company to do all things necessary to carry out the business and affairs of the Company except as otherwise limited by this Agreement.

4.2    **Limitation on Powers of Members**. No act shall be taken, obligation incurred, or power exercised by the Company, Member, employee, or any agents of the Company on behalf of the Company with respect to any of the following, except with the unanimous written approval of its Members:

4.2.1   The lease, transfer, encumbrance, or other disposition by the Company of all or substantially all of its assets;

4.2.2   Any merger or consolidation involving the Company;

4.2.3   Any split, combination, or reclassification of any Member's interest;

4.2.4   The issuance by the Company of any additional interests or equity interests of the Company, or the admission of any person as a Member of the Company;

4.2.5   Require the Members to make any capital contribution in addition to the initial capital contributions as set forth in this Agreement;

4.2.6.   Require any Member to provide any personal guaranty except as set forth and referenced in this Agreement;

4.2.7   Remove or replace a Member;

4.2.8   Any change of the Company's name or any amendment of the Certificate of Formation or this Agreement, including, without limitation, any change in the purposes of the Company; or

4.2.9   The purchase, lease, exchange, or acquisition of any equity interest or assets of any other person, other than in the ordinary course of business.

4.2.10  The purchase, lease, exchange, or otherwise obtaining any interest in real property (including office space);

4.2.11  Borrowing, lending, or loaning any funds, assets, or other tangible property of the Company.

4.2.12  Personnel decisions including hiring or termination of employees, contractors, or agents of the Company;

4.2.13  Hiring contractors, consultants, or other service providers where the amount of services rendered exceeds $500.

4.2.14  Accepting representation of a client in which the Company will be expected to provide costs of litigation in excess of $1000; and

4.2.15  Any other action that will have a material effect on the Company or its Members including any changes to the Practice Management Principles (Exhibit 1).

Operating Agreement – [FIRM NAME], PLLC

4.3     **Deadlock of Members**. The Members shall make all efforts to resolve differences within the membership. In the event that the Members are not able to agree on an appropriate resolution, then the Member _____.

4.4     **Standard of Care.** The Members shall fulfill their duties as Members in good faith, with the care an ordinary prudent person in a like position would exercise under similar circumstances, and in a manner he or she reasonably believes to be in the best interest of the Company.

## ARTICLE V
## BANKING, PAYMENT OF EXPENSES, AND COMPENSATION

5.1     **Bank Accounts.** All funds of the Company will be deposited in a bank or brokerage account(s) in the Company's name. The Members shall determine the institution(s) where the accounts will be opened and maintained, the types of accounts, and who has authority with respect to the accounts and the funds therein.

5.2     **Organization Expenses.** All expenses incurred in connection with the organization of the Company shall be paid by the Company.

5.3     **Legal and Accounting Services.** The Company may obtain legal and accounting services to the extent reasonably necessary for the conduct of the Company's business.

5.4     **Compensation.** The Members shall be entitled to compensation. Compensation shall be made in an amount and at such time as determined by the Members.

## ARTICLE VI
## MEETING AND RECORDS

6.1     **Place of Meeting**. Meeting of the Members shall be held at such place and manner as determined by the Members, inside or outside the State of _____, pursuant to proper notice.

6.2     **Annual Meeting.** An annual meeting of the Members of the Company shall be held each year on the date and at the time as determined by the Members, who may, in their sole discretion, elect not to hold an annual meeting. Failure to hold an annual meeting at the time stated does not affect the validity of any action taken by the Company.

6.3     **Special Meeting.** Special meetings of Members, for any purpose or purposes may be called by any Member.

6.4     **Quorum.** Members holding not less than the majority (50%) in interest represented in person or by proxy shall constitute a quorum at any meeting of Members.

Operating Agreement – [FIRM NAME], PLLC

6.5    **Notice of Meetings.** A notice of all meetings, stating the place, date, and time of the meeting, shall be provided to each Member at his or her address, as shown on Schedule A, by mail at least seven (7) days prior to the meeting or by personal, telephonic, or electronic delivery at least three (3) days prior to the meeting.

6. 6    **Waiver of Notice.** Attendance of a Member at a meeting shall constitute a waiver of notice of the meeting. Notification of a meeting may also be waived in writing.

6.7    **Action without a Meeting**. Any action required or permitted to be taken by a Member, may be taken without a meeting or notice thereof, provided that such action is detailed in writing and is signed by the Member or all Members who are required to vote on such action.

6.8    **Conference Telephone Meeting**. Meetings of the Members may be held by means of conference telephone or similar communications.

6.9    **Records.** The Members shall cause the Company to keep at the principal place of business the following:
1. Current list of names and address of the Members;
2. A copy of this Operating Agreement and all attached Schedules;
3. A copy of the Certificate of Formation; and
4. Copies of the Company's federal tax returns, reports, and other financial statements for the past three (3) years.

Each Member may inspect during ordinary business hours and at the principal place of business of the Company any or all of the above records of the Company.

## ARTICLE VII

## LIMITATION OF LIABILITY, INDEPENDENT ACTIVITIES AND INDEMNIFICATION

7.1    **Limitation of Liability**.  To the extent permitted by the applicable law, this Agreement, and any applicable rules governing attorney conduct, the Members shall not be personally liable for damages, indebtedness, liability, or obligations or otherwise to the Company or any other Member, for any act, omission, breach of duty, or error in judgment performed, omitted or made by it or them in good faith and in a manner reasonably believed by it or them to be within the scope of authority granted by this Agreement, provided that such act, omission, or error in judgment does not constitute bad faith, fraud, gross negligence, intentional misconduct, or knowing violation of the law.

7.2    **Limitations to Third Parties**. The debts, obligations, and liabilities of the Company, whether arising in contract, tort, or otherwise, shall be solely the debts, obligations, and liabilities of the Company, and no Member of the Company shall be obligated personally for any such debt, obligation, or liability by reason of being a Member of the Company.

7.3    **Independent Activities.** Members may engage in or possess an interest in other businesses of any nature or description, including, but not limited to, ownership, employment by,

Operating Agreement – [FIRM NAME], PLLC

or financing, except for businesses that provide legal services substantial similar to the services of the Company.

7.4    **Indemnification by the Company**. To the extent permitted by law, Members, spouses of Members, employees, or any other agent ("Covered Persons") thereof shall be entitled to indemnification from the Company from and against any judgments, settlements, penalties, fines, or expenses of any kind incurred in a proceeding to which such Covered Person is a party because he or she is or was a Member, or was serving at the request of the Company, provided that such Covered Person acted in good faith and in a manner reasonably believed to be in the best interest of the Company, except that no Covered Person shall be entitled to indemnification from or on account of acts or omissions of the Covered Person adjudged to be gross negligence, intentional misconduct, or a knowing violation of the law.

7.5 **Indemnification by Members**. Each Member agrees to indemnify and hold the Company and its attorneys harmless from and against any and all losses, damages, or liability, including reasonable attorneys' fees and expenses, due to or arising out of any fraudulent misrepresentation or breach of any of the representations and warranties stated in Sections 2.7 and 4.4 made in this Agreement.

ARTICLE VIII
TRANSFERS, ASSIGNMENT, AND WITHDRAWAL

8.1    **Transfers Prohibited.** Except as otherwise provided in this Agreement, no Member may voluntarily or involuntarily transfer, sell, convey, encumber, assign, or otherwise dispose of (collectively, "Transfer") an interest in the Company without the prior written consent of all non-transferring Members.

8.2    **Right of First Refusal**. Notwithstanding Section 8.1, a Member ("Transferring Party") may transfer all or part of the their interest ("Interest") in the Company provided they do so in compliance with the terms below:

8.2.1    The Transferring Party must provide written notice to all other Members, stating the price and terms on which the Member is prepared to sell his/her interest ("Offer").

8.2.2    The Company shall have the first option to purchase the Interest from the transferor on the terms listed in the Offer. The Company shall have thirty (30) days after the receipt of the Offer to exercise its option to purchase by providing written notice to the transferor.

8.2.3    If the Company fails to notify the transferring party of its desire to exercise its option, then the Company will be deemed to have waived its right to acquire the Interest on the terms described in the Offer and the transferring Member may sell and convey the Interest consistent with the Offer to another Member of the Company; provided, however, if the sale to another Member is made on terms

Operating Agreement – [FIRM NAME], PLLC

that are more favorable then stated in the original Offer, the transferring Member must reoffer the sale of the Interest to the Company at the new terms and price prior to offering it to another Member.

8.2.4 The Member desiring to purchase the Interest from the transferring party shall have thirty (30) days after the receipt of the Offer to exercises his or her option by providing written notice to the transferor. If the Member fails to notify the transferring party of his or her desire to exercise his or her option, then the Member will have waived his or her right to acquire the Interest on the terms described in the Offer, and the transferring party may sell and convey the Interest consistent with the Offer to any other person or entity with the approval of the non-transferring Member(s); provided, however, if the sale to another person or entity is made on terms that are more favorable than stated in the original Offer, the transferring Member must reoffer the sale of the Interest first to the Company and, if the Company does not exercise its option, then to the Member at the new terms and price prior to offering it to another person or entity.

8.2.5 In the event that neither the Company nor the other Members elect to purchase the Interest, the transferring party may sell and convey the interest consistent with the Offer to any other person licensed to practice law in the state in which he/she practices or entity with the approval of the non-transferring Members, provided that such Transfer shall be made on terms no more favorable than offered to the Company and its Members. The transferee shall retain only economic rights in the Company and shall not be admitted as a full Member without the unanimous written approval of the non-transferring Member(s).

8.2.6 Notwithstanding the foregoing provisions of Section 8.2, should the remaining Member(s) be entitled to and elect to acquire all the Interests of the other Members of the Company in accordance with the provisions of 8.2, such that the Company becomes a single Member Limited Liability Company, the acquiring Member may assign the right to acquire Interests to a spouse, lineal descendent, or an affiliated entity if the assignment is reasonably believed to be necessary to continue the existence of the Company as a Limited Liability Company.

8.3 **Invalid Transfer of Interest.** Each Member hereby acknowledges that any transfer of any Interest or portion thereof in violation of the terms of Section 8.1 shall be deemed invalid, null and void, and of no force or effect.

8.4 **Withdrawal.** A Member may not withdraw from the Company prior to dissolution and winding up of the Company. However, in the event a Member chooses to withdraw prior to dissolution that Member shall receive his or her share of the fair market value of the business in payments over a period of five (5) years beginning on the effective date of withdrawal unless the Company and Members agree otherwise. The Company and the withdrawing Member shall mutually agree on fair market value, and all expenses associated with making such determination shall be shared equally by the Company and the withdrawing Member.

Operating Agreement – [FIRM NAME], PLLC

8.4.1 If any Member becomes legally disqualified to practice law, such Member shall automatically withdraw from the Company and all its interests (other than interests as creditor or vested rights under a bona fide retirement program if any). Such disqualification to practice law shall be deemed to constitute an irrevocable offer by such disqualified Member to sell his or her Membership interest to the Company pursuant to Section 8.4 of the Agreement.

8.4.2 In the event a Member withdraws as a result of section 9.1.3 below, then the Terminating Member or his or her estate shall receive its share of the fair market value of the business. Payments shall be made yearly but such amounts shall not in exceed fifteen percent (15%) of net revenues available each year. In such circumstances, the Company shall determine fair market value of the Company, and expenses associated with making such determination shall be borne by the Company. The Company shall make payments to withdrawing Member in a timely manner.

8.4.3. At the time of withdrawal, for any reason whatsoever, the withdrawing Member agrees to carry tail end attorney malpractice insurance for five/seven/ten (5/7/10) years. The withdrawing Member shall provide proof of such insurance to the Company and shall list [Firm Name], PLLC as a named insured.

## ARTICLE IX
## DISSOLUTION AND LIQUIDATION

9.1 **Events of Dissolution**. The Company shall be dissolved upon the happening of any of the following events:

9.1.1 Unanimous written consent of all the Members;

9.1.2 Any event that makes it unlawful or impossible to carry on the business of the Company;

9.1.3 Death, expulsion, bankruptcy, or the occurrence of any event that terminates the continued membership of a Member to the Company, unless the remaining Member(s) within 120 days after the date of that event, elects to continue the business of the Company and such Member(s) are licensed in the state in which one of the Company's principal office resides. In the event a Member elects to continue the business, the Terminating Member or his or her estate shall be deemed a withdrawn Member for purposes of this Agreement and Section 8.4 shall apply;

9.1.4 Sale, transfer, or other disposition of all or substantially of the Company's assets; or

9.1.5 Any other event causing dissolution under the laws of the State of _____.

9.2 **Procedure for Winding up and Dissolution.** If the Company is dissolved, the Members shall wind up its affairs by taking a full account of the Company's assets and

Operating Agreement – [FIRM NAME], PLLC

liabilities. Upon winding up, the Company and its assets shall be distributed first to creditors who are not Members of the Company in satisfaction of any debts of the Company, then to Members or Interest Holders in discharge of any debts owed to the Members or Interest Holders, and any excess amount available after the Members have paid all of the Company's claims and obligations shall be distributed to the Members in accordance with Section 3 of this Agreement.

9.3    **Termination.** The Members shall comply with any applicable law pertaining to the winding up of the affairs of the Company and the final distribution of assets. Upon the completion of the winding up, liquidation, and distribution of assets, and the filing of a Certificate of Cancellation, the Company shall be deemed terminated.

ARTICLE X
GENERAL PROVISIONS

10.1    **Amendment.** Amendments to this Agreement may be proposed by any Member. A proposed amendment will be adopted and made effective only with the unanimous written approval of all the Members.

10.2    **Modification.** No modification or amendment of any provision of this Agreement shall be binding on any Member without the prior written consent of all the Members.

10.3    **Governing Law.** This Agreement and the rights and obligations of the parties under it are governed by and interpreted in accordance with the laws of the State of _____.

10.4    **Dispute Resolution.** Any dispute, controversy, or claim arising out of or relating to this Agreement, or the breach thereof, shall be settled first by non-binding mediation and if a party is not satisfied by the results thereof, then by binding arbitration in accordance with the commercial arbitration rules of the American Arbitration Association ("AAA") unless all Members agree otherwise. The arbitration proceedings shall be conducted in _____ County, _____, or such other location as the parties may mutually agree upon. The parties shall mutually agree on an arbitrator. If the parties are not able to mutually agree on a single arbitrator, each party will select an arbitrator who, working together, will appoint a third arbitrator to serve as the sole arbiter of the dispute. The prevailing party may enter any judgment or award rendered by the arbitrator in any court having jurisdiction thereof.

10.5    **Complete Agreement**. This Agreement constitutes the entire and exclusive understanding and agreement of its Members. It supersedes all prior written and oral statements, including any prior representation, statement, condition or warranty.

10.6    **Severability.** In the event any provision of this Agreement is held to be illegal, invalid, or unenforceable to any extent, the legality, validity and enforceability of the remainder of this Agreement shall not be affected thereby and shall remain in full force and effect and shall be enforced to the greatest extent permitted by law.

Operating Agreement – [FIRM NAME], PLLC


    10.7    **Notice**. All notices required to be given by this Agreement shall be in writing and sent to the appropriate address as listed on <u>Schedule A</u> and will be effective upon receipt.

Operating Agreement – [FIRM NAME], PLLC

LIMITED LIABILITY COMPANY OPERATING AGREEMENT
OF
[Firm Name], PLLC

SIGNATURE PAGE

IN WITNESS WHEREOF, the parties hereto have executed this Agreement as of the date and year first written above.

COMPANY
[Firm Name], PLLC

MEMBERS


By _____
[NAME], Member, [Firm Name], PLLC


By _____
[Name], Member, [Firm Name], PLLC

Operating Agreement – [FIRM NAME], PLLC

LIMITED LIABILITY COMPANY OPERATING AGREEMENT
OF
{Firm Name], PLLC

SCHEDULE A

MEMBERS

| MEMBERS NAME/ADDRESS | CAPITAL CONTRIBUTIONS | PERCENTAGE INTEREST |
|---|---|---|
| | | |
| TOTAL | $ | 100% |

Operating Agreement – [FIRM NAME], PLLC

LIMITED LIABILITY COMPANY OPERATING AGREEMENT
OF
[Firm Name], PLLC

SCHEDULE B
"PRINCIPAL OFFICE"

State of [_____]

Operating Agreement – [FIRM NAME], PLLC

LIMITED LIABILITY COMPANY OPERATING AGREEMENT
OF
[Firm Name], PLLC

SCHEDULE C
"CONSENT TO SERVE AS REGISTERED AGENT"

     I, _____, hereby consent to serve as Registered Agent in the State of _____ for [Firm Name], PLLC. I understand that as agent for the limited liability company named above, it will be my responsibility to receive service of process in its name; to forward mail to the limited liability company; and immediately notify the Office of Secretary of State in the event of my resignation or any changes in the registered office of the limited liability company for which I am an agent.

     By: _____

     Date: _____ 2015.

Operating Agreement – [FIRM NAME], PLLC

LIMITED LIABILITY COMPANY OPERATING AGREEMENT
OF
[Firm Name], PLLC

EXHIBIT 1

PRACTICE MANAGEMENT PRINCIPALS

The following provisions shall govern the law practice of the Company. The Members may mutually agree on updates to these principals from time to time. The Practice Management Principles are governed by the Company Operating Agreement and are incorporated in the Company Operating Agreement by reference. In the event of a conflict between these principals and the Company Operating Agreement, the Company Operating Agreement shall govern.

1. Business Purpose. The Members intend for the Company to be a for-profit [insert description].

2. Work Hours and Location. The Members agree to work full time from their respective professional offices during the business week. The Members shall be permitted to work from home as their schedule and client matters permit. The Members acknowledge the time and attention certain client and Company matters may require, and shall work additional hours as may be needed.

3. Vacation. The Members shall endeavor to schedule vacations and any other time off to avoid disruptions in the affairs of the business or schedules of other members.

4. Distributions. The Members shall endeavor to evaluate distribution potential every quarter and shall issue such distributions in accordance with the Company Operating Agreement.

5. Management. The Members, shall share in the day to day management activities of the Company. When applicable, the parties shall seek additional contractors, consultants, or employees to help support the business of the Company.

6. Control of Docket. Each Member shall control and be responsible for his/her legal work. Subject to the limitations in Section 4.2 of the Company Operating Agreement and any applicable rules of professional conduct, each Member may decide for himself/herself what cases to take and what clients to represent. To avoid conflicts of interest and friction within the Company, Members shall use best efforts to confer with each other before agreeing to take on a new matter or expand representation on an existing matter.

# Table of Contents of Employee Manual

## EMPLOYEE MANUAL CONTENTS

1.   Introduction
2.   Equal Employment Opportunity, Harassment & Sexual Harassment
3.   Orientation Period
4.   Categories of Employment
5.   General Employment Policies
6.   Code of Conduct
7.   Compensation & Hours of Work
8.   Holidays and Leaves of Absence
9.   Americans With Disabilities Act
10.  Employment Standards
11.  Confidentiality of Employee Records
12.  Social Security Privacy Protection Policy
13.  New Hires, Rehires, Promotions and Transfers
14.  Payroll Procedure
15.  Medical Benefits
16.  Pension Benefits
17.  Vacation and Other Benefits
18.  Termination & Exit Interview
19.  Confidentiality Agreement
20.  Severance
21.  Health Insurance Upon Resignation, Termination or Disability
22.  Smoking
23.  Jury Duty
24.  Dress Code
25.  Drugs and Alcohol Policy
26.  Electronic Communications
27.  Blogging & Online Personal Communication Policy
28.  Nondisclosure Agreement
29.  Safeguarding Agreement
30.  Receipt of Employee Handbook

## Non-Engagement Letter: Declining Representation

Reprinted with permission of Lawyers Mutual
from Attorney-Client Agreements Toolkit

RISK MANAGEMENT HANDOUTS OF LAWYERS MUTUAL

## NON-ENGAGEMENT LETTER: DECLINING REPRESENTATION FOLLOWING REVIEW

[Date]

[Client Name]
[Client Address]
[Client Address]

Re: Confirmation of Non-Representation
    File ID:

Dear [Client's Name]:

You recently requested that [Law Firm] evaluate your claim against [Opposing Party] to decide whether or not the firm would like to represent you in this matter. Unfortunately, after a review of the documents provided, I have concluded that [Law Firm] will be unable to serve as your counsel. However, we appreciate the opportunity to review your situation and would encourage you to contact us again with any future legal needs.

Please understand that [Law Firm] is not expressing any opinions on the validity or merits of your claim, nor are we attempting to convey any likelihood that you will or will not prevail. We strongly suggest that you obtain a second opinion and want to emphasize that you should not be deterred from seeking another attorney simply because we were unable to provide our services.

Statutes of limitation place limits on the amount of time that you have to file a claim, and delay can potentially bar you from bringing suit against [Opposing Party] or recovering any damages to which you may be entitled. If you do not have another attorney in mind, we recommend that you immediately contact the [State/County] Bar Association's Lawyer Referral Service at [Phone Number] .

You have not been charged any fees in connection with our evaluation of this matter. All documents provided to us have been returned with this letter. Thank you again for the opportunity to evaluate your situation and please do not hesitate to contact us with any questions regarding this letter.

Sincerely,

[Attorney's Name]
[Law Firm]

## Non-Engagement Letter: Conflict of Interest

ATTORNEY-CLIENT AGREEMENTS TOOLKIT

Reprinted with permission of Lawyers Mutual
from Attorney-Client Agreements Toolkit

## NON-ENGAGEMENT LETTER: CONFLICT OF INTEREST

[Date]

[Client Name]
[Client Address]
[Client Address]

Re: Confirmation of Non-Representation
    File ID:

Dear [Client's Name]:

Thank you for your visit yesterday regarding _____ _____
_____. It was a pleasure to speak with you.  Regrettably, however, [Law Firm] will not be able to assist you in this matter.

As we discussed yesterday, [Law Firm] would not be able to formally offer our services until we had the opportunity to investigate whether any of our current or former clients would be adversely affected by our participation in your matter. After we spoke, this formal search was performed and I learned that a conflict of interest does exist.  Unfortunately, this situation cannot be resolved in a way that would permit [Law Firm] to represent you in this matter.

Please understand that [Law Firm] expressing no opinions on the merits of your claim. Any comments made were offered based solely on memory of the law and without the benefits of research, a complete understanding of the facts or time to reflect on the issue. Because of this, any such comment was not intended to serve as definitive legal advice.  We strongly urge you to seek other counsel in this matter and remind you that you must not delay because of the legal time limits that can bar you from raising your claim once lapsed.  If you do not have another attorney in mind, we recommend that you immediately contact the [State/County] Bar Association's Lawyer Referral Service at [Phone Number].

Thank you again for your consideration, but we must decline representation.  Please do not hesitate to contact us with any questions regarding this letter.

Sincerely,

[Attorney's Name]
[Law Firm]

*Note: This is a sample form only and is written for the general purposes of facilitating clear expectations and avoiding misunderstandings between an attorney and client. It is not intended as legal advice or opinion and will not provide absolute protection against a malpractice action.*

# Intake Sheet (general)

## __Client Intake__          Date: _____

Name: _____

Address: _____

_____

Telephone  Business: _____ ☐ Preferred Method of Contact

           Mobile: _____ ☐ Preferred Method of Contact

           Home: _____ ☐ Preferred Method of Contact

           _____ ☐ Confidential Method of Contact

E-mail
Address:  Personal: _____

        Business: _____

Does anyone have access to your telephone or e-mail? _____

Name of Business: _____

Business Address: _____

_____

Name of All Business Entities: _____

Name of all Business Owners: _____

Insurance Information:    Client    _____
                                      (Insurance Carrier)

Type of Legal Matter: ☐ Litigation   ☐ Corporate  ☐ Real Estate  ☐ Matrimonial
                         ☐ Personal Injury  ☐ Insurance  ☐ IP        ☐ T&E
                         ☐ Municipal     ☐ L&T                ☐ Environmental

Statute of Limitations and/or critical dates: _____

Referred by: _____

Preferred Method of Payment: _____ Cash _____ Check _____ Credit Card

**Office Use Only**

Consultation Attorney(s)/Notes: _____

_____

_____

_____

_____

_____

_____

_____

_____

_____

_____

_____

_____

_____

_____

_____

_____

_____

_____

_____

_____

_____

_____

Recommendation: _____

Fee Arrangement: _____

☐ Conflict Check
☐ Added to CP
☐ Confirmation letter sent

# Intake Sheet (accident)

## INTAKE (Accident)

Intake Date: _____      Intake by:      _____
Attorney: _____      Approved:      _____
Assign to: _____      Input:      _____
Ref by: _____      Relation to client:      _____
Prior Atty: _____Consent: _____
_____
_____

**Client data:**

Name: _____
Address: _____
_____

Home Phone: _____      Work Phone: _____
Cell Phone: _____      E Mail: _____
Facebook: _____      My Space: _____
Twitter: _____      Others: _____
DOB: _____      Driver's Lic.: _____
Marital status: _____      Spouse: _____
Children: _____      Parents: _____
Emergency contact: _____      Phone: _____
Primary language: _____      Other lang.: _____
Translator required: _____      Sex: Circle one: Male or Female

**Social Security:**
Social Security No.: _____

I am on social security disability: _____
I am collecting social security: _____
I will collect at age 66: _____

Criminal record: Yes___    No___    Details: _____

**Accident Type** (check appropriate type): -Auto: _____ circle one-Driver/Passenger
–Slip and Fall: ___          -Pedestrian: ____          -Other: _____

Date: _____    Time: _____    Weather: _____
Location: _____
Description: _____
_____

## AUTO ACCIDENT

Defendant Driver:
Name: _____          Make: _____
Address: _____       Model: _____
          _____       Color: _____
Phone: _____         Year: _____
Plate No.: _____                   Damage: _____


Defendant Owner:
Name: _____
Address: _____
Phone: _____

Defendant Insurance:
Name: _____
Address: _____
          _____
Claim rep: _____


Plaintiff Passengers:
_____
_____

Witnesses:
_____
_____

Surveillance cameras at/or near scene?      Yes___      No___

Police: _____      Report No.: _____

Police Description: _____
                     _____
                     _____

MV-104 Report Filed:          Yes__ No__

Vehicle damage: _____      Photographs: _____      Collision Ins. _____

No Fault Insurance: _____

_____

_____

Policy Number: _____

Claim Number: _____

Adjuster: _____      Phone Number: _____

Adjuster Fax Number: _____

Application Filed:     Yes_____     No_____

UM/SUM Insurance:

      Client owned auto:

           Insurer: _____      Policy No.:_____

      Resident/relative owned auto:

           Insurer: _____      Policy No.:_____

Umbrella Insurance:

           Insurer: _____      Policy No.:_____

**Is the No-Fault Open**? _____

Accident diagram:

## PREMISES ACCIDENT

Defendant:

        Name: _____

        Address: _____

         _____

        Phone: _____

Defendant homeowner:

        Name: _____

        Address: _____

        Phone: _____

Defendant Homeowner Insurance:

        Name: _____

        Address: _____

         _____

         _____

        Claim rep: _____

        Claim no.: _____

        Phone: _____

Other potential defendants:

_____

_____

_____

Municipal defendants:

_____

_____

_____

Notice witnesses:

_____

_____

_____

Actual witnesses:

_____

_____

Photos:     \_\_Yes     \_\_No     If yes, please provide.

## DAMAGES/INJURIES

**Injuries:** _____
_____
_____
_____

**Client's Private Health Insurance:**

_____
_____

Claim No: _____  Policy No.: _____

**Worker's Comp:** In scope of employment on date of accident?
Yes_____  No_____

**Medicare/Medicaid:** Recipient of benefits?
Yes_____  No_____
Medicare/Medicaid No.: _____

**Hospital:** _____
_____
_____

Date(s) of treatment: In _____  Out_____

**Doctors:**

Name: _____  Phone: _____
Address: _____  Specialty: _____
_____  Referred: _____

Name: _____  Phone: _____
Address: _____  Specialty: _____
_____  Referred: _____

Name: _____  Phone: _____
Address: _____  Specialty: _____
_____  Referred: _____

**Economic Loss:**

Employer: _____        Phone: _____
Address: _____        Fax: _____
_____        Wage: _____
Job title: _____

Time Lost
From Work: _____

Were you on the job at the time of the accident? Yes____ No____
Were you heading to or from work at the time of the accident? _____
If on the job at the time of the accident, do you have a Workers Compensation attorney?

**Prior Injuries and Claims:**

Prior Injuries/Disabilities: _____

Date Occurred and Facts: _____
_____
_____

Treating Physicians: _____
_____
_____
_____

Hospitals: _____
_____
_____

**Prior Claims/Suits:**

Date of accident: _____
Nature of claim: _____
Attorney: _____
_____
_____

Suit Filed: _____        Date: _____        Index No.: _____

Result of Claim: _____

# Intake Sheet (criminal)

## CRIMINAL CLIENT FACT SHEET

Last Name/Corp.: _____ First:_____ Middle:_____

Address: _____

City: _____ State: _____ Zip: _____

Home Tel. No.: _____ Work Tel. No.: _____

Cell No.: _____ E-mail Address: _____

Driver I.D. No.: _____ DOB: _____ Age: _____

Social Security No.: ___ ___ ___ - ___ ___ - ___ ___ ___ ___

File Name: People/USA v. _____

Referred by: _____ Ref. Fee: _____

    Address: _____

Attorney(s) Assigned: _____

Date Opened: _____

Next Court Appearance Date: _____ Time: _____

County: _____ Courthouse: _____

Judge/Courtroom: _____ Docket/Indict. No.: _____

Type of Matter: _____

### SUB-CATEGORY MENU

0 – CRIMINAL – FELONY COMPL.       5 – TRAFFIC – DWI/FEL
1 – CRIMINAL – MISD.               6 – FEDERAL
3 – CRIMINAL INDICT/SCI          7 – MISD/FEL ENV./CON/LAW
4 – TRAFFIC – DWI/MISD          8 – SUBPOENAS/INVEST
                                9 – MISC.

_____ Demand Served _____
_____ Notice Served _____
_____ Discovery Notice Served _____

### CRIMINAL CLIENT FACT SHEET

Marital Status: _____ Spouse's Name: _____ No. of Children: ___

Employment: _____

_____

Nature: _____ Length of Emp.: _____ Salary: _____

If a minor, parent's names and employment: _____

_____

Military Service: _____

Charges: _____ Docket #: _____

_____ Docket #: _____

_____ Docket #: _____

_____ Docket #: _____

_____ Docket #: _____

Bail:     Amount: _____ How posted: _____

Name of Bondsman: _____

Bail Assignment: _____

Opposing Attorney Info.:

Office/Agency: _____

Name: _____

Address: _____

Tel.: _____ Fax: _____

CO-DEPENDANTS:  Name: _____ Atty.: _____

Tel.: _____

Name: _____ Atty.: _____

Tel.: _____

## **CRIMINAL CLIENT FACT SHEET**

Date and Time of Arrest: _____

Place of Arrest: _____

Does Client Reside at Place of Arrest? _____

Criminal Case Pending at Time of Arrest? Yes _____ No _____

Confession: Written: _____ Oral: _____ None: _____

Search Warrant: Yes _____ No _____ Unknown _____

Presently on: Probation/Parole _____

Name of Probation/Parole Officer: _____

| Year | Charge | Location | Disposition | Comments |
|------|--------|----------|-------------|----------|
| _____ | _____ | _____ | _____ | _____ |
| _____ | _____ | _____ | _____ | _____ |
| _____ | _____ | _____ | _____ | _____ |
| _____ | _____ | _____ | _____ | _____ |

FACTS: _____
_____
_____
_____
_____
_____
_____
_____
_____
_____

# Intake Sheet (will/estate plan)

### WILL INTAKE FORM

Full legal name: _____

Address: _____ City: _____ Zip: _____

Home Telephone: (____)_____ Social Security No.: _____

Cell Number: (____)_____ Date of Birth: _____

E-mail : _____ indicate if private ___ or public____

Do you have an existing ___will _____healthcare proxy ____living will _____power of atty

Who prepared these documents? _____

Marital Status:
_____ single _____ married _____ divorced ____ widowed ____ domestic partner relationship

If married, name of spouse _____

If domestic partnership, name of domestic partner _____

If divorced, date of divorce if you know it _____state and county of divorce_____

CHILDREN:

1)Name_____ birthday_____

Address_____

2) Name _____ birthday _____

Address_____

3) Name _____ birthday _____

Address_____

4) Name_____ birthday_____

Address_____

PARENTS (if living):

Father: _____

Address_____

Mother: _____

Address_____

SIBLINGS (if living)

1) Name _____

Address_____

2) Name _____

Address_____

3) Name_____

Address_____

4) Name _____

Address_____

Will and Trust Information:

ANY SPECIFIC BEQUESTS?

Name: _____ City: _____ State:_____

Description of Bequest _____

Name: _____ City: _____ State:_____

Description of Bequest: _____

Name: _____ City: _____ State:_____

Description of Bequest: _____

WHAT DO YOU WANT TO DO WITH THE BALANCE OF YOUR ESTATE?

_____

_____

Executor: _____ Telephone: (___) _____

Address: _____ City: _____ Zip:_____

Alternate Executor: _____ Telephone:(___)

Address: _____ City: _____ Zip:_____

Guardian for Children:_____Telephone_____

Address:_____

Alternate Guardian for Children: _____Telephone_____

Address:_____

ISSUES TO TALK ABOUT:

_____

_____

Contest Anticipated?      □No      □Yes      Explain:

_____

_____

Post-Death Instructions:

□Burial  Where: _____City: _____ State:_____

Memorial service or funeral?  Describe:

_____

_____

□Cremation      Disposition of remains:

_____

_____

Person who will make arrangements:      □Executor      □Other (see below)

Name: _____      Telephone: (___) _____

Address: _____      City: _____ Zip:_____

Has client pre-arranged any post-death services? _____

_____

SUMMARY OF ASSETS

1) REAL PROPERTY: _____

Who owns it? _____

2) _____

Who owns it? _____

LIFE INSURANCE

1) (Company and policy number if you have it):

_____

Face amount:_____

Benficiaries:_____

2)  (Company and policy number if you have it)_____

Face Amount:_____

Beneficiaries:_____

BANK ACCOUNTS

Bank_____

Account name and number_____

Approx. amount_____

Bank_____

Account name and number

Approximate amount

Additional accounts, numbers and values:_____

RETIREMENT, 401Ks, IRAs, PENSION.:

1)Institution_____

Value:_____

2)Institution:_____

Value:_____

3)Institution:_____

Value:_____

STOCKS, BONDS, MUTUAL FUNDS, ETC.:

Institution_____

Value;_____

Institution: _____

Value:_____

Institution: _____

Value:_____

Additional account info:

OTHER ASSETS (INCLUDING COLLECTIBLES, TIME SHARES, ART WORK, EXPENSIVE JEWELRY, BOATS, EXPENSIVE VEHICLES, ETC.):

FOR LIVING WILL AND HEALTHCARE PROXIES

Wishes re: healthcare if ill:

# Consultation Sheet (matrimonial/family)

**CONSULTATION SHEET**


**DATE OF CONSULT:** _____


**NAME OF CLIENT:** _____

**ADDRESS:** _____

**TELEPHONE:** _____

**SPOUSE'S NAME:** _____


**BRIEF DESCRIPTION:** _____

_____

_____

_____

_____

_____

_____

_____


**FEE QUOTED:** _____

**REFERRED BY:** _____

# Retainer Agreement (for formation of LLC)

## [FIRM LETTERHEAD]

[Date]

[Client Names]
123 Any Street
Anywhere, New York 10111

Re: <u>Retainer Agreement</u>

Dear [Client Names]:

Thank you for your interest in retaining [**Firm**] in connection with the formation of a limited liability company (the "LLC"). This letter will confirm the scope and terms of our representation and will ensure that we have a clear understanding of these matters from the outset.

SCOPE OF REPRESENTATION

We will be representing the LLC and we will not be representing either of you individually. There may be substantial conflicts of interests between you and the LLC and between each of you. Accordingly, we recommend that each of you consider retaining separate counsel.

The scope of this representation will include meeting with you to discuss the significant [**tax and**] legal issues regarding the formation of the LLC. We will prepare and draft the Articles of Organization and Operating Agreement of the LLC for your review and approval and, assuming you decide to form a New York LLC, file the Articles of Organization with the Secretary of State, obtain the necessary affidavit of publication and file the affidavit of publication with the Secretary of State. [**We recommend that you discuss the tax and accounting issues regarding the LLC with an accountant. We will not obtain the tax identification number for the LLC or make the necessary tax election.**]

FEES AND COSTS

Our fees for services will be based upon a variety of facts, including the time and labor involved; the difficulty of the questions and the skill required to perform those services properly; time limitations imposed either by you or by the circumstances; the nature and length of the professional relationship between us; and the experience of the lawyers assigned to do the work. The hourly billing rates for attorneys in our firm vary and are re-adjusted periodically. Our current schedule of fees is annexed. [**Alternate: We will bill you for our work in this matter based upon our normal hourly rates. My hourly rate is $ _____ and I anticipate that I will perform most of the services on this matter. We estimate the total fee will be approximately $_____.**]

Beyond hourly fees, certain other costs and expenses may be incurred in this representation. We estimate that filing fees in the amount of $_____ and publication fees in the amount of $_____ will be incurred. **[Other disbursements might include corporate service fees, messenger and overnight courier fees, investigation fees, charges for obtaining copies of records, photocopying expenses, computerized legal research, travel expenses, and similar items.]** These costs and expenses will be billed in the same manner as our fees or we may ask you to make direct payment to the party making the charge.

INITIAL RETAINER AND PERIODIC STATEMENTS

We will require an initial retainer of $_____ to be held in escrow and applied to payment of fees and disbursements. We will render a **[monthly]** statement to you for services rendered at the conclusion of this matter. Our statement[s] will indicate the nature of the work done **[during the time period covered by the statement]**, and the fees for those services, as well as costs advanced by us and credits applied toward those costs and disbursements. Invoices are payable upon receipt.

TERMINATION OF REPRESENTATION

Our representation may be terminated by you or this law firm at any time. If this firm wishes to withdraw from the representation for any reason, you will not unreasonably withhold consent for us to do so. If at any time you wish to terminate our representation, please advise us in writing, and we will then deliver a final statement to you and return the balance of the escrow deposit, adjusted for work done and costs advanced through the date of termination. If we should determine to withdraw as counsel, we will return the adjusted balance with a final statement in the same manner.

APPROVAL

If you agree to the terms of our representation as set forth in this letter, please sign on the lines provided at the close of this letter and return the signed copy with a check in the amount of the initial retainer to us as soon as possible. By signing this letter each of you will also be agreeing to pay our invoice directly and to seek reimbursement from the LLC.

Thank you very much again for having asked us to undertake this representation. Should you have any questions concerning our fees and costs, or the scope of the legal services we will provide, please call me at your convenience.

Very truly yours,
[Name of Attorney]

Enclosure

READ AND AGREED TO:

_____        _____
[Client Name]                          [Client Name]

# Retainer Agreement (lump sum retainer with replenishment)

## Retainer Agreement
(Lump Sum Retainer With Replenishment)

[DATE]

**VIA ELECTRONIC MAIL**

ADDRESS
ADDRESS
ADDRESS
ADDRESS

           Re:      **[DESCRIBE MATTER].**

Dear [CLIENT NAME]:

       Thank you for deciding to retain [FIRM NAME], PLLC ("[FIRM NAME]") to represent you regarding the referenced matter. This letter formalizes this retention as required by applicable Rules of Professional Conduct as well as setting forth how [FIRM NAME] proposes to staff the matter, describes the fee arrangement, discusses certain confidentiality obligations, and addresses conflict of interest understandings. This letter also will be applicable to all other matters in which you may engage us. [FIRM NAME] makes no guarantees, promises, or representations as to the success or failure of this endeavor.

       1.     Staffing. [Partner] will have primary responsibility for your legal matter with assistance as required from others in the firm. [FIRM NAME] will provide those legal services reasonably required to represent you in connection with the matters set forth in the preceding paragraph, and [FIRM NAME] ordinarily does not charge attorney's fees to meet, correspond, or otherwise communicate with you unless the meeting, correspondence, or communication relates to performing legal services, *i.e.*, preparing for a negotiation, deposition, testimony, or other communications related to specific legal work [FIRM NAME] will perform. [FIRM NAME] reserves the right to assign any of our attorneys or staff to perform services related to the matter. [FIRM NAME] will take reasonable steps to keep you informed of the progress for the matter, and to respond to your inquiries.

       2.     Basis of Legal Services. The standard hourly rates currently range from approximately $250 per hour for its junior associates to approximately $450 for its partners. [FIRM NAME] will bill for [Partner]'s time at $450.00 per hour, and the hourly rate for [FIRM NAME] associates will be $250 per hour. Paralegals will be billed at $100.00 per hour. The legal fees apply only to the referenced matter, and do not have any effect on other matters to which you may elect to have [FIRM NAME] represent you. You must provide [FIRM NAME] with a Retainer in the amount of $15,000.00. Each month, [FIRM NAME] will deduct from the Retainer the legal fees and costs incurred. [FIRM NAME] will deliver to you an invoice reflecting the legal fees and costs deducted from the Retainer, and you agree each month to

[CLIENT NAME]
[DATE]
Page 2 of 4

replenish the Retainer by the amount deducted. At the conclusion of the matter, [FIRM NAME] will return to you the balance remaining in the Retainer account. [FIRM NAME] may at any time request you increase the amount of funds held in the Retainer, and you agree to provide such additional funds upon request.

3.     Payment of Fees and Other Charges. If third-party charges are incurred in connection with the representation, such as printing bills, filing fees, court reporting fees, and expert witness fees, [FIRM NAME]'s normal practice is to forward such statements directly to you for payment. Otherwise, [FIRM NAME] may advance certain fees and seek reimbursement from you. [FIRM NAME] will incur various costs and expenses in performing legal services under the Engagement Letter. You agree to pay for those costs and expenses in addition to the legal fees. For purposes of illustration, the costs and expenses commonly include long-distance telephone calls, messenger and other delivery fees, postage, parking and other travel expenses, photocopying and other reproduction costs, clerical staff overtime, word processing charges, charges for computer time, and other similar items. All costs and expenses will be charged at Smith Jones' cost.

4.     Conflicts and Confidential Information. [FIRM NAME] is a full service law firm that frequently introduces existing clients to other clients or potential clients. Therefore, other present or future clients of the firm may have contact with you at some point. To prevent any future misunderstanding, and to preserve the firm's ability to represent you and its other clients, this paragraph 4 confirms the following understanding about certain conflicts of interest issues:

a.     [FIRM NAME] will not represent any other client in any matter in which they also represent you unless [FIRM NAME] has your express agreement that [FIRM NAME] may do so. Nor will [FIRM NAME] represent any other client in a matter where [FIRM NAME]'s other client is substantially and adversely related to you in a matter that the firm is handling for you unless you expressly agree that we may do so.

b.     In the absence of a conflict as described in subparagraph (a) above, you acknowledge that [FIRM NAME] will be free to represent any other client either generally or in any specific matter in which you may have an interest.

c.     The effect of subparagraph (b) above is that [FIRM NAME] may represent another client on any issue or matter in which you might have an interest, including, but not limited to:

     (i)     Preparation and negotiation of agreements; licenses; mergers and acquisitions; joint ventures; loans and financings; securities offerings; bankruptcy or insolvency; patents, copyrights, trademarks, trade secrets, or other intellectual property; real estate; government contracts; the protection of rights; representation before regulatory authorities; and

[CLIENT NAME]
[DATE]
Page 3 of 4

          (ii)     Representation and advocacy with respect to legislative issues, policy issues, administrative proceedings, or rulemakings.

     d.     [FIRM NAME] does not view this advance consent to permit unauthorized disclosure or use of any client confidences. Under applicable Rules of Professional Conduct, [FIRM NAME] remains obligated to, and shall, preserve the confidentiality of all confidential information you provides to them. [FIRM NAME] may obtain nonpublic personal information about you or nonpublic information about You in the course of this representation, and they will restrict access to all such information to [FIRM NAME] personnel who need to know that information in connection with the representation, and, as appropriate, to third parties assisting in that representation. [FIRM NAME] maintains appropriate physical, electronic, and procedural safeguards to protect all such information. [FIRM NAME] does not disclose nonpublic personal information about its clients or former clients to anyone, except as required or provided by law and applicable Rules of Professional Conduct.

     e.     [FIRM NAME] will not disclose to you or you, or use on your behalf any documents or information with respect to which [FIRM NAME] owes a duty of confidentiality to another client or person.

     f.     The fact [FIRM NAME] may have your documents or information, which may be relevant to another matter in which they represent another client, will not prevent [FIRM NAME] from representing that other client in that matter without any further consent from you. But in such a case, [FIRM NAME] will put in place screening or other arrangements to ensure and maintain the confidentiality of your documents or information.

     5.     Client Identification. This confirms [FIRM NAME]'s understanding that you is their client for the specific matters on which it has engaged us, and [FIRM NAME] shall not be deemed to represent any of your affiliates unless we expressly agree in writing to do so. Any proposed expansion of your representation to include any other affiliated entities is subject to and contingent upon executing an engagement letter directly with any such affiliated entity.

     6.     Client Duties. You agree to be truthful with [FIRM NAME], to cooperate, to keep [FIRM NAME] informed of developments to abide by this letter, to pay any amounts due on time, and to keep [FIRM NAME] advised of your address, telephone number, and your whereabouts.

     7.     Application of these Terms. This letter governs [FIRM NAME]'s relationship with you, even if you do not sign and return a copy of the letter. If you retain [FIRM NAME] as agent for a third party, you confirm that you have authority to retain us on such terms. If you

[CLIENT NAME]
[DATE]
Page 4 of 4

disagree with any of the terms, you should so advise me immediately by return correspondence. This letter supersedes any prior agreement with respect to this engagement to provide professional services to you. This Agreement is governed by Florida law, and any dispute arising under or relating to this Agreement will be resolved in Florida.

      8.    <u>Discharge and Withdrawal</u>. You may discharge [FIRM NAME] at any time. [FIRM NAME] may withdraw with your consent or for good cause. Good cause includes your breach of this letter, its refusal to cooperate with [FIRM NAME] or to follow [FIRM NAME]'s advice on a material matter or any fact or circumstance that would render its continuing representation unlawful or unethical. Further, you hereby irrevocably authorizes [FIRM NAME] to immediately suspend or terminate its services if any statement is not paid on a timely basis. When [FIRM NAME]'s services conclude, all unpaid fees and costs will immediately become due and payable without regard to whether the representation fruitful. To the extent [FIRM NAME] must commence an action to recover any fees owed to it, [FIRM NAME] shall be entitled to recover its reasonable attorneys' fees and costs. After [FIRM NAME]'s services conclude and it has received payment of any outstanding fees and costs, they will, upon your request, deliver a copy of the file to you, along with any funds or property belonging to you in [FIRM NAME]'s possession.

      [FIRM NAME] looks forward to working with you on your matter. Please sign and return this letter to us at your earliest convenience.

                    Sincerely,

                    */s/*

                    [Partner]
                    for [FIRM NAME], PLLC

By:_____
     [CLIENT NAME]

Date:_____

# Retainer Agreement (lump sum with replenishment)

## Retainer Agreement
### (Lump Sum With Replenishment)

## [FIRM NAME]
123 Any Street
Anywhere, U.S. 11111

### AGREEMENT TO EMPLOY ATTORNEY

This AGREEMENT TO EMPLOY ATTORNEY is entered into between XXX ("Client"), and [FIRM NAME] ("Attorney").

**1. CONDITIONS.**

This agreement will not take effect, and Attorney will have no obligation to provide legal services, until Client returns a signed copy of this Agreement and pays the initial retainer deposit of $10,000.

**2. SCOPE AND DUTIES.**

Client hires Attorney for the purpose of domestic relations litigation.

Attorney shall provide those legal services reasonably required to represent Client, and shall take reasonable steps to keep Client informed of progress and to respond to Client's inquiries. Client shall be truthful with Attorney, cooperate in the preparation and trial of the case, appear on reasonable notice for depositions and Court appearances, keep Attorney informed of developments, abide by this Agreement, pay Attorney's bills on time and keep Attorney advised of Client's address, telephone number, and whereabouts. Client agrees not to compromise the claim without discussing the matter with Attorney, in advance, and Attorney is not authorized to compromise the claim without Client's consent.

**OTHER TERMS:** None.

**3. CONTACTS, COMMUNICATION, AND ASSIGNMENTS.**

Client acknowledges that the normal operation of Attorney's office has been explained, and specifically that communications are normally maintained through the paralegal staff, and that the "team approach" utilized in Attorney's office makes it likely that different tasks will be attended to by different people. Client understands that calls should normally be placed to, and normally will be returned by, the paralegal case manager assigned by Attorney.

Client authorizes Attorney to use associate counsel, legal assistants, or paralegals for such work on this case as Attorney might deem appropriate. Such persons shall be billed at their regular billing rate. Client acknowledges and agrees that such staff personnel may be utilized whenever deemed appropriate, and directs Attorney to apportion work, and alter who works on which matters at any time, at Attorney's discretion.

Client understands that documents will frequently be drafted by one member of Attorney's office staff (often a paralegal), and then reviewed or edited by another (usually an attorney), sometimes going through multiple drafts or reviews until completed, depending on the nature of the document.

Client has been informed that Attorney's usual mode of keeping clients informed about the status of pending matters in this office is to copy all incoming and outgoing written communications, and Client has been directed to retain all such copies, and periodic billing statements, so that Client's file should be virtually identical to Attorney's file as the case progresses.

Unless Client has opted out in writing, Client has further expressly given Attorney authorization to utilize electronic means to communicate using either a facsimile or an e-mail address provided to Attorney for that purpose. Said communications shall include the billing statements sent to Client, unless specific alternative arrangements have been made with the Firm Administrator.

Client understands that for the purpose of preserving attorney/client confidentiality, and other reasons, all contacts between Client and any member of Attorney's staff are to be conducted *at the office*, whether in person or by phone, and not at the home of a member of Attorney's staff, or a cell phone, etc., except where strictly necessary and where advance arrangements for such contacts have been made at the office. It is understood that any meetings outside of normal office hours (i.e., 8:00 a.m. to 5:00 p.m.) or phone calls to a member of Attorney's staff at home or by cell phone are extraordinary events, and are discouraged. Where Client's schedule or other requirements necessitate phone calls or meetings outside of regular office hours, or at the home or cell phone of any member of Attorney's staff, a premium rate of 2 times the normal billing rate for that staff member applies to all time taken for such meeting or phone call.

Client understands that Attorney's office works by appointment and scheduling, such that all client meetings must be by appointment. In the absence of other arrangement made in advance by an attorney in Attorney's office, appointments for office visits should be made through the paralegal case manager assigned to the case.

As a general proposition, *everything* you tell us, or we tell you, is and will be treated as confidential information, protected by the "attorney-client privilege" against disclosure. There are certain rare exceptions. For example, we might be required to reveal information necessary to prevent death or substantial bodily harm. However, if Client shares privileged information with a third party, it generally loses that protection – the third party (even relatives or financial backers) can be deposed or examined at trial as to what they know and why they know it. Additionally, the applicable ethics rules *prohibit* us from taking direction from, or giving confidential information to, a third party who happens to be supporting the client, or paying the client's legal costs.

In certain *extremely* rare circumstances, we permit contact by, and either taking information from, or giving information to, such third parties, at our sole discretion. The normal rule, however, and what you should expect, is that we will not respond to inquiries from any third party, no matter how trusted they might be by Client, and third parties may not normally be the conduit for the passing of confidential information between Attorney and Client, in either direction.

## 4.    LEGAL FEES.

Client agrees to pay for legal services at the following rates: $550 per hour for [Partner], Esq., $350 to $500 per hour for Senior associates, $250 to $350 per hour for Junior associates, and $110 to $250 per hour for paralegals/legal assistants. All personnel billing for their time will do so in 1/10 of an hour (i.e., six minute) increments, and will round to the nearest such increment.

Client agrees that these fees are reasonable on the basis of Attorney's ability, training, education, experience, professional standing and skill, and the difficulty, intricacy, importance, and time and skill required to perform the work to be done.

It is understood by Client that **ALL** time expended by personnel in Attorney's office on Client's case should be expected to be billed at the rate for those personnel. It is not possible to list all the work that may be required in working on Client's case, but it is understood that such work (by attorneys, or legal assistants/paralegals) includes time spent on phone calls to or from Client, or on Client's behalf, reviewing or handling incoming documents from Client, the opposing party, the Court, or any third party, and drafting, preparing, editing, reviewing, etc., pleadings, letters, documents, or materials, etc., performing legal or factual research, travel to or from hearings or meetings, depositions, time actually spent in such hearings and meetings (including time spent waiting for the matter to be called) and any other activities related to this matter.

In short, Client is informed and understands that the time spent by the personnel of Attorney's office attending to Client's case will normally be billed at the rate of the persons who spent the time.

Under certain circumstances, more than one member of Attorney's staff may work on a matter for Client simultaneously, in which case both members of Attorney's staff should be expected to bill for the time spent. An example would include a trial or contested evidentiary hearing, during which in Attorney's discretion the participation of more than one person is necessary to properly attend to Client's case.

The same rules apply to sequential or duplicative work. For example, it might be necessary to charge Client for a paralegal or attorney to review some or all of the case file, where immediate familiarity with the facts is required in preparation for a hearing, etc. However, Client will normally not be charged for time spent that is attributable to Attorney's internal staffing assignments, etc., such as one case manager reviewing a file when taking over a file from another case manager, or Attorney's alteration of the lead attorney in a case.

Notwithstanding the expectation that all time spent on Client's case will be billed, Attorney may, at Attorney's discretion, elect to "write off" or "no charge" certain time actually expended by attorneys or legal assistants/paralegals on Client's behalf. Client acknowledges being on notice that any such write-offs are **discretionary** by Attorney, and are expressly **contingent** on there being no dispute regarding payment of the remaining items billed to the Client. As specified below in the section of this Agreement labeled "BILLING INQUIRIES, AND FORMAL FEE DISPUTES," all "no charge" or "written off" costs, expenses, and fees for legal services will be considered payable in full in the event of a formal dispute or adjudication of a lien, regarding Client's bill.

The hourly fees quoted above are subject to increase from time to time. Attorney will give notice in writing at least thirty days prior to any increase in hourly fees. If Client does not wish to be charged at the new rates, Client agrees to pay Attorney in full for services up to the date of the expected increase and terminate representation by Attorney. Client understands that if Attorney continues to represent Client past the date of the increase, the new fees will be in effect and Client agrees to pay those increased fees for all services rendered thereafter. Likewise, Attorney may modify other terms of this Agreement, similarly notifying Client thirty days in advance of the change, and with the same options for Client to terminate representation, and the same result (the new Agreement goes into effect) if Client does not terminate representation and Attorney continues to represent Client past the date of the proposed change.

If a Court awards attorney's fees to Client (or to Attorney on Client's behalf), and such sums are actually collected, they shall be applied against any outstanding charges on Client's bill. Client, however, remains responsible for payment of the costs, expenses, and fees for legal services incurred in Client's case. A court order awarding attorney's fees from the opposing party does **not** relieve Client of the primary responsibility for paying Attorney's bill, or make any work done to collect the attorney's fees awarded any different from any other work performed by Attorney. Any attorney's fees awarded and actually collected that are not needed to pay the costs, expenses, and fees for legal services incurred in Client's case, or replenish the retainer fee deposit, shall be paid to Client.

Likewise, Client is aware that the Court could order Client to pay fees or costs to the other side of a case.

## 5.     COSTS AND EXPENSES.

### A.     INITIAL AND CONTINUING COSTS

An initial, non-refundable, $25 will be billed to Client, from the first funds deposited with Attorney, to purchase initial file materials, etc., and to pay for access to the computer-assisted legal research service reserved for all cases in the event access to the service is needed.

Client agrees that if Attorney advances or incurs any costs in this case, including but not limited to costs of investigation, filing fees or other court fees, depositions, process server or witness fees, photographs, exhibits, outside photocopying, expenses incurred incident to travel on Client's behalf (including lodging and meals), messenger and other delivery fees, parking, consultant's fees, express mail charges, timed-increment computer research charges, or other similar items, such charges will be paid by Client out of funds on retainer or promptly upon being billed.

### B.      EXPERTS, CONSULTANTS, AND INVESTIGATORS

It may become necessary for Attorney to hire expert witnesses, consultants, and/or investigators. Attorney will not hire such persons unless Client agrees to pay their fees and charges, but Attorney will select which such persons should be hired. It is understood that Client's refusal to authorize hiring of such persons, when considered necessary by Attorney, could greatly injure Client's case, and if the absence of such persons makes it impossible, in Attorney's discretion, to continue with the case, Attorney may withdraw from the case.

### C.      RETURNED CHECK FEE

Should Client remit a payment to this office by way of check and it is returned for insufficient funds or stop payment, a $25 returned check fee will be assessed to Client.

### 6.      DEPOSITS AND STATEMENTS.

Client agrees to pay Attorney an initial retainer fee deposit at the time Attorney is hired, which money is to be held in trust. A normal retainer fee deposit is $10,000. Cases in which hearing dates are already set and pending, or that will otherwise require extraordinary immediate efforts, may require a larger initial retainer fee deposit.

Attorney will send Client periodic statements, normally twice per month, for costs, expenses, and fees for legal services incurred. Client hereby authorizes Attorney to withdraw sums from the trust account to pay the costs, expenses, and fees for legal services incurred during each billing cycle in Client's case. All such charges against Client's account are to be replenished within 14 days from the date of each statement.

It is intended that the retainer fee deposit will be held and used as a security deposit until the conclusion of the case and payment of all outstanding costs, expenses, and fees for legal services in Client's case. Client has been advised that the provided credit card on the last page of this Agreement shall be used to replenish Client's retainer the day prior to the following billing cycle, unless prior arrangements have been made with the Firm Administrator.

Interest at the rate of 18 percent annually ($1\frac{1}{2}$ percent per month) will be charged on any unpaid balance in excess of the sum held as a retainer fee deposit, beginning on the date of a statement showing such an unpaid balance.  This interest provision is **not** an agreement to extend credit, but is a method of compensating Attorney for delayed payment.

In addition to the Semi-Monthly replenishment of the retainer fee deposit, Attorney may from time to time require additional deposits of retainer funds in anticipation of an evidentiary hearing, lengthy deposition, trial, or other large cost, whenever Attorney reasonably believes that the sum on retainer is insufficient to cover the expected costs, expenses, and fees for legal services likely to be incurred through the next billing cycle.  Client acknowledges being informed that firm policy is to never proceed to a contested hearing or trial without adequate funds on deposit to pay the fees and costs anticipated to be expended in that hearing or trial.

Failure by the Client to replenish the retainer fee deposit to its original amount within 14 days from the date of each statement, or to deposit an additional retainer deposit if requested will be cause for and permit, but not require, Attorney to immediately withdraw from the case.

In other words, Client agrees to pay Attorney in advance for all work to be performed, by maintaining at all times a retainer fee deposit which is to be replenished within 14 days of the date of each statement during the course of Attorney's representation.

The retainer fee deposit is fully refundable.  Any money not used for costs, expenses, and fees for legal services will be refunded to the Client at the conclusion of the case, except that no portion of any "flat fee" specified in this Agreement for specific items will be refunded, even if the accrued costs and fees are less than the non-refundable fee.

The initial retainer and any replenishing or additional payments must be remitted to the Firm Administrator only, unless specifically directed otherwise by [Partner] personally.  Client acknowledges being informed that no additional, or alternative, arrangements as to any economic matter may be made with *any* person other than [Partner] or the Firm Administrator.

## 7.     BILLING INQUIRIES AND FORMAL FEE DISPUTES.

Obviously, it is possible for mistakes to happen, and Client is not expected to pay for any charges that are incorrect.  Client may call or e-mail Attorney's office with an inquiry concerning billing statements, directing the inquiry to the Firm Administrator.  Most actual errors can be resolved with a simple phone call, and the Firm Administrator will inform Client whether a mistake is acknowledged, and promptly send an amended statement showing any adjustment or correction resulting from any such call.

In the absence of written confirmation from Attorney's office showing such an adjustment or correction, each statement remains as the record of Client's account.  Any dispute as to the accuracy or validity of any charges, or requests for adjustment of any costs, expenses, or fees for legal services billed to Client must be made in writing to the Firm Administrator within 30 days of the date of the statement containing that cost, expense, or fee for legal services.  If Client does not do so within 30 days of a billing statement, the statement will be conclusively presumed to be correct.

In other words, **if Client does not contact us in writing within 30 days of a billing statement, Client will have irrevocably agreed that the statement is accurate and correct.** Any person ever reviewing any dispute regarding charges on a billing statement is asked to honor this provision, since it is an essential term to Attorney's agreement to represent Client in this case.

As stated above, while Client should presume that all time spent attending to Client's case by any member of Attorney's staff will be billed, Attorney may elect to "write off" or "no charge" some costs, expenses, and fees for legal services. Any such write-offs are **discretionary** by Attorney, and are expressly **contingent** on there being no dispute regarding payment of the remaining items billed to Client, initiated by either Attorney or Client.

If Attorney files a lien to recover unpaid fees and/or costs incurred on client's behalf, or if Client seeks to formally dispute Attorney's billings, by initiating mediation, arbitration, litigation, or a fee dispute in any forum, all "write off" or "no charge" costs, expenses, and fees for legal services reflected on any statement to Client will revert to being fully billed, and be **additional** sums owed to Attorney by Client, in **addition** to the sum disputed by Client.

These provisions are explicitly written to **prevent** a situation in which Attorney reduces Client's bill by writing off costs, expenses, or fees for legal services during a case, and then Client seeks to reduce the sums owed further by disputing Client's responsibility to pay the reduced sum. They are intended to provide incentives for both Attorney and Client to resolve, informally and **promptly**, any questions or concerns about the legitimacy of any item billed on any statement, and to provide certainty that once a statement is 30 days old, the costs, expenses, and fees for legal services reflected on that statement are agreed by Attorney and Client to have been accurate and correct.

In accordance with the Uniform Commercial Code, no payments made to Attorney for less than the full sum owed shall constitute payment in full, even if that notation is placed on the payment instrument, unless Attorney and Client both sign a separate written agreement specifically permitting such payment to constitute a payment-in-full.

Client agrees to pay any fees and costs that are incurred by Attorney to collect fees, costs, or expenses from Client, including reasonable attorney's fees.

## 8.    LIENS AND ADJUDICATION.

Client hereby grants Attorney a lien on any and all claims or causes of action that are related to the subject of Attorney's representation under this Agreement. Attorney's lien will be for any sums due and owing to Attorney at the conclusion of Attorney's services, whether or not the case has been concluded. The lien will attach to any recovery Client may obtain, whether by arbitration award, judgment, settlement, or otherwise. Any amounts received by Attorney's office on Client's behalf may be used to pay Client's account.

Attorney will retain possession of Client's file and all information therein until full payment of all costs, expenses, and fees for legal services, subject to turnover or destruction of the file as set out in Paragraph 10. Client consents to the district court's adjudication of any such lien and during the pendency of the underlying action without requiring the filing of a separate action, regardless of whether any other action might be or has been filed by either Attorney or Client against the other, including any action alleging malpractice.

## 9.     DISCHARGE AND WITHDRAWAL.

Client may discharge Attorney at any time, although Client understands that court rules might still require Attorney to file a motion to withdraw. Attorney may withdraw at any time at Attorney's discretion. In either such circumstance, Client agrees to sign the documents necessary to permit Attorney to withdraw.

Client has been informed that among the events that should be expected to cause Attorney's withdrawal from this case are Client's breach of any portion of this Agreement (including its payment provisions), Client's refusal to cooperate with Attorney or to follow Attorney's advice on a material matter, or any other fact or circumstance that would render Attorney's continuing representation unlawful, unethical, or impractical.

Specifically, while it is the province of the Client to identify the "objectives of representation," a lawyer is not required to pursue objectives or employ means simply because a client may wish that the lawyer do so. The terms of a lawyer's representation may exclude specific objectives or means, including those that a lawyer regards as repugnant or imprudent.

If Client shall desire to retain other counsel, then Attorney shall be paid the amount then due and owing for costs, expenses, or fees for legal services incurred in Client's case.

## 10.     CONCLUSION OF SERVICES; TURNOVER, STORAGE, AND DESTRUCTION OF FILES.

When Attorney's services conclude, all unpaid charges shall become immediately due and payable. Attorney will normally formally withdraw from the case at its conclusion.

After payment of all sums due and upon Client's request, Attorney will deliver Client's file (other than Attorney's personal notes, briefs, and work product that Attorney elects to retain) to Client, along with any Client funds or property in Attorney's possession. If Attorney is not instructed otherwise, Client's file will be kept in Attorney's office for a limited time after completion of the case. **Files are digitized, stored as PDF files and then destroyed upon completion of a case. If you want your file, or anything out of your file, you should obtain it promptly upon conclusion of your case.**

## 11. DISCLAIMER OF GUARANTEE; TOTAL FEES AND COSTS; TAX CONSEQUENCES.

Nothing in this Agreement and nothing in Attorney's statements to Client will be construed as a promise or guarantee about the outcome of Client's matter. Attorney makes **no such promises or guarantees**. Attorney's comments about the outcome of Client's matter, if any, are expressions of opinion only.

**It is understood that it is impossible to predict how long a case will take, how much it will cost, or what the resulting outcome may be.** Attorney does not make and has not made any guarantees to Client about the length or expense of Client's case. Attorney has not made and will not make any guarantee as to the outcome of Client's case. Client has been informed and acknowledges that it is quite likely that the costs, expenses, and fees for legal services incurred in Client's case will substantially exceed the initial retainer fee deposit.

No advice is given regarding tax consequences, and Attorney specifically is **not** providing tax advice, although questions relating to tax matters may very well come up during the course of the case. Client agrees to seek tax advice elsewhere, and to hold Attorney harmless from any tax effects.

## 12. EFFECTIVE DATE; SEVERABILITY; [STATE] LAW.

This agreement will take effect when Client has performed the conditions stated in paragraph 1, but its effective date will be retroactive to the date Attorney first provided services, if earlier. Even if this Agreement does not take effect, Client will be obligated to pay Attorney the reasonable value of any services Attorney may have performed for Client.

The provisions of this Agreement are severable. This means that if one or more provisions of this Agreement are found to be void or unenforceable for any reason, the remaining provisions of this Agreement will still apply.

This Agreement is entered into in accordance with the law of the State, and [State] law will apply to any questions relating to the meaning of any provision of this Agreement.

\* \* \* \* \* \* \* \* \*
\* \* \* \* \* \* \* \* \*
\* \* \* \* \* \* \* \* \*
\* \* \* \* \* \* \* \* \*
\* \* \* \* \* \* \* \* \*
\* \* \* \* \* \* \* \* \*
\* \* \* \* \* \* \* \* \*
\* \* \* \* \* \* \* \* \*
\* \* \* \* \* \* \* \* \*
\* \* \* \* \* \* \* \* \*

**PLEASE READ THIS CAREFULLY:**

This Agreement is a formal legal contract for Attorney's services. It protects both you and your attorney, is intended to prevent misunderstandings, and it may vary the law otherwise applicable to attorney's liens and resolution of fee disputes. **DO NOT SIGN THIS AGREEMENT UNTIL YOU HAVE READ IT THOROUGHLY AND ARE SURE YOU UNDERSTAND ITS TERMS.** If you do not understand it or if it does not contain all the agreements discussed, please call it to our attention and be sure this written Agreement contains **all** terms you believe are in effect between us. You have an absolute right to discuss this agreement with independent counsel (or any other advisor) before entering into this agreement, and we encourage you to do so.

CLIENT                         [FIRM NAME]

_____    _____

XXX                          [Partner], Esq.

_____    _____

Date                          Date

**CREDIT CARD AUTHORIZATION:**

I authorize the [FIRM NAME] to keep my signature on file and charge my legal fees, costs, and expenses as incurred on my Visa, MasterCard, American Express, or Discover in accordance with the terms stated above as to fees, costs, expenses, and retainer fee deposits, as of the 14$^{th}$ day after any statement.

I understand that this authorization is valid and cannot be canceled while a financial obligation is outstanding to the [FIRM NAME] under the terms set out above. I further understand that if this card is canceled or replaced (including issuance of a card with an updated expiration date), I am obligated to supply the [FIRM NAME] with the new credit card information.

*Please fill out the information (including the address to which your credit card is billed and the security code), and return the original signed document to our office. Thank you.*

_____

Client's name

_____    _____

Card Holder's name, as it appears on the card     Credit Card #

_____   _____    _____

Security Code     Expiration      Signature           Date

_____

Address to which this credit card's bill is sent

_____

Email (or other) address to which you would like a receipt sent

## Engagement Letter (corporate)

Reprinted with permission of Lawyers Mutual
from Attorney-Client Agreements Toolkit     RISK MANAGEMENT HANDOUTS OF LAWYERS MUTUAL

## ENGAGEMENT LETTER: CORPORATE

[Date]

[Client Name]
[Client Address]
[Client Address]

Re: Confirmation of Engagement
    File ID:

Dear [Client's Name]:

We are pleased that you have asked the firm to serve as your counsel. This letter will confirm our discussion with you regarding your engagement of this firm and will describe the basis on which our firm will provide legal services to you.

Accordingly, we submit for your approval the following provisions governing our engagement. If you are in agreement, please sign the enclosed copy of this letter in the space provided below. If you have any questions about these provisions, or if you would like to discuss possible modifications, do not hesitate to call. Again, we are pleased to have the opportunity to serve you.

*Scope of Representation*
Our client in this matter will be [Name of Corporation]. We will be engaged to advise the Company solely in connection with [Describe Matter and Scope of Representation].

*Client Responsibilities*
You agree to cooperate fully with us and to provide promptly all information known or available to you relevant to our representation. You also agree to pay our statements for services and expenses in accordance with the fee agreement outlined in this document.

*Conflicts*
As we have discussed, you are aware that the firm represents many other companies and individuals. It is possible that during the time that we are representing the Company, some of our present or future clients will have [disputes or transactions] with the Company. The Company agrees that we may continue to represent or may undertake in the future to represent existing or new clients in any matter that is not substantially related to our work for you even if the interests of such clients in those other matters are directly adverse. We agree, however, that your prospective consent to conflicting representation contained in the preceding sentence shall not apply in any instance where, as a result of our representation of you, we have obtained proprietary or other confidential information of a non-public nature, that, if known to such other client, could be used in any such other matter by such client to your material disadvantage. You should know that, in similar engagement letters with many of our other clients, we have asked for similar agreements to preserve our ability to represent you. [Note: If possible, and if not prevented by considerations of confidentiality, insert disclosures about prior or existing relationships with other parties and the probable nature of any anticipated adverse relationships.]

You have agreed that our representation of the Company in this matter does not give rise to an attorney-client relationship between the firm and [Parent Corporation's Name] any of the Company's affiliates. You also have agreed that the firm, during the course of its representation of the Company, will not be given any confidential information regarding any of the

ATTORNEY-CLIENT AGREEMENTS TOOLKIT

Company's affiliates. Accordingly, representation of the Company in this matter will not give rise to any conflict of interest in the event other clients of the firm are adverse to [Parent Corporation's Name] or any of the Company's other affiliates.

It is understood that our client for purposes of this representation is [Company's Name], and not any of its individual members or any other entities whose interests in this matter are being represented by those individual members.

Once again, we are pleased to have this opportunity to work with you. Please call me if you have any questions or comments during the course of our representation.

*Fees and Expenses*

Our fees will primarily be based on the billing rate for each attorney and legal assistant devoting time to this matter. Our billing rates for attorneys currently range from $____ per hour for new associates to $___ per hour for senior partners. Time devoted by legal assistants is charged at billing rates ranging from $___ to $___ per hour. Other factors may be taken into consideration in determining our fees including the responsibility assumed, the novelty and difficulty of the legal problem involved, particular experience or knowledge provided, time limitations imposed by the client or the matter, the benefit resulting to the client, and any unforeseen circumstances arising in the course of our representation. These billing rates are subject to change from time to time.

[Include language on reimbursement of disbursements and Administrative Expenses.]

[Include language attaching firm Billing and Fee Policy and incorporate it by reference.]

If you request us to do so, we will provide to you with each bill the detailed information maintained in our accounting database concerning time expended by each attorney and legal assistant in connection with the work covered by the bill as well as each charge item by the firm.

Statements normally will be rendered monthly for work performed and expenses recorded on our books during the previous month. Payment is due promptly upon receipt of our statement. If any statement remains unpaid for more than 90 days, we may suspend performing services for you [until arrangements satisfactory to us have been made for payment of outstanding statements and the payment of future fees and expenses].

As we have discussed, the fees and costs relating to this matter are not predictable. Accordingly, we have made no commitment to you concerning the maximum fees and costs that will be necessary to resolve or complete this matter. It is also expressly understood that payment of the firm's fees and costs is in no way contingent on the ultimate outcome of the matter.

*Retainer*

Our representation shall commence upon your execution of this letter and our receipt of an initial retainer of $_____. At the conclusion of this engagement and after payment of all of our fees and expenses, we will return to you, without interest, any unearned portion of the retainer.
or

This will acknowledge receipt of your check for $_____ as an advance for fees to be rendered in connection with our representation. Such advance will be deposited in our general trust account and we will charge our fees against the advance and credit them on our billing statement. In the event our fees exceed the advance deposited with us, we will bill you for the excess. Any unused portion of the advance will be refundable at the conclusion of our services. We will have the right to request additional advances from time to time based on our estimates of future work to be undertaken. If you fail to pay promptly any additional advance requested, we will have the right to withdraw from further representation.

*Term of Engagement*

Either of us may terminate the engagement at any time for any reason by written notice, subject on our part to applicable rules of professional conduct. In the event that we terminate the engagement, we will take such steps as are reasonably practicable to protect your interests in the above matter, including consultations with subsequent counsel and providing him or her with whatever papers you have provided to us. If permission for withdrawal is required by a court, we will promptly apply for such permission, and you agree to engage successor counsel to represent you.

*Conclusion of Representation; Retention and Disposition of Documents*

Unless previously terminated, our representation of the Company will terminate upon our sending you our final statement for services rendered in this matter. Following such termination, any otherwise non-public information you have supplied to us which is retained by us will be kept confidential in accordance with applicable rules of professional conduct. At your request, your papers and property will be returned to you promptly upon receipt of payment for outstanding fees and costs. Our own files pertaining to the matter will be retained by the firm. These firm files include, for example, firm administrative records, time and expense reports, personnel and staffing materials, and credit and accounting records; and internal lawyers' work product such as drafts, notes, internal memoranda, and legal and factual research, including investigative reports, prepared by or for the internal use of lawyers. All such documents retained by the firm will be transferred to the person responsible for administering our records retention program. For various reasons, including the minimization of unnecessary storage expenses, we reserve the right to destroy or otherwise dispose of any such documents or other materials retained by us within a reasonable time after the termination of the engagement.

*Post Engagement Matters*

You are engaging the firm to provide legal services in connection with a specific matter. After completion of the matter, changes may occur in the applicable laws or regulations that could have an impact upon your future rights and liabilities. Unless you engage us after completion of the matter to provide additional advice on issues arising from the matter, the firm has no continuing obligation to advise you with respect to future legal developments.

Very truly yours,


[Attorney Name]
[Law Firm Name]
[Date]

Agreed and accepted:     _____

                         [Name of Corporation]
                         _____

                         [Name of Individual Signing]
                         _____

                         [Title of Individual Signing]
                         _____

                         [Date]


*Note: This is a sample form only and is written for the general purpose of facilitating clear expectations and avoiding misunderstandings between an attorney and client. It is not intended as legal advice or opinion and will not provide absolute protection against a malpractice action.*

# Engagement Letter (alternate clauses – corporate)

ATTORNEY-CLIENT AGREEMENTS TOOLKIT

Reprinted with permission of Lawyers Mutual
from Attorney-Client Agreements Toolkit

## ENGAGEMENT LETTER: ALTERNATE CLAUSES - CORPORATE

### Scope of Representation

Add for Business Transaction:
We will prepare, negotiate and revise documentation required to consummate [state transaction].

Add for litigation:
We will prepare and file necessary documentation in connection with [brief description of matter] and pursue such matter to an ultimate conclusion, either by order of court or by settlement. You may limit or expand the scope of our representation from time to time, provided that any substantial expansion must be agreed to by us.

For use with federally regulated financial Institutions:
It is our understanding that our engagement for this and other financing transactions will consist solely of assisting you with the structuring, negotiating, documenting and closing of your financings, and conducting a legal review (the scope of which will be defined at the commencement of each transaction) of certain due diligence matters pertaining to each prospective borrower's business. In connection with the foregoing, we will also assist you with the federal regulatory aspects of your receipt of equity enhancements (e.g., warrants and success fees) in connection with your financings and the effect on, and applicability to, your financings of federal margin stock laws and regulations; however, because we are not your counsel with respect to general corporate compliance matters, we will not otherwise undertake any responsibility for assuring that, with respect to any of the financing transactions, you will be complying with applicable state or federal laws and regulations because of your legal or regulatory status or because of the general nature of your business, including, without limitation, capital adequacy requirements, lending limits, restrictions on affiliate and insider transactions, rules regarding interlocking boards of directors, governmental reporting and licensing requirements, and federal, state or local tax matters. Of course you may limit or expand the scope of our representation from time to time, provided that any such expansion is agreed to by us.]

### Fees and Expenses

Retainer as Security:
Our representation will not commence until we receive from you a [certified] [cashier's] check in the amount of $_____. These funds will remain in our client trust account for the duration of our representation, and any remaining balance will be returned to you immediately upon termination of our representation. We reserve the right to use any part of said funds to satisfy a delinquent payment, and to discontinue our representation until you forward funds to restore the full retainer.

Retainer To Be Drawn Down:
Our representation will not commence until we receive from you a [certified] [cashier's] check in the amount of $_____. Those funds will be deposited in our client trust account, and we will draw against those funds to satisfy our monthly statements, copies of which will be sent to you for your information. Upon depletion of the retainer, we will so advise you, and you agree to pay all further statements upon receipt.

Additional Damages:
Papers we file may request that the court award you [attorneys' fees] [treble damages] [punitive damages] [prejudgment interest] as part of your claim. These types of damages are rarely granted. Therefore, you should not, unless we advise you to the contrary, assume that any such recovery is forthcoming, nor should you assume that those items realistically will be part of any settlement negotiation. That means that in any settlement or favorable court judgment you will most likely have to bear your own attorneys' fees [and that you will not receive interest on amounts due you up to the date of judgment].

## Engagement Letter (litigation)

Reprinted with permission of Lawyers Mutual
from Attorney-Client Agreements Toolkit    RISK MANAGEMENT HANDOUTS OF LAWYERS MUTUAL

## ENGAGEMENT LETTER: LITIGATION

[Date]

[Client Name]
[Client Address]
[Client Address]

Re: Engagement For Legal Services
    File ID:

Dear [Client's Name]:

Thank you for selecting [Law Firm] to represent you in connection with the action entitled [Case Name] pending in [Court Name] as [Case Number]. We have agreed that our engagement is limited to performance of services related to this action. Because we are not your general counsel, our acceptance of this engagement does not involve an undertaking to represent you or your interests in any other matter. In particular, our present engagement does not include responsibility for review of your insurance policies to determine the possibility of coverage for the claim asserted in this matter, for notification of your insurance carriers about the matter, or for advice to you about your disclosure obligations concerning the matter under the federal securities laws or any other applicable law.

I will have primary responsibility for your representation and will utilize other firm lawyers and legal assistants as I believe appropriate in the circumstances. We will provide legal counsel to you in accordance with this letter and in reliance upon information and guidance provided by you. We will endeavor to keep you reasonably informed of progress and developments, and to respond to your inquiries.

To enable us to represent you effectively, you agree to cooperate fully with us in all matters relating to your case, and to fully and accurately disclose to us all facts and documents that may be relevant to the matter or that we may otherwise request. You also will make yourself reasonably available to attend meetings, discovery proceedings and conferences, hearings and other proceedings. You also agree to pay our statements for services and other charges as stated below.

Either at the commencement or during the course of our representation, we may express opinions or beliefs concerning the litigation or various courses of action and the results that might be anticipated. Any such statement made by any partner or employee of our firm is intended to be an expression of opinion only, based on information available to us at the time, and should not be construed by you as a promise or guarantee.

Our fees will be based primarily on the amount of time spent on your behalf. Each lawyer and legal assistant has an hourly billing rate based generally on experience and special knowledge. The rate multiplied by the time expended on your behalf, measured in tenths of an hour, will be the initial basis for determining the fee. Our billing rates currently range from $_____ an hour for new associates to $_____ an hour for senior partners. My time is billed at $_____ an hour. Time devoted by legal assistants is charged at rates currently ranging from $_____ to $_____ an hour. Our billing rates are adjusted from time to time.

Other factors may be taken into consideration in determining our fees, including the novelty and difficulty of the questions involved; the skill requisite to perform the services properly; the experience, reputation and ability of those performing the services; the time limitations imposed by you or the circumstances; the amount involved and results obtained; and any other factors that may be relevant in accordance with applicable rules of professional conduct. However, these factors will not result in our fees exceeding the indicated amounts based on our hourly rates without prior discussion with you.

ATTORNEY-CLIENT AGREEMENTS TOOLKIT

You authorize us to retain any investigators, consultants or experts necessary in our judgment to represent your interests in the litigation. At our option, we may forward third-party charges in excess of $_____ directly to you for payment.

Statements normally will be rendered monthly for work performed and expenses recorded on our books during the previous month. Payment is due promptly upon receipt of our statement. If any statement remains unpaid for more than _____ days, we may suspend performing services for you [until arrangements satisfactory to us have been made for payment of outstanding statements and the payment of future fees and expenses).

Once a trial or hearing date is set, we will require you to pay all amounts then owing to us and to deposit with us the fees we estimate will be incurred in preparing for and completing the trial or arbitration, as well as jury fees and arbitration fees likely to be assessed. If you fail to timely pay any additional deposit requested, we will have the right to cease performing further work and to withdraw from the representation.

As we have discussed, the fees and costs relating to this matter are not predictable. Accordingly, we have made no commitment to you concerning the maximum fees and costs that will be necessary to resolve or complete this matter. Any estimate of fees and costs that we may have discussed represents only an estimate of such fees and costs. It is also expressly understood that payment of the firm's fees and costs is in no way contingent on the ultimate outcome of the matter.

You may terminate our representation at any time by notifying us. Your termination of our services will not affect your responsibility for payment of outstanding statements and accrued fees and expenses incurred before termination or incurred thereafter in connection with an orderly transition of the matter. If such termination occurs, your papers and property will be returned to you promptly upon receipt of payment for outstanding fees and costs. Our own files pertaining to the matter will be retained. These firm files include, for example, firm administrative records, time and expense reports, personnel and staffing materials, and credit and accounting records; and internal lawyers' work product such as drafts, notes, internal memoranda, and legal and factual research, including investigative reports, prepared by or for the internal use of lawyers.

We may withdraw from representation if you fail to fulfill your obligations under this agreement, including your obligation to pay our fees and expenses, or as permitted or required under any applicable standards of professional conduct or rules of court, or upon our reasonable notice to you.

Please review this letter carefully and, if it meets with your approval, please sign the enclosed copy of this letter and return it to me [with retainer or fee advance] so that we may begin work. Please call me if you have any questions.

Very truly yours,

[Attorney Name]
[Law Firm]
[Date]

Agreed and accepted:

_____
[Client's Name]

Date: _____

Note: This is a sample form only and is written for the general purposes of facilitating clear expectations and avoiding misunderstandings between an attorney and client. It is not intended as legal advice or opinion and will not provide absolute protection against a malpractice action.

## Engagement Letter (alternate clauses – litigation)

Reprinted with permission of Lawyers Mutual
from Attorney-Client Agreements Toolkit          RISK MANAGEMENT HANDOUTS OF LAWYERS MUTUAL

# ENGAGEMENT LETTER: ALTERNATE CLAUSES - LITIGATION

### Fees and Expenses

Retainer as Security:

Our representation will not commence until we receive from you a [certified] [cashier's] check in the amount of $_____. These funds will remain in our client trust account for the duration of our representation, and any remaining balance will be returned to you immediately upon termination of our representation. We reserve the right to use any part of said funds to satisfy a delinquent payment, and to discontinue our representation until you forward funds to restore the full retainer.

Retainer to Be Drawn Down:

Our representation will not commence until we receive from you a [certified] [cashier's] check in the amount of $_____. Those funds will be deposited in our client trust account, and we will draw against those funds to satisfy our monthly statements, copies of which will be sent to you for your information. Upon depletion of the retainer, we will so advise you, and you agree to pay all further statements upon receipt.

Additional Damages:

Papers we file may request that the court award you [attorneys' fees] [treble damages] [punitive damages] [prejudgment interest] as part of your claim. These types of damages are rarely granted. Therefore, you should not, unless we advise you to the contrary, assume that any such recovery is forthcoming, nor should you assume that those items realistically will be part of any settlement negotiation. That means that in any settlement or favorable court judgment you will most likely have to bear your own attorneys' fees [and that you will not receive interest on amounts due you up to the date of judgment].

Fee Based on Factors Other Than Straight Time:

As indicated above, the principal basis for computing our fees will be the time spent on the matter by various lawyers multiplied by their individual hourly rates. However, as we discussed, you understand that in a matter of this kind it may be appropriate to take into account in establishing our fees additional factors, such as the complexity of the work, the efficiency with which it is accomplished, the extent to which we may have forgone other client opportunities in order to satisfy your requirements, and the nature of the results that we ultimately achieve on your behalf. We will discuss any such special factors with you whenever we believe it is appropriate to do so.

### Multiple Parties to a Business Transaction

Single Representation:

As we discussed in my office on _____, this firm will be counsel only for A. We will not be counsel for B or C. They are encouraged to retain other counsel. As this matter proceeds, we will be seeking to protect A's interests as best we can, which may mean taking action that might eventually disadvantage B or C. If a dispute arises among A, B and C, we will have the right to represent A in that dispute, if A so chooses.

Joint Representation:

As we discussed in my office on _____, the "perfect" way to proceed would be for each of you to have separate counsel. There are many issues where you may or will have conflicting or potentially conflicting interests: compensation, ownership shares, control of the enterprise-just to name a few. Notwithstanding the above, you have each said that, to keep legal costs to a minimum, you may wish our law firm to represent all three of you.

ATTORNEY-CLIENT AGREEMENTS TOOLKIT

Our bills will be sent to _____, but all of you will be jointly and severally responsible for their payment. If you disagree on any issue, we will ask you to resolve your differences among yourselves, without our assistance. If you cannot resolve your differences, we will not be able to represent any one of you as to that issue. If the differences are serious enough, we may be required by applicable ethics rules to withdraw from the matter completely.

We have agreed that there will be no confidences among us regarding the work we do for you. In other words, if we receive information from or about one of you that we believe the others should have in order to make decisions regarding the subject of our representation, we shall give the others that information.

Represent Entity Only:

Until the [corporation] [partnership] is functioning, we will send our statements to _____, who will be responsible for their payment.

When the [corporation] [partnership] begins functioning, we will send our statements to the [corporation] [partnership]. From that point forward our only client will be the [corporation] [partnership], and we will not be counsel for any of you individually. Absent a specific future understanding, we will not be representing any of you individually or jointly.

**Representing Employer and Employee**

Because we believe that Employee's interests and Employer's interests are identical, or nearly so, we believe we can represent both. Employer agrees to pay all our fees and expenses. We urge Employee, however, to consult with another lawyer of his choice about our representing both Employer and Employee, and about Employee's signing this agreement.

**Trade Association or Group Type Client**

It is understood that our client for purposes of this representation is [name of trade association or other group-type client], and not any of its individual members or any other entities whose interests in this matter are being represented by those individual members.

**Waiver of Future Conflicts**

As we have discussed, you are aware that the firm represents many other companies and individuals. It is possible that during the time that we are representing the Company, some of our present or future clients will have [disputes or transactions] with the Company. The Company agrees that we may continue to represent or may undertake in the future to represent existing or new clients in any matter that is not substantially related to our work for you even if the interests of such clients in those other matters are directly adverse including, for example, representing adverse parties in litigation. We agree, however, that your prospective consent to conflicting representation contained in the preceding sentence shall not apply in any instance where, as a result of our representation of you, we have obtained proprietary or other confidential information of a non-public nature, that, if known to such other client, could be used in any such other matter by such client to your material disadvantage. You should know that, in similar engagement letters with many of our other clients, we have asked for similar agreements to preserve our ability to represent you. [*Note:* If possible, and if not prevented by considerations of confidentiality, insert disclosures about prior or existing relationships with other parties and the probable nature of any anticipated adverse relationships.]

# Retainer Letter (accident New York)

---

## RETAINER AGREEMENT

1. _____, the undersigned residing at
_____ hereby employ and engage the law firm of
[FIRM NAME]     ("the attorneys"), with offices at     [ADDRESS]     , to
represent the undersigned in connection with any and all claims which I/we may have against any and all
persons, arising out of _____

_____.

### SERVICES PROVIDED

2. The attorneys are authorized to fully investigate my claim with regard to any legal and/or medical basis, and should they elect to do so, file suit or other legal proceedings on my/our behalf, and to fully prepare for and prosecute the same. After reasonable legal and/or medical investigation of such claim or claims the attorneys may, at their sole discretion, decline to prosecute such claim. Upon notification to me of such fact, the attorneys may withdraw from representation under this agreement.

I/We understand that the legal representation that the attorneys will provide will include all aspects of the handling of my lawsuit from the commencement of the suit through entry of judgment. I/We further understand that the services to be provided through this agreement will not extend through the prosecution of an appeal or representation on an appeal brought by any of the parties to the lawsuit.

### LEGAL FEES

3. For such professional services I/we hereby agree to pay     [FIRM NAME]     , a percentage of the amount of any judgment recovered or any moneys received through settlement or compromise. The amount of such percentage shall be Thirty Three and one-third (33 1/3 %) of the sum recovered as the result of any claim or action or as otherwise provided by law.

Page 2 of 3

       I/We understand that if this retainer is for the benefit of an infant or incompetent the Court will fix the fee.

       4. The attorneys will pay on their own account the case expenses, disbursements and the costs of the litigation pursuant to NYS Judiciary Law §488 (2) d.

**Select by initialing your choice of option paragraph 5(a) or 5(b):**

_____ 5(a). The legal fee percentage shall be computed on the **net** sum recovered after deducting from the amount recovered: case expenses, disbursements and the costs of litigation for expert testimony and investigative or other services properly chargeable to the enforcement of the claim or prosecution of the action. In computing the legal fee, the costs as taxed, including interest upon a judgment, shall be deemed part of the amount recovered. For the following or similar items there shall be no deduction in computing the legal fee: liens, assignments or claims in favor of hospitals, for medical care and treatment by doctors and nurses, or of self-insurers or insurance carriers, and such items shall remain the sole responsibility of the client. If client(s) elects this option, then in the event the action is lost, **the client(s) shall** be responsible to reimburse to the attorney the case expenses, disbursements and the costs of lititgation advanced by the attorney.

_____ 5(b). The legal fee percentage shall be computed on the **gross** sum recovered without deduction for case expenses, disbursements and the costs of litigation for expert testimony and investigative or other services properly chargeable to the enforcement of the claim or prosecution of the action. Said case expenses, disbursements and the costs of litigation will be reimbursed to the attorney out of the recovery after deducting the attorneys' fee. In computing the fee, the costs as taxed, including interest upon a judgment, shall be deemed part of the amount recovered. If client(s) elects this option, **the client(s) will not** be responsible for any case expenses, disbursements or the costs of the litigation in the event the action is lost. Liens, assignments or claims in favor of hospitals, for medical care and treatment by doctors and nurses, or of self-insurers or insurance carriers, and similar items, shall remain the sole responsibility of the client(s).

| **EXAMPLE:** | | **EXAMPLE:** | |
|---|---|---|---|
| Gross Recovery | $10,000.00 | Gross Recovery | $10,000.00 |
| Expenses | $400.00 | Legal Fee | $3,333.33 |
| Net Sum recovered | $9,600.00 | Expenses | $400.00 |
| Legal Fee (33 1/3%) | $3,200.00 | Amount to Attorneys | $3,733.33 |
| Net to Client | $6,400.00 | Net to Client | $6,366.67 |

Page 3 of 3

Please note that by choosing Option 5b the legal fee is larger, but the client is **never** responsible for the expenses even if the case is lost.  On the other hand, by choosing Option 5a the legal fee is smaller, but the client is **always** responsible for the expenses even if the case is lost.

6.  I/We further agree that from the proceeds of any such recovery, whether by settlement, judgment or otherwise, you may deduct the attorneys' fees to which you are entitled, and all costs and expenses incurred by you.  Should this matter be concluded on the basis of a "structured settlement" your entire fee plus all costs advanced on my behalf shall be deducted from the initial cash payment.

7.  I/We am aware that the following lawyers/law firms will be participating in the investigation and possible prosecution of my claim and will all be participating in the single legal fee: - [FIRM NAME]  _____

8.  I/We acknowledge, before signing this contract, that I/we have received and read it and understand each of the statements made herein.

Dated:  _____

SUBJECT TO MEDICAL and LEGAL INVESTIGATION

_____        (X)_____
Witness                                  Client

                                         (X)_____
                                         Client

# Retainer Agreement (accident)

## RETAINER AGREEMENT

The undersigned Client, residing at _____ hereby retains [FIRM NAME], P.C. (hereafter called the "Firm") to prosecute or adjust a claim for damages arising from: personal injuries sustained by _____ loss of services of _____ property damage to _____ _____ through the negligence of _____ or other persons and/or entities.

The client hereby gives the Firm the exclusive right to take all legal steps to enforce this claim through trial and appeal.

**Appeal:** The Firm shall have the right but not the obligation to represent the Client on appeal. The Client will be responsible for the expenses of the appeal.

**Fee:** The Firm's fees shall be paid as "contingency compensation" which means that the Firm shall be compensated a percentage of the sum recovered by settlement, verdict or appeal. The Firm offers two options pursuant to 22 NYCRR 691.20:

> Option "A" All disbursements, expenses, and litigation costs are paid, advanced and/or forwarded by the client. The Firm will be compensated 33 and 1/3% of the net sum recovered by settlement, verdict, or appeal after reimbursement to the Client for disbursements, expenses, and litigation costs advanced or forwarded are deducted from the gross recovery.

> Option "B" All disbursements, expenses and litigation costs are advanced or forwarded by the Firm. The Firm will be compensated 33 and 1/3% of the gross (or entire) sum recovered by settlement, verdict or appeal.

The Client acknowledges that the Firm has the option, but not the obligation to advance disbursements. Said disbursements and litigation costs are to be repaid by the Client upon the resolution of the case. Trial disbursements will be advanced by the Firm at its discretion. There shall be no deduction in computing such percentages for the following or similar items: liens (for example: Medicare & Medicaid), assignments or claims in favor of hospitals, for medical care and treatment by doctors and nurses, or of self-insurers or insurance carriers.

**Costs and expenses** required in prosecuting the case will be either advanced by the client under Option "A" or by the Firm, under Option "B". The client may choose either option. If the client elects to advance the money for costs and expenses, the client must pay each cost and expense as it is incurred. If the client elects to have the Firm advance the money for costs and expenses, the money will be borrowed by the Firm on the client's behalf at an interest rate not to exceed the maximum allowable by New York State law. At the conclusion of the case, all such monies, both principal and interest, shall be reimbursed by the client to the firm.

_____ I elect Option "A" and will pay for all disbursements, expenses, or litigation costs. I want to be billed for each disbursement as incurred. I understand that by paying the disbursements as they are incurred, I will receive a greater amount of the settlement. The disbursements will be subtracted from the gross settlement.

_____ I elect to Option 'B" and authorize [FIRM NAME], P.C. procure a third party lending company to advance the money for costs and expenses at an interest rate not to exceed the maximum allowed by New York State law. I do not want to be billed for each disbursement as incurred. I understand that [FIRM NAME] will receive a greater amount of the settlement at the conclusion of the case because the disbursements will be charged to my portion of the recovery.

**Other services**: The services to be provided do not include settlement or litigation of any lien, creation and administration of supplemental needs trusts or guardianships, Surrogates court proceedings and withdrawal of funds deposited pursuant to an Infants Compromise Order. The services to be provided in prosecuting or adjusting this personal injury claim do not include legal services relative to the negotiation or litigation of any Medicaid lien under Anlborn. In the event that the firm is requested to and does perform services for Client which are not directly related to the third party tort action for personal injury, then those services, unless otherwise agreed, shall be performed at the hourly rate of $250 and shall be paid in advance or shall be a lien on the file.

**No-fault:** A flat fee of $350 is charged for Personal Injury Protection (no fault) benefits administration, payable in advance or as a lien. This flat fee does not include Attorney time for investigating no-fault claims, appearances at Examinations Under Oath for No-fault benefits and arbitrating denials which will be billed at $250 per hour.

**Property Damage**: Any monies recovered for property damage shall be subject to a twenty-five percent (25%) legal fee to be deducted from said proceeds.

**Bankruptcy Provisions**: Client represents to the Firm that they are not presently, nor do they contemplate filing for Bankruptcy protection; that they will inform the Firm should such a course of action be contemplated in the future. Client acknowledges that any fees garnered as result from this claim are subject to such proceedings wherein they are to be scheduled as an asset by Client. Client further acknowledges that any expense which the Firm may incur to protect attorney fees from said shall be subtracted from fees which normally would flow to Client as their share of any recovery.

**Cooperation of Client:** Client agrees to cooperate with the Firm at all times and to comply with all reasonable requests in the prosecution of this matter. Client agrees to cooperate with the Firm at all times and to comply with all reasonable requests in the prosecution of this matter. Client agrees to be truthful, to always disclose complete and accurate facts, to provide the most complete information possible. Client agrees to report any changes in Client's personal or professional life which may affect representation such as divorce, death of a spouse of interest party, subsequent accidents or re-injury, substantial improvement in condition, surgical recommendation; to provide whatever information is necessary (in the attorney's estimation) in a timely and competent manner. **Client shall notify Firm in writing of any address or telephone changes.** Failure to meet these obligations is a basis for the Firm to withdraw from representation of client.

**Client has Been Advised of Consequence of Fraud:** Any person who knowingly and with intent to defraud any insurance company or other person brings a claim containing any materially false information, or conceals for the purpose of misleading, information concerning any fact material thereto, and any person who knowingly makes or knowingly assists, abets, solicits or conspires with another to make a false report of the theft, destruction, damage or conversion of any motor vehicle to a law enforcement agency, The Department of Motor Vehicles or an insurance company commits a fraudulent insurance act, which is a crime, and shall also be subject to a civil penalty not to exceed five thousand dollars ($5,000) and the value of the subject motor vehicle or stated claim for each violation.

**Power of Attorney to Settle Claim and Endorsement Authorization Where Client is Missing**: In the event Firm is unable to contact Client through ordinary efforts via mail or via telephone, Client grants Firm the authority to take all action which Firm deems necessary, including the authority to negotiate and settle Clients claim for an amount which the firm deems reasonable under the circumstances. Firm may settle the case without client's approval, negotiate the Release and settlement Check in Client's name, and hold client's net proceeds in Firm's Escrow Account, whereupon Firm may take only the portion of the proceeds to which they are entitled.

**If Client Settles Case Without Attorney:** If the cause of action is settled by the Client without the consent of the Firm, Client agrees to pay the Firm the above percentage of the full amount of the settlement for benefit of the Client, to whomever paid or whatever called. The Firm shall have, in the alternative, the option of seeking compensation on a quantum meruit basis to be determined by the court. In such circumstances, the court would determine the fair value of the service. Firm shall have, in addition, Firm's taxable costs and disbursements. In the event the Client is represented on appeal by another attorney, Firm shall have the option of seeking compensation on a quantum meruit basis to be determined by the court.

**Client agrees that the Firm has made no promises or guarantees regarding the outcome** to the Client's claim and if after so investigating, claim does not appear to have merit or appears that the defendant have no insurance coverage, then Firm shall have the right to cancel this agreement and reject this case, provided that Client is informed by ordinary mail sent to Client's Last-Known-Address that the firm is abandoning this matter and that the client may seek other counsel.

**Client's receipt of Agreement and Acknowledgement of Terms:** Clients acknowledge that they have read and fully understand all of the terms and conditions of this Agreement before signing it, and that they have received a copy of this Agreement upon execution thereof.

The client authorizes the firm to retain other lawyers if the firm deems it appropriate to assist in the resolution of any lien asserted by workers compensation carriers, medicare, medicaid, private health insurers or others, on a settled claim. The fee associates with the retention of the lawyers or lawyers to handle the resolution of said liens, including the expenses (i.e. costs and disbursements) of said lawyer or lawyers, may be forwarded by the firm and, if so, will be treated like a cost and disbursement. In other words, these costs and disbursements will be repaid by the client to the firm at the conclusion of the claim. Any such fee will be reasonable and will never exceed the amount of the asserted items.

Dated: _____            _____ L.S.

Witness: _____            _____ L.S.

Sworn to before me this
_____ day of _____ 201

_____
Notary Public

## Fee Agreement and Authority to Represent (contingency fee)

Reprinted with permission from
the Louisiana State Bar Association (LSBA)

## Fee Agreement and Authority to Represent (Contingency Fee)

(In accordance with amended Rule 1.5 (c) of the Louisiana Rules of Professional Conduct, effective date April 1, 2006)

I, _____, the undersigned client (hereinafter referred to as "I," "me" or the "Client"), do hereby retain and employ _____ and his law firm (hereinafter referred to as "Attorney"), as my Attorney to represent me in connection with the following matter:

_____

This claim is not in litigation; and I specifically authorize Attorney to undertake negotiations and/or file suit or institute legal proceedings necessary on my behalf. As used herein, the term "suit" includes, where applicable, the institution of proceedings to impanel a medical review panel. I further authorize Attorney to retain and employ, at my expense, the services of any experts, including physicians and doctors, as well as the services of other outside contractors, as Attorney deems necessary or expedient in representing my interests. I also authorize Attorney to retain and employ other attorneys with my prior knowledge and written consent; however, the combined fee of Attorney and all other attorneys shall be limited as set forth herein below.

1. **ATTORNEY'S FEES.** As compensation for legal services, I agree to pay my Attorney as follows:

   **Contingency Fee**

   Attorney shall receive the following percentage of the amount recovered before the deduction of costs and expenses as set forth in Section 2 herein:

   _____ % in the event of settlement before the suit is filed;
   _____ % in the event the suit is filed and the matter settles before a trial on the merits;
   _____ % in the event of settlement after the start of a trial on the merits;
   _____ % in the event a judgment is rendered at a trial on the merits and no appeals are filed by any party;
   _____ % in the event an appeal is filed by any party after conclusion of a trial on the merits.

   It is understood and agreed that this employment is upon a contingency fee basis and, if no recovery is made, I will not be indebted to my Attorney for any sum whatsoever **as Attorney's Fees**. (However, I agree to pay all costs and expenses as set forth in Section 2 herein, regardless of whether there is any recovery in this matter. In the event of recovery, costs and expenses shall be paid out of my share of the recovery.)

2. **COSTS AND EXPENSES.** In addition to paying Attorney's Fees, I agree to pay all costs and expenses in connection with Attorney's handling of this matter. Costs and expenses shall be billed to me as they are incurred, and I hereby agree to promptly reimburse Attorney. If an

advance deposit is being held by Attorney, I agree to promptly reimburse Attorney for any amount in excess of what is being held in advance. These costs may include (but are not limited to) the following: long distance telephone charges, photocopying ($        per page), postage, facsimile costs, Federal Express or other delivery charges, deposition fees, expert fees, subpoena costs, court costs, sheriff's and service fees, travel expenses and investigation fees.

**Advance required**          ____ Yes ____ No

I agree to advance $ _____ for costs and expenses, which amount shall be deposited in Attorney's trust account and shall be applied to costs and expenses as they accrue. Should this advance be exhausted, I agree to replenish the advance promptly upon Attorney's request. If I fail to replenish the advance within ten (10) days of Attorney's request, Attorney shall have, in addition to other rights, the right to withdraw as my Attorney.

3. **NO GUARANTEE.** I acknowledge that Attorney has made no promise or guarantee regarding the outcome of my legal matter. In fact, Attorney has advised me that litigation in general is risky, can take a long time, can be very costly and can be very frustrating. I further acknowledge that Attorney shall have the right to cancel this agreement and withdraw from this matter if, in Attorney's professional opinion, the matter does not have merit, I do not have a reasonably good possibility of recovery, I refuse to follow the recommendations of Attorney, I fail to abide by the terms of this agreement, and/or if Attorney's continued representation would result in a violation of the Rules of Professional Conduct, or at any other time as or if permitted under the Rules of Professional Conduct.

4. **STATUTORY ATTORNEY'S FEES.** In the event of recovery under the provisions of the Longshore and Harbor Workers' Compensation Act, or under Louisiana Workman's Compensation laws, or under any other laws which specify attorney's fees to be paid, then Attorney's fees shall be paid in accordance with the maximum allowed by law.

5. **PRIVILEGE.** I agree and understand that this contract is intended to and does hereby assign, transfer, set over and deliver unto Attorney as his fee for representation of me in this matter an interest in the claim(s), the proceeds or any recovery therefrom under the terms and conditions aforesaid, in accordance with the provisions of Louisiana Revised Statute § 37:218, and that Attorney shall have the privilege afforded by Louisiana Revised Statute § 9:5001.

[Optional]
[6. **ALTERNATIVE DISPUTE RESOLUTION.** In the event of any dispute or disagreement concerning this agreement, I agree to submit to arbitration by the Louisiana State Bar Association Legal Fee Dispute Resolution Program.]

**NOTICE: By initialing in the space below, you are agreeing to have any dispute arising out of the matters included in the "Alternative Dispute Resolution" provision decided by neutral binding arbitration as provided by Louisiana Arbitration Law; and you are giving up your right to have the dispute decided in a court or jury trial. By initialing in the space below, you are also giving up your rights to discovery and appeal. If you refuse**

to submit to arbitration after agreeing to this provision, you may be compelled to arbitrate under the authority of the Louisiana Arbitration Law.

I have read and understand the foregoing and agree to submit to neutral binding arbitration disputes arising out of the matters included in the "Alternative Dispute Resolution" provision.

Client's Initials _____
Attorney's Initials_____

7. **ADDITIONAL TERMS.** Attorney and Client agree to the following additional terms:

_____
_____

8. **LOUISIANA LAW.** This contract shall be governed by Louisiana law.

9. **TERMINATION OF REPRESENTATION.** I understand that I have the right to terminate the representation upon written notice to that effect. I understand that I will be responsible for any fees or costs incurred prior to the discharge or termination.

10. **ENTIRE AGREEMENT.** I have read this agreement in its entirety, a copy of which I have received, and I agree to and understand the terms and conditions set forth herein. I acknowledge that there are no other terms or oral agreements existing between Attorney and Client. This agreement may not be amended or modified in any way without the prior written consent of Attorney and Client.

**This agreement is executed by me, the undersigned Client, on this ____ day of _____ , 20 ____ .**

CLIENT _____

The foregoing agreement is hereby accepted on this ____ day of _____, 20 ____ .

ATTORNEY_____

## Engagement Letter (contingency fee)

ATTORNEY-CLIENT AGREEMENTS TOOLKIT

## ENGAGEMENT LETTER: CONTINGENCY FEE

[Date]

[Client Name]
[Client Address]
[Client Address]

Re: Confirmation of Engagement
    File ID:

Dear [Client's Name]:

We are pleased that you have asked [Law Firm] to serve as your counsel. At the outset of any engagement, we believe it is appropriate to confirm in writing the nature of the engagement and the terms of our representation, and that is the purpose of this letter. If you have any questions about this letter or any of its provisions, do not hesitate to call. Otherwise, this letter [and the attached Policy] will represent the terms of our engagement. Again, we are pleased to have the opportunity to serve you.

*Client(s)*. [Name Client(s)] will be our only client(s) in this matter.

### *Scope of Representation*

Our representation will be limited to the specific matters described in this paragraph. [Law Firm] has been engaged to represent [Client's Name] for the purpose of _____ _____
_____
_____, hereinafter referred to as the "matter" or "engagement." However, engagement does not include_____ _____
_____.

### *Nature of Relationship*

Our objective is to provide high quality legal services to our clients at a fair and reasonable cost. The attorney-client relationship is one of mutual trust and confidence. If any of you has any questions at all concerning the terms of this engagement, our ongoing handling of this legal matter, we invite your inquiries.

### *Fee Agreement*

You have agreed with us that the firm will undertake this engagement on a contingency fee basis. Our fee will be based upon all amounts recovered on your behalf, including actual damages, punitive or exemplary damages, treble damages, interest, and attorneys fees, but excluding any recovery of costs awarded to reimburse out-of-pocket expenses incurred in bringing your claims. Our fee will be _____ percent ( %) of all amounts recovered on your behalf by any settlement(s) made prior to filing legal action, and our fee will be _____ percent ( %) of all amounts recovered on your behalf after legal action is filed, whether by settlement, jury verdict, or otherwise, unless there is an appeal of an award in your favor. If any award by a trial court in your favor is appealed, our fee will be [percentage] percent (__%) of all amounts ultimately recovered if there is a single appeal, and our fee will be [percentage] percent (__%) of all amounts ultimately recovered on your behalf if there is more than one appeal. Unless the Termination of Services provisions apply as set out below, the contingency fee would only be due and paid in the event you recover damages or other amounts as a result of the Accident.

In addition to any contingency fee we earn in the event of a recovery, you are responsible for out-of-pocket expenses, including deposition charges, medical records charges, Federal Express and similar charges, large copying projects and messenger services. We would bill these charges separately, generally during the month following the month in which out-of-pocket expenses are incurred. We may advance out-of-pocket expenses and defer billing for them until the conclusion of this matter, in which event you agree that we may deduct and retain those amounts from any recovery, or you will pay them at the time of any recovery, in addition to the contingency fee described above.

We have attached our Billing and Fee Policy which applies to this engagement, except to the extent that this letter provides differently. In that regard, the administrative expense charge described in the attached Billing and Fee Policy, for which we ordinarily charge a fixed amount per hour of services rendered, will not be charged separately, and these are covered by the contingency fee set out above.

*Termination of Legal Services; Fees and Expenses Due*
We are confident that we can work together in a manner satisfactory to you, but you are free to terminate our services at any time. However, if you terminate this engagement before a final settlement or conclusion of this matter, you agree that our fee has been earned, and you agree to pay [Law Firm], at our option, an amount equal to (a) the hourly rate for the services of the attorneys and paralegals who work on this matter, based upon their standard hourly rates as adjusted from time to time during this engagement, plus all out-of-pocket expenses and all of the administrative expense charges as described in the Billing and Fee Policy, or (b) that percentage of any settlement or other recovery for your claims that would have applied had the recovery been made at the time we last represented you (for example, if you terminate our firm before legal action is filed, and you ultimately make a recovery, we would be entitled to ____%; if you terminate our firm after legal action is filed but before a settlement or trial verdict, and you ultimately make a recovery, we would be entitled to ____%), plus all out-of-pocket expenses we incurred.

Although we do not contemplate at this time any reason why we would seek to withdraw from representing you, should we determine in our discretion that we should withdraw and we are ethically permitted to do so, we retain the right to do so subject to such court approval, if any, that may be required, and in that event you would only be required to pay or reimburse any out of pocket expenses we incurred on your behalf that you had not previously paid, and you would not owe any fee to us unless our withdrawal was caused by your refusal to cooperate or communicate with us in the pursuit of your claims. If our withdrawal was caused by your refusal to cooperate or communicate with us in the pursuit of your claims, you agree that this shall be treated as if you had terminated our services, and our fee would be deemed earned in accordance with the preceding paragraph. Again, we certainly hope and expect that there will be no reason for either of us to want to terminate the engagement, and we look forward to representing you to the conclusion of this matter.

*General Waiver of Conflicts.*
As we have discussed, you are aware that the firm represents many other companies and individuals. You agree that we may continue to represent or may undertake in the future to represent existing or new clients in any matter that is not substantially related to our work for you, even if the interests of such clients in those other matters may be directly or indirectly adverse to you. We agree, however, that your prospective consent to conflicting representation contained in the preceding sentence shall not apply in any instance where, as a result of our representation of you, we have obtained proprietary or other confidential information of a non-public nature, that, if known to such other client, could be used in any such other matter by such client to your material disadvantage. You should know that, in similar engagement letters with many of our other clients, we have asked for similar agreements to preserve our ability to represent you.

*Conclusion of Representation; Retention and Disposition of Documents.* Unless previously terminated, our representation of you will terminate upon the conclusion of this matter by the resolution of all claims by recovery of your damages and other amounts as a result of the Accident whether as a result of an award of damages at trial, a settlement, a mediation or arbitration, or any combination thereof. Following such termination, any otherwise non-public information you have supplied to us which is retained by us will be kept confidential in accordance with applicable rules of professional conduct. All documents retained by the firm will be transferred to the person responsible for administering our records retention program. For various reasons, including the minimization of unnecessary storage expenses, we reserve the right to destroy or otherwise dispose of any such documents or other materials retained by us within a reasonable time after the termination of the engagement.

*Acknowledgment*

If you read, understand and are in agreement with the terms of our engagement as outlined above and in the attachment, sign and return a copy of this letter in the enclosed self-addressed envelope. We cannot begin to represent you until we have received the signed confirmation of our engagement. Once again, we are pleased to have this opportunity to work with you. Please call me if you have any questions or comments during the course of our representation.

Very truly yours,


[Attorney Name]
[Law Firm Name]
[Date]

Enclosure

The foregoing letter and the attachment accurately state the terms of our engagement of [Law Firm] to represent us in connection with the matter and under the circumstances described above, including the contingency fee agreements, and this confirms our waiver of any existing conflicts and our waiver of future conflicts as described in the preceding letter.

_____
[Client's Name]

Date: _____

*Note: This is a sample form only and is written for the general purposes of facilitating clear expectations and avoiding misunderstandings between an attorney and client. It is not intended as legal advice or opinion and will not provide absolute protection against a malpractice action.*

# Retainer Agreement (matrimonial)

## RETAINER AGREEMENT

### This is a legally binding Contract

### Please read it carefully

1.   I, _____, hereby retain _____, hereinafter referred to as the "the Firm" to represent me in the following matter: _____.

2.   I agree to pay a minimum fee of $_____. I understand that the Firm's representation of me shall not commence until the Firm has received a signed copy of this Agreement, a signed Statement of Client's Rights and Responsibilities and payment of the minimum fee as set forth above.

3.   I understand that if the Firm disposes of my matter either by way of settlement or litigation without having used up my entire minimum fee, I will nonetheless not receive any refund. I acknowledge that the establishment of a minimum fee is based on more than just the time to be devoted to my file, but also, among other things: the experience and expertise of the collective attorneys handling the case, the reputation of the Firm, and/or the individual attorneys handling my case, the complexity of the case and the security of the availability of the Firm to handle my matter.

4.   The hourly rates for the attorneys and paralegals working on my file are as follows:

5.   I understand that the present hourly rates may change from time to time. However there will be no more than one rate increase per year (except for the addition of partners and experienced attorneys) and such increase will not exceed more than ten percent (10%) of the then hourly rates applicable. Time applied to your file (computed in units of six (6) minutes) will be charged against the retainer at the hourly rates shown in the preceding paragraph and any increase thereof.

6.   I understand that I will be billed for all time spent on my case including, but not limited to: conferences in the office and/or in Court, information gathering while assisting in filling out financial affidavits and pleadings, preparing and answering complaints, counterclaims, motions, discovery proceedings, telephone calls whether with me or someone else involved in my case such as opposing counsel, experts and witnesses, examinations before trial, trial preparation, Court appearances and preparation, review of agreements, judgments and other documents, negotiations, correspondence, research and travel to and from locations away from the Firm's offices.

7.   This Retainer Agreement does not cover services relative to Family Court or District Court unless specifically set forth within this retainer agreement, and the Firm without a further retainer agreement is not required to do any of the following: provide legal services after a judgment is outlined, handle any appeal, enforce any judgment or agreement, represent me in the purchase of or sale of my home or other property, or prepare my will. An additional retainer may provide for any of the above or additional services by mutual written agreement except for the rendering of tax advice, which the Firm cannot give.

8.    The Firm agrees to send me an itemized billing statement at least once every sixty (60) days. I agree to promptly review my bill; and if I have any questions concerning same, I will contact the Firm. The Firm will not charge me for time spent in discussing billing questions. Bills not disputed within thirty (30) days of mailing are presumed accurate and shall be paid within such thirty (30)-day period. All outstanding balances in excess of thirty (30) days shall accumulate interest at the rate of six (6%) percent annually which will be charged on a monthly basis at the rate of .5% on the entire outstanding balance.

9.    I recognize that I am responsible for the immediate payment of all disbursements which include but are not limited to:  process service fees, filing fees, court fees, expert witnesses, consultants, accountants, actuaries, appraisers, overnight mailings, witness fees, long distance telephone calls, facsimile transmissions, messengers, stenographic fees and/or costs of transcripts associated with the case, postage, supplies, and copies. Failure to pay disbursements may result in a delay of my case.  No deposition will be undertaken without a payment of at least five hundred dollars ($500.00) in advance.  Disbursements are a separate charge and will not be credited against my retainer.

10.    If an expert or outside service provider such as an appraiser, accountant, actuary, expert or other outside consultant is needed and authorized by me I will pay the cost of same.  This cost is not the obligation of the Firm and is solely my obligation.  However, no such expert will be utilized without my approval.  The client however agrees to retain such experts as are necessary for the case to properly proceed acknowledging that failure to do so may either result in a loss of an important issue in the case or may be the basis for the Firm to seek to be relieved.

11.    Should the time expended on my behalf exceed the amount of the retainer I paid, I agree to pay additional fees incurred within 30 days of receipt of a bill.  After all monies paid by me have been used, the Firm has the right to request and receive additional lump sum payments.  No advance lump sum payment shall exceed the minimum fee.  At no time shall my outstanding fee to the Firm exceed one thousand dollars ($1,000).

12.    In the event there is an outstanding obligation for legal services rendered at any time during the prosecution or defense or at the conclusion of my case and I cannot pay my outstanding bill, I understand that the Firm may apply to the court for a mortgage or other security device on notice to my spouse and his or her attorney.  This applies whether or not the Firm is continuing to represent me. Court approval is required for the Firm to obtain a security device.  I have been advised that any mortgage given to the Firm on my house will not be foreclosed upon so long as I continue to own and occupy any portion of the house.

13.    I am aware that I have the right to cancel this Retainer Agreement at any time if I decide not to pursue the case (other than the effectuation of a settlement) or if the opposing party drops the case or I discharge the Firm or the Firm discontinues my representation.  I will be entitled to receive back money for any time not used minus all costs and disbursements incurred in setting up my file, and in representing me up to the date of discontinuance. The Firm agrees to provide me with any refund due within fifteen (15) business days of my request for discontinuance of services.

14.    It is specifically understood and agreed that failure to pay fees to the Firm as agreed herein is failure to cooperate in the Firm's representation of me and shall be a basis for the Firm to seek to discontinue representing me.  Further, being less than candid with the Firm, lying to staff and in failing to keep appointments or supply information requested, shall serve as a basis for the Firm to be relieved as my attorneys.  The Firm has a right to seek what is called a charging lien against me to

cover fees at the time of withdrawal or if the Firm is discharged. The Court may determine how such a charging lien will be paid which the firm will seek to have paid out of settlement proceeds. I have been advised that no lien may attach to child support or maintenance. I also understand that a retaining lien may be attached to my file until payment arrangements are agreed upon between the Firm and me.

15.   The Firm shall make its best efforts on my behalf but I understand that no results are guaranteed.

16.   I understand that I have the right to be kept apprised of the status my case. I understand that I have a right to receive copies of all motions and correspondence as well as pleadings upon my request.   It is my right to choose to receive copies of such papers and if I choose to receive copies I understand that I will be charged reasonable copying costs, which will be included as a disbursement on my bill.

17.   I am aware that any of the attorneys associated with the Firm may be assigned to handle all or a portion of my case. I am aware that I have retained the Firm and understand that the use of more than one attorney on my file gives me the benefit of the collective experience and strategic judgment of multiple attorneys at the Firm and, in certain situations, may be a cost saving to me.

18.   I understand that the nature of the Firm's practice requires a great deal of conference and court time by the attorneys and therefore all calls may not always be returned within twenty four (24) hours. However I promise to leave a message with specific details and/or questions and to advise if the situation is an emergency so that some one may respond as quickly as possible.

19.   I have also been advised that pursuant to Court Rules my attorneys are required to certify all papers submitted by me to a court, which contain statements of fact. The attorney must certify that he or she is aware of no inaccuracies in the papers submitted. I therefore agree to provide the Firm with complete and accurate information, which I recognize will be included in my papers. I agree to certify to the Firm that there are no inaccuracies in the papers that the Firm has prepared on my behalf and to correct any inaccuracies.

20.   If counsel fees are awarded in my case, or if my spouse agrees to pay any portion of my counsel fees, I understand that these payments are subject to collection and that I must continue to pay my bill for services rendered.   However, if the funds awarded are received, such sums will be credited to my account and if on the completion of my case, there is any overpayment, the amount of such overpayment will be returned to me.   The Firm shall not be obligated to bring proceeding to collect any fees awarded unless I retain the Firm to specifically do so.

21.   While the Firm seeks to avoid any fee disputes with its clients, in the event of such a dispute, I have been advised that all such fee disputes shall be resolved under Part 137 of the Rules of the Chief Administrator of the Courts (22NYCRR). I acknowledge my right, at my election, to seek arbitration to resolve the fee dispute and should I seek arbitration, I will notify the Firm in writing and the Firm will provide me with information necessary to file for arbitration.   Also, in accordance with Part 137 of the Rules of the Chief Administrator, the Firm may likewise, at its election, initiate arbitration proceedings to resolve a fee dispute should I decline to do so. The decision resulting from arbitration shall be binding upon both you and the Firm and you and the Firm agree to waive the right to reject the arbitration award by commencing a lawsuit on the merits (trial de novo) in a court of law within thirty (30) days after the arbitration decision has been mailed.   By signing this agreement, both

parties hereto acknowledge that they have received and read the official written Rules and Regulations of Part 137 entitled New York State Fee Dispute Resolution Program. This agreement does not foreclose the parties' attempting to resolve this fee dispute at any time through voluntary mediation.

    22.   Balances due upon completion of the Firm's work shall, like monthly bills, be paid within thirty (30) days. Bills unpaid after thirty (30) days shall incur interest and handling charges of .5% per month. The interest charges shall in no way limit the Firm's rights should litigation be required to collect fees.

    23.   I have read this Agreement and have received a copy of this and the Statement of Clients Rights and Responsibilities. I understand the terms of this Retainer Agreement and by signing below I authorize the Firm to act as counselors on my behalf.

Dated: _____, New York        This ___ day of _____, 2015

_____

_____        **Client's Signature**

**Client's Legal Address**

                                    _____

                                      **Client's Social Security Number**

_____

_____        _____

**Mailing Address if different than above**        **(Firm)**

                                      By:_____

# Retainer Letter (matrimonial)

## Retainer Agreement
(Matrimonial)

[FIRM ADDRESS]
[FIRM ADDRESS]
[FIRM ADDRESS]
(###) ###-####
Fax: (###) ###-####
www.firm.com

**[FIRM NAME]**
**(###) ###-####**
**Attorney@firm.com**

DATE

<u>**VIA EMAIL**</u>

[CLIENT NAME]
[CLIENT ADDRESS]
[CLIENT ADDRESS]

       RE:     Dissolution of Marriage

Dear [CLIENT NAME]:

       This letter describes the basis on which our firm will provide legal services to you and bill for services.

       1.     <u>Professional Undertaking</u>:   Specifically, you have retained the firm of [FIRM NAME] to represent you in the matter of a dissolution of your marriage, including any temporary agreements or orders that need to be in place. We practice as a team at our firm, recognizing our respective strengths, and we staff our cases by placing the correct attorney and/or paralegal on the task at hand. You hire us, not just one of us.

       Please review the following information carefully and, if it meets with your approval, sign the enclosed copy of the letter and return it to me in the envelope provided. It is important that we receive a signed copy of this letter back from you in a timely fashion in order to begin work on your case, and accordingly, we ask that you please return this letter within ten (10) days of receipt so that your file can be processed.

       2.     <u>Fees</u>:  We bill our clients on an hourly rate basis only. Statements for services are simply the product of the hours worked multiplied by the hourly rates for the attorneys and legal assistants who did the work along with any disbursements we have made on your behalf.

       Our schedule of hourly rates for attorneys and other members of the professional staff is based on years of experience, training and practice, and level of professional attainment. Currently, my rate is $200.00 per hour. The rates for other attorneys in the

[DATE]
Page 2

firm are $150.00 to $340.00. The schedule is reconsidered annually with changes effective on January 1$^{st}$ of each year.

3.     Costs: Often it is necessary for us to incur expenses for items such as travel, lodging, meals, long-distance telephone calls and photocopying. Similarly, some matters require substantial amounts of ancillary services such as computer research services. In order to allocate these expenses fairly and keep billable rates as low as possible for those matters which do not involve such expenditures, these items are separately itemized on our statements as "disbursements." Also, we may need to engage experts such as real estate appraisers, CPA's, pension evaluators or mental health experts. The engagement of those experts will be a matter of contract between you and the expert. It is our firm policy to bill such items directly to the client and you will be expected to pay directly to the vendor the costs of any such services.

4.     Billings: Our statements are prepared and mailed during the month following the month in which services are rendered and costs advanced. We expect payment within 15 days after the statement date. **If for any thirty-day billing cycle you fail to make a payment, we reserve the right to immediately withdraw.** Payments are accepted by cash, check, Visa, MasterCard and Discover. We do not accept American Express. We now have a link where clients can make payments by credit card online: [LINK FOR ONLINE PAYMENT.]

5.     Retainer: We have received a retainer of $[RETAINER FEE] which will show as a credit on your monthly statement. Thereafter, you will receive a monthly bill and when the fees and costs exceed the amount of the retainer you will be expected to pay any amount due upon billing.

6.     Termination: Either of us may terminate this engagement or any phase of it at any time for any reason by written notice, subject on our part to the [STATE] Rules of Professional Conduct. If our representation is terminated for any reason, we will take steps to the extent reasonably practicable to protect your interests in the matter and, if you so request, we will provide any successor counsel you engage with whatever papers you have provided us.

Our representation will conclude upon completion of the matters identified in this letter. Any future legal work will require that you separately engage us for that purpose.

Once our engagement in this matter ends, we will send you a written notice advising you that this engagement has concluded. You may thereafter direct us to return, retain or discard some or all of the documents pertaining to the engagement. If you do not respond to the notice within sixty (60) days, you agree and understand that any materials left with us after the engagement ends may be retained or destroyed at our discretion. Notwithstanding the foregoing, and unless you instruct us otherwise, we will return to you any original wills, deeds, contracts, promissory notes or other similar

[DATE]
Page 3

documents, and any documents we know or believe you will need to retain. You should understand that "materials" include paper files as well as information in other mediums of storage including voicemail, email, printer files, copier files, facsimiles, dictation recordings, video files, and other formats. We reserve the right to make, at our expense, certain copies of all documents generated or received by us in the course of our representation. When you request copies of documents from us, copies that we generate will be made at your expense. We will maintain the confidentiality of all documents throughout this process.

Our own files pertaining to the matter will be retained electronically by the firm (as opposed to being sent to you) or destroyed. These firm files include, for example, pleadings, correspondence, firm administrative records, time and expense reports, personnel and staffing materials, and credit and account records. For various reasons, including the minimization of unnecessary storage expenses, we reserve the right to destroy or otherwise dispose of any documents or other materials retained by us within a reasonable time after the termination of the engagement and after the necessary documents have been scanned and retained electronically.

Please review the foregoing and, if it meets with your approval, sign a copy of the letter and return it to me in the enclosed envelope. If you have any questions, please feel free to call me.

With kindest regards,

FIRM PLLC

**APPROVED AND AGREED:**

By: _____     Date:_____
      [CLIENT NAME]

**Attorney-Client Fee Agreement (hourly with advance deposit, domestic)**

Reprinted with permission from
the Louisiana State Bar Association (LSBA)

# Attorney-Client Fee Agreement
## (Hourly with Advance Deposit, Domestic)

DATE _____

CLIENT NAME _____

We appreciate the confidence you have shown in retaining our firm to represent you. This letter sets forth our respective participation and responsibilities in your case. You have hired us to handle the following matter for you:

### DIVORCE, CHILD CUSTODY, CHILD SUPPORT, SPOUSAL SUPPORT AND COMMUNITY PROPERTY PARTITION

Legal services on your case will not begin until after we have received your deposit for fees *and* a signed copy of this agreement, unless the attorney decides otherwise. You have paid a deposit of $ _____ to secure the services of our firm, to compensate us for assuming responsibility for your case, and to ensure our availability to represent you.

The deposit will be applied toward payment of legal services rendered on your behalf. You authorize us to transfer expenses incurred and fees earned from our client trust account to our business account. When your credit balance with us falls below 50% of the amount of the deposit, you agree to replenish your deposit, so that you maintain a minimum credit balance on deposit with the firm at all times in the amount of at least 50% of your original advance fee. At the conclusion of the case, any unused portion of the advance will be refunded to you. We will send you itemized statements each month. If your statement shows a balance due to the firm, you agree to pay both that balance due and to replenish your advance deposit each time you receive a statement from us. You agree to make these required payments no later than ten (10) days from the date of the statement.

**This firm does not finance legal services**. If you fail to maintain the terms of this agreement, and to pay fees as expressly set forth herein, we may file a Motion to Withdraw as your counsel of record.

You agree to pay the firm for attorneys' services at the rate of $ _____ per hour. You also agree to pay $ _____ per hour for paralegal services rendered to you. The time expended on your matter will be computed on the basis of one-tenth of an hour increments.

Any figures we quote you for the total cost of our services are merely estimates. The opposing party, the opposing attorney or others may engage in activities beyond our control, requiring us to expend additional time not originally contemplated.

In addition, you will be responsible for all costs which we may incur on your behalf. These costs include filing fees, service of process, depositions, appraisals, witness fees, court reporter fees, copy and telephone expense, and fees for accountants, investigators, psychologists and other experts. We will consult with you prior to employing any such services. We will mutually decide whether such expert fees are paid out of the advance deposit or directly by you. You authorize us to hire other attorneys, with your prior knowledge and written consent, to work with us on this engagement, at your expense.

Our representation does not include preparation of Qualified Domestic Relations Orders to divide community retirement or profit-sharing benefits. This requires extra specialized work which will usually be referred to another attorney.

We also do not give advice on the tax consequences in community property, spousal support, child support and succession cases. We advise you to confer with a tax attorney or Certified Public Accountant to determine the tax consequences of any proposed action prior to settlement or trial.

We make every reasonable effort to settle contested issues without the emotional and financial burden of trial. Sometimes, though, it is not possible to reach agreement. If it becomes apparent that your case will have to go to trial, you agree to pay the firm a **trial deposit** in an amount to be determined by the attorney, within one week after we notify you of the amount required. If your case is subsequently resolved without the necessity of a trial, any unused portion of your deposit will be refunded to you. If you do not pay the trial deposit within one week of notification, we may file a Motion to Withdraw in your case.

We reserve the right to terminate this agreement for any of the following reasons:
1. You fail to pay fees, costs, advance fee replenishment or trial deposits in accordance with this agreement.
2. You fail to cooperate and comply fully with all reasonable requests of the firm in reference to your case.
3. You insist on pursuing an objective that the firm considers repugnant, illegal or imprudent, or contrary to your legal best interest.
4. You engage in conduct which makes it unreasonably difficult to carry out the purposes of this employment.
5. Any other reason allowed under the Rules of Professional Conduct.

You have the right to terminate our services upon **written** notice to that effect. You will be responsible for any fee for services performed or costs expended prior to our withdrawal or discharge, including time and costs expended to duplicate the file, turn over the file, and withdraw as counsel of record.

You understand and agree that this contract is intended to and does hereby assign, transfer, set over and deliver unto us as the fee for representing you, an interest in the claims, proceeds or any recovery therefrom under the terms and conditions above, and that our firm shall have a privilege afforded by [STATE] Revised Statute § [STATUTE].

We have explained to you that the court dockets are crowded, and that it might take a long time to have a contested matter heard. While most cases will settle, some do not. You acknowledge that we have made no promises regarding when the matter will be concluded or any particular results. We will work as quickly as possible to get the matter concluded, consistent with our caseload and the proper protection of your rights.

New fee arrangements will be required at our discretion for appellate work and the collection of amounts which the opposing party may be required to pay to you. This agreement is only for services to be performed through the trial court level and does not extend beyond the entry of judgment or motion for new trial.

[Optional]
[**ALTERNATIVE DISPUTE RESOLUTION.** In the event of any dispute or disagreement concerning this agreement, I agree to submit to arbitration by the [STATE] State Bar Association Legal Fee Dispute Resolution Program.]

**NOTICE: By initialing in the space below, you are agreeing to have any dispute arising out of the matters included in the "Alternative Dispute Resolution" provision decided by neutral binding arbitration as provided by [STATE] Arbitration Law; and you are giving up your right to have the dispute decided in a court or jury trial. By initialing in the space below, you are also giving up your rights to discovery and appeal. If you refuse to submit to arbitration after agreeing to this provision, you may be compelled to arbitrate under the authority of the [STATE] Arbitration Law.**

**I have read and understand the foregoing and agree to submit to neutral binding arbitration disputes arising out of the matters included in the "Alternative Dispute Resolution" provision.**

Client's Initials _____
Attorney's Initials _____

**ADDITIONAL TERMS.** Attorney and Client agree to the following additional terms:

_____

**FILE RETENTION.** Our office will maintain your file for a minimum of five years after termination of representation, after which your file may be destroyed without further notice.

Please read this document carefully. It sets forth all the terms of our agreement. If you agree with these terms, please sign in the place provided for your signature and return one signed copy to the firm. You should also retain a copy for your files so that you will have a memorandum of your agreement.

APPROVED AND AGREED TO THIS _____ DAY OF _____ , 20 \_\_\_\_ .

**CLIENT** _____
**ATTORNEY**_____

# Attorney-Client Fee Agreement (hourly with advance deposit, criminal)

## Attorney-Client Fee Agreement
### (Hourly With Advance Deposit, Criminal)

### RETAINER AGREEMENT

**Re:    INVESTIGATION**

This agreement is made between [CLIENT NAME] and the law firm of [FIRM NAME] regarding representation in the above matter.

It has been explained to me that by retaining the firm of [FIRM NAME], I authorize both partners and attorneys they employ to appear in court, if necessary, on my behalf or otherwise handle this matter.

I agree to pay [FIRM NAME] a minimum initial retainer of $[RETAINER FEE] for the services to be performed regarding this matter.   Time spent on my case, which includes services, telephone calls and correspondence, will be billed against the retainer at an hourly rate of $450 for partners and $50 for interns.  If the retainer is depleted, an additional retainer may be required.

### Defaults

I also understand, that if I do not pay the fee as agreed upon, or make other arrangements to do so, this will be interpreted as my decision to discontinue the services of [FIRM NAME], relieving them as my attorneys.  If I fail to pay as agreed upon and action to collect the fee is taken, I agree that I will be responsible for any expenses incurred by [FIRM NAME] relating to such collection, including reasonable attorney's fees.

### Additional Expenses

It has been explained to me that some times additional charges are incurred in the defense of a case. These include, but are not limited to, the cost of obtaining official reports, discovery material, audio and video tapes and minutes of court proceedings, investigative costs for interviewing witnesses and taking statements, subpoenaing witnesses and records, etc.  I will be told in advance what fees are likely to be incurred, and if I agree to the expense(s), I agree to pay any and all reasonable expenses incurred by [FIRM NAME] on my behalf, apart from the fee.

### Additional Criminal Charges

If, during the course of my representation on the above case, I require services on other matters, or it is discovered that I have additional matters outstanding or under investigation, I realize that I will be asked to sign a separate retainer for the new matter if I wish the firm of [FIRM NAME] to represent me on it.

## Civil Forfeiture

If there is a separate civil forfeiture action in regard to my case, the fee for representation on that shall be by separate retainer, and nothing in this retainer shall obligate the firm of [FIRM NAME] to litigate such matter absent a retainer. I understand that the firm may, as a courtesy, file paperwork to answer the initial complaint, to preserve my rights, or to negotiate the forfeiture as part of the disposition in my criminal case. This shall not be construed as an obligation of the firm to litigate the forfeiture on a continuing basis unless a separate retainer is signed with regard to that. I understand that if the criminal case is disposed of without disposition of the forfeiture, I will be responsible for retaining either [FIRM NAME] or another firm to litigate it upon my sentencing. Under no circumstances will the firm of [FIRM NAME] have any post-sentencing obligation to litigate forfeitures absent a signed retainer. In addition, nothing in this retainer requires that [FIRM NAME] undertake any civil forfeiture litigation regarding preliminary remedies without compensation and a signed specific retainer.

## Notice Regarding Arbitration

You may be entitled to arbitrate a fee dispute under this retainer pursuant to 22 NYCRR Section 137 depending upon the nature of the case.

ALL FEES ARE PAYABLE IN FULL PRIOR TO DISPOSITION OF THE CASE.

The undersigned hereby agrees to be fully responsible for and to answer for payment of the above fee to [FIRM NAME], as set forth above.


Dated: _____           _____

# Retainer Agreement (criminal)

## Retainer Agreement
(Criminal)

[DATE]


[CLIENT NAME]
[ADDRESS]
[ADDRESS]


    Re:  **People v. [CLIENT NAME]**
         District Court, Suffolk County Family Court, Suffolk County
         New York State DMV Refusal Hearing
         New York State Bureau of Professional Licensing

Dear [CLIENT NAME]:

This will serve to confirm that you have retained our office to represent you in the above matters.

It is agreed that we shall receive a minimum fee retainer in the amount of [RETAINER FEE]. This amount shall be the minimum cost of our representation of you and does not represent the amount of the total fee which you may incur for our services. The amount of the total fee shall be determined finally by the amount of hourly time expended by our firm in representing you.

Our billing rate shall be $475 per hour for attorney services. If the minimum fee charged is exhausted by our billable time, you shall be billed on a monthly basis for additional legal fees earned. Billable time commenced as of [DATE].

Your payment of [AMOUNT] received on [DATE] will be credited to your account. The balance of [AMOUNT] shall be due by [DATE].

Legal fees will be incurred when attorney's time is expended relative to your case, including by way of example, but not limited to legal research and writing, office meetings, telephone calls and conferences (either placed by or placed to you or otherwise made or received on your behalf, or related to your matter), preparation, review and revision of correspondence, file review, preparation time, travel time and any other attorney's time expended on behalf or in connection with your case.

It is further agreed that this sum is exclusive of expenses and disbursements incurred. Such expenses and disbursements may include, but are not limited to, fees for investigators, expert witnesses, fees for photographs, fees for copies, and any and all necessary expenses incurred. Disbursements will be billed to you as they are incurred and are to paid directly to the firm. Disbursements are not legal fees and are not deductible from your retainer.

It is further understood and agreed that this retainer does not include the legal services to be rendered in connection with any additional criminal charges you may face or any appellate proceeding. Said representation shall be subject to a separate retainer agreement.

Additionally, I reserve the right to terminate this agreement for non-payment of fees or costs upon fifteen (15) days' notice in writing. In the event this retainer is terminated by either party, it is specifically agreed between us that the firm shall be compensated at the rate as specified above. Any amounts paid toward the fee shall be retained as payment towards said services rendered and you shall remain liable for any balance due and owing.

It is further understood that I have made no promises to you as to the outcome of my representation other than our promise to render services to the very best of our ability.

If you should have any questions regarding the terms of this retainer agreement, please call me. If the terms herein are acceptable to you, kindly return a signed copy of this agreement to my office at your earliest opportunity.

Very truly yours,


[ATTORNEY NAME]

XXX:xx

I have read the foregoing retainer agreement, understand the same, and agree to all the provision thereof, and guarantee payment of all fees set forth herein.


_____     _____
[CLIENT NAME]                      Date

# Retainer Letter (criminal)

## Retainer Letter
(Criminal)

_____           _____

_____

_____

Dear

        Re:  People  v. [CLIENT NAME]
        Court:

This will serve to confirm that you have retained my office to represent [CLIENT NAME] on the following charge(s) pending in the [COURT NAME] Court of [COUNTY NAME] County:

It is agreed that I shall receive the amount of $[AMOUNT] for the non trial disposition of this matter. This retainer amount shall constitute payment for my representation including all legal research, preparation of all pre-trial motions, calendar calls, argument of motions, conferences with the Court, conferences with expert witnesses and conferences with you. In the event of a trial, I will charge an additional sum of $[AMOUNT] per day for each day of trial. A trial day consists of any day in which sworn testimony is taken of a witness during pre trial hearings, trial, jury selection, jury charge, jury deliberation and sentencing, if applicable.

I have received payment of $[AMOUNT]. The balance of $[AMOUNT] is due as follows:

        $_____ due by _____

        $_____ due by _____

        $_____ due by _____

        $_____ due by _____

        $_____ due by _____

        $_____ due by _____

It is further agreed that this sum is exclusive of expenses and disbursements incurred. Such expenses and disbursements may include, but are not limited to, fees for investigators, expert witnesses, fees for photographs, fees for court reporters, transcripts, and any and all necessary expenses incurred.

It is further understood and agreed that this retainer does not include the services to be rendered in connection with any appellate proceedings that may have to be taken hereinafter. Such services are subject to a separate retainer with my office or such other counsel as you may select.

Additionally, I reserve the right to terminate this agreement for non-payment of fees or costs upon twenty-one (21) days' notice in writing by certified mail, return-receipt requested. In the event this retainer is terminated by either party, it is specifically agreed between us that I shall be compensated at the rate of $450 per hour. Any amounts paid toward the fee shall be retained as payment towards said services rendered and you shall remain liable for any balance due and owing.

It is further understood that I have made no promises to you as to the outcome of this case other than my promise to render my services to the very best of my ability.

If you should have any questions regarding the terms of this retainer agreement, please call me. If the terms herein are acceptable to you, kindly return a signed copy of this agreement to my office at your earliest opportunity.

Very truly yours,

_____
[ATTORNEY NAME]

XXX:xx

        I have read the foregoing retainer agreement, understand the same, and agree to all the provision thereof, and guarantee payment of all fees set forth herein.

        _____     _____
        [CLIENT NAME]              Date

        _____
        Social Security No.

# Retainer Agreement (Chapter 7 bankruptcy)

### CHAPTER 7 RETAINER AGREEMENT

I (We), <u>Debtor & Joint Debtor</u>. have retained the Law Office of _____, to represent me (us) in a Chapter 7 Bankruptcy proceeding. I (We), <u>Debtor & Joint Debtor</u>, agreed that the fee for representation in this proceeding is the sum of $\underline{\$_____}$ plus the court filing fee of $335.00.

Any fee paid for pre-petition services must be paid at the time the Chapter 7 bankruptcy proceeding is executed.

The remaining fee due is for post-petition services and must be paid no later than the chapter 7 341 meeting of creditors which is approximately held thirty (30) days after the bankruptcy filing date. This fee is based upon the following assumptions. The Debtor(s) provided complete and accurate information. If the assumption set out above is not accurate, the fee shall be increased to compensate for additional time and expense in providing legal services.

I (We), understand that it is my (our) responsibility to provide a complete list of creditors including the names, addresses. amounts and account numbers to my attorneys reflecting all monies due and owing to creditors prior to the bankruptcy filing date.

In addition it is understood that the Law Office of _____, may receive legal fees paid after filing for certain post-petition bankruptcy legal services, including but not limited to telephone conferences with client; discussions with secured creditors to obtain reaffirmation agreements and execution of related documents; ensuring that Debtors have completed Pre-Discharge education course and filing the appropriate certificates with the court; appearance at a discharge hearing if applicable and all copy charges, fax charges and postage related to the above services.

I (We) understand that the above services are all that are necessary, in most cases. Representation after Discharge, if necessary, is <u>not</u> included in this fee. In the event that additional services are necessary, I (we) agree to pay the following fees for the following services:

1. Attend any adjourned Section 341 caused by my failure to come to Court or failure to provide necessary documents for the progress of the case - $250.00 per appearance.

2. Represent me in regards to a Motion to Lift/Dismiss due to my failure to make mortgage/loan/lease payments or due to my failure to appear at any Court proceedings - $450.00

3. Amending schedules prior to Discharge, to include an asset or a debt I failed to reveal to the Law Office of _____ prior to the filing of my Petition - $250.00 plus $30.00 Court filing fee.

4. Motions on my behalf to expunge or reduce claims or to avoid liens - $750.00 and up.

5. Conversion to Chapter 13, including preparation of schedules, plan and attendance at Chapter 13 Section 341 and Confirmation hearing - $2,500.00.

6. All other contested matters including 11 U.S.C. 707(b) inquiries, except for the defense of an adversary proceeding, will be billed hourly at $495.00 per hour for partner time and $350.00 for a Senior Associate and $275.00 for a Junior Associate.

    7. Auto reaffirmation agreement. redemption or return of collateral securing a consumer loan- $250.00.

    8. An additional fee of $250.00 may be charged if the petition is filed on an emergency basis and outside the regular course of the Law Office of _____'s practice of filing petitions in bulk.

    This retainer agreement excludes the defense of an adversary proceeding and such a defense is not within the agreed scope of representation as set forth in this retainer agreement. Absent our firm being retained under a separate retainer agreement by you and our firm being compensated pursuant to a new retainer agreement as to the fees and costs involved in the defense of the adversary proceeding, we will either have to obtain separate counsel for the defense of the adversary proceeding or alternatively defend such an action yourself. In the event our firm is not retained as counsel in the adversary proceeding, the nature of the adversary proceeding and the claims asserted against you will be discussed with you and you will be advised that it is your obligation to file and serve an appropriate response to the complaint and the consequences if you fail to timely answer the complaint. We will also explain to you the requirements and time limits applicable for the preparation, filing and service of a responsive pleading and/or answer to the complaint. Representation will be provided under a separate retainer agreement agreed to by you and our law office.

    I (We) understand that if I (we) fail to pay the Law Office of _____, any fee agreed upon in this Retainer Agreement when it becomes due, then the Law Office of _____ will stop all work on my case and ask the Court to be relieved as my attorney. I (We) understand that all legal fee payments are not refundable.

    I (We) understand that certain taxes, fines, penalties, student loans, support and maintenance may not be dischargeable, as well as any debts not listed on the petition.

    I (We) understand that after the petition is filed, it is my (our) responsibility to complete an instructional course in personal financial management (Debtor Education Program). I (We) agree to complete this course within thirty (30) days after the petition is filed.

    **SPECIAL NOTE:** I (We) understand there is **NO PROTECTION** against foreclosure/eviction/garnishment until the Petition is filed in Court. I (We), <u>Debtor & Joint Debtor</u>, understand that my Petition will not be filed until I (we) have paid the Law Office of _____ _____. Additionally, if any payment is paid by personal check, I (we) understand that the Law Office of _____, will not file this Chapter 7 Petition until the check clears the bank.

LAW OFFICE OF _____

_____
By:

**AGREED & CONSENTED TO:**
this _____ day of _____, 2015

_____
Debtor-

_____
Debtor-

# Retainer Agreement (contingent, judgment collection)

**[FIRM NAME], A Professional; Corporation**
**RETAINER AGREEMENT (Judgment Collection – Contingent Fee)**

**THIS AGREEMENT** between [FIRM NAME], A P.C. ("Law Firm") and _____("Client") is made at [CITY], [STATE] as of _____, 20__.

**Conditions.** This Agreement will not take effect, and Law Firm shall have no professional responsibility or obligation to render legal services, until Client signs this Agreement and pays any required retainer.

**Legal Services To Be Provided.** Client as judgment creditor engages Law Firm as counsel to collect the following judgment(s): _____

_____

Services rendered for a contingent fee include: (i) domestication of the judgment(s) if rendered in a state other than [STATE]; (ii) preparation and filing of an abstract of judgment and business personal property lien; (iii) online investigation; (iv) realizing upon property subject to enforcement of the judgment by levy, garnishment and other lawful judicial remedies; (v) conducting a judgment debtor examination; ; (vi) filing a proof of claim in any bankruptcy case; (vii) defending, any judicial lien against avoidance motions under 11 U.S.C. § 522(f), if a defense is warranted and economically practical in Law Firm's business judgment; and (viii) reporting significant developments to Client. Services which will not be rendered for a contingent fee, but which may be rendered for an hourly fee, in addition to the contingent fee, include: (a) defending any action commenced against Client, including avoidance actions in bankruptcy; (b) prosecuting or defending any appeal or petition for an extraordinary writ; (c) prosecution of actions against third parties, including claims to avoid fraudulent transfers; (d) prosecution of a complaint to determine dischargeability in bankruptcy; and (e) making any motion to withdraw as counsel which is granted by the court. Except with respect to services relating to termination of Law Firm's employment, no services to be rendered for an hourly fee shall be performed by Law Firm without the consent of Client. Law Firm will do only what is reasonable in light of the amounts at issue and the likelihood of recovery. Unless otherwise indicated below ("Special Provisions") Client has not called to Law Firm's attention any facts indicating the need for secrecy, or for extraordinary or emergency relief. Law Firm is not qualified, and has not been retained, to give tax advice. Client has the responsibility to consult with a tax specialist as to the tax effect of any event, including actions which Law Firm advises Client to take.

**Law Firm's Responsibilities.** Law Firm promises to abide by this Agreement, and to:
- Competently and diligently provide the legal services described above.
- Keep Client informed of its progress, and of any important developments.
- Respond promptly to Client's telephone calls and letters.
- Cooperate with Client so that Client may be effectively represented.

**Client's Responsibilities.** Client promises to abide by this Agreement, and to:
- Pay the contingent fee and the costs provided for under this Agreement.
- Keep Law Firm advised of Client's current address, telephone number, and whereabouts.
- Inform Law Firm promptly of any dissatisfaction with Law Firm's services or with its fees.
- Cooperate with Law Firm so that Client may be effectively represented. Client agrees to inform Law Firm of all relevant facts, whether or not Client believes that any fact is unfavorable, and to provide copies (or originals if requested and available) of all relevant documents.

**Fees.** Law Firm's contingent fee shall be computed as twenty five percent (25%) of the total gross recovery obtained in relation to the matter in which Law Firm is engaged. Fees shall be owing as to all collections made after retention of Law Firm, regardless of whether: (i) payment is tendered to Law Firm or directly to Client; (ii) collection was the result of services provided by Law Firm, or (iii) a "Closing Notice" has been given closing Law Firm's file as described below. In the event that rights in property are obtained pursuant to settlement, judgment or execution, Law Firm's shall be entitled to an undivided twenty five percent (25%) ownership interest in such property (irrespective of any different percentage set forth in this Agreement). Such interest shall be deemed to have been created at the time Client acquires rights in such property. Such interest is not intended by the parties for purposes of security. Client agrees to execute, at Law Firm's request, all documents reasonably required to evidence such interest, including, e.g., quitclaim deeds.

**Costs And Expenses.** Client agrees to pay Law Firm's out of pocket expenses in relation to collection of the judgment, including but not limited to: (i) court filing fees; (ii) service of process; (iii) online research; (iv) court reporters; (v) copy services; (vi) postage and courier services; and (vii) travel expenses. Client will provide an advance retainer for costs as provided for below. Such expenses shall not exceed in total $_____ except as authorized by Client. Law Firm is not required to advance any costs exceeding the amount of the retainer then on hand.

**Retainer For Costs.** Client initials: _____ Law Firm initials (or "N/A"): _____ Concurrently with the execution hereof, Client shall pay to Law Firm a retainer for costs and expenses in the amount of $_____. Such sum shall be held in a non-interest bearing trust account by Law Firm and drawn upon as costs are incurred. Law Firm is authorized to, at any time, and without further notice to Client, draw on any trust balance to pay costs directly, or to pay sums owing to Law Firm under this Agreement. At the conclusion of Law Firms's employment, any unused portion of the retainer shall be refunded to Client.

**Security Agreement.** Client grants to Law Firm a security interest in any retainer paid in trust to Law Firm, and in any and all claims, causes of action, general intangibles, contract rights and rights to payment of any kind which arise under or relate to the subject of Law Firm's representation. Such lien will attach, without implied limitation, to the judgment itself, and to any recovery Client may obtain by levy, settlement or otherwise. **THIS PROVISION CREATES A CHARGING LIEN IN FAVOR OF LAW FIRM AS SECURITY FOR ITS FEES.** In the event of a dispute between Law Firm and Client, this lien could significantly impair Client's interest by delaying payment of funds owing to Client until the dispute can be resolved. Client authorizes Law Firm to file a financing statement to perfect such lien. Client authorizes Law Firm to negotiate checks and drafts and otherwise receive funds in Client's name and to disburse from those funds all amounts owing to Law Firm under this Agreement prior to remitting the balance to Client.

**Client Trust Funds.** Funds deposited in Law Firm's trust account for the benefit of Client, including retainers, will not bear interest. Client may request in writing that an interest bearing account be established, providing Client's social security number or tax identification number for reporting purposes.

**Termination of Services.** The attorney-client relationship is one of mutual trust, confidence and respect. For this reason, Client retains the right to discharge Law Firm at any time for any reason, and Client assents to the withdrawal of Law Firm at any time for any reason, provided that Law Firm has taken reasonable steps to avoid reasonably foreseeable prejudice to the rights of Client. Client agrees to execute any Substitution of Attorney necessary to effect the withdrawal. If Law Firm withdraws for "cause," Client will remain liable for all fees and expenses incurred under the terms of this Agreement, including the required percentage of any recovery subsequent to Law Firm's withdrawal, whether or not such subsequent collection is due to the efforts of Law Firm. If Law Firm withdraws without "cause," Client will be responsible to reimburse Law Firm for costs advanced. "Cause" includes: (i) Client's breach of this Agreement: (ii) failure to pay fees or costs when due; (iii) failure to cooperate such that it becomes unreasonably difficult for Law Firm to carry out its employment; or (iv) any other fact or circumstance under which Law Firm may withdraw under the Rules of Professional Conduct.

**File Closing.** Law Firm may determine that further active efforts to collect are unlikely to yield results and would not be economically practical for Law Firm as a matter of business judgment. In that case, Law Firm may notify Client that Law Firm is closing its file (a "Closing Notice"). After giving a Closing Notice, Law Firm shall have no further professional responsibility to continue to make active attempts to locate the debtor or the debtor's assets, conduct further investigation, renew any judgment or judgment lien, or report to the Client. Law Firm may in its business judgment, but is not required to, renew any judgment or judicial lien after a Closing Notice is given.

**Return of Client's File.** Upon client's written request Law Firm will, whether or not all fees owing under this Agreement have been paid, make Client's file (with the exception of Law Firm's work product) available for pickup by Client at Law Firm's office. Law Firm may at any time request in writing that Client take possession of all or a portion of Client's file. If Client does not take possession within 30 days after mailing of such request, Law Firm may thereafter destroy the file. In any case, Law Firm is authorized to destroy the file without notice five years after termination of Law Firm's employment.

**No Guaranties of Outcome.** Most commercial claims referred to collection lawyers are not collected due to the disappearance of debtors, the lack of available assets, or bankruptcy. Nothing in this Agreement, and no statement made to Client before or after this Agreement is signed, is intended as a promise or guaranty of collection Law Firm's comments about the anticipated outcome are expressions of opinion only.

**General Provisions.** This Agreement contains the entire agreement and understanding between Law Firm and Client as to the terms of Law Firm's engagement. It cannot be modified except in writing signed by the party against which the modification is to be enforced. The venue of any action arising under or relating to this Agreement or Law Firm's representation of Client shall be in [CITY], [STATE].
**THE PROVISIONS OF THIS AGREEMENT (INCLUDING THE PERCENTAGE FEE) ARE NOT SET BY LAW, BUT ARE NEGOTIABLE BETWEEN LAW FIRM AND CLIENT PRIOR TO EXECUTING THIS AGREEMENT. CLIENT MAY SEEK THE ADVICE OF AN INDEPENDENT LAWYER OF CLIENT'S CHOICE** before signing this Agreement.
(Set forth special provisions here or refer to any Addendum to be attached to this Agreement.)_____

**READ THIS AGREEMENT CAREFULLY. AMONG OTHER THINGS, IT PROVIDES FOR:**
- **COMPENSATION OF LAW FIRM BASED ON A CONTINGENT (PERCENTAGE) FEE;**
- **REIMBURSEMENT OF LAW FIRM FOR COSTS WHETHER OR NOT THERE IS A RECOVERY;**
- **CREATION OF A CHARGING LIEN IN FAVOR OF LAW FIRM.**

"CLIENT"                                                        "LAW FIRM"
                                                               [FIRM NAME], A P.C.


_____
_____          Client acknowledges receipt          By:_____
Print Name and Title                        of a duplicate copy of this
                                            Agreement

# Fee Agreement and Authority to Represent (flat fee)

# Fee Agreement and Authority to Represent (Flat Fee)

I, _____, the undersigned client (hereinafter referred to as "I," "me" or the "Client"), do hereby retain and employ _____ and his law firm (hereinafter referred to as "Attorney"), as my Attorney to represent me in connection with the following matter:

_____

The firm will provide all services necessary to the representation of the above matter, including court appearances, investigation, pretrial discovery, negotiations with opposing counsel and trial on the merits, if necessary. I also authorize Attorney to retain and employ other attorneys with my prior knowledge and written consent; however, the entire fee of Attorney and such other attorneys shall be limited as set forth hereinbelow.

1. **ATTORNEY'S FEES.** As compensation for legal services, I agree to pay my Attorney as follows:

   **Flat Fee**

   I understand that the flat fee for these legal services is $ _____ , which amount is due and payable before _____. The fee reflects not simply the number of hours which individual lawyers may devote to my representation, but also the experience, reputation, skill and efficiency of the attorneys, as well as the potential inability of the firm to accept other employment during the pendency of the representation. I understand that if all of the flat fee is not received by _____, then this agreement is null and void. This agreement pertains to the representation through trial only. Any writ, appeal, new trial motion or any other kind of post-trial relief must be the subject of a new written fee agreement.

2. **COSTS AND EXPENSES.** In addition to paying Attorney's fees, I agree to pay all costs and expenses in connection with Attorney's handling of this matter. Costs and expenses shall be billed to me as they are incurred, and I hereby agree to promptly reimburse Attorney. If an advance deposit is being held by the Attorney, I agree to promptly reimburse the Attorney for any amount in excess of what is being held in advance. These costs may include (but are not limited to) the following: long distance telephone charges, photocopying ( ____ per page), postage, facsimile costs, Federal Express or other delivery charges, deposition fees, expert fees, subpoena costs, court costs, sheriff's and service fees, travel expenses and investigation fees.

   **Advance required**        ____ Yes ____ No

   I agree to advance $ ____ for costs and expenses, which amount shall be deposited in Attorney's trust account and shall be applied to costs and expenses as they accrue. Should this advance be exhausted, I agree to replenish the advance promptly upon Attorney's request. If I fail to replenish the advance within ten (10) days of Attorney's request, Attorney shall have, in addition to other rights, the right to withdraw as my Attorney.

3. **NO GUARANTEE.** I acknowledge that Attorney has made no promise or guarantee regarding the outcome of my legal matter. In fact, Attorney has advised me that litigation in general is

risky, can take a long time, can be very costly and can be very frustrating. I further acknowledge that Attorney shall have the right to cancel this agreement and withdraw from this matter if, in Attorney's professional opinion, the matter does not have merit, I do not have a reasonably good possibility of recovery, I refuse to follow the recommendations of Attorney, I fail to abide by the terms of this agreement, and/or if Attorney's continued representation would result in a violation of the Rules of Professional Conduct.

[Optional]
[4. **ALTERNATIVE DISPUTE RESOLUTION.** In the event of any dispute or disagreement concerning this agreement, I agree to submit to arbitration by the [STATE] State Bar Association Legal Fee Dispute Resolution Program.]

**NOTICE: By initialing in the space below, you are agreeing to have any dispute arising out of the matters included in the "Alternative Dispute Resolution" provision decided by neutral binding arbitration as provided by [STATE] Arbitration Law; and you are giving up your right to have the dispute decided in a court or jury trial. By initialing in the space below, you are also giving up your rights to discovery and appeal. If you refuse to submit to arbitration after agreeing to this provision, you may be compelled to arbitrate under the authority of the [STATE] Arbitration Law.**

**I have read and understand the foregoing and agree to submit to neutral binding arbitration disputes arising out of the matters included in the "Alternative Dispute Resolution" provision.**

Client's Initials _____

Attorney's Initials _____

5. **ADDITIONAL TERMS.** Attorney and Client agree to the following additional terms:

_____

6. **ENTIRE AGREEMENT.** I have read this agreement in its entirety and I agree to and understand the terms and conditions set forth herein. I acknowledge that there are no other terms or oral agreements existing between Attorney and Client. This agreement may not be amended or modified in any way without the prior written consent of Attorney and Client.

**This agreement is executed by me, the undersigned Client, on this ____ day of _____, 20 __ .**

                   **CLIENT** _____

**The foregoing agreement is hereby accepted on this ___ day of _____, 20 __ .**

                   **ATTORNEY** _____

## Retainer Agreement (hybrid)

## Retainer Agreement
### (Hybrid)

I _____ hereby retain The Law Office _____
(hereinafter referred to as my attorney) to represent me with regard to the following
matter:_____
_____.


RESTRICTIONS ON SETTLEMENT

It is agreed that my attorney will not settle this action in any manner without my (our)
consent.


LEGAL FEES

1. Simultaneously with the signing of this agreement I am paying the Law Offices of
_____ the sum of $10,000.00 as and for a minimum
fee with regard to the above referenced matter.

2. I further agree that should the Law Offices of _____ be successful and
obtain a recovery in this matter, the attorney shall receive a total sum of thirty-
three and one-third per cent of the net (after expenses) recovery. The minimum
retainer that I have paid will be credited against that recovery. So by way of
example, if the attorney settles my case for $100,000.00, the attorney shall be
entitled to the sum of $33,333.33 as and for attorney's fees. My retainer payment
of $10,000.00 shall be credited to me and thus my attorney shall be entitled to an
additional $23,333.33 from the settlement proceeds.

3. I further agree that should either I or the attorney terminate our relationship prior to a
settlement or verdict in this matter, my attorney shall be entitled to retain so much
of the retainer payment as he has earned for time spent at the following hourly
billing rates:

Attorney Name _____
Associates _____
Paralegals _____

In addition, I agree that my attorney shall be entitled to be paid quantum meruit
for any additional sums to which he/she may be entitled from any recovery. The
attorney shall be entitled to a charging lien against any recovery.

4. My attorney shall send me a statement at least every sixty days as to time spent on my matter and for what purpose.

## CLIENT'S ADDITIONAL FINANCIAL RESPONSIBILITIES

1. I understand that I am fully and solely responsible for paying for all disbursements associated with this litigation including but not limited to the following: cost of investigation, expert fees, reports, index numbers and filing fees, transcripts, depositions and any other costs associated with the investigation and or pursuit of this matter. I understand that my failure to pay any of the said expenses when requested will absolve my attorneys of any obligation to incur said expense. It is agreed that should the court ultimately award monies for the cost of such expenses, and monies are in fact collected, I will be reimbursed for expense payments I have made for costs for which the attorney has been paid.

2. My attorney shall send all requests for disbursements to me in writing, and I understand I am responsible for paying same in a timely fashion, and more particularly such that I do not prejudice my case.

3. Returned check fee: Should client remit a payment to this office by way of check, and it is returned for insufficient funds or stop payment, a $20.00 returned check fee will be assessed to client.

## CLIENT'S RESPONSIBILITIES (NON-FINANCIAL)

A. At attorney's request, to provide and to help Attorney obtain all information (in whatever form it may appear) that I or someone to whom I may make an appropriate request possesses;

B. To make myself available for any meetings, interviews, or other events that attorney requires, including at attorney's office if requested;

C. To carefully consider attorney's advice before making any major decisions.

D. To make myself available to provide sworn testimony, e.g., in a deposition, affidavit, trial or other proceedings, when attorney requests this.

E. To immediately tell attorney if and when I move change residences), change jobs, change my phone number or other electronic means of communication, or otherwise make it difficult for attorney to communicate with me;

F. To inform attorney about any new developments or information in the matter, e.g., court notices, letters from the opposing party, new factual developments, or other similar developments;

G. To respond to attorney's communications (letters, telephone calls, or other forms of electronic forms of communication) as soon as reasonably possible;

H.     To otherwise, as indicated by attorney, help attorney provide the services identified above in the scope of services and to effectively represent client; and

## BASES FOR ATTORNEY TO WITHDRAW

I have been informed that any of the following shall be a basis for my attorney to be able to withdraw from my representation:

- My breach of any portion of this agreement (including its payment provisions).
- My refusal to cooperate with my attorney or to follow my attorney's advice on a material matter;
- Or any other fact or circumstance that would render the attorney's continuing representation unlawful, unethical, or impractical.

## POSSIBLE CONFLICTS OF INTEREST

If attorney determines that he/she represents another client whose interests conflict, or are likely to conflict, with client's interests, Attorney reserves the right to terminate this agreement, while protecting the confidentiality of any privileged information that client has provided to attorney.

## GROUND TO TERMINATE THIS AGREEMENT

A.     Client may terminate this agreement for any or no reason, although Client still will be 1legally obligated under this agreement to meet Client's obligations to attorney, including the obligation to pay to attorney the agreed-upon attorney's fee to the extent it has been earned.

B.     Attorney may terminate this agreement if, in attorney's sole judgment, client has failed to fulfill one of client's material obligations under this agreement, or for other good cause, or for any other reason authorized by law including the ethical rules that govern attorneys.

## NO PROMISES

Other than agreeing to work diligently on the client's behalf, I understand that my attorney is making no promises with regard to the outcome of this matter.

CLIENT'S INFORMED CONSENT

Client has carefully read this agreement and considered the additional information and advice that attorney has provided to client. Client understands the possible risks and benefits of the limited-service representation described in this agreement. Understanding those possible risks and benefits, client voluntarily, knowingly and intentionally enters into this agreement with attorney.


Dated: _____


Client's Signature


_____
Client's Name (handwritten)


_____
Attorney Signature

# Retainer Agreement (civil rights)

CIVIL RIGHTS RETAINER

AUTHORIZATION TO PROSECUTE

The undersigned _____ residing at ADDRESS being an aggrieved party and prospective charging party and/or Plaintiff in a Complaint, hereby retains The Law Office of _____ to prosecute or adjust a claim for damages and/ or any other relief relating to a violation of civil rights, to wit: _____

_____

_____ the same which may constitute negligence, civil rights violations, constitutional violations or violations of any rights to which the clients are entitled. Included in these rights is the right to free speech, protection from seizure, beating and use of excessive and unreasonable force, unfair and improper practices, procedures, actions or otherwise by said individuals, corporations and municipalities. Also the client seeks protection from injury to the client's reputation, and retaliation at the hands of said parties and/or their employees, agents or servants and/or any other body, person or persons who have participated in wrongful acts against me. The undersigned client hereby gives you, The Law Offices of _____, Attorney, the exclusive right to take all legal steps to enforce the said claim.

RESTRICTIONS ON SETTLEMENT

It is agreed that Attorney will not settle this action in any manner without the consent of the client.

LEGAL FEES

In consideration of the services rendered and to be rendered by Attorney, the undersigned hereby agrees to pay you and you are authorized to seek payment as follows:

1.      Seven thousand five hundred dollars ($7,500.00) as an initial retainer fee.

2.      It is agreed that Attorney will bill against the initial retainer fee at the hourly rate stated herein.

3.      The hourly rate which your office will charge for your services is five hundred dollars ($500.00), and the balance of your staff will charge an hourly rate equal to, or less than, three hundred fifty dollars ($350.00).

4.      Client understands that he/she will be billed periodically for the services being provided, and that they are ultimately responsible for the attorney's fees and costs incurred as part of this case. In addition, client agrees that the attorney may seek further litigation, trial fees, and costs at a later time for which I am responsible.

5.       It is understood that you may seek such attorney's fees that are due you for work performed through proper application to the Court.

6.       Client agrees to pay Attorney thirty-three and one-third percent (33-1/3%) of any amount recovered by settlement and/or trial, but if the total hourly fee is greater than said percentage, Client is responsible for paying any balance.

CLIENT'S ADDITIONAL FINANCIAL RESPONSIBILITIES

There may be additional costs and expenses in this matter, for example, filing fees; the costs of transcribing testimony taken at a hearing or trial; subpoena costs; an expert's fees (if appropriate for the matter); the costs of an investigator or of other methods to discover and obtain factual information; document-reproduction expenses; discovery costs (including those of depositions); out-of-jurisdiction travel, lodging, meal, and related expenses; the costs of long-distance phone calls, facsimile transmissions; other forms of communication; and the costs required to reasonably conduct on-line legal research (if necessary). Client, not Attorney, is responsible for these costs. It is agreed that Client's failure to bear or assist bearing said expenses when requested will absolve Attorney of any obligation to incur said expense. It is agreed that should the court ultimately award the cost of such expenses, the client will be reimbursed for expense payments they have made.

Returned check fee: Should Client remit a payment to this office by way of check, and it is returned for insufficient funds or stop payment, a $20.00 returned check fee will be assessed to Client.

STATEMENTS, INVOICING AND BILLING INQUIRIES

Attorney will send Client periodic statements every sixty days (60) for costs, expenses, and legal services incurred. The sum indicated on such statements is owed upon generation of the statement, and must be paid within thirty days (30) of the statement date. In the event Client does not pay the statement amount, Attorney shall have the option of immediately withdrawing from representation if permitted by law. If court permission is required for withdrawal, then in that event, the failure to timely make payment shall be deemed a basis for attorney seeking to withdraw as counsel.

CAUSES FOR ATTORNEY WITHDRAWAL

Client has been informed that among the events that should be expected to cause Attorney's withdrawal from this case are:

• Client's breach of any portion of this agreement (including its payment provisions).
• Client's refusal to cooperate with attorney or to follow Attorney's advice on a material matter;
• Or any other fact or circumstance that would render Attorney's continuing representation unlawful, unethical, or impractical.

OBLIGATIONS OF CLIENT

To help Attorney represent Client effectively, and to reduce the costs of the representation, Client agrees:

A.    At Attorney's request, to provide and to help Attorney obtain all information (in whatever form it may appear) that Client or someone to whom Client may make an appropriate request possesses;

B.    To make himself or herself available for any meetings, interviews, or other events that Attorney requires, including at Attorney's office if requested;

C.    To carefully consider Attorney's advice before making any major decisions;

D.    To make himself/herself available to provide sworn testimony, e.g., in a deposition, affidavit, trial or other proceedings, when Attorney requests this.

E.    To immediately tell Attorney if and when Client moves (changes residences), changes jobs, changes a phone number or other electronic means of communication, or otherwise makes it difficult for Attorney to communicate with Client;

F.    To inform Attorney about any new developments or information in the matter, e.g., court notices, letters from the opposing party, new factual developments, or other similar developments;

G.    To respond to Attorney's communications (letters, telephone calls, or other forms of electronic forms of communication) as soon as reasonably possible;

H.    To otherwise, as indicated by Attorney, help Attorney provide the services identified above in the scope of services and to effectively represent Client; and

POSSIBLE CONFLICTS OF INTEREST

If Attorney determines that he represents another client whose interests conflict, or are likely to conflict, with Client's interests, Attorney reserves the right to terminate this Agreement, while protecting the confidentiality of any privileged information that Client has provided to Attorney.

GROUND TO TERMINATE THIS AGREEMENT

A.    Client may terminate this Agreement for any or no reason, although Client still will be legally obligated under this Agreement to meet Client's obligations to Attorney, including the obligation to pay to Attorney the agreed-upon attorney's fee to the extent it has been earned.

B.      Attorney may terminate this Agreement if, in Attorney's sole judgment, Client has failed to fulfill one of Client's material obligations under this Agreement, or for other good cause, or for any other reason authorized by law (including the ethical rules that govern lawyers.

CLIENT'S INFORMED CONSENT

Client has carefully read this Agreement and considered the additional information and advice that Attorney has provided to Client. Client understands the possible risks and benefits of the limited-service representation described in this Agreement. Understanding those possible risks and benefits, Client voluntarily, knowingly and intentionally enters into this Agreement with Attorney.

Dated:_____

_____L.S.
CLIENT'S NAME

_____
LAW OFFICES OF

# Engagement Letter: Limited Scope Retainer

Reprinted with permission of Lawyers Mutual
from Attorney-Client Agreements Toolkit          RISK MANAGEMENT HANDOUTS OF LAWYERS MUTUAL

## ENGAGEMENT LETTER: LIMITED SCOPE RETAINER AGREEMENT

This Agreement is made between the Attorney and Client named at the end of this agreement.

1. **Nature of Agreement**. This Agreement describes the relationship between the Attorney and Client. Specifically, this Agreement defines:

    a. The general nature of the Client's case;

    b. The responsibilities and control that the Client agrees to retain over the case;

    c. The services that the Client seeks from the Attorney in his/her capacity as attorney at law;

    d. The limits of the Attorney's responsibilities;

    e. Methods to resolve disputes between Attorney and Client; and

    f. The method of payment by Client for services rendered by the Attorney.

2. **Nature of Case**. The Client is requesting services from the Attorney in the following matter:

_____

_____

3. **Client Responsibilities and Control**. The Client intends to handle his/her own case and understands that he/she will remain in control of the case and be responsible for all decisions made in the course of the case. The Client will:

    a. Cooperate with the Attorney or Attorney's office by complying with all reasonable requests for information in connection with the matter for which the Client is requesting services;

    b. Keep the Attorney or Attorney's office advised of the Client's concerns and any information that is pertinent to the Client's case;

    c. Provide the Attorney with copies of all correspondence to and from the Client relevant to the case; and

    d. Keep all documents related to the case in a file for review by the Attorney.

4. **Services Sought by Client**. The Client seeks the following services from the Attorney (please indicate services sought with check mark):

    ____ a. Legal advice: office visits, telephone calls, fax, mail, electronic mail.

    ____ b. Advice about the availability of alternative means to resolve the dispute, including mediation and arbitration.

    ____ c. Evaluation of the Client's self-diagnosis of the case and advice about the Client's legal rights.

    ____ d. Guidance and procedural information for filing or serving documents.

    ____ e. Review of correspondence and court documents.

    ____ f. Preparation of documents and/or suggestions concerning documents to be prepared.

    ____ g. Factual investigation: contacting witnesses, public record searches, in-depth interview of Client.

    ____ h. Legal research and analysis.

    ____ i. Discovery: interrogatories, depositions, requests for document production.

    ____ j. Planning for negotiations, including role playing with the Client.

    ____ k. Planning for court appearances to be made by Client, including role playing with the Client.

    ____ l. Backup and trouble shooting during the trial.

    ____ m. Referrals to other counsel, experts, or professionals.

    ____ n. Counseling the Client about an appeal.

    ____ o. Procedural help with an appeal and assisting with substantive legal argumentation in an appeal.

    ____ p. Preventive planning and/or legal check-ups.

    ____ q. Other: _____

5. **Attorney's Responsibilities**. The Attorney shall exercise due professional care and observe strict confidentiality in providing the services identified by a checkmark in Paragraph 4 above. In providing those services, Attorney SHALL NOT:

    a. Represent, speak for, appear for, or sign papers on the Client's behalf;

    b. Provide services listed in Paragraph 4 that are not identified by a checkmark; or

    c. Make decisions for the Client about any aspect of the case.

ATTORNEY-CLIENT AGREEMENTS TOOLKIT

---

6. **Method and Payment for Services.**

a. *Hourly fee.* The current hourly fee charged by the Attorney for services under this agreement is as follows:

Senior Partner:   $_____$
Junior Partner:   $_____$
Associate:       $_____$

Unless a different fee arrangement is specified in clauses (b) or (c) of this Paragraph, the hourly fee shall be payable at the time of the service.

b. *Payment from Retainer.* The Client shall have the option of setting up a deposit fund with the Attorney. Services are then paid for from this retainer account as they occur. If a retainer is established under this clause, the Attorney shall mail the Client a billing statement summarizing the type of services performed, the costs and expenses incurred, and the current balance in the retainer after the appropriate deductions have been made. Client may replenish the retainer or continue to draw the funds down as additional services are delivered. If the retainer becomes depleted, the Client must pay for additional services as provided in clauses (a) or (c) of this Paragraph.

c. *Flat Rate Charges.* The Attorney has the option of agreeing to provide one or more of the services described in Paragraph 4 for a flat rate. Any such agreement shall be set out in writing, dated, signed by both Attorney and Client, and attached to this Agreement.

d. *Attorneys' Fees.* Should it be necessary to institute any legal action for the enforcement of this Agreement, the prevailing party shall be entitled to receive from the other party all court costs and reasonable attorneys' fees incurred in that action.

7. **Resolving Disputes Between Client and Attorney.**

a. *Notice and Negotiation.* If any dispute between Client and Attorney arises under this Agreement, both Attorney and Client agree to meet and confer within ten (10) days of written notice by either Client or Attorney that the dispute exists. The purpose of this meeting and conference will be to negotiate a solution short of further dispute resolution proceedings.

b. *Mediation.* If the dispute is not resolved through negotiation, the Client and Attorney shall attempt, within fifteen (15) days of failed negotiations, to agree on a neutral mediator whose role will be to facilitate further negotiations within fifteen (15) days. If Attorney and Client cannot agree on a neutral mediator, they shall request that the [local or state] bar association select a mediator. The mediation shall occur within fifteen (15) days after the mediator is selected. The Attorney and Client shall share the costs of mediation, provided that payment of the costs and any attorneys' fees may also be mediated.

c. *Arbitration.* If mediation fails to produce a full settlement of the dispute satisfactory to both Client and Attorney, Client and Attorney agree to submit to binding arbitration under the rules of the [governing] bar association. This arbitration must take place within sixty (60) days of the failure of mediation. Costs and attorneys' fees for arbitration and prior mediation may be awarded to the prevailing party.

8. **Amendments and Additional Services.** This written Agreement governs the entire relationship between the Client and Attorney. All amendments shall be in writing and attached to this Agreement. If the Client wishes to obtain additional services from the Attorney as defined in Paragraph 4, a photocopy of Paragraph 4 that clearly denotes which extra services are to be provided must be signed and dated by both Attorney and Client and attached to this Agreement. Such a photocopy shall qualify as an amendment to this agreement.

9. **Statement of Client's Understanding.** I have carefully read this Agreement and believe that I understand all of its provisions. I signify my agreement with the following statements by initialing each one:

_____ I have accurately described the nature of my case in Paragraph 2.

_____ I will remain in control of my case and assume responsibility for my case as described in Paragraph 3.

_____ The services that I want the Attorney to perform in my case are identified by check marks in Paragraph 4. I take responsibility for all other aspects of my case.

___ I accept the limitations on the Attorney's responsibilities identified in Paragraph 5.

___ I shall pay the Attorney for services rendered as described in Paragraph 6.

___ I will resolve any disputes I have with the Attorney under this Agreement in the manner described in Paragraph 7.

___ I understand that any amendments to this Agreement shall be in writing, as described in Paragraph 8.

___ I acknowledge that I have been advised by the Attorney that I have the right to consult another independent Attorney to review this Agreement and to advise me on my rights as a Client before I sign this Agreement.

_____          _____

Client                                          Attorney

_____

Date

* This model agreement is derived from an agreement in *Lawyer's Guide to Being a Client Coach* (1994), published by the California State Bar Committee on Delivery of Legal Services for Middle Income Persons.

*Note. This is a sample form only and is written for the general purposes of facilitating clear expectations and avoiding misunderstandings between an attorney and client. It is not intended as legal advice or opinion and will not provide absolute protection against a malpractice action.*

# Notice and Consent to Limited Representation (example from Missouri)

## Notice and Consent to Limited Representation

To help you with your legal matters, you, the client, and_____, the lawyer, agree that the lawyer will limit the representation to helping you with a certain legal matter for a short time or for a particular purpose.

The lawyer must act in your best interest and give you competent help. When a lawyer and you agree that the lawyer will provide limited help:

• The lawyer DOES NOT HAVE TO GIVE MORE HELP than the lawyer and you agreed; and

• The lawyer DOES NOT HAVE TO HELP WITH ANY OTHER PART of your legal matter.

While performing the limited legal services, the lawyer:

• Is not promising any particular outcome; and

• Is relying entirely on your disclosure of facts and will not make any independent investigation unless expressly agreed to in writing in this document.

If short-term limited representation is not reasonable, a lawyer may give advice, but will also tell you of the need to get more or other legal counsel.

I, the lawyer, agree to help you by performing the following limited services listed below and no other service, unless we revise this agreement in writing.

[INSTRUCTIONS: Check every item either Yes or No - do not leave any item blank. Delete all text that does not apply.]:

Y N

a) \_\_ \_\_ Give legal advice through office visits, telephone calls, facsimile (fax), mail or e-mail

b) \_\_ \_\_ Advise about alternate means of resolving the matter including mediation and arbitration

c) \_\_ \_\_ Evaluate the client's self-diagnosis of the case and advise about legal rights and responsibilities.

d) \_\_ \_\_ Review pleadings and other documents prepared by you, the client

e) \_\_ \_\_ Provide guidance and procedural information regarding filing and serving documents

f) __ __ Suggest documents to be prepared

g) __ __ Draft pleadings, motions and other documents

h) __ __ Perform factual investigation including contacting witnesses, public record searches, in-depth interview of you, the client

i) __ __ Perform legal research and analysis

j) __ __ Evaluate settlement options

k) __ __ Perform discovery by interrogatories, deposition and requests for admissions

l) __ __ Plan for negotiations

m) __ __ Plan for court appearances

n) __ __ Provide standby telephone assistance during negotiations or settlement conferences

o) __ __ Refer you, the client, to expert witnesses, special masters or other attorneys

p) __ __ Provide procedural assistance with an appeal

q) __ __ Provide substantive legal arguments in an appeal

r) __ __ Appear in court for the limited purpose of _____

_____

s) __ __ Other: _____

I will charge to the Client the following costs: _____

_____

I will charge to the Client the following fee for my limited legal representation:

_____

_____      _____
[Type Lawyer's name)                     Date:

**CLIENT'S CONSENT**

I have read this Notice and Consent form and I understand it. I agree that the legal services listed above are the ONLY legal services to be provided by the lawyer. I understand and agree that the lawyer who is helping me with these services is not my lawyer for any other purpose and does not have to give me more legal help. If the lawyer is giving me advice or is helping me with legal or other documents, I understand the lawyer will stop helping me when the services listed above have been completed. The address I give below is my permanent address where I can be reached. I understand that it is important that the court handling my case and other parties to the case be able to reach me at the address after the lawyer ends the limited representation. I therefore agree that I will inform the Court and other parties of any change in my permanent address.

In exchange for the Lawyer's limited representation, I agree to pay the attorney's fee and costs described above.

Sign your name: _____

Print your name: _____

Print your address: _____

Phone number:_____FAX: _____

Message Phone:_____Name: _____

Email address: _____

# Limited Representation Agreement (example from Maine)

**LIMITED REPRESENTATION AGREEMENT**

To Be Executed in Duplicate

Date: _____, 20___

1. The client, , retains the attorney, , to perform limited legal services in the following matter: __**[DESCRIBE MATTER]** __.
2. The client seeks the following services from the attorney (indicate by writing "yes" or "no"):

a. _____ Legal advice: office visits, telephone calls, fax, mail, e-mail;

b. _____ Advice about availability of alternative means to resolving the dispute, including mediation and arbitration;

c. _____ Evaluation of client self-diagnosis of the case and advising client about legal rights and responsibilities;

d. _____ Guidance and procedural information for filing or serving documents;

e. _____ Review pleadings and other documents prepared by client;

f. _____ Suggest documents to be prepared;

g. _____ Draft pleadings, motions, and other documents;

h. _____ Factual investigation: contacting witnesses, public record searches, in depth interview of client;

i. _____ Assistance with computer support programs;

j. _____ Legal research and analysis;

k. _____ Evaluate settlement options;

l. _____ Discovery: interrogatories, depositions, requests for document production;

m. _____ Planning for negotiations;

n. _____ Planning for court appearances;

o. _____ Standby telephone assistance during negotiations or settlement conferences;

p. _____ Referring client to expert witnesses, special masters, or other counsel;

q. _____ Counseling client about an appeal;

r. _____ Procedural assistance with an appeal and assisting with substantive legal argument in an appeal;

s. _____ Provide preventive planning and/or schedule legal check-ups:

t. _____ Other:

    1. The client shall pay the attorney for those limited services as follows:

a. Hourly Fee: The current hourly fee charged by the attorney or the attorney's law firm for services under this agreement are as follows:

i. Attorney:

ii. Associate:

iii. Paralegal:

iv. Law Clerk:

Unless a different fee arrangement is established in clause b.) of this paragraph, the hourly fee shall be payable at the time of the service. Time will be charged in increments of one-tenth of an hour, rounded off for each particular activity to the nearest one-tenth of an hour.

b. Payment from Deposit:

For a continuing consulting role, client will pay to attorney a deposit of $_____, to be received by attorney on or before _____, and to be applied against attorney fees and costs incurred by client. This amount will be deposited by attorney in attorney trust account. Client authorizes attorney to withdraw funds from the trust account to pay attorney fees and costs as they are incurred by client. The deposit is refundable. If, at the termination of services under this agreement, the total amount incurred by client for attorney fees and costs is less than the amount of the deposit, the difference will be refunded to client. Any balance due shall be paid within thirty days of the termination of services.

c. Costs:

Client shall pay attorney out-of-pocket costs incurred in connection with this agreement, including long distance telephone and fax costs, photocopy expense and postage. All costs payable to third parties in connection with client case, including filing fees, investigation fees, deposition fees, and the like shall be paid directly by client. Attorney shall not advance costs to third parties on client behalf.

1.  The client understands that the attorney will exercise his or her best judgment while performing the limited legal services set out above, but also recognizes:

a. the attorney is not promising any particular outcome.

b. the attorney has not made any independent investigation of the facts and is relying entirely on the client limited disclosure of the facts given the duration of the limited services provided, and

c. the attorney has no further obligation to the client after completing the above described limited legal services unless and until both attorney and client enter into another written representation agreement.

1.  If any dispute between client and attorney arises under this agreement concerning the payment of fees, the client and attorney shall submit the dispute for fee arbitration in accordance with Rule [RULE NO.] of the [STATE] Bar Rules. This arbitration shall be binding upon both parties to this agreement.

WE HAVE EACH READ THE ABOVE AGREEMENT BEFORE SIGNING IT.

_____

Signature of client

_____

Signature of attorney

# Notice and Consent to Limited Representation (example from Wyoming)

### NOTICE AND CONSENT TO LIMITED REPRESENTATION
#### NOTICE

To help you with your legal problems, a lawyer may agree to give you some of the help you want, but not all of it. In other words, you and the lawyer may agree that the lawyer will limit his representation to helping you with a certain legal problem for a short time or for a particular purpose. Limited representation is available only in civil cases.

When a lawyer agrees to help you for a short time or for a particular purpose, the lawyer must act in your best interest and give you competent help. When a lawyer and you agree that the lawyer will provide such limited help,

   --- The lawyer DOES NOT HAVE TO GIVE MORE HELP than the lawyer and you agreed.

   --- The lawyer DOES NOT HAVE TO help with any other part of your legal problem.

If short-term limited representation is not reasonable, a lawyer may give advice, but will also tell you of the need to get another lawyer.

If you agree to have this lawyer give you limited help, sign your name at the bottom of this form. The lawyer will also sign to show that he or she agrees. If you and the lawyer both sign, the lawyer agrees to help you by performing the following <u>limited services,</u> and need not give you any more help.

[ ] Advise you about the following issues:

[ ] Write or read and advise you about the following legal documents:

[ ] Go to court to represent you only in the following matter(s):

_____
Attorney's Name

#### Consent

I have read this Notice and Consent form and I understand what it says. I agree that the legal services specified above are the ONLY legal help this lawyer will give me. <u>I understand and agree that the lawyer who is helping me with these services is not my lawyer for any other purpose and does not have to give me any more legal help.</u> If the lawyer is giving me advice, or is helping me with legal or other documents, I understand the lawyer may decide to stop helping me whenever the lawyer wants. I also understand that if the lawyer goes to court for me, he or she does not have to help me after he goes to court unless we both agree in writing. I agree that the address I give below is my permanent address where I may be reached. I understand that it is important that both the opposing party and the court handling my case be able to reach me at this address in the event my attorney ends his limited representation. I therefore agree that I will inform the Court and the opposing party of any change in my permanent address.

_____    _____
Print Your Name                          Mailing Address

_____    _____
Sign Your Name                           City State and Zip Code

_____    _____
Date                                 Phone Number

# Notice of Limited Scope Representation (example from California)

Reprinted with permission from
the Judicial Council of California

FL-950

| ATTORNEY OR PARTY WITHOUT ATTORNEY *(Name, state bar number, and address)*: | FOR COURT USE ONLY |
|---|---|
| TELEPHONE NO.:      FAX NO *(Optional)*: <br> E-MAIL ADDRESS *(Optional)*: <br> ATTORNEY FOR *(Name)*: | |

| SUPERIOR COURT OF CALIFORNIA, COUNTY OF | |
|---|---|
| STREET ADDRESS: <br> MAILING ADDRESS: <br> CITY AND ZIP CODE: <br> BRANCH NAME: | |

| PETITIONER/PLAINTIFF: <br><br> RESPONDENT/DEFENDANT: <br><br> OTHER PARENT/CLAIMANT: | |
|---|---|

| NOTICE OF LIMITED SCOPE REPRESENTATION <br> ☐ Amended | CASE NUMBER: |
|---|---|

1.  Attorney *(name)*:
    and party *(name)*:
    have a written agreement that attorney will provide limited scope representation to the party.

2.  Attorney will represent the party
    ☐ at the hearing on:         ☐ and for any continuance of that hearing
    ☐ until submission of the order after hearing
    ☐ until resolution of the issues checked on page 1 by trial or settlement
    ☐ other *(specify duration of representation)*:

3.  Attorney will serve as "attorney of record" for the party **only** for the following issues in this case:
    a.   ☐ Child support:    (1) ☐ Establish    (2) ☐ Enforce    (3) ☐ Modify *(describe in detail)*:

    b.   ☐ Spousal support:   (1) ☐ Establish    (2) ☐ Enforce    (3) ☐ Modify *(describe in detail)*:

    c.   ☐ Restraining order: (1) ☐ Establish    (2) ☐ Enforce    (3) ☐ Modify *(describe in detail)*:

    d.   ☐ Child custody and visitation:    (1) ☐ Establish    (2) ☐ Enforce    (3) ☐ Modify *(describe in detail)*:

    e.   ☐ Division of property *(describe in detail)*:

    f.   ☐ Pension issues *(describe in detail)*:

Page 1 of 3

Form Adopted for Mandatory Use
Judicial Council of California
FL-950 [New July 1, 2003]      **NOTICE OF LIMITED SCOPE REPRESENTATION**      *www.courtinfo.ca.gov*

Martin Dean's
ESSENTIAL FORMS™

| PETITIONER/PLAINTIFF: | CASE NUMBER: |
|---|---|
| RESPONDENT/DEFENDANT: | |
| OTHER PARENT/CLAIMANT: | |

g. ☐ Contempt *(describe in detail)* :

h. ☐ Other *(describe in detail)* :

i. ☐ See attachment 3i.

4. By signing this form, the party agrees to sign form MC-050, *Substitution of Attorney-Civil* at the completion of the representation as set forth above.

5. The attorney named above is "attorney of record" and available for service of documents only for those issues specifically checked on pages 1 and 2. For all other matters, the party must be served directly. The party's name, address, and phone number are listed below for that purpose.

Name:
Address *(for the purpose of service)* :

Phone:                      Fax:

This notice accurately sets forth all current matters on which the attorney has agreed to serve as "attorney of record" for the party in this case. The information provided herein is not intended to set forth all of the terms and conditions of the agreement between the party and the attorney for limited scope representation.

Date:

_____    ▶    _____
(TYPE OR PRINT NAME)                    (SIGNATURE OF PARTY)

Date:

_____    ▶    _____
(TYPE OR PRINT NAME)                    (SIGNATURE OF ATTORNEY)

*Martin Dean's*
**ESSENTIAL FORMS™**

| PETITIONER/PLAINTIFF: | CASE NUMBER |
|---|---|
| RESPONDENT/DEFENDANT: | |
| OTHER PARENT/CLAIMANT: | |

**PROOF OF SERVICE BY** ☐ **PERSONAL SERVICE** ☐ **MAIL**

1. At the time of service I was at least 18 years of age and **not a party to this action.**

2. I served a copy of the *Notice of Limited Scope Representation* as follows *(check either a. or b. below)* :
   a. ☐ **Personal service.** The *Notice of Limited Scope Representation* was given to:
      (1) Name of person served:
      (2) Address where served:

      (3) Date served:
      (4) Time served:

   b. ☐ **Mail.** I placed a copy of the *Notice of Limited Scope Representation* in the United States mail, in a sealed envelope with postage fully prepaid. The envelope was addressed and mailed as follows:
      (1) Name of person served:
      (2) Address:

      (3) Date of mailing:
      (4) Place of mailing *(city and state)* :
      (5) I live in or work in the county where the *Notice* was mailed.

3. Server's information:
   a. Name:
   b. Home or work address:

   c. Telephone number:

I declare under penalty of perjury under the laws of the State of California that the information is true and correct.

Date:

_____ ▶ _____
(TYPE OR PRINT NAME)          (SIGNATURE OF PERSON SERVING NOTICE)

Martin Dean's
ESSENTIAL FORMS™

# Notice of Limited Scope Representation (example from Illinois)

**Form for Limited Scope Appearance in Civil Action**

IN THE CIRCUIT COURT OF THE _____ JUDICIAL CIRCUIT

_____ COUNTY, ILLINOIS

(OR, IN THE CIRCUIT COURT OF COOK COUNTY, ILLINOIS)

| | |
|---|---|
| _____ | ) |
| Plaintiff/Petitioner | ) |
| | ) |
| v. | )   No. |
| | ) |
| | ) |
| _____ | ) |
| Defendant/Respondent | ) |

**NOTICE OF LIMITED SCOPE APPEARANCE**

1. The _____ attorney, _____, and _____ the _____ Party, _____ , have entered into a written agreement dated _____ providing that the attorney will provide limited scope representation to the Party in the above-captioned matter in accordance with Paragraphs 3 and 4, below.

2. The Party is Plaintiff Petitioner Defendant Respondent in this matter. (Circle one)

APPENDIX B: RULES OF ETHICS AND PROCEDURE

3.  The attorney appears pursuant to Supreme Court Rule 13(c)(6). This appearance is limited in scope to the following matter(s) in which the attorney will represent the Party (check and complete all that apply):

☐      In the court proceeding (identify) on the following date: _____

☐      And in any continuance of that proceeding

☐      At the trial on the following date: _____

☐      And in any continuance of that trial

☐      And until judgment

☐      At the following deposition(s): _____

☐      If a family law matter, specify the scope and limits of representation:
       _____

☐      Other   (specify   the   scope   and   limits   of   representation):
       _____

4.  If this appearance does not extend to all matters to be considered at the proceeding(s) above, identify the discrete issues within each proceeding covered by this appearance:
_____
_____
_____

5.  The attorney may withdraw following completion of the limited scope representation specified in this appearance as follows:

APPENDIX B: RULES OF ETHICS AND PROCEDURE

a. orally move to withdraw at a hearing attended by the Party, at which the Party may object to withdrawal if the Party contends that the limited scope representation specified in this appearance has not been completed; or

b. file a Notice of Withdrawal of Limited Scope Representation in the form attached to Supreme Court Rule 13. If the attorney files such a Notice, the attorney shall serve it upon the Party and upon all counsel of record and other parties not represented by counsel unless the court excuses service upon other counsel and other unrepresented parties, and upon the judge then presiding over this case. The method of service shall be as provided in Supreme Court Rule 11 unless the court orders otherwise. If the Party objects to the withdrawal, the Party may, within 21 days after the date of the attorney's service of the Notice of Withdrawal of Limited Scope Appearance, file an Objection to Withdrawal of Limited Scope Appearance in the form attached to Supreme Court Rule 13. The attorney will provide a copy of the form of Objection to the Party with the attorney's Notice, including instructions for filing and service of an Objection. If the Party timely serves an Objection, the attorney shall notice the matter for hearing to rule on the Objection.

6.   Service of pleadings on the attorney and party named above shall be made in accordance with Supreme Court Rule 11(e).

7.   By signing below, the Party being represented under this Limited Scope Appearance:

a. agrees to the delivery of all court papers to the addresses specified below; and

b. agrees to inform the court, all counsel of record, and all parties not represented by counsel of any changes to the Party's address information listed below during the limited scope representation.

_____          _____

Signature of Attorney                               Name of Attorney

_____          _____

Attorney's Address                                    Attorney's Telephone Number

_____          _____

Attorney's E-Mail Address                        Attorney Number

APPENDIX B: RULES OF ETHICS AND PROCEDURE

_____     _____

Signature of Party                  Name of Party


_____     _____

Party's Address                     Party's Telephone Number


_____

Party's E-Mail Address


_____

Date

# Notice of Withdrawal of Limited Scope Appearance (example from Illinois)

**Form for Notice of Withdrawal of Limited Scope Appearance**

IN THE CIRCUIT COURT OF THE _____ JUDICIAL CIRCUIT

_____ COUNTY, ILLINOIS

(OR, IN THE CIRCUIT COURT OF COOK COUNTY, ILLINOIS)

| | |
|---|---|
| _____ ) | |
| Plaintiff/Petitioner ) | |
| ) | |
| v. ) | No. |
| ) | |
| ) | |
| _____ ) | |
| Defendant/Respondent ) | |

**NOTICE OF WITHDRAWAL OF LIMITED SCOPE APPEARANCE**

I withdraw my Notice of Limited Scope Appearance for _____ [party], pursuant to Supreme Court Rule 13(c)(7).

I have completed all services within the scope of the Notice of Limited Scope Appearance, and I have completed all acts ordered by the court within the scope of that appearance.

Service of documents upon me under Supreme Court Rule 11(e) will no longer be required upon the later of: (a) 21 days after service of this Notice or, (b) if _____ [party] files and serves an Objection to Withdrawal of Limited Scope Appearance within 21 days after service of this Notice, entry of a court order allowing my withdrawal. Service of documents on _____ [party] continues to be required.

**NOTICE TO** _____**[party]:** You have the right to object to my withdrawal as your lawyer if you believe that I have not finished everything that I had agreed to do. To object, you must:

1. Fill in the blanks in the attached form of Objection to Withdrawal of Limited Scope Appearance, including the Certificate of Service and sign where indicated.

2. File the original Objection with the court by _____ __, ____, [date to be filled in by lawyer] which is 21 days after the date that I am filing and serving this Notice.

3. On the same day that you file the Objection with the court, send copies of it to me and to the other persons listed in the Certificate of Service attached to the Objection. Also, check the boxes in the Certificate of Service to show how you sent the copy to each person.

If you file and serve an Objection within the 21-day period, I will arrange to have a hearing date set by the court. I will send you notice of the date. You must appear at the hearing and explain to the judge why you believe that I have not finished everything that I had agreed to do for you.

_____          _____

Signature of Attorney            Name of Attorney

_____          _____

Attorney's Address               Attorney's Telephone Number

_____          _____

Attorney's E-Mail Address        Attorney Number

_____

Date

**Proof of Filing and Service**

I certify that this Notice has been filed with the court on the ___ day of _____, 20__, and on the same day I served this Notice on the following, including the Party that I represented, all counsel of record and parties not represented by counsel, and the judge now presiding over this case, by the method checked below for each.

[List Name and Address of Each]       [Check Method of Service}

The Honorable _____      [ ] US Mail, Postage Prepaid [ ] Messenger

_____      [ ] Personal Delivery    [ ] Facsimile

_____      [ ] Email

_____

[Client]_____      [ ] US Mail, Postage Prepaid [ ] Messenger

_____      [ ] Personal Delivery    [ ] Facsimile

_____      [ ] Email

_____

[Repeat Same Information for Each Other Counsel of Record and Unrepresented Party]

_____

Signature of Attorney

# Payment Options: Credit Card Authorization

### PAYMENT OPTIONS

For your convenience, this office accepts VISA, Mastercard, Discover, and American Express credit cards. If you would like to satisfy your balance by credit card, please complete the required information below, and return this form to our office.

Thank you.

**CLIENT'S NAME
AND ADDRESS:** _____
_____
_____

**VISA** _____  **MASTERCARD** _____  **DISCOVER** _____  **AMERICAN EXPRESS** _____

**NAME OF CARDHOLDER:** _____

**ADDRESS OF CARDHOLDER:** _____
_____

**CREDIT CARD NUMBER:** _____

**EXPIRATION DATE:** _____

**AMOUNT OF PAYMENT:** _____

**CARDHOLDER'S SIGNATURE:** _____

# Thank You for Being Our Client (letter and instructions)

## Thank You for Being Our Client (and Instructions)

Dear

Re:  Your Legal Matter Date of Accident:


I want to take this moment to thank you for selecting our office to represent you in connection with the accident on the above date.  Our firm has experienced attorneys, as well as an excellent staff, all dedicated to the overall goal of complete client satisfaction.  I am pleased to report that I will be jointly handling your case with my colleague, _____.  Please give her your full cooperation.

If you have any questions about something particular regarding your case, or just want to inquire about the status of the lawsuit, please contact me or _____ at any time.  We encourage your active participation in your case and want you to be informed at every stage of your lawsuit.  Therefore, never hesitate to call our office.

Please remember not to discuss this pending matter with anyone, except with a representative of our firm.  Of course, you must speak with your doctors about your injuries, try not to discuss the details of the accident to any great extent.  You may be contacted by different organizations, including insurance companies, from time to time.  Simply explain that you are represented by an attorney and that they should contact us directly.  Any legal questions relating to this accident should be directed to us.  If you are losing time from work, please make sure that you file the disability claim form which we gave you at the interview within (30) days of the date of your accident with your employer.

You may also receive certain items in the mail, including hospital bills, medical bills or any request for information.  Please send those things directly to our office and we will submit them for you.  Take care of your medical treatment by following the instructions of your treating physicians, including referrals to specialists, MRI's or other testing.  Please keep a record of the names and addresses of all doctors that treated you and the treatment dates for each.  Please forward the names of any new doctors to our attention.  In the event that you move or change your telephone number, be sure to notify our office with the new information.

It will ordinarily take us as long as nine months to obtain the necessary information including all your medical reports before we will start a law suit on your behalf.  During that time, we maintain continuous contact with the insurance company for the offending driver.  After we commence a law suit, which is done by issuing a Summons and Complaint, the attorney representing the insurance company will submit an Answer with various legal demands.  At that point, we attend a conference at the Supreme Court of the State of New York.  At the conference, the Court issues an order dictating the necessary discovery information.  At some point in the litigation, you will be required to give an oral statement called an Examination Before Trial, and you will be requested to attend one or two physical examinations by doctors of defendant's choosing. You must attend these physical examinations or your case will be dismissed by court. The entire process takes time, and will be followed closely by the Courts. Ultimately, if the case cannot be resolved between the parties, the Court will schedule a trial of your case.

Again, if you have any questions during your pending case, please do not hesitate to contact our office.

I look forward to working towards a successful resolution of your case. Thank you again, and welcome to _____.

Very truly yours,

**Conference-Scheduling and Re-Scheduling (for court use/matrimonial)**

## CONFERENCE – SCHEDULING AND RE-SCHEDULING

FROM: _____     TO: _____

DATE: _____

CASE: _____
        We represent the __ Husband __ Wife

BY: _____     BY: _____

JUDGE: _____     Who was
                                 (     )     Husband present
                                   (     )     Wife present

Today I conferenced the above.

The case has been:
(     )     settled
(     )     inquest taken
(     )     adjourned to _____

INSTRUCTIONS:

(     )     Notify client by letter _____ weeks before adjourned date.
(     )     Opposing counsel
(     )     Judge's Chambers: Attn: _____
                                      (Law Secretary)
(     )     Time spent on case _____ Please record.

MEMO:

_____

_____

_____

_____

## Disengagement Letter (unpaid fees)

ATTORNEY-CLIENT AGREEMENTS TOOLKIT

Reprinted with permission of Lawyers Mutual
from Attorney-Client Agreements Toolkit

## DISENGAGEMENT LETTER: UNPAID FEES

[Date]

[Client Name]
[Client Address]
[Client Address]

Re: Confirmation of Disengagement
     File ID:

Dear [Client's Name]:

Throughout the past [State Time Frame], it has been the pleasure of [Law Firm] to represent you in [Case Name]. In the course of representation, you have paid us approximately $_____ in legal fees and expenses. Unfortunately, contrary to the terms set forth in the engagement agreement, the retainer account has not been replenished in a timely manner. The outstanding balance has now reached $_____ and this amount is [State Time Frame] past due.

[Law Firm] values our relationship and appreciates the opportunity to have served as your counsel in this matter. It is for this reason we have continued representation while your balance continued to increase. Nonetheless, we are unable to finance your case any longer and respectfully request your permission to withdraw. We believe that the tribunal will grant us this permission since there is still sufficient time for you to retain another attorney without jeopardizing the case or adversely affecting the court's calendar.

Please be advised that you should not hesitate in contacting other counsel if you wish to continue pursuit of this matter. Important legal deadlines do exist and failure to meet these time limits will permanently bar your legal claim and any recovery to which you may be entitled. If you do not have another attorney in mind, we recommend that you immediately contact the North Carolina Bar Association's Lawyer Referral Service at (800) 662-7660.

Because of the great deal of time we have invested in researching and preparing for this case, it would be to your advantage to have your new lawyer consult with us. We would be more than happy to do this, but before this can be accommodated we will need to reach an agreement regarding compensation for additional time and expenses incurred. Furthermore, arrangements will need to be made for gradual reduction and payment of the outstanding balance.

Enclosed is a petition to withdraw from the case, which will be filed with the court [State Time Period] from the date of this letter. I would also like to direct your attention to an enclosed form requesting your consent. Should you wish for us to continue representation in this matter, we would be pleased to do so, provided the balance has been settled and the retainer account has been replenished in accordance with our initial agreement.

I look forward to hearing from you and genuinely hope that our relationship can continue.

Sincerely,

[Attorney's Name], Attorney at Law
[Law Firm]

*Note: This is a sample form only and is written for the general purposes of facilitating clear expectations and avoiding misunderstandings between an attorney and client. It is not intended as legal advice or opinion and will not provide absolute protection against a malpractice action.*

# Disengagement Letter (concluding case/matrimonial)

Dear Client:

We would like to thank you for having given us the opportunity to represent you with regard to your matrimonial matter. We have enjoyed working with you and are pleased that we were able to conclude this matter favorably.

We are enclosing the following documents which we suggest you keep in a safe location:_____

_____

_____

_____.

Although we have served a copy of the judgment of divorce upon opposing counsel and we have also served the QDRO upon your ex-husband's employer, we suggest that you make sure to notify your former husband's employer of your entitlement if you should become aware of his retirement. Even if you are not aware of any retirement details, we would suggest that if your ex-husband is still working when he turns 64, that you send a note to the Human Resources Department of his company along with a copy of the QDRO, reminding them of their obligation to make payment to you.

In addition, as you are aware, the law does allow for adjustments in support payments in the future. Should you need or wish to utilize our services in this regard in the future, please do not hesitate to call us.

As you recall, you provided us with many records and documents during the course of our representation of you. Now that your matter is concluded, we no longer have any need for these documents and want to suggest you retrieve whichever of the items you wish to keep. Because of the number of cases we handle, we are unable to store your documents beyond 6 months of the date of this letter. Please call our office within that time frame to make arrangements to pick up whatever you would like to keep. Please allow this letter to serve as notice to you that upon the expiration of 6 months from the date hereof, we may destroy your records. We will keep an electronic copy of your file in our possession for at least the next 7 years, but this file will not include copies of your records and will be limited to copies of the work we performed on your behalf as well as correspondence, agreements, judgments and orders.

You have a modest outstanding balance of $563.00 due to us on your file of and ask that you satisfy same as soon as possible.

Once again, we thank you for having allowed us to be of help to you and wish you all the best in the future.

Very truly yours,

# Grievance Packet (sample complaint, background questionnaire and response)

## GRIEVANCE PACKET

### Sample Complaint

Please be advised that pursuant to the Dishonored Check Reporting Rules for Attorney Special, Trust and Escrow Accounts (22 NYCRR part 1300), this Committee has received from the Lawyer's Fund for Client Protection a dishonored check report pertaining to an account purportedly maintained by you. The report (copy enclosed) reflects that the designated check (or debit) was drawn against insufficient available funds in an account related to your practice of law.

Based upon this information, this Committee has initiated a complaint and investigation *sua sponte,* concerning your professional conduct pursuant to Section 691.4© of the Rules of the Appellate Division, Second Department (22 NYCRR part 691 et seq.). As part of this investigation, you are hereby requested to submit to the undersigned, within twenty (20) days of your receipt of this letter, your written answer, setting forth any explanation of the circumstances which caused the subject check (or debit) to be drawn against insufficient funds. With your answer, you are requested to produce the following required bookkeeping records , as specified in the Rules of Professional Conduct (22 NYCRR part 1200 [Rule 1.15]), for the six (6) months preceding the date that the check (or debit) in question was dishonored (copies of the records will suffice at this time):

1.      Records of all deposits in and withdrawals from the account, which specifically identify the date, source and description of each item deposited, as well as the date, payee and purpose of each withdrawal or disbursement;

2.      A record showing the source of all funds deposited in the account, the names of all persons for whom the funds are or were held, the amount of such funds, and description and amount, and the names of all persons to whom such funds were disbursed; and

3.      All checkbooks and check stubs, bank statements, pre-numbered canceled checks (front and back), and duplicate deposit slips.

In addition, we ask that you identify the source(s) of the funds (i.e., what amount belongs to what client) that comprise the opening balance in the earliest banking statement being provided pursuant to this request, as well as the identity of all signatories on the account and the attorney(s)/partner(s) responsible for maintaining and managing the account.

Please feel free to include with your answer any additional information or materials which you consider relevant.

Also enclosed is a Background Questionnaire, which you are requested to complete and submit with your written answer.

Please note that this sua sponte complaint is against you, not your law firm. Therefore, the response should be from you, and not delegated.

You are advised that an unexcused failure to timely respond or otherwise properly cooperate in this matter constitutes "professional misconduct" independent of the underlying investigation. In addition, an unexcused failure to produce the required bookkeeping records specified above may be deemed a violation of the Rules of Professional Conduct and may subject you to disciplinary proceedings (see 22 NYCRR part 1200 [Rule 1.15(i) and (j)]).

Enclosures

**Sample Response from Attorney**

Please accept this original response (together with enclosed additional copy of same) to the *sua sponte* complaint initiated against me by the Committee upon receipt of a dishonored check report from _____ regarding "_____ Trust Account", _____ (the "_____ Account"). Please note that the requested bank records were sent to the Committee last week under separate cover. Thank you for your courtesies in providing an extension of time in which to submit my response.

I was admitted to practice law in the State of New York in ____, after graduating from _____. I have practiced law for over _____, for the past _____ with my own firm, _____ (the "Firm"). My practice focuses on providing creditors with debt collection services.

I am a founding member, former vice president, former member of the Board of Directors (a position that I held for ten (10) years), and former chairman of the legislative committee of the _____). _____ is an organization comprised of approximately _____ law firms, whose mission, among other things, is to set new and higher standards for the _____.

The firm mainly represents national _____, including (_____), many of which regularly audit the Firm's _____ procedures to ensure that they comply with the clients' own internal policies as well as a myriad of other regulations. As a result, we have developed _____ procedures which govern the manner in which our attorneys and non-lawyer employees conduct business. Some of these procedures are relevant to this Complaint, which are explained below.

After giving due consideration to the Complaint, reviewing the pertinent files maintained in the matter and reacquainting myself with the chronology of events that took place, I respectfully submit that I did not commit any professional misconduct with respect to _____ and would like to emphasize that at no time did I or any member of the Firm act with venality or intend to harm anyone.

For several reasons – namely, to comply with the Rules of Professional Conduct, to preclude even the possibility of co-mingling client funds, to maintain the integrity of client funds while handling such a large volume of collections and pursuant to specific direction from the Firm opened and currently maintains a segregated escrow account for _____ in which only funds for the benefit of _____ are deposited.

On _____, a wire transfer was made from the Firm to our client, in the amount of $_____. On _____, a report was issued by our bank, to the Lawyers Fund for Client Protection, indicating that the _____ transfer brought the _____ Account balance negative by _____.

Occasionally, as happened on _____ check does not clear and funds that the bank has credited to must be reversed. When that occurs, ____ is notified electronically and returns the already-credited funds to the _____ Account the following day.

I would like to note here that the Firm's wire transfer to our client was paid, as indicated on the face of the _____ report, although the account balance did go negative as a result of a _____.

Significantly, _____, there was and is no risk that payment made to _____ could be from other client funds, and there is no risk that any of the Firm's other clients could have been harmed.

My understanding of Rule 1.15(a) of the Rules of Professional Conduct is that a lawyer must not misappropriate client funds or co-mingle client funds with the lawyer's own funds. Here, as my banking records demonstrate, there was no misappropriation or co-mingling of client funds. In fact, I made careful efforts to avoid any possibility of co-mingling by creating separate escrow accounts for each client. Funds belonging to _____ were not deposited into an account of any other client, nor were other client funds deposited into the account designated for _____.

My Firm maintains our accounts with _____ Bank located in _____, New York and, as evident by its report to the Lawyer's Fund for Client Protection, provided a dishonored check report. The _____ Account is maintained in the name of my law firm "_____ _____ Trust Account".

The Firm has never made any withdrawals from the _____ Account to cash. In further compliance with the Rules of Professional Conduct, the only authorized signatories on the _____ Account were lawyers admitted to practice law in New York State, namely, _____ is the attorney responsible for maintaining and managing the account.

For the foregoing reasons, together with the accompanying bank and financial records, I respectfully request that the Committee dismiss in its entirety the *sua sponte* Complaint issued in response to correspondence from the Lawyer's Fund for Client Protection. Thank you for your consideration.


Enclosures

## Sample Response by Counsel

We represent _____ with respect to the above-referenced matter. Enclosed please find an original and copy of Mr. _____'s response to the Committee's letter dated _____ ("Complaint"), and a copy of _____'s background questionnaire. _____ is sending the original background questionnaire to your attention under separate cover. I have reviewed the Complaint, have read _____'s response and have discussed the facts and circumstances surrounding the Complaint with _____. Based on those discussions and the information provided to me, I respectfully submit this letter in conjunction with _____'s response.

Pursuant to the Complaint, received by my office on _____, enclosed please find three (3) boxes containing records related to _____ Bank, _____, Trust Account, Escrow Management Account No. -----____ ("_____ Account"), dating from _____ through _____.

As _____ sets forth in his response to the Complaint, _____ ("_____") is a client of _____. Among other things, _____ is a creditor that retained _____ to provide legal services in connection with its efforts to collect unpaid balances from many individuals ("Account debtors").

The accompanying records consist of _____ Account bank statements that reflect all deposits into and withdrawals from the account. _____ has also provided copies (and in some cases originals) of each and every check and money order that was deposited into the _____ Account. Those checks and money orders are accompanied by a covering spreadsheet containing a list of the amounts collected from the specified account debtor in each particular day, as well as reference to _____'s internal account number to which each payment corresponds. _____ sent all of that information to _____ on a daily basis.

As _____'s bank account was first opened, all of the funds therein have belonged only to _____ and not to any other party. Accordingly, the entire amount of the opening balance in the earliest bank statement provided pursuant to the Committee's request belonged to _____.

_____'s response and the accompanying bank account records make clear that he did not breach his ethical duties in relation to the _____ Account and that he did not violate the Rules of Professional Conduct.

As _____ Bank has indicated in the accompanying letter dated _____, it issued the _____ dishonored check report in error as _____ did not remit a $_____ electronic funds transfer to its client, _____. Shortly thereafter, when the Bank discovered that a previous deposit by one of _____'s account debtors did not clear due to insufficient funds in the debtors' account, the Bank reversed the electronic funds transfer, i.e., _____ repaid those funds back into its account.

22NYCRR § 1300.1(c) sets forth a bank's reporting requirements, and provides:

> A dishonored check report by a banking institution shall be
> required whenever a properly payable instrument is

> presented against an attorney special, trust or escrow account which contains insufficient available funds, <u>and the banking institution dishonors the instrument for that reason</u>. A properly payable instrument means an instrument which, if presented in the normal course of business, is in a form requiring payment under the laws of the State of New York.

<u>Id.</u> emphasis added. Clearly then, since the bank paid on and did not dishonor _____ electronic funds transfer, the bank was not required to and should not have issued the dishonored check report that formed the basis for the instant complaint.

Rule 1.15(a) of the Rules of Professional Conduct prohibits a lawyer from misappropriating client funds or from co-mingling client funds with the lawyer's own funds. The purpose of the rule "is to maintain a complete wall of separation between the lawyer's own funds. The purpose of the rule "is to maintain a complete wall of separation between the lawyer's property and property belonging to others." <u>Simon's New York Rules of Professional Conduct Annotated</u>, (2014 Ed., p. 789).

Here, as _____'s banking records demonstrate, there was no misappropriation or co-mingling of client funds, and he maintained "a complete wall of separation" between the firm's funds and the client's funds. In fact, _____ made careful efforts to avoid even the possibility of co-mingling by creating separate escrow accounts for each client. Funds belonging to _____ were only deposited into the _____ Account, and at no time were other client funds deposited into that account. In this regard, there was never a risk that one client's funds would be used to cover a payment made to or on behalf of another client, and all of _____'s client's funds were protected.

Rule 1.15 §(b) (1) of the Rules of Professional Conduct requires a lawyer to maintain client funds in a bank within New York State that agrees to provide dishonored check reports in accordance with 22 NYCRR § 1300. _____'s firm maintains its accounts with _____ Bank located in _____, New York and, as evident by its report to the Lawyer's Fund for Client Protection in this instance, _____ Bank appears to comply with 22 NYCRR § 1300. The account at issue here was in compliance with RPC § 1.15(b) (1) in that it is maintained in the name of the law firm "_____."

RPC 1.15 § (b) (2) has been complied with as well as the _____ Account is identified as "_____ Trust Account." As _____ has indicated in his accompanying letter, the client directed the Firm to transfer all funds belonging to the client via electronic funds transfer directly to the client. For that reason, no checkbooks exist for this account. This too serves to protect the client's funds in that it removes all possibility of malfeasance that is otherwise present when checks exist that could be drawn on a client account. Without checks, that possibility does not exist.

_____ clearly complied with RPC § 1.15(c) by promptly notifying his client of the receipt of funds in which it had an interest. In fact, _____ notified _____ of funds received on a daily basis, via an e-mail containing a pdf with that information. In addition, it maintained complete records of those funds that came into its possession, rendering appropriate accounts to _____. _____, then promptly delivered the funds that _____ was entitled to receive, without even withholding the legal fee earned for the collection of those funds, pursuant to the agreement that _____ required _____ to abide by.

In compliance with RPC § 1.15(d) (1), the Firm has maintained the banking records for the _____ Account, which reflect **all** deposits in and withdrawals from that account by date and amount of each transaction. The Firm has maintained records that identify the date, source and description of each item deposited, as well as the date, payee and purpose of each withdrawal or disbursement.

All of the funds in the _____ Account were held for one client only -- _____ -- which is borne out by the accompanying records.

In compliance with RPC § 1.15(d) (2), _____ has maintained accurate entries of all financial transactions relating to the _____ Account in its accounting records.

In compliance with RPC § 1.15(e), all withdrawals for the _____ Account were made by bank transfer pursuant to prior approval of _____.

_____ did not make any withdrawals from this account to cash.

In further compliance with RPC § 1.15(e), only a lawyer admitted to practice law in New York State, _____, was an authorized signatory on the _____ Account.

In light of the above, on _____'s behalf, we respectfully request a dismissal of the *sua sponte* Complaint issued as a result of the _____ dishonored check report. Should you require any additional information or clarification of the above matters, please feel free to contact me at any time.


Enclosures

<u>PLEASE TYPE OR PRINT CLEARLY USING BLACK INK</u>

SEND THIS FORM TO:     STATE OF NEW YORK GRIEVANCE COMMITTEE
                       TENTH JUDICIAL DISTRICT
                       150 MOTOR PARKWAY – SUITE 102
                       HAUPPAUGE, NEW YORK 11788
                       (631) 231-3775

DATE: _____
      Mr.   ( )
      Mrs.  ( )
      Ms.   ( )

YOUR NAME: _____
             (First)           (Initial)         (Last)

YOUR ADDRESS: _____
                   (No. and Street)

_____
  (City)           (County)          (State)       (Zip Code)

TELEPHONE: (Home) _____     (Office) _____

     ATTORNEY COMPLAINED OF:

     NAME: _____
            (First)         (Initial)      (Last)

     ADDRESS: _____
                (No. and Street)

_____
  (City)           (County)          (State)       (Zip Code)

     TELEPHONE: (Home) _____     (Office) _____

DATE YOU HIRED/RETAINED THE ATTORNEY: _____

HAVE YOU CONTACTED ANY OTHER AGENCY REGARDING THIS MATTER? _____

IF SO, NAME OF AGENCY AND WHAT ACTION TAKEN _____
_____
_____
_____

PLEASE SIGN

_____

### Sample Grievance Response

Please accept this original response (together with enclosed additional copy of same) to the complaint filed against me by _____ ("Complainant"), alleging that her phone calls to my office went unreturned for approximately a three (3) month period.

I.     Summary and Background of My Representation of the Complainant

The Complainant filed a complaint against me with the Grievance Committee ("Committee"), on _____ which I believe originates from _____ frustration with the fact that our efforts to obtain a home loan modification have not yet achieved the desired result, and because she was not able to speak to me personally when she called my office.

After giving due consideration to the allegations in the complaint, reviewing the pertinent files maintained in the matter and reacquainting myself with the chronology of events that took place, I respectfully submit that I never intended to commit any professional misconduct in relation to my representation of the Complainant.

The Complainant retained my firm in _____ for the sole purpose of trying to obtain a home loan modification that she was seeking on her residence _____. After our initial telephone conversation, my office faxed an authorization letter to the Complainant's home mortgage lender, _____, giving us permission to speak with the Bank about her loan. Thereafter, we requested, and the Complainant provided, various documents regarding her financial circumstances. (See Exhibit 1.) We began the process of communicating with the Bank to obtain a modification of her loan. _____, we are continuing in our efforts to obtain a modification of her loan.

When the Complainant first retained me, _____ explained the long and disturbing history _____. _____
_____
_____
_____
_____
_____, due
to an inability to care for ____ self, the Complainant's _____ designated the Complainant as attorney-in-fact over ____ affairs by way of a Power of Attorney. (See Exhibit _____
_____.) (See Exhibit 3.) That year, _____
bought the _____ house together. (See Exhibit 4.)

Prior to the time that the Complainant retained me, _____ had obtained a loan modification offer from _____; however, as the Complainant explained to me _____ had taken active steps to sabotage the Complainant's attempt to modify the mortgage. (See Exhibit 3; _____. In response to requests from my office regarding this loan modification application, _____ confirmed with us that _____ made numerous calls to the Bank directing it to "cancel" the pending application for loan modification. (See annexed Fax Cover Sheet.) Unfortunately, _____ interference had the effect that the Bank deemed the loan modification application cancelled.

Prior to receiving this Complaint from the Grievance Committee, I was never made aware that the Complainant was attempting to reach me for discussion of her matter. As I have subsequently learned, during the first several months of representation, the Complainant had called my office several times asking to speak with _____ (one of my employees) or me, who were not in the office or available to speak at that time. Regrettably, the Complainant's request to speak with me was not conveyed to me and the first I learned of it was when I received this complaint. If it had been conveyed to me, I would certainly have called ___ to discuss _____ matter or, if ___ preferred, met with ___ in person.

As I explain herein, while I acknowledge that I should have done certain things differently (and have instituted new office procedures to prevent same from happening again), I believe that this Complaint was filed before the Complainant and I discovered all of the facts surrounding _____ loan modification request, and that the Complaint has since largely been rendered moot.

In sum, my office is continuing to work on obtaining a loan modification on the Complainant's behalf; however, _____ has _____.
After receiving this Complaint and speaking with the Complainant, I refunded to her the _____ legal fee that ___ had paid me and am currently continuing to represent her on a *pro bono* basis, both with respect to obtaining a loan modification as well as in a foreclosure action commenced by ___ lender.

## II.    Mitigation

I am disappointed with the fact that I was not made aware that the Complainant was trying to speak with me to discuss ___ matter. However, it appears that the time period asserted in the complaint was about three (3) months.

I truly did not intend to harm the Complainant in any way or to violate the Rules of Professional Conduct. I did not do anything with venality, and returned the entire $1,000 legal fee to the Complainant as soon as I learned that _____ was unhappy.

A.    I have tried to demonstrate my contrition for any violations unintentionally committed.

I refunded the entire _____ legal fee paid as soon as I learned of the Complainant's request for same. Despite the fact that I believed I had earned that fee, I did so as a courtesy to the Complainant, based upon what I felt were extraordinary circumstances surrounding our attempt to obtain a home loan modification for her.

Additionally, as part of my volunteer work, I receive a schedule of conferences wherein the parties request pro-bono representation. I noted that _____ foreclosure action was scheduled for a court appearance at _____ in Supreme Court, _____ County. I requested the assignment, as it would provide me with an opportunity to personally meet with _____. I appeared to personally apologize and to determine the status of the action. _____ gracefully accepted my apology and we agreed that I would represent ___ on a *pro bono* basis going forward.

Even though I will continue to work on ___ action *pro bono*, I have attempted to make amends with the Complainant by refunding ____ $1,000 payment, meeting with ___ personally in my office and apologizing to ___ for not getting back to ___, and agreeing to represent her *pro bono* regarding both ___ loan modification application and a pending foreclosure action in which ___ is a defendant. Significantly, the foreclosure action will involve extensive discovery requests, the filing of written motions and appearances in the _____ County Supreme Court. If necessary, we may even have to file a cross-claim against _____ in an effort to require _____ to comply with requests that ___ allow the Complainant to assume full responsibility for the loan.

B.     I have instituted improved procedures in my office for recognizing and addressing client <u>concern in a timely manner.</u>

_____ investigated the matter and discovered that a staff member from my office failed to communicate the Complainant's concerns to me. I am very unhappy with my staff member's failure to inform me of the Complainant's requests, but hope to remedy the situation in the future through careful attention to my clients and an affirmative effort to ensure that such an event does not happen again.

Although I have told my staff in the past to inform me immediately of any client requests to speak with me, I realized in light of this complaint, that I needed to do more to ensure that I will be notified immediately of client concerns. To start, I investigated how this particular complaint arose and I disciplined the employee who failed to bring the Complainant's requests to my attention.

In addition, to prevent this situation from happening again, I have created and instituted an active, real-time online forum for my employees to use to document client concerns, client requests for in-office conferences with me, and any other client-related matter. This forum is accessible to all members of my staff through any computer that is connected to the Internet. I have instructed my employees to input all client requests or concerns into this forum immediately. I now check this forum on a regular basis, which will allow me to address any client issue without delay.

C.     I have attempted to demonstrate my commitment to the Bar and residents of <u>New York State through my pro bono work.</u>

Over the past several years, I have devoted approximately 100 hours or more of my time to volunteering with the _____ County Bar Pro Bono Foreclosure Settlement Project ("Project"), a pro bono program created as a response to the nationwide foreclosure crisis and concern about how New York State Courts would be able to handle the enormous number of foreclosure cases pending before them. More specifically, I have dedicated my time to counsel those in need of legal assistance with respect to imminent and pending foreclosure actions, as well as appearing in court as their attorney. There is no compensation for work as a volunteer attorney with the Project.

I have personally observed the devastating effects that the foreclosure crisis has had on residents of Long Island, as well as the burden it has placed on the courts. I believe that the Project serves an important purpose and I am proud to be a part of it.

I also work with the _____ County Bar Association's "Modest Means Panel", which provides representation for low-income persons.

Additionally, in the past several months I have made concerted efforts to become more familiar with the Rules of Professional Conduct and my ethical obligations as any attorney. In that vein, I attended three (3) continuing legal education courses with an emphasis in Ethics: "The Grievance Process in the 10<sup>th</sup> Judicial District (3.0 credits); "Escrow Issues and Account Management" (2.0 credits); and "Real Estate Ethics" (3.0 credits). (See Exhibit 9.) I intend on paying close attention to the Rules of Professional Conduct and my ethical obligations to my clients in my day to day practice from this point forward.

III.     Conclusion

My firm and I, together with the Complainant, are diligently working on _____ request for a loan modification. Unfortunately, however, this application may be somewhat challenging due to her sister's interference and past direction to cancel the application. Notwithstanding _____ intervention, my firm is doing exactly what we were hired to do; prepare the documents that _____ requires to process an application for a loan modification and negotiate for loan terms satisfactory to the Complainant.

It bears highlighting that during the three (3) months in which I represented the Complainant, we were waiting for the Bank to process our authorization and we did communicate with the Complainant several times on the telephone and in person. For these reasons, any implication of neglect is not warranted. While I acknowledge that one of my employee's did not appropriately inform the staff member who was handling the Complainant's matter (or me) that she wanted to speak with one of us, we are making all appropriate efforts to obtain a loan modification for the Complainant.

I do understand the Complainant's frustration with her situation, however, I do not believe that I violated the Rules of Professional Conduct in representing her. Also, although I refunded it, I do not believe that my fee was unjustified considering the work that my firm did on the Complainant's behalf.

As I have explained in this letter, I have changed the way I run my office so that a client's request to speak with me will not go unanswered in the future. I truly hope that the Committee Members recognize the entirety of the circumstances surrounding the Complaint and are able to dismiss it in its entirety.

GRIEVANCE COMMITTEE, NINTH JUDICIAL DISTRICT
APPELLATE DIVISION:  SECOND JUDICIAL DEPARTMENT

BACKGROUND QUESTIONNAIRE

1.  Name:_____    _____
             (Last)                                  (First)                       (Initial)              (Date of Birth)

2.  Department and Date of Admission in New York:  _____
    Name Under Which Admitted:  _____

3.  Other Jurisdictions Where Admitted (Federal, State, Special Courts or Agencies):
    _____
    _____
    _____

4.  Home Address and Telephone Number:  _____
    _____
    _____

5.  Present Address(es) and Telephone Number(s) for the Practice of Law:
    _____
    _____
    _____

6.  Other than the addresses in #5, have you within the last ten (10) years, maintained an
    office for the practice of law in any other judicial district?  If so, where?  _____
    _____
    _____
    _____

7.  If you have ever been censured, suspended or disbarred from the practice of law, provide
    the name of the court, or jurisdiction, the discipline imposed and the date of imposition.
    If you were suspended or disbarred, provide the date you were readmitted to practice:
    _____
    _____
    _____

8.  Have you ever been convicted of a crime in any jurisdiction, subsequent to your
    admission to practice in the State of New York?  If so, give particulars:  _____
    _____
    _____
    _____

9.  Subsequent to your admission to practice in the State of New York, have you ever been directed to pay sanctions or costs pursuant to 22 NYCRR Part 130? If so, provide the name of the matter and the court in which you were sanctioned, the amount you were directed to pay, and the date: _____

    _____
    _____

10. Have you ever had a complaint of attorney misconduct filed against you which resulted in any disposition, other than a dismissal, by any agency or body other than the Grievance Committee for the Ninth Judicial District? If so, provide the name and address of the agency, and the nature and date of final disposition: _____

    _____
    _____
    _____

11. If you are currently the subject of any complaint before any attorney disciplinary agency or bar association other than the Grievance Committee for the Ninth Judicial District, provide the name and address of the agency and a brief description of the complaint:

    _____
    _____
    _____
    _____

12. Are you now or have you ever served as a member of the judiciary in any capacity in any court? If so, please state your position, the court(s) wherein you served, and the starting and ending dates of your service: _____

    _____
    _____

      I certify that the statements made herein are true and correct. I further understand that I have a continuing duty to notify the Grievance Committee for the Ninth Judicial District of any change in information provided herein that may occur during the pendency of an investigation or proceeding regarding my conduct as an attorney and counselor-at-law.

_____    _____
           Signature               Date

# APPENDIX B

## PRACTICE/CASE MANAGEMENT SOFTWARE COMPARISON CHART FOR SOLO/SMALL FIRM

This document includes two charts: a Practice/Case Management Software Comparison Chart for Solo/Small Firm, and a Time & Billing Software Comparison Chart for Solo/Small Firm. Scroll down to view the Time & Billing chart. Last updated: May 2015.

## Practice/Case Management Software Comparison Chart for Solo/Small Firm

(Note: May include time/billing features. See below for Time & Billing specific chart.)

| | Pricing | Technical Requirements | Front Office Tasks | Back Office Tasks | Software Compatibility (import/export, etc.) | Mobile Access | Technical Support |
|---|---|---|---|---|---|---|---|
| AbacusLaw | AbacusLaw from just $47/month/user<br><br>Abacus Private Cloud™ (full virtual law practice) starts at just $197/month<br><br>Custom, no risk proposal: http://www.abacuslaw.com/pricing/<br><br>ABA members save 15% on AbacusLaw through ABA Member Advantage | AbacusLaw: Windows 8, Windows 7, Windows Vista Business or Ultimate or Windows Server 2003-2012<br><br>Abacus Private Cloud™: Any modern device with an Internet connection.<br><br>(more info) | Fully integrated rules-based calendaring, case, contact and document management, email document assembly, auto-fill court forms, instant messaging, Professional Services: The experienced Professional Services team offers law practice solutions that increase firm productivity and mitigate risks by customizing how you use the powerful AbacusLaw™ | Available in AbacusLaw Gold. One-click time tracking, billing, accounting, trust accounting, general ledger, check writing, payroll, integrated credit card processing and ACH billing and more.<br><br>(more info) | Abacus Private Cloud™ is software agnostic so you can use any applications, per your firm's requirements.<br><br>Abacus Law, Microsoft Word, Outlook, WordPerfect<br><br>Data Migration: Abacus Professional Services provides expert data migration from existing Case Management Software systems to the AbacusLaw platform (or platform for your choice)<br><br>(more info) | Access your practice anytime, anywhere and from any device<br><br>Abacus offers both In-Office or Virtual Practice Environments. Not sure which is right for your needs? Let our experts help you access your options with a no-obligation Technology Readiness Assessment<br><br>(more info) | Abacus Private Cloud includes fully managed IT, 24x7 monitoring, managed backups, inherent disaster recovery, antivirus and malware protection, firewall & intrusion prevention, unlimited technical support and more all from the U.S.<br><br>AbacusLaw offers U.S. based support, M-F from 6am-5pmPST, by remote desktop, telephone, email and fax. |

1

| | | | | | | | |
|---|---|---|---|---|---|---|---|
| | | | | | | | platform to meet your firm's specific needs. (more info) |
| Actionstep | Monthly subscription: $60/month per user per month (includes Time and Billing) | Web-based, requires any internet browser: Internet Explorer FireFox Chrome Safari Mac or PC | Workflow, Document Management, Document Assembly, Time Recording, Email, Calendar, Contacts, Tasks, Integrated Accounting, Website Integration, Client Portal, Secure Document Exchange | Time tracking, billing and reporting, trust accounting | Microsoft Office Microsoft Outlook Google Calendar/Exchange Gmail (Google Apps) Calendar sync Xero HotDocs | Actionstep is web-based, and accessible on any mobile device including smartphones, iPad and other tablets. | Technical support is included free as a part of Actionstep's monthly subscription. Support options include email, telephone support and knowledge center |
| Amicus Attorney | **Amicus Attorney Premium Edition 2014:** $999 1st license, $699 additional licenses. Optional (Standard/Enterprise) additional fees for annual maintenance ($350/$295 respectively), annual tech support ($195/$595 respectively). | **Premium Edition:** SQL Server 2012/2008 R2/2008 R2/2003 Windows Server 2012 R2/2012/2008 R2/2008/2003 R2/2003 SBS 2011/2008 R2/2008/2003 R2/2003 Windows 8.1/8/7/Vista (more info) | Matter management, contact relationship management, knowledge management, calendaring & docketing, universal communication inbox, document assembly, document management, conflict checking, to-do lists, deadline management. | Time tracking and reporting. Additional back office features available in Amicus Small Firm Accounting (see Time & Billing chart below). | Microsoft Exchange* Microsoft Outlook Google Calendar* Microsoft Word/Excel WordPerfect Adobe Acrobat/Reader HotDocs Compulaw Worldox* Dropbox* SQL Reporting Services Amicus Premium Billing* Amicus Small Firm Accounting* Timeslips PCLaw QuickBooks Tabs3 Juris Plus numerous other accounting and billing applications (more info) | Amicus Anywhere* provides a secure live connection through a web browser. (more info)<br><br>Amicus TimeTracker lets you do time entries on your smartphone. (more info)<br><br>Contacts and Calendar sync with any mobile device via Outlook, Exchange* or Google*. (more info) | Annual technical support plans offer unlimited telephone & email support, web-based remote desktop assistance, access to experts, convenient hours. (more info)<br><br>Annual maintenance plans offer access to Amicus Anywhere, Amicus TimeTracker, automatic software upgrades and updates in addition to technical support. (more info) |
| | **Amicus Attorney Small Firm Edition 2014:** $499 1st license, $399 additional licenses. Optional additional fees for annual maintenance ($240/$160) | **Small Firm Edition:** Windows Server 2012/2008 R2/2008/2003 R2/2003 | | | * Premium only | | |

| | | | | | | | |
|---|---|---|---|---|---|---|---|
| **Amicus Cloud** | SBS 2011/2008 R2/2008/2003 Windows 8.1/8/7/Vista respectively), annual tech support ($195/$95 respectively). (more info) | Web-based – Use with any modern browser. Internet Explorer 9 or above, Firefox 9 or above, Safari 5 or above, Chrome 16 or above (more info) | Matter management, contact relationship management, calendaring & docketing, universal communication inbox, document assembly, document management, conflict checking, task & deadline management. | Time tracking and reporting, billing and trust accounting | Microsoft Outlook Dropbox Box.com QuickBooks | * Premium only * Small Firm only | Unlimited technical support is included with the Amicus Cloud subscription. Support options include toll free phone, email and live chat. |
| | $45/month per user when paid annually $49.95/month per user (more info) | | | | Electronic time entry posting to accounting systems, with pre-set templates for QuickBooks, Timeslips and PCLaw. (more info) | Amicus Cloud is web based and accessible from any device with a modern web browser. (more info) Amicus TimeTracker lets you do time entries on your smartphone. (more info) | Completely integrated email, calendaring, contacts and tasks on your PC (or in most apps on your smartphone or tablet). Everything you see/do in Outlook, Mail, Calendar, Reminders & Contact on the Mac, iPad or iPhone is instantly in Amicus Cloud, and vice versa. (more info) |
| **Cosmolex** | 1st Month Free (no obligation) Thereafter, $49/month per user when paid annually $59/month per user Pricing includes unlimited US | Web-based, accessible from any mobile device with an Internet connection. Mac, PC, Tablets or Smartphones. | Workflow, Docket Control, Document Management, Calendar & Tasks, Case Notes, Matter Management, Contacts, Conflict Checking | Time & Expense Tracking, Billing, Payment Reminders, Low Retainer Reminders, Legal Accounting, General Ledger, Trust (IOLTA) Accounting, AR, Check Printing, Bank | Cosmolex is a single login, all inclusive system that combines practice management, billing & accounting, including trust accounting. All reports can be saved in Excel or PDF formats. Cosmolex also | Web-based, accessible from any mobile device with an Internet connection. Mac, PC, Tablets or Smartphones. (more info) | Live unlimited U.S. based support. |

| | Based support & training. (More Info) | | | | integrates with: | | |
|---|---|---|---|---|---|---|---|
| | | | | Reconciliations, Management & Financial Reporting. Cosmolex users do not need a separate accounting software. (More Info) | DropBox Box Google Calender (More Info) | | |
| Clio | Monthly subscription: $65 dollars per account. ABA Members save 25% on their first six months of Clio through ABA Member Advantage. Additional discounts available with an annual subscription. | Web-based, requires Google Chrome, Firefox, Internet Explorer 10.0+ or Safari | Matter/case management, document management, client/contact management, calendaring, task scheduling, practice performance metrics, document assembly and sharing/collaboration, secure communications and client portal. | Time tracking, billing and invoice generation, trust accounting, accounts receivable, firm-wide and individual attorney reporting, receive online bill payments via Paypal and other legal specific credit card processors. (more info) | Microsoft Outlook QuickBooks Xero Accounting Google Mail with built-in time-tracking, task assignment, and email archiving Google Calendar Google Drive and Apps for Business Apple iCal Apple Contacts Box DropBox NetDocuments for firm-wide knowledge management gUnify for automatic phone call tracking Fujitsu ScanSnap for instant document scanning and uploading All integrations with other services are provided at no additional costs from Clio. (more info) | Clio has an iPhone and Android app. (more info) Clio can be accessed via mobile-optimized versions as well on tablets, Blackberry phones, and other mobile devices. | Technical support is included free as a part of Clio's monthly subscription. Support options include phone (800-number), chat, social media, and e-mail. Support agents are available 17 hours a day to help with any questions. |
| Credenza | Credenza Basic: Free | Requires Outlook 2013 | Credenza Basic: Matter | Credenza Basic: Time tracking, | Microsoft Office 2013/2010/2007/200 | Contacts and Calendar sync with any mobile device via | Online Help Online Knowledge Base & Troubleshooter. |

Note these charts do not provide a comprehensive comparison of all Practice Management/Time & Billing products on the market. Inclusion in the chart should not be construed as an endorsement or recommendation. If you have an update to a listing or if you'd like to submit a product for consideration in future chart revisions, please contact the LTRC at ltrc@americanbar.org

| | Price | System Requirements | Features | Billing / Accounting | | Time Entry | Support |
|---|---|---|---|---|---|---|---|
| **Credenza Pro:** $24.95/month per user (more info) | | (32-Bit)/2010 (32-Bit)/2007/2003 running on Windows 8/7/Vista/XP (more info) | management, contact relationship management, call recording, phone calendaring, task management, document management. **Credenza Pro:** Includes all features of Credenza Basic, but adds sharing/collaboration, system-wide search. (more info) | reporting. **Credenza Pro:** Billing, payment posting to accounting systems, trust accounting, reporting, posting to popular accounting systems. (more info) | 3 | Outlook. **Credenza Pro:** Electronic time entry posting to accounting systems, with pre-set templates for QuickBooks, Timeslips and PCLaw. (more info) | Unlimited technical support and all upgrades are included with the Credenza Pro monthly subscription. |
| **Firm Central** | $35/user/month | Web-based Windows 7 or Windows 8 Internet Explorer 8 or later, Firefox 7.0 or later, Safari 5.0 or later, or Google Chrome 7 or later Mac OS 10.5 or later running Safari 5.0 or later, Firefox 7.0 or later, or Google Chrome 7 or later JavaScript and cookies enabled Adobe Reader (more info) | Matter and document management, calendaring, task management, client/contact management, secure client portal, indexing documents, global search, document sharing, conflict checker, custom fields for contact/clients and matters (more info) | Preloaded ABA Billing codes, hourly, flat-rate and retainer billing options, trust accounting, billing by client, matter, activity and firm member, invoicing, batch time/expense tracking, trust accounting, online bill paying (more info) | Time and Billing (see Time and Billing Comparison Chart) Westlaw/Next Practical Law Westlaw Doc & Form Builder Custom Forms Drafting Assistant Microsoft Outlook & Windows Explorer Microsoft Excel Data import/export is available through Microsoft Excel (more info) | Firm Central is web-based and accessible from any device with a web-browser. A smartphone optimized version is also available (more info) | Technical Support is available 24/7 Product how-to videos and webinars are also available (more info) |

| | Pricing | System Requirements | Practice Management Features | Time & Billing Features | Integrations | Mobile Access | Support |
|---|---|---|---|---|---|---|---|
| | | 9.4 or Adobe Flash 10.0 installed 1024 x 768 screen resolution (or higher) recommended | | | | | |
| **HoudiniESQ**<br>(more info) | SaaS/Cloud: $64/month per seat (more info)<br>5 seat on-premise license–also web-based: $2240 ($1280 one time, $960 annually) (more info)<br>Free for solo practitioners, including support | Web-based, runs in most modern web browsers (i.e. Safari, FireFox, Chrome and Opera)<br>On-premise install runs on Windows, OSX and Linux. (on-premise is also web-based)<br>Some router configuration required. | Matter, email, document, contacts, and to-do/tasks management; group calendaring and scheduling, document assembly/generation; alerts and reminders; web-based client access; IM and chat; matter reports; AR reports; call center dashboards; trust accounting report dashboard. (more info) | Time tracking and reporting; trust accounting ant export/import required) billing; batch invoicing, ad-hoc invoicing; staff performance reports; (more info) | MS Outlook MS Word MS Excel Intuit QuickBooks (no PDF plugin Calendar Rules All plug-ins are included at no additional cost | Included. Supports iPhone, Android and Blackberry | Included at no additional cost. |
| **Legal Files**<br>(more info) | Contact sales team for quote. 1.800.500.0537 or sales@legalfiles.com | Legal Files is a web client that utilizes a browser on the desktop. Use the link below to see more information on the technical environment. | Case/contact management, email, document assembly and management, relationship management, conflict checking, calendaring, automatic notification system for tasks and to-do's. | Time management, budgeting, expense tracking and management and eBilling module (more info) | Microsoft Office suite Numerous popular document management and accounting programs. | In addition to accessing Legal Files from anywhere through your browser, Legal Files Mobile provides an iOS application designed for the iPhone and iPad devices. | |
| **MyCase** | Monthly subscription: $39/month per attorney $29/month per attorney | Web-based, requires any internet browser: IE9 or later | Legal Practice Management includes: Client & Team communication in a receives online | Time & billing, time tracking, trust accounting, | Microsoft Outlook Plugin Google Calendar Google Docs Apple iCal | MyCase is web-based and accessible on any mobile device including smartphones, iPad, and other tablets. | Technical Support and Getting Started Help are included free with the monthly subscription. Support options include email, |

Note: these charts do not provide a comprehensive comparison of all Practice Management/Time & Billing products on the market. Inclusion in the chart should not be construed as an endorsement or recommendation. If you have an update to a listing or if you'd like to submit a production for consideration in future chart revisions, please contact the LTRC at ltrc@americanbar.org

| | Pricing | System Requirements | Features | Financial / Billing | Integrations | Mobile / Remote | Support |
|---|---|---|---|---|---|---|---|
| | paralegal/staff ABA members save 20% on their subscriptions to MyCase through ABA Member Advantage. | Firefox 3.5 or later Safari 4 Chrome Mac or PC | secure portal, calendar management, client message, document management / collaboration / storage, matter/case management, task & to-do scheduling. | payments, firm reporting. | Apple Contacts QuickBooks Email integration | MyCase has an app built for Android and iPhones. MyCase customer support is available 6am-5pm PT Monday-Friday. | telephone support, and knowledge center. |
| **Needles** | Licenses 1-10: $1,000 per user. Annual support, Sybase, and implementation/training at additional cost. Pricing calculator available on website. (more info) | Workstation: Windows 2000, XP, Vista. Server: Windows 2003, 2008. (more info) | Notes, calendar, document management, case status, e-mail, IM, case files, conflict checking, statute tracking. (more info) | Marketing, expense tracking, reporting, import/export to other Needles firms. (more info) | Acrobat Corel WordPerfect Docs Open Hot Docs Microsoft Suite QuickBooks Timeslips Worldox (more info) | Remote access (more info) | New Needles clients must undergo initial training and implementation with certified training consultant. Annual support provides technical support M-F, 8:30-5:15pm EST. (more info) |
| **PracticeMaster** | $600 for first user ($280 per add'l user). Platinum version: $1,320 for first user ($365 per add'l user). All prices include one year of maintenance (free telephone support, software updates and more). | Basic/Premier: Windows 8, 7, Vista, XP, 2000 Platinum: STI Server on Windows 7, Vista, XP, 2000 (comparison chart) | Matter & contact database, firm-wide calendaring, conflict checking, document management, common task templates, document assembly, document management integration, area of practice customization, etc. (more info) | Fee and cost entry, Tabs3 products can be purchased for back office billing, accounting, A/R, A/P, trust accounting and check writing. (more info here and here) | Tabs3 Billing, Paperport, Outlook, HotDocs, Worldox, Microsoft Word, WordPerfect, CompuLaw court rules. (more info) | Tabs3 Connect is available for those who use the Platinum version of both Tabs3 and PracticeMaster. (more info) | Free knowledge base, free telephone support for first 60 days, annual maintenance plans available which include unlimited telephone support and free updates (more info) |
| **ProLaw** | Contact Prolaw for pricing. Information request form available on web page, or call 1-800-977-6529. | Workstation: Windows 2000 Pro, XP Pro, Vista Business/Ultimate. | Matter management, contacts, document assembly/mgmt, email, appointments/tasks, docketing. | Time/expense tracking, budgeting, collections, billing, cost recovery, contingency | Microsoft Suite Lotus Domino/Notes GroupWise Acrobat HotDocs DOCS Open OpenText | | ProLaw offers support for planning & implementation, training & adoption, and technical support. (more info) |

Note: these charts do not provide a comprehensive comparison of all Practice Management/Time & Billing products on the market. Inclusion on the chart should not be construed as an endorsement or recommendation. If you have an update to a listing or if you'd like to submit a product for consideration in future chart revisions, please contact the LPEC at ltrc@americanbar.org

7

| Company | Pricing | Compatibility / Server Requirements | Features | Calendaring & Time | Compatible Software / Billing | Mobile Access | Technical Support |
|---|---|---|---|---|---|---|---|
| *(continued)* | (more info) | Server: Windows Server 2000, Server 2003 R2, Server 2008 running Microsoft SQL Server 2000/2005/2008. (more info) | calendaring, in-context Westlaw research, records management. Specialized practice area modules available. (more info) | analysis & disposition, integrated accounting. (more info) | Interwoven Worldox PeachTree QuickPayroll | | |
| **Rocket Matter** | 1st User: $65/Month, Additional Users: $55/Month. Pricing includes modem web browser, mobile access, upgrades, backups, security, support, and training. (more info) | Web based, cross-platform. Runs on any operating system with a modern web browser. Requires Internet Explorer 7 or above, Safari 3 or above, Firefox 2 or above, Chrome, or Opera. (more info) | contact management, phone messaging, conflict checking, document storage, document assembly using custom fields, timer (stopwatch), billing, invoicing, matter-based ledgers and accounting, trust accounting, ledgers, AR reports, batch invoice creation. (more info) | Individual and firm-wide calendaring, to-do and task tracking, matter management, time and expense tracking, flexible user rates, online calendaring programs. (more info) | Hourly, flat fee, and contingency matter support, 2007, iCal, Sunbird, Google Calendar, and most other compliant calendaring programs. iPad app. (more info) | Any mobile device capable of running a full browser. Optimized for usage on tablets, the iPhone, Android, Windows Mobile, and modern BlackBerry devices. (more info) | Unlimited phone and email technical support. Support hours from 8 AM to 8 PM EST, M-F. Our support representatives are located in the U.S. and are native English speakers. Support in Spanish is also available. We respond to most issues within the hour, and guarantee a 1 business day response time. Rocket Matter subscriptions include free training sessions and 24-hour access to online support videos to help with most common questions. |
| | One-time fee starting at $995 per user license. Software updates are included in a maintenance and support contract. | Server Requirements: Windows Server 2008/2012, MS SQL Server 2008 R2/2012 (Standard/Enterprise). | Case Management; Contact Relationship Management; Document Management; Document Assembly; Critical Deadline Work Plans which automate document generation. | Reporting; Document Merging; Time Tracking; Expense Tracking; Work Plans | eLaw Integration; Microsoft Exchange; Microsoft Outlook; Google Calendar; Microsoft Word; Microsoft Excel; Adobe Acrobat; SQL Reporting Services; QuickBooks. Mail merge with Microsoft Word for form letter/label generation. Invoices can be created in WordPerfect, Word, or PDF. Reports and data can be backed up to CSV files readable with Excel. (more info) | Access your practice anytime, anywhere and from any device through browser. (more info) | Unlimited technical support is included with the SmartAdvocate Maintenance and Support Plan which include toll free phone, email and live remote support provided by in house technicians. Email |

Note: these charts do not provide a comprehensive comparison of all Practice Management/Time & Billing products on the market. Inclusion in the charts should not be construed as an endorsement or recommendation. If you have an update to a listing or if you'd like to submit a product for consideration in future chart revisions, please contact the LTRC at ltrc@americanbar.org

| | Training / Price | System Requirements | Features | Time capture | Integrations | Support |
|---|---|---|---|---|---|---|
| **SMARTADVOCATE** | Initial software training is required and will be included in the initial price quote. (more info) | MS IIS 7.0/8.0 MS Office 2010/2013 **WorkStation Requirements:** Windows 7/8 MS Office 2010/2013 Internet Explorer 11 Chrome 16 or above. (more info) | Barcode Document Scanning; Email Management, Note Management; Case and Firm Calendaring that integrates with Outlook; Knowledge Management; Conflict Check; Detailed Reporting with Subscription; Case Timeline, Productivity and Practice Management; Mail Merge; Task Management; Specialized practice areas. Professional Services to increase law firms efficiency and effectiveness available. (more info) | note creation, email creation and case status changes. (more info) | | support@smartadvocate.assist.com or call 1-877-438-7627 24 hours/7 days a week. http://www.smartadvocate.com/support |
| **Time Matters** | 1ˢᵗ user: $950 Additional users: $525 (includes 1ˢᵗ year maintenance plan) (more info) | Workstation: Windows XP, Vista, Windows 7/8, MS Office 2010/2013 Business/Pro edition recommended. Server: Windows Server 2003/2008 SQL Server 2005/2008 with Microsoft SQL 2005/2008. (more info) | Contacts, matter management, docketing, calendaring, document management, communications, data import/sync (more info) | Time capture (more info) | PCLaw Juris Timeslips QuickBooks Other "billing, document management, e-mail management and other desktop business applications." (more info) | Online support center with articles/FAQs. (more info) Online service center available for licensed customers. (more info) Live-answer telephone support available M-F, 8am-8pm for strictly technical issues. (more info) |

Note: these charts do not provide a comprehensive comparison of all Practice Management, Time & Billing products on the market. Inclusion in the chart should not be construed as an endorsement or recommendation. If you have an update to a listing or if you'd like to submit a product for consideration in future chart revisions, please contact the LPC at ltrc@americanbar.org

## Time and Billing Software Comparison Chart for Solo/Small Firms

| | Pricing | Technical Requirements | Key Accounting and Billing Tasks | Types of Billing Supported | Software Compatibility | Data Conversion Available | Mobile Access | Technical Support |
|---|---|---|---|---|---|---|---|---|
| **Amicus Premium Billing** / **Amicus Premium Accounting** | **Amicus Premium Billing:** $199 per license. (Works with Amicus Premium Edition 2014) (more info) **Amicus Premium Accounting:** $399 1st license, $299 additional licenses. Optional additional fees for annual maintenance ($70/$70 respectively), annual tech support ($100/$50 respectively). (more info) | **Amicus Premium Billing:** SQL Server 2012/2008 R2/2008 (Standard/Enterprise) Windows Server 2012 R2/2012/2008 R2/2008/2003 SBS 2011/2008 R2/2008/2003 Windows 8.1/8/7/Vista | **Amicus Premium Billing:** Billing, collections, trust accounting, time tracking, expenses, consolidated billing, e-billing. **Amicus Premium Accounting:** productivity reporting (more info) | **Amicus Premium Billing:** Hourly, flat fee, contingency, consolidated billing, e-billing. | **Amicus Premium Billing:** QuickBooks 2014, Amicus Attorney Premium Edition 2014, Adobe Acrobat/Reader, Microsoft Word, SQL Reporting Services | **Amicus Premium Billing:** Yes – please call our Services Department at 800-472-2289. (more info) | **Amicus Premium Billing:** Premium Billing provides secure live connection through a web browser with Amicus Anywhere. (more info) | **Amicus Premium Billing:** Annual technical support plans offer unlimited telephone & email support, web-based remote desktop assistance, access to experts, convenient hours. (more info) **Amicus Premium Accounting:** Annual maintenance plans offer access to Amicus Anywhere, Amicus TimeTracker, Amicus automatic software upgrades and updates in addition to technical support. (more info) |
| **Amicus Small Firm Accounting** | **Amicus Small Firm Accounting:** (more info) | **Amicus Small Firm Accounting:** Windows Server 2012/2008 R2/2008/2003 SBS 2011/2008 R2/2008 R2/2008/2003 Windows R2/2003 Windows 8.1/8/7/Vista (more info) | **Amicus Small Firm Accounting:** Time tracking, billing and full General Ledger accounting. Includes check writing, accounts payable and productivity reporting. (more info) | **Amicus Small Firm Accounting:** Hourly, split, flat fee, consolidated, e-billing. (more info) | **Amicus Small Firm Accounting:** Amicus Attorney Small Firm Edition 2014 (more info) | **Amicus Small Firm Accounting:** Guide to migrating from another accounting system available: see PDF. (more info) | **Amicus Small Firm Accounting:** Amicus TimeTracker lets you do time entries on your smartphone. (more info) | |
| **Bill4Time** | Free (1 user, 3 active clients, 5 open projects). | All operating systems – the software is online | Mobile time and expense tracking, customer service. | | Uploads all formats for file management. | Pre-existing database conversion easily | iPhone, Android and BlackBerry mobile app | All subscribers get free technical support. Lite and |

| Product | Cost | Platform / OS | Features | Billing methods | Integrates with | Conversion / Support | Remote access | Support / Training |
|---|---|---|---|---|---|---|---|---|
| | Lite - $19.99 per month for first user, $9.99 per month for additional users (20 active clients, 30 open projects). Pro - $39.99 per month for first user, $19.99 per month for additional users (unlimited clients and projects). Students (with .edu email) free while in school. Business start-ups (within 1st year of business) – Free pro account for 9 months, new customers only. (more info) | so isn't subject to specific operating systems. For both Mac and PC. All browsers – Internet Explorer 7+, Firefox, Safari, Chrome. (more info) | scheduling, time attendance, project management, business productivity, control, reporting, invoicing, billing, accounting, firm management. (more info) | | Integrates with QuickBooks. Exports firm data in CSV. | possible with Bill4Time free technical support. (more info) | Laptops disconnected from the internet can use a desktop widget to track time. | Pro users get priority. Free system updates and daily back-ups. Free tutorials, webinars, scheduled weekly, and group tutorials upon request. Free access to video tutorials and knowledgebase |
| BillQuick | Free 30-Day Trial Basic edition starts at $14.95/user/month | Available as a stand-alone solution (BillQuick Desktop), hosted on-premise solution (BillQuick Web Suite) or SaaS, on the cloud (BillQuick Online). Stand-alone version runs on all windows operating systems (Win XP, Vista, 7 and 8). Browser- | Intuitive Time & Expense Tracking – Time card in calendar, spreadsheet and stopwatch formats. Unlimited multiple timers. Attach files and links. Simplified Billing & Accounts Receivable – Over 150 customizable invoice templates. Retainer, | Hourly, Recurring, Fixed fee, Retainer, Task-based, Automatic | QuickBooks Sage50 Microsoft Office Microsoft Outlook Crystal Reports LEDES Electronic Exchange | Free Built-in Timeslips conversion Seamless QuickBooks Integration LEDES Electronic Exchange Excel Import/Export Custom Conversion | Access via all web browsers Native mobile apps for iOS, Android and Windows8 Phones Web access via tablet devices | Unlimited email, web-based and phone support included in all plans. Free access to monthly training webinars Free access to Knowledgebase Support hours: 7:00am – 3:00pm Pacific Time |

| Product | Price | System Requirements | Features | Billing Types | Compatibility / Integration | Support / Notes |
|---|---|---|---|---|---|---|
| | | based/Cloud version runs in IE 7 or later, Chrome 7 or later, Firefox 4 or later, Opera 11 or later, Safari 5 or later | (more info) | Powerful Reporting: Over 500 templates. Automatic report delivery. Memorize reports. | recurring, fixed, hourly, or more. | |
| **PCLaw** (more info) | Including first year maintenance plan: 1st User: $950 Add'l users: $455 (more info) — Without first year maintenance plan: 1st User: $600 Add'l users: $400 (more info) | Workstation: Windows 2000, XP, Vista, 7; Server: Windows 2000, Windows 2003 Server (more info) | Time tracking, billing, accounts receivable, integrated credit card processing, trust accounts, ledgers, comprehensive reporting, integrated payroll (more info) | Flat-fee, task-based, split, contingency, retainer, electronic billing. (more info) | LexisNexis Total Practice Advantage, Time Matters, Amicus Attorney, PCLaw Timer, LexisNexis Research Microsoft QuickBooks, Timeslips, Compulaw, Esilaw, Manac, and Tabs3. (more info) | Free utilities and paid services offered to ease transition. Data has been converted from (more info) — PCLaw Travel Edition module for Palm OS 3.5+, BlackBerry OS 4.0+ (more info) — Online support provided via LexisNexis Total Practice Solutions Support Center. (more info) |
| **Tabs3 Billing** PracticeMaster Basic is included with purchase of Tabs3. (more info) — All prices include one year of maintenance (free | $675 (two attorneys) $1340 (five attorneys) (more info) — Platinum version: $1770 (5 users) $2665 (9 users) (more info) — Please click here for full technical requirements | Tabs3 and PracticeMaster Software is compatible with all supported versions of Windows and Windows Server. Separate Tabs3 software available for trust, general ledger, accounts payable. | Time tracking, accounts receivable, reports (more info) | Hourly, flat-fee, contingency, UTMBS/electronic billing, split-fee, retainer, task based billing, pro bono, billable, non-billable (more info) | Tabs3 financial software, PracticeMaster, QuickBooks (more info here and here) | Tabs3 Connect is available for those who use the Platinum version of both Tabs3 and PracticeMaster. (more info) — Free knowledge base, free telephone support. Platinum maintenance plans available which include unlimited telephone support and free updates (more info) |

12

## Time and Billing

| Product | Cost | Operating Systems | Features | Integration / Supported Formats | Data Conversion | Mobile Access & Support |
|---|---|---|---|---|---|---|
| *(continued)* | telephone support, software updates and more). $25/user/month | All operating systems. All browsers are supported | Time/expense tracking, online invoicing, trust accounting, online bill pay (more info) | Preloaded ABA Billing codes, hourly, flat-rate and retainer billing options, trust accounting, billing by client, matter, activity and firm member, invoicing, batch invoicing, time tracking, trust accounting, online bill paying, custom codes, LEDES 19988 Format | Firm Central Microsoft Outlook | Pre-existing database conversion is possible in most cases. Call 1-888-287-8537 for more information |
| | | | Convert your emails and calendar events into time entries from Microsoft Outlook | | | Native App for iPhone/iPad and Android. Desktop Widget for Mac and PC to track time when offline |
| **Sage Timeslips** | 1 user: $519.99 Additional workstations: $295.99 each. For more than 10 additional workstations, call Sage Timeslips at 877-816-7829. Includes 30 days of support starting from date of purchase – new customers only. On-demand test drive is available. (more info) ABA members save 15% on Timeslips through ABA Member Advantage. | Windows 8, 7 Ultimate or Professional, Windows Vista Business or Ultimate, Windows XP SP3 (more info) Various add-on products available. | Time/expense tracking, automatic time capture, calendar sync, bill generation, 988 and Litigation Advisor, billing administrators may choose if a slip requires approval before being invoiced to the customer, A/R reports included with the invoicing software may integrate with 20 software packages including QuickBooks, Sage 50 Accounting and practice management software packages, define aging periods, allocate payments. accounts receivable, report design & customization, scheduled backups, alerts, custom fields, networking options. (more info) | Industry standard electronic billing formats are supported, including LEDES Business, Time Matters, Amicus Attorney and more. (more info) QuickBooks, Sage 50 Accounting, Microsoft Outlook, Excel, Time Matters, Amicus Attorney and more. | Built-in data import feature can import data from delimited text files. (more info) Tools offered for conversion of older Timeslips databases. Conversion from other databases may be possible via Timeslips Certified Consultant. | Sage Timeslips eCenter is a Web-based time and expense entry portal that works with any mobile device with an Internet connection, including laptops, smartphones, older Timeslips, iPads and tablets. Apple Macs and Available as a monthly subscription per license. (more info) Free technical support for 30 days. Basic and premium support plan options available. Knowledgebase and community assistance is available through Sage City or the Sage Timeslips LinkedIn user group. (more info) Enter time from any web-connected computer using Timeslips eCenter add on. |

Note these charts do not provide a comprehensive comparison of all Practice Management/Time & Billing products on the market. Inclusion in the chart should not be construed as an endorsement or recommendation. If you have an update to a listing or if you'd like to submit a product for consideration in future chart revisions, please contact the TRC at ltrc@americanbar.org

| Product | Price | System Requirements | Features | Integration / Export | Devices / Data | Support |
|---|---|---|---|---|---|---|
| TimeSolv Legal (more info) | $35.00 per timekeeper/per month or $29 per user/month with an annual plan. No charge for non-timekeepers. Includes initial setup, support and one-on-one online Training. Discounts available for 10+ users (more info) | Windows XP, Vista, Macintosh, Linux, Unix, etc. Software is browser based and not subject to specific operating system. Browsers: Internet Explorer, Firefox, Safari, Chrome (more info) | Billing: LEDES billing, batch bill creation, flat fee, contingency, consolidated billing, multiple global rates, matter specific rates, time entry specific rates, templates, five bill delivery options, online bill presentment and outsourced billing, LEDES billing, print and mail service. (more info) Hourly by timekeeper/task, ... to timekeepers, set up discount rules for early payments. (more info) Narrative replacement codes for quick notes entry, multiple timers, ABA UTBMS codes. Accounting: Accounts receivable, trust accounting, financial reports, auto reports, project management, conflicts management, approval workflow. (more info) Additional electronic billing formats available for insurance companies, such as Chubbs, Litigation Advisors, etc. (more info) | Quickbooks, MYOB, AccountEdge, CSV Export, PayPal WorkTRAKR for automatically capturing time from phone calls and emails (more info) | Quickbooks Access through TimeSolv Mobile systems including Timeslips. No charge for data conversion and help with data upload. Supported devices include * iPhone * Blackberry * Windows Mobile * Palm (more info) | Toll Free Telephone and Email support included in subscription. Response time of less than 2 hours. Support personnel located in the US. Includes free one-on-one online training, initial setup and configuration. Laptop based mobile access through TimeSync, a desktop application for tracking time and expenses. (more info) |
| TurboLaw Time and Billing | $29 per month for the first license. $19 per month for each additional | Cloud, Mac, or PC For PC: Windows 98, ME, | Time keeping, payment entry, stop watch, bill creation, account creation, account (more info) Custom interval, hour, half hour, quarter | Microsoft Outlook, Turbolaw Document Software | The Cloud and Mac version are web based and can be used | Unlimited support including US based toll free phone. Online support site available for self help. (more info) |

| | | | | | |
|---|---|---|---|---|---|
| license. Volume discount available for 5+ licenses. No contract term. Free trial available. | 2000, XP, Server 2003, Vista XP or higher recommended for best results. Internet connection required for setup, updates, and activation. | history, financial reports, LEDES billing, client/staff information entry (including billing rates), application of finance charges, dozens of customizable bill/statement templates, multiple matter support, IOLTA reconciliation. | hour, tenth hour, exact time, flat fee. | PDF (built in), HTML, Text, CSV, MHT, Excel, RTF, Image (BMP, GIF, JPEG, PNG, TIFF, EMF, WMF) (more info) | with any mobile device with an Internet connection, including iPads, laptops, smartphones, Macs and tablets. (more info) |
| **BillingTracker Pro** <br><br> 1 user: $179. <br> 3 users: $358. <br> 5 users: $448. <br> Total Care Maintenance/Online Backup Subscription: $10/month for 1st user, $5/month for each user thereafter (more info) | Windows XP/Vista/7/8 (more info) | Time tracking, billing, expenses, accounts receivable, detailed reporting, online backup, alerts, unpaid bills tracking (ageing.) | Hourly, flat fee, contingency, retainer, recurring, billable/non-billable | Exports statements and reports to PDF, RTF (can be opened by Word), and CSV (can be opened by Excel) | support and email for active subscribers. Free training webinars and help center also available. <br><br> Online backup of data file can be accessed by any Windows laptop so user can work while outside of office <br><br> Total Care subscription provides technical support, new versions of the software, replacement registration codes, and online backup of data file. Online backup can be encrypted. |

# INDEX

[References are to sections.]

## A

**ALARM SYSTEMS**
Generally . . . 9.02

## B

**BANKING** (See ORGANIZATION OF LAW OFFICE, subhead: Banking)

**BROCHURES**
Generally . . . 9.04; 12.06[G]

**BUSINESS CARDS**
Generally . . . 9.03
Support staff, for . . . 12.06[C]

**BUSINESS ENTITY, CREATION OF**
Consultants . . . 4.01
Malpractice considerations . . . 4.02
Multiple attorneys, business with . . . 4.04
Solo practitioner with entity . . . 4.03[B]
Solo practitioner with no entity . . . 4.03[A]
Steps, common . . . 4.05

## C

**CLIENT RELATIONS** (See MANAGING CLIENTS)

**CLIENTS, POTENTIAL**
Conflict checks . . . 14.05
Declining case
   Generally . . . 15.05
   Letter of non-engagement . . . 15.05[A]
Friends or relatives of potential client attending consultation . . . 15.02
Initial phone call
   Generally . . . 14.01
   Information to obtain during . . . 14.02
Interviewing
   Generally . . . 15.01; 15.03
   Friends or relatives of potential client attending consultation . . . 15.02
   Notetaking during . . . 15.03[B]
   Purpose of initial interview . . . 15.03[D]
   Recording during . . . 15.03[C]
   Road map of procedure, explaining to client . . . 15.03[F]
   Scripted questions . . . 15.03[A]
   Strategy for . . . 15.03[E]
   Sympathy/empathy, expressing . . . 15.03[G]
   "Whole story," advice for eliciting . . . 15.03[H]
Price shoppers, handling . . . 14.09
Scheduling appointments . . . 14.06
Screening . . . 14.04
Steps for moving forward with case . . . 15.04
Walk-in appointments . . . 14.08

**CLIENTS, POTENTIAL**—Cont.
Website, initial contact through
   Generally . . . 14.03; 14.03[B]
   Responsibility for legal advice . . . 14.03[A]
Work hours, meeting with clients during set . . . 14.07

**COMPENSATION ISSUES**
Generally . . . 5.01
"Eat-what-you-kill" systems . . . 5.02[E]
Equal distribution of profits . . . 5.02[A]
Equal draws with subjective distribution of profits . . . 5.02[B]
Equal partnerships, possibility of . . . 5.03[A]
Growth, opportunity for . . . 5.03[C]
Incentive-based compensation
   Limited . . . 5.02[D]
   Percentages allocated to different functions, where . . . 5.02[C]
Timing of financial distributions . . . 5.03[B]

**CONSULTATION FEES**
Generally . . . 11.04; 11.04[A]

**CREDIT CARD PAYMENT OF FEES**
Generally . . . 11.07
Ethical and professional considerations
   Generally . . . 11.07[A]
   Automatic payments . . . 11.07[A][2]
   Confidentiality, client . . . 11.07[A][1]
   Disputed fees . . . 11.07[A][4]
   Risk of commingling of operating account and trust funds . . . 11.07[A][3]
Selection of credit card processor
   Generally . . . 11.07[B]
   Bank, processing offered through . . . 11.07[B][2]
   Processing companies . . . 11.07[B][1]

## D

**DISSOLUTION OF PARTNERSHIPS**
Generally . . . Ch. 21

## E

**EMPLOYEES ISSUES** (See PERSONNEL ISSUES)

**EQUIPMENT, OFFICE**
Generally . . . 6.06[C]; 9.06

## F

**FEE ARRANGEMENTS**
Contingency fees
   Generally . . . 11.01[C]
   Reverse contingency fees . . . 11.01[D]
Credit card payment of fees (See CREDIT CARD PAYMENT OF FEES)

I-1

[References are to sections.]

[References are to sections.]

# M

**MALPRACTICE INSURANCE**
Generally . . . 4.02; 19.01
Application information, accuracy of . . . 19.05
Avoiding malpractice
    Generally . . . 19.06[E]
    Calendar system, maintaining superior
      . . . 19.06[B]
    Conflict checks . . . 19.06[A]
    Documenting client's actions contrary to advice
      . . . 19.06[D]
    Limiting scope of representation . . . 19.06[C]
Cooperating with carrier regarding potential claim
    . . . 19.07[B]
Coverage, necessary . . . 19.04
Deductible, recommended . . . 19.04
Notifying carrier of potential claim . . . 19.07[A]
Obtaining . . . 19.02
Partner's mistake, avoiding personal liability for
    . . . 19.08
Related insurance . . . 19.03

**MANAGING CLIENTS**
Altering and reusing documents themselves, clients
    . . . 16.04
Bad news, communicating . . . 16.11
Demanding clients
    Generally . . . 16.02
    Controlling . . . 16.02[A]
    Identifying . . . 16.02[B]
Difficult clients . . . 16.01
Ending relationship with problem client . . . 16.10
Legal researchers, clients behaving as . . . 16.06
Lying for client . . . 16.09
Second-guessing advice, client . . . 16.05
Strange behaviors, clients exhibiting . . . 16.08
Time-consuming clients . . . 16.03
Unresponsive clients . . . 16.07

**MARKETING**
Generally . . . 12.01
Advertising . . . 12.04[A]
Article writing . . . 12.04[D]
Blogs . . . 12.04[C]
Brochures . . . 12.06[G]
Business cards for support staff . . . 12.06[C]
Choices . . . 12.02
Community organizations and events, sponsoring
    . . . 12.06[D]
Greeting cards . . . 12.06[J]
Internet . . . 12.04[B]
Newspaper reporters
    Cultivating relationships with . . . 12.06[H]
    Responding to . . . 12.06[I]
"Off-duty" marketing . . . 12.05
Referrals, cultivating relationships for . . . 12.06[E]
Social media . . . 12.04[E]
Speaking engagements . . . 12.06[F]
Strategies . . . 12.03
Testimonials . . . 12.06[B]
Volunteering . . . 12.06[A]

# N

**NAMING PRACTICE**
Multiple lawyers, with . . . 3.01

**NATURAL DISASTERS**
Generally . . . 22.01

# O

**OFFICE SPACE**
Buying building or condominium . . . 8.02
Home offices (See HOME OFFICES)
Incubator programs for recent law school graduates
    . . . 8.04
Physical appearance (See ORGANIZATION OF
    LAW OFFICE, subhead: Physical appearance)
Renting
    Generally . . . 6.03; 6.06[A]; 8.01
    Double-net lease . . . 8.01[C]
    Gross lease . . . 8.01[B]
    Triple-net lease . . . 8.01[A]
Time-for-space arrangement
    Generally . . . 8.03
    Calculating . . . 8.03[A]

**OFFICE SUPPLIES**
Generally . . . 9.07

**ORGANIZATION OF LAW OFFICE**
Backup systems . . . 10.04
Banking
    Disbursement account . . . 10.06[D]
    Escrow/trust account . . . 10.06[C]
    IOLA/IOLTA account . . . 10.06[B]
    Operating account . . . 10.06[A]
    Petty cash account . . . 10.06[E]
Checklist for procedures, creating . . . 10.05
Filing systems . . . 10.03
Physical appearance
    Generally . . . 10.01
    Layout . . . 10.01[A]
    Waiting area . . . 10.01[A], [B]
Technology . . . 10.02

# P

**PARTNERSHIPS**
Balanced . . . 2.02
Business entity, creation of . . . 4.04
Classmates, with . . . 2.01[B]
Compensation issues (See COMPENSATION IS-
    SUES)
Dissolution of . . . Ch. 21
Family, with . . . 2.01; 2.01[A]
Friends, with . . . 2.01[B]
Misconduct of partner, professional . . . Ch. 21
Mistake of partner, avoiding personal liability for
    . . . 19.08
Naming firm . . . 3.01
Professional acquaintances, with . . . 2.01[C]

[References are to sections.]